ISBN 978-1-333-00273-2
PIBN 10447450

1 MONTH OF
FREE
READING

at

www.ForgottenBooks.com

By purchasing this book you are eligible for one month membership to ForgottenBooks.com, giving you unlimited access to our entire collection of over 1,000,000 titles via our web site and mobile apps.

To claim your free month visit:

www.forgottenbooks.com/free447450

English
Français
Deutsche
Italiano
Español
Português

www.forgottenbooks.com

Mythology Photography **Fiction**
Fishing Christianity **Art** Cooking
Essays Buddhism Freemasonry
Medicine **Biology** Music **Ancient
Egypt** Evolution Carpentry Physics
Dance Geology **Mathematics** Fitness
Shakespeare **Folklore** Yoga Marketing
Confidence Immortality Biographies
Poetry **Psychology** Witchcraft
Electronics Chemistry History **Law**
Accounting **Philosophy** Anthropology
Alchemy Drama Quantum Mechanics
Atheism Sexual Health **Ancient History**
Entrepreneurship Languages Sport
Paleontology Needlework Islam
Metaphysics Investment Archaeology
Parenting Statistics Criminology
Motivational

NEW BOOKS

IN THE COURSE OF PUBLICATION

BY

J. G. & F. RIVINGTON,

ST. PAUL'S CHURCH YARD, AND WATERLOO PLACE, PALL MALL,

I.

A SCRIPTURAL VINDICATION of CHURCH ESTABLISH-
MENTS; with a Review of the Principal Objections of Non-Conformists.
By the Rev. GEORGE HOLDEN, M.A.
Small 8vo. 7s. 6d.

II.

CHRISTIAN INSTITUTES:
A SERIES of DISCOURSES and TRACTS, systematically. arranged,
Designed to be subservient to the Religious Portion of a Liberal
Education for the Upper Classes and the Learned Professions.
By CHRISTOPHER WORDSWORTH, D.D.
Master of Trinity College, Cambridge.
In 4 Vols. 8vo. (In the Press.)

III.

The DOCTRINE and PRACTICE of REPENTANCE.
Extracted and Abridged from the larger Work upon the same subject; by
Bishop JEREMY TAYLOR.
By the Rev. WILLIAM HALE HALE, M.A.
Prebendary of St. Paul's, Preacher of the Charter House, and Chaplain to
the Lord Bishop of London.
Small 8vo. 6s. 6d.

IV.

A COMPENDIUM of the RUDIMENTS of THEOLOGY:
Containing a Digest of Bishop Butler's Analogy; an Epitome of Graves
on the Pentateuch; and an Analysis of Bishop Newton
on the Prophecies. For the Use of Students.
By the Rev. J. B. SMITH, B.D.
Of Christ's College, Cambridge; Head Master of Horncastle Grammar School,
12mo. (In a few Days.)

V.

A NEW EDITION OF
MEMORIALS of a DEPARTED FRIEND.
" She being dead, yet speaketh."—Heb.
12mo. 7s. (In a few Days.)

VI.

TWENTY PAROCHIAL SERMONS:—Third Series.

On PARTICULAR OCCASIONS; for the most part referring to Charitable Collections. With an Appendix of Notes and Illustrations.

By the Rev. CHARLES GIRDLESTONE, M.A.

Vicar of Sedgley, Staffordshire.

12mo. 5s. 6d.

VII.

SOME ACCOUNT of the WRITINGS and OPINIONS of JUSTIN MARTYR.

By the Right Rev. JOHN KAYE, D.D.

Lord Bishop of Lincoln.

Second Edition, revised. 7s. 6d.

VIII.

The LIFE of ARCHBISHOP LAUD.

In Continuation of the Series of Lives of British Divines in the Theological Library, and printed uniformly with *Wiclif, Cranmer,* and *Jewel.*

By CHARLES WEBB LE BAS, M.A.

Professor in the East India College, Herts; and late Fellow of Trinity College, Cambridge.

In small 8vo. *With Portrait.* 6s.

IX.

S E R M O N S:

Preached before the University of Cambridge, in February, 1836; to which are added, Two Sermons preached in Great St. Mary's, at the Evening Lecture.

By HENRY MELVILL, M.A.

Late Fellow of St. Peter's College, Cambridge.

Second Edition. 8vo. 5s.

X.

THE CLERICAL GUIDE and ECCLESIASTICAL DIRECTORY;

Containing a Complete Register of the Dignities and Benefices of the Church of England, with their respective Value, founded on an Average of Three Years; and exhibiting the Names of the Incumbents, Patrons and Impropriators, County, Diocese, Archdeaconry, Population, and Church Accommodation of the Livings: compiled from the Report of the Commissioners to inquire into the Revenues and Patronage of the Established Church in England and Wales, and presented to both Houses of Parliament in June, 1835, by Command of his Majesty. To which are added, an Alphabetical List of the Dignitaries and Beneficed Clergy; and the Ecclesiastical Patronage at the Disposal of the King, Lord Chancellor, Archbishops and Bishops, Deans and Chapters, and the Universities.

Edited by RICHARD GILBERT, M.R.S.L.

Compiler of the " Clergyman's Almanack" and the " Liber Scholasticus."

Royal 8vo. 1l. 2s.

XI.

'A NEW VOLUME of SERMONS.
By the Rev. EDWARD BERENS, M.A.
Archdeacon of Berks.
12mo. *(In the Press.)*

XII.

A SKETCH of the CHURCH of the FIRST TWO CENTURIES
after CHRIST, drawn from the Writings of the Fathers down to Clemens
Alexandrinus inclusive, in a COURSE of SERMONS preached
before the University of Cambridge, in January, 1836.
By the Rev. JOHN J. BLUNT,
Late Fellow of St. John's College.
Small 8vo. 6s. 6d.

XIII.

A NEW EDITION OF THE
Rev. G. TOWNSEND'S HISTORICAL and CHRONOLOGICAL
ARRANGEMENT of the OLD TESTAMENT. With Annotations.
In Two Vols. 8vo. *(Nearly ready.)*

XIV.

The DIVINE GLORY Manifested in the CONDUCT and DIS-
COURSES of our LORD; EIGHT SERMONS preached before
the University of Oxford, at the Bampton Lecture for 1836.
By CHARLES A. OGILVIE, M.A.
Domestic Chaplain to his Grace the Archbishop of Canterbury, and late
Fellow of Balliol College.
8vo. 7s. 6d.

XV.

A VIEW of the CREATION of the WORLD, in Illustration of
the Mosaic Record.
By the Rev. CHARLES JAMES BURTON, M.A.
Vicar of Lydd, Kent; and late Michel Fellow of Queen's College, Oxford.
In 8vo. 9s.

XVI.

DEATH DISARMED of his TERRORS:
A COURSE of LECTURES preached in Lent, 1836.
By the Rev. R. C. COXE, M.A.
Minister of Archbishop Tenison's Chapel, Regent Street, and formerly Fellow of
Worcester College, Oxford.
12mo. 4s. 6d.

XVII.

SERMONS on some of the SOCIAL and POLITICAL DUTIES
of a CHRISTIAN. With a Preface on the Usefulness of Preaching
on such Subjects.
By the Rev. W. GRESLEY, M.A.
Late Student of Christ Church, and Author of Ecclesiastes Anglicanus, a
Treatise on Preaching.
12mo. 7s. 6d.

XVIII.

The BOOK of PSALMS, according to the Two Authorized
Translations of the Holy Bible and Common Prayer; together
with the Marginal Notes.

Edited by the Rev. CHARLES GIRDLESTONE, M.A.
Vicar of Sedgley, Staffordshire.

Small 8vo. 4s. 6d.

Lately published by the same Editor, and uniformly printed, A CONCORDANCE
to the Prayer-book Translation of the Psalms. 4s. 6d.

XIX.

HOMERI ILIAS.

Chiefly from the Text of HEYNE.

With copious ENGLISH NOTES, illustrating the Grammatical Construction,
the Manners and Customs, the Mythology and Antiquities of the
Heroic Ages: and Preliminary Observations on Points
of Classical Interest and Importance connected
with Homer and his Writings.

By the Rev. WILLIAM TROLLOPE, M.A.
Of Pembroke College, Cambridge; and formerly one of the Masters of Christ's
Hospital.

SECOND EDITION, revised and improved. In one large Volume, 8vo. 18s.

XX.

The SECOND EDITION of

DISCOURSES on ELIJAH and JOHN the BAPTIST.

By the Rev. J. S. M. ANDERSON, M.A.
Chaplain in Ordinary to the Queen, and Perpetual Curate of St. George's Chapel,
Brighton.

8vo. 10s. 6d.

XXI.

DANIEL'S PROPHECY of the SEVENTY WEEKS.

Interpreted by a LAYMAN.

12mo. 5s.

XXII.

NOMENCLATOR POETICUS:

Or the Quantities of all the Proper Names that occur in the Latin Classic Poets
from B.C. 190, to A.D. 500, ascertained by Quotations, including
Examples of every Species of Metre used by them.

By LANCELOT SHARPE, M.A.

12mo. 6s. 6d.

XXIII.

A THIRD VOLUME of PAROCHIAL SERMONS.

By the Rev. JOHN HENRY NEWMAN, M.A.
Vicar of St. Mary the Virgin's, Oxford, and Fellow of Oriel College.

8vo. 10s. 6d.

Lately published, VOLS. I. and II. 8vo. 1l. 1s.

XXIV.

HINTS to YOUNG CLERGYMEN,

On Various Matters of FORM and DUTY; to which are prefixed, Hints for a
simple Course of Study preparatory and subsequent to taking Holy Orders.

By the INCUMBENT of a COUNTRY PARISH.

THIRD EDITION. 12mo. 2s.

XXV.

TRACTS for the TIMES.

By MEMBERS of the UNIVERSITY of OXFORD.

VOL. II. For 1834-5. 8vo. 7s. 6d.

CONTENTS:—1. Liturgical.—2. On Ordinances.—3. On the Apostolical Succession.—4. On the Doctrines of the Church.—5. On the History of the Church.
—6. Records of the Church; or Extracts translated from the Writings of the
Fathers.

Lately published, The FIRST VOLUME. 8vo. 8s. 6d.

XXVI.

DEVOTIONS for FAMILY USE.

By the Rev. CHARLES GIRDLESTONE, M.A.
Vicar of Sedgley, Staffordshire.

Small 8vo. 2s.

Also, DEVOTIONS for PRIVATE USE. By the same Author. 2s.

XXVII.

A GREEK HARMONY of the GOSPELS;

In which the ARRANGEMENTS of NEWCOME, TOWNSEND and
GRESWELL are incorporated. The Verbal Parallelisms, occurring
at different Periods of the Evangelical History are placed in
Juxta-Position; their Chronological Situation being either
preserved or distinctly pointed out. With NOTES.

By the Rev. RICHARD CHAPMAN, B.A.
Formerly of St. John's College, Cambridge.

4to. 1l. 1s.

XXVIII.

SERMONS, chiefly PRACTICAL.

By the Rev. CHARLES J. FURLONG,
Vicar of Warfield, Berks; and late Curate of Bath Easton, near Bath.

8vo. 8s.

XXIX.

ENOCH RESTITUTUS;

Or an Attempt to separate from the Books of Enoch, the Book quoted by St.
Jude; also a Comparison of the Chronology of Enoch with the Hebrew
Computation and with the Periods mentioned in the Book of
Daniel and in the Apocalypse.

By the Rev. EDWARD MURRAY,
Vicar of Stinsford, and Chaplain to the Bishop of Rochester.

XXX.

A LATIN SYNTAX and FIRST READING BOOK for
BEGINNERS; being an Adaptation of BROEDER'S " LITTLE LATIN
GRAMMAR" to the Eton Syntax; and intended as a Companion and
Supplement to that Work.

12mo. 3s.

XXXI.

PRIVATE PRAYERS.

Compiled by the Rev. WALTER FARQUHAR HOOK, M.A.
Vicar of Trinity Parish, Coventry, and Chaplain in Ordinary to his Majesty.

Small 8vo. 2s.

XXXII.

A SECOND SERIES of PLAIN SERMONS.

By the Rev. F. W. FOWLE,
Rector of Allington, and Perpetual Curate of Amesbury, Wilts.

12mo. 5s.

Lately published, the FIRST SERIES. 12mo. 5s. 6d.

XXXIII.

A FEW REMARKABLE EVENTS in the LIFE of the Rev.
JOSIAH THOMPSON, a Secession Minister; showing the Evil
Effects of Voluntary Churches in general, and the Secession
Church in the North of England in particular.

12mo. 3s. 6d.

XXXIV.

On the WHOLE DOCTRINE of FINAL CAUSES.
A Dissertation in Three Parts. With an Introductory Chapter on the
Character of Modern Deism.

By WILLIAM J. IRONS, M.A.

Of Queen College, Oxford, and Curate of St. Mary's Newington, Surrey.

8vo. 7s. 6d.

XXXV.

The ART of READING GREEK according to ACCENT as well
as according to QUANTITY; or a Second Companion to the Eton
Greek Grammar.

By the Rev. ROBERT COLE,
Late Master of the Free Grammar School, Andover.

12mo. 5s.

XXXVI.

THE THIRD VOLUME OF THE

PENNY SUNDAY READER; January to June, 1836.

Edited by the Rev. J. E. N. MOLESWORTH,
Rector of St. Martin's Canterbury, and one of the Six Preachers of Canterbury
Cathedral.

Small 8vo. 2s. 9d.

₄ *This Work is continued in Weekly Numbers.*

XXXVII.

A DEFENCE of CHRISTIANITY, or CONFERENCES on RELIGION; being a Translation of *Défense du Christianisme, ou Conferences sur la Religion, par M. D. Fraysinnous.*

By J. B. JONES, Esq.

In 2 vols. 8vo. 1*l.* 1*s.*

XXXVIII.

The SOLDIER'S HELP to the KNOWLEDGE of DIVINE TRUTH.

A SERIES of DISCOURSES delivered in the Chapel of the Military Hospital, Chelsea.

By the Rev. G. R. GLEIG, M.A. Chaplain.

12mo. 6*s.*

XXXIX.

SERMONS.

Preached in the Parish Church of St. Andrew the Great, Cambridge.

By the Rev. TEMPLE CHEVALLIER, B.D.

Late Vicar and Lecturer of St. Andrew the Great, Cambridge; Professor of Mathematics in the University of Durham; and Perpetual Curate of Esk, Durham.

12mo. 6*s.*

XL.

ECCLESIASTICAL RECORDS of ENGLAND, IRELAND, and SCOTLAND, from the Fifth Century till the Reformation: being an Epitome of BRITISH COUNCILS, the Legatine and Provincial Constitutions, and other Memorials of the Olden Time. With Prolegomena and Notes.

By the Rev. RICHARD HART, B.A.

Vicar of Catton, in the Diocese of Norwich.

8vo. 7*s.* 6*d.*

XLI.

OBSERVATIONS on RELIGIOUS SUBJECTS, originally addressed to a Young Person. With Notes: to which are added a few pages on the Geological Schemes of Creation.

By a DISCIPLE of BISHOP HACKETT.

Third Edition, enlarged. 12mo. 2*s.* 6*d.*

XLII.

PRIVATE DEVOTIONS for SCHOOL BOYS; together with some Rules of Conduct, given by a Father to his Son, on his going to School.

By a LAYMAN.

Third Edition, enlarged, 6*d.*

IN UNIFORM VOLUMES, PRICE 6*s.* EACH, THE

THEOLOGICAL LIBRARY.

EDITORS.

The VEN. ARCHDEACON LYALL, M.A.
The REV. HUGH JAMES ROSE, B.D.

VOLUMES PUBLISHED:

I.

The LIFE of WICLIF.

By CHARLES WEBB LE BAS, M.A.
Professor in the East India College, Herts; and late Fellow of Trinity College, Cambridge.
Portrait. 6*s.*

II.

The CONSISTENCY of the whole SCHEME of REVELATION with ITSELF and with HUMAN REASON.

By PHILIP NICHOLAS SHUTTLEWORTH, D.D.
Warden of New College, Oxford; and Rector of Foxley, Wilts.
6*s.*

III. VI. VIII.

HISTORY of the REFORMED RELIGION in FRANCE.

By EDWARD SMEDLEY, M.A.
Late Fellow of Sidney Sussex College, Cambridge.
In Three Volumes. *With Fourteen Portraits.* 18*s.*

IV. V.

The LIFE of ARCHBISHOP CRANMER.

By CHARLES WEBB LE BAS, M.A.
Professor in the East India College, Herts; and late Fellow of Trinity College, Cambridge.
2 Vols. *Portrait.* 12*s.*

VII. XII.

SCRIPTURE BIOGRAPHY.

By R. W. EVANS. M.A.
Fellow and Tutor of Trinity College, Cambridge; and Author of the " Rectory of Valehead."
2 Vols. 12*s.*

IX. X.

HISTORY of the CHURCH in SCOTLAND.

By the Rev. M. RUSSELL, D.D.
Author of the " Connection of Sacred and Profane History."
2 Vols. *Portraits.* 12*s.*

XI.

The LIFE of BISHOP JEWEL.

By CHARLES WEBB LE BAS, M.A.
Professor in the East India College, Herts; and late Fellow of Trinity College, Cambridge.
Portrait. 6*s.*

XIII.

The LIFE of ARCHBISHOP LAUD.

By CHARLES WEBB LE BAS, M.A.
Professor in the East India College, Herts; and late Fellow of Trinity College, Cambridge.
Portrait. 6*s.*

RIVINGTONS, ST. PAUL'S CHURCH YARD, & WATERLOO PLACE.

THE

𝕭𝖗𝖎𝖙𝖎𝖘𝖍 𝕮𝖗𝖎𝖙𝖎𝖈,

QUARTERLY THEOLOGICAL REVIEW

AND

ECCLESIASTICAL RECORD.

No. XXXIX.—JULY, 1836.

ADVERTISEMENTS.

Just published, price 2s. 9d. in cloth boards, the Third Volume of

THE PENNY SUNDAY READER. Edited by the Rev. J. E. N. MOLESWORTH, Rector of St. Martin's Canterbury, and one of the Six Preachers of Canterbury Cathedral.

The first two Volumes complete the observations on the Collects, Epistles, and Gospels, for every Sunday in the Year, and, the Editor hopes, will form, what has been much wanted, an interesting and various collection of Sunday Reading, which every master may place in the hands of his servants, children, friends, and neighbours, with a view to give them amusing and instructive occupation, suitable to the sacred character of the Lord's Day, and to increase their love and admiration of the Services of the Church. The Work is continued in Numbers. The leading subjects for each Number, in 1836, are the "Proper Lessons" for the several Sundays, of which the harmony and connection with each other, and with the service of the day, are shown, in the same original and practical manner as that in which the Collects, &c. were explained.

Lately published, by the same Author,

1. The PARSON: reprinted from "*The Penny Sunday Reader.*" Price 2d.

2. GOD'S GLORY DECLARED in the HEAVENS: a Sermon, on the Solar Eclipse, May 15th, 1836. Price 3d.

Rivingtons, St. Paul's Church Yard and Waterloo Place.

Just published. Price 1s.

THE LEAVEN OF CHRISTIAN TRUTH: a SERMON, Preached in St. Lawrence Church, Reading, March 24, 1836.

By the Rev. J. HITCHINGS, M. A. Vicar of Wargrave, Berks.

Published by Desire of the District Committee of the Society for Promoting Christian Knowledge.

Rivingtons, St. Paul's Church Yard, and Waterloo Place, Pall Mall; and E. Blackwell, Reading.

Price 6d. The Third Edition of

PRIVATE DEVOTIONS FOR SCHOOL BOYS: together with some Rules of Conduct given by a Father to his Son, on his going to School.

By a LAYMAN.

Rivingtons, St. Paul's Church Yard and Waterloo Place.

In the Press.

REMARKS on that Part of Mr. KING'S PAMPHLET entitled "MAITLAND NOT AUTHORIZED TO CENSURE MILNER," which relates to the WALDENSES: including a REPLY to Mr. FABER'S SUPPLEMENT, entitled "RENERIUS AND MAITLAND."

By the Rev. S. R. MAITLAND.

Rivingtons, St. Paul's Churchyard and Waterloo Place.

DR. ADAM CLARKE'S MISCELLANEOUS WORKS.

On the First of June will be published, elegantly printed in Duodecimo, price 6s. in boards, Vol. 1. of

THE MISCELLANEOUS WORKS of DR. ADAM CLARKE; including his Memoirs of the Wesley Family; Sermons; Sturm's Reflections, &c. &c. The whole printed from the corrected copies left by the Author for publication, embellished with Portraits, Views, Autographs, &c. The work will be published Monthly, and completed in about Fifteen Volumes.

London: Printed for Thomas Tegg & Son, 73, Cheapside; and sold by J. Mason, 14, City Road; R. Griffin & Co. Glasgow; Tegg, Wise & Co. Dublin; and all other Booksellers.

OVID—SALLUST—CICERO—WITH ENGLISH· NOTES, BY THE
REV. WILLIAM TROLLOPE.

EXCERPTA ex OVIDII METAM, et EPISTOLÆ. With
English Notes, and an Introduction, containing Rules for Construing, a Parsing
Praxis, &c. 12mo. 3s. 6d. bound.

The BELLUM CATILINARUM of SALLUST, and CICERO'S FOUR
ORATIONS against CATILINE. With English Notes and an Introduction; to-
gether with the BELLUM JUGURTHINUM of Sallust. The Second Edition, with
Emendations, and an Appendix. 12mo. 3s 6d. bound.

By the Rev. WILLIAM TROLLOPE, M.A.

Printed for J. G. & F. Rivington, St. Paul's Church Yard, and Waterloo Place,
Pall Mall.

In 8vo. price 12s. boards, the Second Edition, of

ÆSCHYLUS. Recensuit JACOBUS SCHOLEFIELD, A.M.
Coll. SS. Trin. nuper Socius, et Græcarum Literarum Professor Regius.

Cantabrigiæ: Veneunt apud J. et J. J. Deighton; et J. G. et F. Rivington, Londini.

GORDON ON LOCOMOTION.—THIRD EDITION.

In One Volume, 8vo. embellished with Thirteen Engravings, Price 10s. 6d. boards,

A TREATISE UPON ELEMENTAL LOCOMOTION and
Interior Communication, wherein are explained and illustrated the History,
Practice, and Prospects of Steam Carriages; and the comparative value of Turnpike
Roads, Railways, and Canals. Third Edition, improved and enlarged, with an
Appendix and a new set of Plates. By ALEXANDER GORDON, Esq., Civil
Engineer.

London: Printed for Thomas Tegg & Son, 73, Cheapside; R. Griffin & Co., Glasgow;
and Tegg, Wise, & Co., Dublin.

This day is published, a New Edition, in 1 vol. royal 8vo. price 21s· in cloth, with a
Portrait (by Vandyke,) of

SIR JOHN SUCKLING'S WORKS, with a Life of the Author,
and Critical Remarks on his Writings and Genius, by the Rev. ALFRED
SUCKLING, L.L.B.

London: Longman & Co.; and John Stacy, Norwich.

Price One Shilling,

A SERMON preached at the General ORDINATION of the
Honourable and Right Reverend RICHARD, LORD BISHOP of OXFORD,
in the Cathedral of Christ Church, Oxford, on Trinity Sunday, May 29, 1836. By
FREDERICK OAKELEY, M.A. Fellow of Balliol College, Oxford. Published at
the Request of the Lord Bishop.

Oxford: J. H. Parker; J. G. & F. Rivington, London.

Price Seven Shillings and Sixpence.

THE DIVINE GLORY MANIFESTED in the CONDUCT and
DISCOURSES of OUR LORD. Eight SERMONS preached before the
University of Oxford, in the year 1836, at the Lecture founded by the late Rev. John
Bampton, M.A. Canon of Salisbury. By CHARLES A. OGILVIE, M.A. Domestic
Chaplain to his Grace the Archbishop of Canterbury, and late Fellow of Balliol College.

Oxford: J. H. Parker; J. G. & F. Rivington, London.

CONTENTS

OF

No. XXXIX.

———◆———

THE

BRITISH CRITIC,

Quarterly Theological Review,

AND

ECCLESIASTICAL RECORD.

JULY, 1836.

ART. I.—1. *Maynooth in* 1834. By Eugene Francis O'Beirne, late Student of Maynooth College. Dublin. 1835.

2. *Ireland. Popery and Priestcraft the Cause of Misery and Crime.* By J. C. Colquhoun, Esq. of Killermont, Glasgow.

3. *The present Position and Duties of the Church of England: A Sermon preached in Canterbury Cathedral, &c. &c.* By William Grant Broughton, M. A., Archdeacon of New South Wales. London. 1835.

WE have placed at the head of this paper the pamphlet of Eugene Francis O'Beirne, because it professes to tell us a great deal about the College of Maynooth—a subject, respecting which every Protestant, who is at all in earnest, must be impatiently desirous of information. And Mr. O'Beirne *does* tell us a great deal. But, unfortunately, there is one awkward circumstance, which tends to impair most grievously the value of his testimony. Mr. O'Beirne was expelled from Maynooth College!—for what reason we are altogether ignorant; and the writer declares himself to be quite as ignorant as we. He complains bitterly that he was removed by the arm of " bare-faced power," and that no application or effort on his part has hitherto been sufficient to extort from the collegiate authorities any statement of the delinquency for which he was driven away. We have no thought whatever of questioning the truth of his allegation. For anything that we know to the contrary, he may have been the victim of caprice and tyranny. He may have been goaded by such oppression as makes " wise men mad." But, even wise men, while the madness is upon them, are not, by any means, the most desirable and trustworthy of witnesses, *anent* the sayings and doings of their persecutors. And, therefore, without the slightest disposition to impeach the integrity of the informant, we must frankly pronounce it to be the duty of all prudent and honest men to listen to his charges with considerably more than ordinary caution.

But, further,—we must venture upon the freedom of doubting whether the wisdom of Mr. O'Beirne, even if it had never been disturbed by oppression, would have been sufficiently commanding to secure the confidence of the public, on his appearance before them as the censor of a great public institution. His statements are put forth, not only in the temper of exasperation which may have been inspired by a sense of wrong, but also, for the most part, in a style of dictatorial arrogance, and sometimes, of coarse, but vapid and feeble jocularity. All this is deeply to be lamented. He has been within the *penetralia* of this establishment; and his personal acquaintance with the system might have given a high value to his testimony, if it had been delivered in a tone of modest and dispassionate intelligence. As it is, to say the least, one is strongly tempted to distrust his judgment. One cannot help feeling that it would be scarcely righteous to condemn the establishment, or its conductors, purely on the strength of depositions which manifest so little either of the spirit of charity or of a sound mind.

We trust that we shall not be misunderstood. It will scarcely, we suppose, be suspected that we entertain any profound admiration for the College of Maynooth! On the contrary, we have always been in the habit of regarding it as a nursery of feelings and of principles inveterately and rancorously hostile to every thing that is called Protestant. From the very nature of the Institution, it cannot well be otherwise. Nevertheless, we must repeat, that the voice of its accuser would have been incomparably more " potential," in confirming our opinions, if it had been somewhat more gentle and subdued; and, above all, if it had been uttered by one who had no personal injuries to redress.

The substance of his arraignment is comprised in the following paragraphs:—

" I denounce the system pursue in Maynooth, both as it regards mental instruction and moral discipline. I denounce it as at variance with the best interests of the state. I denounce it as directly opposed to the constitution of the British empire, upon the inborn and secured rights of a portion of whose subjects it is a never-ceasing infringement. I denounce it as the perpetuator of monkish prejudices, and monkish hostility to tolerant and philanthropic views. I denounce it as the fomenter of bigotry—as an enemy to the diffusion of light—as a drag-chain upon the intellectual movement. I denounce its internal government, as contemning the code of laws originally agreed upon between the trustees and the legislature for the regulation of the establishment—as having invented and acted upon a set of arbitrary and cruel regulations, unsanctioned by the laws—inflicting capricious punishment—violating the common constitution of Great Britain and Ireland, by which a fair trial is secured, and the accuser is confronted with the accused; and as setting up in its stead a cruel Dagon, the work of their own hands—an Inquisitional tribunal in the heart of a free country. I denounce it as not only conniving at, but encouraging the infamous trade of the spy and the informer, and selecting by preference, from those who have sustained such a character, the most persevering and most unprincipled, as the worthiest members of the priesthood, and the most befitting guardians of the people's morals. I denounce them as incompetent, some of them from sheer lack of intellect, and others from a total absence of all dignity of character and enlightenment of views, to hold the reins of government in an institution of such vast importance, and to preside over the education of the future Roman Catholic clergy and hierarchy of Ireland.

" This is strong language, but it is no more than the simple and unvarnished truth. The breast of every man who has received his education in Maynooth College, will, when he reads this statement, beat responsively to the just feeling of indignation which I have attempted to convey. If he look back to the period of his leaving the walls of that institution—his *Sæva*, not his *Alma Mater*—whether he left it bearing his credentials as a Roman Catholic priest, or as a layman, he will recollect, with a shudder, the tyranny from whose jaws he then escaped; and while he reflects upon that moment, and confesses it to have been the happiest of his life, he will acknowledge the accuracy of the picture which I have attempted to draw."—pp. 19, 20.

With this extract we shall dismiss the pamphlet of Mr. O'Beirne; adding only this one suggestion,—that, although his allegations are by no means to be received as conclusive evidence, they may safely and advantageously be resorted to, as a manual of instructions, to direct the investigations of other persons, who may, at any time, be authorized to ascertain the condition and the tendency of this formidable Institution.

We now proceed to Mr. Colquhoun, of Killermont. This gentleman, it appears, has swept away from before him the huge pile of conflicting statements, with which a multitude of interested parties have, from time to time, loaded and perplexed the inquiry; and has, very wisely, betaken himself to the vast body of facts, collected by five Parliamentary Committees, who have sat on the State of Ireland since the year 1825, and have published five folio volumes of Evidence. From this enormous mass of documents he has extracted very cogent proof of the following propositions; that the disorders of Ireland are miserably aggravated by the influence of Roman Catholic *agitators* and *priests;* that, by this influence, the lives and property of Protestants are placed in constant danger; and that tranquillity and order are confined, for the most part, to those quarters in which the Protestants predominate. We can very confidently recommend these statements to the serious attention of the public. They seem to us to be the

result of patient, righteous, and dispassionate investigation. There
is about them nothing which leads to the suspicion that they are
the report of one who was seeking for matter of condemnation,
and was, at all events, resolved to find it. In speaking of the
Romish priesthood, for instance, he does not, after the manner of
some, rush into fierce and truculent reprobation of the whole
body, as a brotherhood of selfish and remorseless impostors, a
band of willing conspirators against virtue, liberty, and order.
He proclaims, on the contrary, that there are among them many
simple-minded and honest men, who are infinitely better than the
cause with which they happen unfortunately to be connected.
Mr. Shiel, however, has been pleased to affirm, on the other
hand, that " the Roman Catholic priesthood of Ireland are the
" best, the purest, and the most zealous clerical body in the
" Christian world"—a proposition which, we opine, he will never
establish to the satisfaction of any reasoning man, unless he can
first contrive to drown the five folios of Parliamentary Evidence
" deeper than did ever plummet sound."

The first thing that must strike every one, on examining the
extracts produced by Mr. Colquhoun, is the disastrous fact, that,
potent as this zealous body have been represented for good, they
are, beyond all comparison, more potent for evil. Their influence, in all matters clearly connected with religion, is notoriously
paramount and irresistible. But it would appear that, the instant the priest steps beyond the circle of his spiritual function, to
interfere with the business of life, and to arrest the political madness of the people,—that instant, the spell deserts him, and he
goes forth merely as a common man. In the confessional, at the
altar, in the sick and dying chamber, he is invested with an overpowering and superhuman majesty. With a word he can lift up,
or cast down, the stoutest heart. He appears before men, as one
who, literally, holds the keys of heaven. But let him attempt to
bring the message of peace into the midst of a band of midnight
conspirators, or an infuriate multitude bent on spoil, incendiarism
and blood, and he finds himself suddenly bereft of all power and
dignity. He is in danger of being scowled at, as an emissary of
oppression, and a traitor to his people. The sword of spiritual
rule suddenly becomes " all too massy for his strength, and will
" not be uplifted." He might, indeed, threaten the plunderers
and assassins with suspension from the sacraments of the Church.
But the probable consequence of his temerity would be, a burst
of frantic indignation against him for a tyrannical abuse of his
sacerdotal powers. The sacredness of his person and his office
would, for a time, be utterly forgotten. Godlike as he is, he
would speedily be doomed to learn that his worshippers bear a

strong.resemblance to the devout and superstitious savage, who flogs his idol whenever it displeases him. Even the Protestant parson is scarcely more an object of aversion and of persecution, than a loyal and pacific priest!

.Now this occasional exposure of weakness—this public desecration of himself—this open descent to the ordinary level of humanity—is more than the best-disposed of the Irish priests are long able to endure. They feel—for they have many of them avowed as much—that the success of their exertions in the cause of order and obedience is at all times extremely doubtful; and they know that every instance of failure shears off a lock from the temples of the.Nazarite, and robs him of a portion of his strength. Like wary and prudent wizards, therefore, they abstain from all fruitless attempts to allay the winds, when the tempest is abroad in all the fulness of its irresistible might. They look on—reluctantly and sorrowfully, perhaps, but still inertly and passively —while murder and pillage are in full revelry around them. When the neighbourhood of the Priest of Ballyheagh was distracted with atrocities perpetrated by contending factions, he refused to interfere, because, truly, " it would have diminished his " influence with his flock." In 1832 there was an illegal combination against the rents of the Duke of Buckingham. One might have expected that a member of " the best, the purest, and " most zealous clerical body in the Christian world," would, at once, have planted himself in the breach between the law and its assailants. But, no! The priest himself, Mr. Burke, declares that he did no such thing; for " if he had positively opposed the " attack, he might find that his influence, upon that and other " subjects, might be very weak."—*Colquhoun*, p. 19.

But, if the priesthood in Ireland are thus, comparatively, powerless as auxiliaries to the law, what tongue can tell, what heart can conceive, their terrific omnipotence, as enemies to the law! If the spiritual power mutters out of the dust, when it speaks of quiet and submission, it thunders from the heights of heaven, when it speaks of resistance and of insurrection. Its accents of peace are drowned by the yell of popular and desperate fury. But when its voice mingles, in dreadful harmony, with the outcry of exasperated multitudes, the sound thereof goes forth to the ends of the land, proclaiming woe and desolation to every individual, and to every institution, which stands in the way for an adversary against the march of rebellion. The destructive confederacy becomes at once a holy crusade. The sufferers in the warfare against tithes are virtually exalted to the honours of martyrdom. The Protestants are not only a band of invaders and usurpers, but a proscribed and accursed race, hateful to God and man. And the dissolution of a union with the sacrilegious and heretical Saxon, becomes a blessed consummation, to which the vows and the energies of the faithful ought incessantly to be directed.

· That such is at least the *tendency* of priestly interference, whenever it allies itself with the turbulent passions, and fierce discontents, of the Romish population, is a matter, we presume, sufficiently notorious and manifest to all who collect their knowledge merely from the current intelligence of the time. But it stands out, in all the bold relief of a substantial and appalling fact, before the face of those who laboriously consult the records compiled by the legislature for our information. And let no man imagine that we insist on this, in a spirit of railing and vindictive crimination. From the very same documents, which tell us of these dreadful things, we likewise learn, that, if a large portion of the Irish priesthood are now enlisted in the battle of political agitation, there are many among them who have been actually driven into the ranks; and this, after an honest and vigorous, but ineffectual struggle, against the degradation of such ruffian warfare. There are, scattered through the folios of parliamentary evidence, instances which show that the better feelings of the body frequently shrunk back from an unholy alliance with the apostles of sedition. But the tide was far too mighty for them either to roll back, or to resist. They could no longer buffet the angry billows, with any hope of escaping destruction; and, accordingly, they were fain to swim with the overpowering torrent. In the parish of Castle Pollard, for instance, the people were bitterly incensed against their priest, because, though " he was a very good man, *he was a bad man for his parishioners;*" in other words, because he refused to prostitute his sacred function to the encouragement of insubordination. The general cry, nearly throughout the country, was, that no priest should be upheld who would not lend his authority to designs of outrage and disorder. Among the instruments for bearing down the reluctance of the secular clergy, was the meddling activity of the friars; who, conformably to their immemorial usage, were incessantly on the watch for the unpopularity of the parish priest, and were ready to rush into his parish, and to seize upon his dues, and to ruin his influence and usefulness. And, instances might be produced, where the people themselves carried their threat of revolt from their local minister into savage execution; and where many moderate and upright individuals of the clerical body were exposed to every species of injustice, insult, and persecution. The result was just what might reasonably have been anticipated. In 1824, when the great Catholic question was in agitation, the priesthood were halting between two opinions; and many of their number kept aloof. from the work of social and political distraction. By the year 1830, all their scruples had been dismissed or smothered; and, when another " theme was thrown out for insurrection's arguing," the priests were the foremost and the hottest in the conflict. Then came Dr. Doyle's Letter against tithes. Then came the denunciations from the altar. Then were the Romish chapels repeatedly polluted and profaned by scenes of brutal violence and tumult, which made religion weep.* And thenceforward, too, did Irish murders, from their horrible frequency, come to be regarded almost as *solennial* occurrences; and to excite, by the wearisome iteration and monotony of crime, but little more attention, than the list of promotions, or the catalogue of bankruptcies!

About this period, too, another element of discord had intimately mixed itself with the spreading mass of evil. The College of Maynooth was established, if we recollect right, in the year 1795; and, in 1824, the credulous policy which had sown the wind, began, in ample measure, to reap the whirlwind. We have been somewhat slow to receive the representations of Mr. O'Beirne, relative to this monument of national *liberality*. But there is other testimony in abundance, besides his, before us. We learn from Mr. Wyse that, in 1824, when the Catholic Association was beginning to trouble the waters, and to lash them into fury, there were in Ireland two classes of priests. There were the older clergy, for the most part educated abroad, and, in general, men of cultivated minds, and gentle manners; desirous of avoiding all secular collision, and willing, if it were possible, to live peaceably with all men. On the other hand, there was a large infusion of a very different material, which had been carefully prepared within the walls of the domestic Institution. The disciples of Maynooth, (if we may trust the accounts here presented to us,) from whatever cause, were found to be much unlike their elder brethren. They were keen politicians, and excellent conductors of the electric element which was then fearfully accumulating in the political atmosphere. And, when it was finally resolved that the Romish hierarchy of Ireland should be forced into solemn league and covenant with the *patriotism* of the day, the younger priests, who had all been educated at home, were mostly found to be in a state of surprising aptitude for the adventure; and were, accordingly, exalted into commanding popularity: while all, of whatever sort, who were backward in the glorious cause, were, gradually, frightened, or goaded, or starved

* See Colquhoun, p. 22, &c.

into compliance.   It seems that the bishops, as being of the old
school, were the last to give way.   Dr. Doyle, himself, is known
to have resisted long; but even he was, at length, compelled to
perceive that his influence, however potent it might be in the
work of excitement, was altogether powerless for the purposes of
restraint.   The result was, that the authority of the prelates was,
in time, brought to bear, with all its weight, upon the sluggish
and the refractory; till, at length, nearly the whole clerical body
was formed into one tremendous agency of disaffection.   After
the struggle of 1824, the priests became, very generally, the collectors for the Association; and no less than 2600 of them en-
rolled themselves among its members, with twenty bishops and
four archbishops at their head.   The services of the same body of
publicans, at the present hour, as gatherers of the O'Connell tribute, is a matter perfectly notorious throughout the empire.

See, then, what is the condition of the Romish priesthood in
that wretched country!   They live under a perpetual, and almost
irresistible, temptation, to become political incendiaries!   Every
one remembers the crowd-compelling game of football, in the
Caliph Vathek.   Now, the football is abroad in Ireland: and it
would seem as if Eblis himself presided over the sport.   The
priests, for a time, may stand aloof from the pursuit; but, one
after the other, the madness seizes upon them: till, at last, they
are found to be foremost in the infernal struggle.   And hence it
is that, (as Mr. Colquhoun suggests,) to the eyes of peaceable
men, the country presents an image of Pandemonium, where the
" vassals of perdition" vex, and torment, and lacerate each other.
The worst and most wicked " have the land in empire"—the
ministers of religion are, at once, their spiritual lords and their
political slaves—superstition is almost compelled to minister to
crime—and clouds of stormy hatred and dissension mingle with
the incense which rises from the altar.   The plague is creeping
about in darkness, and the demon is walking abroad at noon-day.
All this while, the Protestants are marked out for extermination;
and the downfal of the heretical church is now no longer in the
distance of the picture which is constantly before the eyes of every
faithful *Catholic*.   " Boys," exclaimed Priest Burke from his
altar, " Boys, the tottering fabric of heresy is falling, and the
" *Catholic* Church is rising in glory.   Ireland was once *Catholic*
" —it *shall* be *Catholic* again."

Every reader of this Journal must be distinctly aware that it
professes to see but little either of charity or wisdom in the proceedings of fierce haranguers, or cyclical rhapsodists, who go about
the country—(it may be with righteous and benevolent intent)—
to enlighten the people of England, by throwing a glare of lurid

torch-light upon the atrocities of Romanism. But, nevertheless, we hold, on the other hand, that it would argue nothing short of downright judicial infatuation, to close our eyes against the *sunlight*, which is rushing in upon us, from a vast collection of irrefragable *facts.* It may be true that Popery is not in a state of *relative* increase, either in England or in Ireland. It may be true—(though this is rather a heavy demand on our credulity)—that the theology of Peter Dens, and the ethics of Maynooth, are mere literary or ecclesiastical curiosities, and not the guides and manuals of living men. It may be true,—(or it may, for the present, be left undisputed,)—that the Church of Rome is immutable in theory alone, while the life and spirit has departed from her: that she is unchangeable, just as the petrifaction of a man would be unchangeable; retaining, rigidly, the original form, although the vitality is gone. It may be true that the day of the Dominics and the Torquemadas, the Gardiners and the Bonners, is departed for ever,—that it is but a poor and sorry fancy to brood over the probable return of the horrors of Smithfield,—and that to look forward to the ferocity of a future Inquisition, is to see with the eye of childhood, and to fear " a painted devil." All this *may* possibly be true. But, let the confidence, with which all this is frequently asserted, be what it may, it can never cause the truth, which is written in these parliamentary folios, " to pale its ineffectual fire." And these folios,—illustrated as they are, day after day, by the perpetual commentary of Irish affairs—show, with irresistible cogency, that *the day of vengeance is in the heart* of Papal Ireland; that she is prepared, if need be, to plead her cause by violence and blood; and that her priesthood,—whether willingly or by compulsion,—must inevitably be foremost in this strife, whenever it may come. We say not this for the purpose of spreading panic-terror (the most blind and cruel of all passions) among our own people. We speak it rather in sorrow than in anger. We declare it, not to rouse the fury, but to awaken the vigilance, of our countrymen. We proclaim it, in order that,—if we have a deadly struggle to encounter,—we may encounter it in the open day; with a full and clear understanding of our position, and the perils which environ it: so that, if the evil hour should arrive, it may not spring suddenly upon us, *like an armed man,* while we are solacing ourselves with visions of peace, and liberality, and conciliation.

How it is that things have fallen into this miserable condition, (whether " by folly, or by fate," by long misgovernment, or by some strange peculiarity of national temperament, or by all these and many other causes working together), it would now be idle and fruitless to inquire. The phenomena are before us. The

advantage of physical exemption from noxious creations, pro-
verbially ascribed to Ireland, is, somehow or other, most cala-
mitously overbalanced by an abundant and pernicious growth of
moral venom. A dreadful and complicated disease is corroding
" the bowels of the land;" and, of that disease, the mighty agitator
himself is rather a symptom, than a cause; though, like other
symptomatic affections, his virulence may aggravate the malady,
and protract its cure, or tend to render it utterly incurable.
" Whether he be man or devil"—(to use the language of his Majesty's prime minister,)—whether he be " a spirit of health or
goblin damned," Daniel O'Connel is, after all, but the creature
of the times; though a creature who may greatly exasperate the
misery and the confusion by which he was engendered. Those
" yelling monsters" who were the progeny of Sin and Death, are
perpetually preying upon the mother that bred them, so " that
rest or intermission finds she none." And thus it is with political
agitators of every description, whether they be laymen, or whether
they be priests. The entrails of the parent who bore them,
supply them with their foul repast. And there is little hope that
she will find either " rest or intermission," unless some means can
be discovered of muzzling or pacifying their " wide, Cerberean
mouths." But this is a task which, hitherto, has baffled all our
legislative benevolence and sagacity. Cake after cake, medicated
with opiates and honey, has been cast before them and eagerly
devoured. But still the brood are as wakeful and as ravenous as
ever? Nay, " increase of appetite has grown by what it fed on."
And, at present, such is the *Bulimia*, that we are utterly unable
to conceive what prey will ever assuage it, unless the whole body
of Irish Protestantism,—Church, property, every thing,—be
tossed into their jaws!

It is notorious, indeed, that in the moment of every concession
made to the *Catholics* of Ireland, there was always a stunning
chorus of grateful profession. And, of the sincerity of these
effusions there cannot be any reasonable doubt,—provided always,
that we adopt the well-known definition of *gratitude; viz.* a profound and lively sense of *future* favours. And so long as any
thing remains to be granted, the *gratitude* of the petitioners will,
of course, be inexhaustible. We, ourselves, have seen a tiger at
Exeter Change crouch and fawn under the hand of his feeder, when
his supper was just about to be thrown into his cage; and the same
symptoms of *mansuetude* would, naturally, occur at every meal!

After all, however, these strange obliquities ought not, perhaps,
much to astonish us, when we consider the manifold and peculiar
infelicities which have been, for ages, besetting that ill-fated land.
And, among these infelicities, we cannot but reckon the fatality

which, to this hour, has disabled her from enjoying the full *benefits* of the principle of freedom. A people must be most disastrously circumstanced, to which the British Constitution is a curse rather than a blessing. And yet—atrocious as the opinion may be deemed by some—we do, with a deep intensity of conviction, believe that this is the simple case with Ireland! We are eternally reminded that, in other parts of Europe, the most perfect equality of civil rights has been granted to Protestants and Romanists; and that nothing but *peace and good will* has been the result of this triumph of liberality. Be it so. But, be it likewise kept in mind, that, in those blessed regions of *peace and good will*, both Protestants and Romanists are all under the constant and overpowering pressure of a despotic domination. Only let any one figure to himself a Romish Priest, in Austria or in Prussia, denouncing, from his altar, this individual as a traitor, and that individual as an apostate—forbidding his people to do any farming labour for one, or stigmatising another as " *a miscreant to be hunted out of the country.*" In short, only let us imagine any minister of religion, in those kingdoms, daring to blow the trumpet of anarchy from the sanctuary of God. Will any intelligent person among us pretend to doubt what would be the fate of the incendiary? Does any man believe that this detestable abuse of the sacerdotal office would enjoy one day's impunity? And, further, will any one venture to affirm that this beautiful and millennial display of *peace and good will* would have a year's duration, if the arm of absolute power were to be lifted off? Now, in Ireland, we know, the arm of absolute power can never be *laid on.* She forms an integral and most important section of the British empire; and, therefore, she *must* be admitted to a participation in the privileges of our British institutions. But what is the consequence? Why, obviously, that they who hold the keys of heaven, hold likewise the prerogative of *binding and loosing* in all secular and civil matters. They virtually have the power of absolving their people from the duty of obedience to the law; and, not only so, but of proclaiming, if it so please them, with irresistible authority, the religious duty of disobedience and insurrection. Tithes, rent, the exercise of the elective franchise, all are at their mercy! And if any member of our legislature should presume to hint the necessity of controlling this prostitution of priestly influence, he would, instantly, be hooted down, as a violator of the rights of conscience; as a narrow-minded, meddling bigot, intent upon the abridgment of religious freedom; in short, as a traitor to the liberties of the human race.

Now, let it not be imagined that we are here contending for the introduction of despotic power into the administration of Ireland. What we *are* contending for is, the necessity of discerning the absence of all analogy between the cases of Continental Catholicism and Irish Catholicism. We are contending for the manifest absurdity of the notion, that a scheme of gentleness and liberality is attended with no dangers here, because it may be found to be innocent and safe abroad. We maintain that, in our political system, the effect of priestly agitation is, as if the disturbing forces in the planetary system should be sufficiently potent to work a ruinous counteraction to the predominance of the central body. How this evil is to be corrected, is another question; a question which hardly will be thought to lie within our province. But, still, we may affirm that nothing but an aggravation of the mischief can arise from our remaining in stupid and contented ignorance of the existence of the evil.

And is not the evil deadly to the peace and prosperity of Ireland? What would be the probable result if the destinies of Ireland were, at this moment, wielded by a paternal and enlightened, but yet a military despotism. Under such a government, the amplest indulgence might be allowed to every form and variety of purely theological opinion. But no set of opinions would be considered as entitled to the immunity of pure theological belief, if it should be converted into an instrument for distracting and convulsing the realm from one end of it to the other. A mere creed, as such, might be invested with the fullest and most liberal protection. But, if the creed should assume the tone and bearing of an armed and aggressive doctrine, it would, at once, be treated, and justly treated, as an institute of rebellion. And how would the people be the *worse* for the suppression of these treasonable developments of any system of religious opinions? How they might be the *better* for it, may be easily imagined. The government would, then, be able to apply itself, with undisturbed free agency, to the redress of substantial grievances,—to the mitigation of national and traditional prejudices,—to the introduction of pacific and industrious habits,—and to the gradual improvement of the social fabric. But this process of amelioration is, under existing circumstances, scarcely practicable in Ireland. The people are free, as they ought to be, to listen to their priests. And their priests are free, as they ought *not* to be, to preach sedition to the people. And, all this while, the position of the priests is such as lays them under almost overpowering temptations to preach sedition, and to perpetuate and inflame the insurrectionary propensities of their flocks. And the result is, that any limited government must be crippled in its attempts to promote the general happiness and peace. And therefore it is that we have said that the people of Ireland are, virtually, excluded from the *benefits* of the British constitution. That which is a blessing to us, seems to be little better than a curse to them. Those very institutions which have conferred grandeur and liberty on us, threaten to keep them down, for ever, in poverty and degradation..

In the mean time, in spite of the gathering shadows, the hopes of many, among the professed friends of Ireland, are gloriously bright. Wonders are to be accomplished by a course of liberal and conciliating policy, and, above all, of even-handed justice. And, doubtless, conciliation and justice are both most eminently commendable. But the worst of it is, that, with the Romanists of Ireland, conciliation *always* means unlimited concession; and that justice means any thing that Daniel O'Connell may be pleased to take into his head. O, but the general education of the people will, eventually, dissipate every delusion, and subdue every prejudice! But how is education to break the power of the priesthood, where the priests themselves are, in effect, the schoolmasters? But, then, infinite good may reasonably be expected from the introduction of a judicious system of poor laws. Let the good, however, be what it may, there is but little chance of its impairing the predominance of the Romish clergy; who will, probably, contrive to become the almoners of the legislative bounty. In short, it really would appear that Popery is now, to Ireland, what the Old Man of the Mountain was to Sinbad. It is difficult to imagine by what merely human effort it is ever to be shaken off. And, so long as it shall keep its seat, so long there *must* be, not only an antagonism of creeds, but a political strife for mastery; and this, too, with no imaginable end, but the total prostration and demolition of the weaker interest. The right hand of Popery must, indeed, have forgotten its cunning, if it can remain satisfied with retaining the crozier alone in its quiet and unambitious grasp. And the ministers of Popery would be more or less than men, if they could, uniformly and constantly, maintain the demeanour of spiritual serenity and peace, while the roar of stormy passion is every where around them, demanding their help, and craving their blessing upon the banners of revolt; and while there is no secular power able or willing to hinder their obedience to that call.

There are, indeed, few things more astonishing to us than the comfortable stagnation into which the public mind of England has settled down, upon the lees of its own ignorance, touching the peculiar genius of the Church of Rome. We are not now speaking of the *merely* theological errors and corruptions which disfigure her scheme of faith. Against these the outcry is, in various quarters, sufficiently audible and vehement. The peculiarity, to which we allude, is her portentous elasticity; the property which enables her to shrink under pressure without being crushed; and to expand—to all appearance with augmented power of recoil—the instant the pressure is removed; which keeps her in perpetual readiness to diffuse herself in every direction; to rush out through the smallest opening; or to go forward, with a full tide of energy, where an entrance is ministered abundantly to her operations. Now there are many, who have never read history at all, and who, therefore, know nothing of this peculiarity; and there are others, who have read history in vain, and, therefore, care for none of these things. And these are the people who talk, with prodigious fluency and complacency, of the marvels to be wrought on the temper of the Romish Church by measures of equity, and of kindness, and of frank and generous confidence. They speak as if they were in possession of some very simple process, by which this active and "thought-executing" element could be reduced, as it were, to the condition of a non-elastic fluid, content with its appropriate measure of cubic inches. And, if any one should attempt to satisfy these persons that the satellites of the Church of Rome, and more especially the order of Jesuits, are, at this moment, deeply and incessantly engaged in a design for the recovery of her supremacy in this empire, he would probably be listened to with a stare of as much compassion, or contempt, as if he had given utterance to a grave prediction of the speedy restoration of the Druidical hierarchy. And yet—whether they will hear, or whether they will forbear—it is most certain that copious materials have been actually collected, relative to the condition of Romanism in this realm of Great Britain, for many years past; the details of which might furnish matter for serious meditation to all, whose trust in the progress and the efficacy of *Useful and Entertaining Knowledge* is not absolutely unlimited. The march of mind, we know, is astonishingly rapid. But yet it might be well, if the swift and the strong would remember the voice of proverbial wisdom; and learn that the race and the battle may, after all, be to an antagonist whom they despise. And this brings us to the Sermon of Archdeacon Broughton, " On the present Position and Duties of the Church of England."

This Discourse is the production of a man eminently distinguished for sobriety of mind, as well as for steadiness of principle. And, yet, he scruples not to affirm, that " there are many and cer- " tain evidences to show a gigantic design has been conceived, " and is in a course of extensive execution, for re-establishing " here those tenets, and that dominion, which were overthrown at

" the Reformation," p. 5. And, in support of this averment, he has subjoined to his Sermon a most important and interesting Appendix, embodying, in a brief narrative, much of the substance of those materials to which we have just adverted, and to which we ourselves have likewise had access. As these pages may, by possibility, meet the eye of some, who have hitherto wrapped themselves up in a superb disdain for the devices of Jesuits and Monks, we shall venture to call the public attention to some few prominent particulars from the collections in question.

It may scarcely, perhaps, be remembered, at the present day, that, in 1793, a small remnant of persons, under the vows of Loyola, were among the exiles who were then driven, by the fury of the French Revolution, to seek an asylum in this country. In 1795, these persons were described, in the Laity's Directory, as " the gentlemen of the Academy of Liege;" and as already settled " at Stonyhurst, near Clithero." This country was, at that time, in the commencement of her long and agonizing conflict for the deliverance of Europe. Her struggle, for the next twenty years, was with the Demon of Jacobinism. With the Powers of the Vatican she had little cause of quarrel. And, accordingly, the " gentlemen of Liege" excited no more suspicion, than if they had been a small brotherhood of crazy astrologers or alchymists. And thus the Order of Jesus, which had been driven from the land in 1604, crept back again, under a lowly disguise, in 1795.

A period of general confusion and warfare was originally favourable to the quiet perseverance of these "*few ancient men,*" as they were termed by their apologist, Mr. Dallas. They had obtained the house and estate of Stonyhurst, under a long and advantageous lease, from the owner, Mr. Weld, a gentleman of an ancient and wealthy Roman Catholic family. The mansion was spacious, and excellently adapted to the purposes of a school or seminary. And what could be more reasonable and praiseworthy, in these aged exiles, than to provide for their own maintenance, by " the education of young gentlemen?" Accordingly, in 1797, came forth the Prospectus of " Stonyhurst College," describing it as prepared for the convenient reception of 150 pupils, and offering to the public the attraction of singularly moderate terms.

It is well known that the training of youth has ever been, as it were, the fulcrum of that lever, by which the Jesuits have essayed to move the world. It now appeared that this philosophy had, never been forgotten in the darkest days of their adversity. And, that their mechanism might be more powerful, a certain number of eleemosynary children were taken into the establishment, with a view to their eventual admission into holy orders. This part of the plan, (which was *not* publicly announced in the prospectus,) was, of course, admirably fitted to provide the governing body with a succession of obedient, devoted, and serviceable agents.

The discipline established at Stonyhurst was in strict accordance with the spirit of the Romish Church, and after the most approved principles of the School of Loyola. It was, inflexibly and constantly, directed to one object—the subjugation of the individual will. The pupil can never, for one moment, escape the inspection of the " Prefect." Whether in the intervals of recreation, or in the hours of study, he is pursued by the same Gorgon look, which, in time, turns the young heart almost to stone. The very walls of the institution seem to have eyes and ears. Even the mode of administering punishment is so contrived, as to exercise a sort of oppressive and mysterious influence on the spirit of the offender; for, the Superior simply announces to him the penalty he is to undergo; and, thereupon, the delinquent is expected to present himself to the Prefect, and respectfully to solicit the appointed number of stripes. In order that this awful discipline of submission might receive the least possible interruption from the influence of the domestic charities and social affections, the only absence allowed from scholastic controul was an annual vacation of one month : and even this was a concession extorted with difficulty from the austere genius of the place. For it was distinctly declared, that, " if the Directors could abso- " lutely enforce their own serious and earnest desire," the children should never be " called home during the course of their educa- " tion." And, lastly, when, by this sort of dark and subterranean process, the school-boy has been well nigh petrified into a student, he is transferred to the custody of the Professors; where the chains of priestly domination are riveted upon his conscience by the terrors of the Confessional: for, no less than once in every fortnight must he disclose his sins, and seek for absolution.

The institution, nevertheless, took root with astonishing rapidity. and firmness. Nearly from the first, there was a large influx of pupils from Great Britain, from Ireland, and from various parts of the continent. The enterprising spirit of the fathers was naturally animated by success. Their scale of operations was enlarged. Their estate was rendered more valuable by a costly series of improvements. Their mansion was put into a condition of complete repair. A large and handsome wing was added to the original fabric. In the course of time, the number of students was doubled. The work of proselytism was vigorously and successfully prosecuted in the neighbourhood of Stonyhurst: and emissaries were constantly issuing from the establishment, to advance the sacred cause in other parts of 'the kingdom.

In 1814 a mighty impulse was given to their hopes, and to their movements, by an event which, at any other period, must have. occasioned an almost convulsive sensation in Christendom. In the month of August, in that year, the Order of Jesus was restored by a bull of Pope Pius VII. It must, here, be remembered, that in the course of little more than two centuries—from 1555 to 1773—this Society had been stigmatized by no less than thirty-seven expulsions from various states. And it is most remarkable, that, during the eighteenth century, most of the European countries, from which they had been driven, were precisely those who were the blindest in their devotion to the Romish faith. They were ejected from Savoy, in 1729; from Portugal, in 1759; from Spain and the two Sicilies, in 1767; from Parma, in 1768; from Malta, also, in 1768. But the last blow was the most astounding of all. In 1773 they were suppressed, not only at Rome, but throughout all Christendom, by a bull of Pope Ganganelli, Clement XIV. Four years did he painfully deliberate before he launched the thunder. But, at last, it fell. The Society was pronounced by him to be inherently mischievous and wicked, dangerous to the peace of the world, and unworthy of longer toleration. It might have been imagined, that, from thenceforth, the whole body would be regarded for ever as a *triste bidental*—a monument of divine vengeance—a vessel of wrath, broken to pieces like the work of the potter. No such thing. Forty years afterwards, the world beheld, with astonishment, another bull, reinstating this same Society in all its plenitude; and this, too, without the slightest notice of the grounds of their condemnation; without denial, or refutation, of the charges which had been so fatally urged against them; without expressing disapprobation of the doctrines and the practices which had been imputed to them; without a word of prohibition, or of caution, against the revival of such practices and doctrines. His solicitude for the security of the Church is the only motive which Pius VII. is pleased to allege in vindication of this seemingly hazardous and desperate edict. He found the bark of St. Peter tossed with continual storms; and, therefore, he deemed that he should be guilty of a great crime towards God, if he should neglect to employ " these vigorous and experienced rowers," who made a voluntary tender of their services. His audacity was well justified by the event. The " vigorous rowers" started up, and seized the oars, with an alacrity, which showed that their vitality had never, for a moment, been suspended.

―――――― κάρυξε δ' αυτοῖς
ἐμβαλεῖν κώπαισι ΤΕΡΑΣΚΟΠΟΣ, ἀ-
-δείας ἐνίπτων ἐλπίδας.
εἰρεσία δ' ὑπεχώ-
-ρησεν ταχειᾶν ἐκ παλαμᾶν ἄκορος.

Among these " vigorous rowers" were the men of Stonyhurst. And there occurred, about this same period, some circumstances, which gave peculiar value to their exertions. By this time, the " gentlemen of Liege," or their associates and successors, were the Superiors of an imposing establishment, the lords of a large territorial domain, and the central power of a still wider circle of predominant influence. In the meanwhile, the munificent national endowment of Maynooth College, had been elating the hearts, and raising the hopes and aspirations, of the Romanists in Ireland. It appears, however, that there was one serious drawback upon the satisfaction excited by the prosperity of that institution. Its theology laboured under certain suspicions of unsoundness. In the first place, it was observed, with deep regret, that the principles of the Gallican Church had been too much countenanced by the conductors of that establishment; and, secondly, that alarming symptoms had been manifested in its lecture-rooms, of a tendency towards the errors of Jansenism. One instance of this, was a declaration, made by Dr. Ferris, one of the professors, to the effect, that " the merits of the saints, when compared with the " merits of Christ, were no more than a drop of water when com- " pared with the ocean." These were sounds of doctrine hardly to be endured by the Romish Hierarchy of Ireland; who were understood to have acquiesced in all the edicts from the Vatican, by which the Papal Supremacy was most extravagantly exalted; and, moreover, to have accepted the celebrated bull *Unigenitus*, which condemned the propositions of Quesnel, and solemnly approved the moral teaching of the Jesuits. In this exigency, the attention of the faithful was turned towards Stonyhurst, whose orthodoxy was always without spot or wrinkle: and, among her disciples, they found a man admirably fitted for the work of reformation—the Rev. Peter Kenney. This gentleman had received his early education at this establishment; and, during his residence in England, had taken the simple vows of the Order of Jesus. And, after that Order had been revived in Sicily, by a Special Brief from Rome, in 1804, he proceeded to Palermo for the express purpose of being formally and solemnly incorporated into the Society. This individual was the person selected to purify the theology of Maynooth. He was, accordingly, appointed to the office of vice-president, the president being Dr. Murray, the present titular Archbishop of Dublin. He was, there, especially entrusted with the charge of conducting the periodical exercises, known by the name of *Retreats;* a word implying certain seasons set apart for the purposes of religious meditation and discussion. This office, from its very nature, gave him an almost unlimited command over the minds of the young men; and the

result was, that the genius of Loyola speedily became predominant at Maynooth.

But there was still further occasion for the inestimable services
of Mr. Kenney. The college of Maynooth was endowed by our
government expressly and *solely* for the education of the priesthood: whereas it is well known that the Order of Jesus has,
evermore, grasped at the education of all mankind. This principle of monopoly was soon found to be in full activity at
Maynooth: for, a design was actually formed for the establishment of a supplementary seminary for the education of laymen;
and this, too, within the very walls of the clerical institution!
The project was defeated by the vigilance and firmness of Mr.
Abbot, afterwards Lord Colchester. But the spirit of the Order
was not to be baffled. In 1813 the estate of Clongowes Wood,
only six miles from Maynooth, was purchased, with a view
to its conversion into a lay college. In *July*, 1814, the building
was opened for the reception of scholars, and Mr. Kenney was
appointed to fill the office of president. In *August*, 1814, (with
memorable coincidence,) the Bull was issued for the restoration
of the Order of Jesus; and the validity of its vows were established throughout the world. The " vigorous and experienced
rowers" were, thus, encouraged to throw themselves lustily upon
their oars. The terrors of the navigation vanished before them.
They were no longer appalled with difficulties and dangers,
threatening, from opposite quarters, to crush them with destructive collision. And their way towards the possession of the
precious mystic fleece was, thenceforth, left, comparatively, without serious impediment.

The affiliation of the younger institution with the parent seminary of " the gentlemen of Liege " being rendered complete, Mr.
Kenney was joined by others of his order, who became his col-
leagues in the task of education. The intercourse between Clongowes and Stonyhurst has, since that time, been intimate, and
without interruption: and, between them, the work of restoring
and extending the dominion of the Romish Church has been
carried on with incomparable harmony, and untiring perseverance.
Some indications of their success appear upon the face of the
parliamentary evidence. Mr. Kenney there states, upon oath,
that, when he became Vice-President of Maynooth, there were
but two members of the Jesuit Order beside himself in the whole
of Ireland. And from a return, ordered by the House of Commons to be printed in 1830, the number of persons in Ireland
bound by the Jesuit vows, appears to be fifty-eight, and in
England one hundred and seventeen. What augmentation may
have taken place in the interval we are unable to say. But, still,

c 2

it must be allowed, we imagine, that the phenomena distinctly before us are sufficiently remarkable to demand some attention. " A. few ancient men "—a small company of destitute and persecuted exiles—appear as the founders of a towering and prosperous institution, with ample funds at its command,—devoted, with all its powers and resources, to the cause of the Romish Church,—and directed by members of the most subtle, ambitious, and indefatigable fraternity, that was ever organized by the ingenuity of man.

It was not to be supposed that the Pilot of St. Peter's bark would look, without deep interest, upon these accessions to his *crew;* and, in order that their exertions might want no encouragement which he could bestow, his most affectionate regards were, at length, emphatically manifested towards a kindred fraternity, which was capable of becoming an eminently valuable auxiliary to their labours—namely, the *English College* at Rome. Accordingly, in October, 1827, his Holiness, *for the first time during several centuries*, was graciously pleased to visit this Society, at their summer retreat, about fourteen miles from the Eternal City. Of this memorable excursion, a very striking account is now extant, written by one who was formerly a pupil of Stonyhurst, and who was himself present on the occasion. Nothing can be more animated than the picture he has given us of the solemnity in question. The affability and condescension of his Holiness were unspeakably gratifying and impressive. He allowed the brethren to kiss his hand and his foot. He blessed their beads. He dined at their table. He conferred on them, as they knelt before him, the animating and pregnantly eloquent appellation of " *the hope of the Church*." After his departure, he sent them, as a present, a beautiful young calf, decorated with flowers ; and, to crown all, he issued directions to his Master of the Ceremonies, to the effect that, in the procession of *Corpus Christi*, he should assign to the students of the *English* College, the honour of holding the Baldacchino, or Canopy, which is borne over the person of the Pontiff, as he carries the holy Sacrament abroad.

It is scarcely possible, one would imagine, to mistake these indications. But, in all directions, there are other keen and well-feathered shafts upon the wing; the sound whereof may be inaudible to the many, but which are whistling, clearly and sharply, in the ears of the intelligent! There is, positively, a " sleet of arrowy shower" abroad. Among these, we may reckon a prodigal application of the resources of the Society *de Propaganda*, &c., to the purposes of the *English Mission*. And then, within the limits of this mission, there are Christian Doctrine

Societies; and there are *Purgatorian* Societies, with circulating libraries attached;* and there are Stations of the Cross for Pil‑ grimages; and there are Dispensations, and Scapulars, and Religious Sale Libraries. And, lastly, there are various Devo‑ tional Sodalities or Confraternities: for instance, the Confraternity of the Secular Priests of St. Paul; the Sodality of the Heart of Mary; and, above all, there is the *Sodality of the Sacred Heart of Jesus.* And,—(to use the language of a most intelligent friend, who has very recently surveyed this multifarious agency in Ire‑ land,)—these contrivances are all interwoven into the Romish system. They belong to it,—they strengthen it,—they extend it, —and, so far as human means can do so, they *universalize* it. To these circumstances it must be added, that, encouraged by the example of the Jesuits, the other regular orders have vigor‑ ously resumed their operations; that six colleges, besides Stony‑ hurst, under the direction of one or other of these orders, are now in activity, on a very extended scale, in various parts of this king‑ dom; that, according to the Laity's Directory for the present year, the number of Roman Catholic chapels in England and Wales is 410; that every newspaper announces a constant acces‑ sion to that number; and that no chapel is erected without pro‑ ducing a large influx of proselytes.

One word, before we proceed, on the last-mentioned of the *Confraternities* above adverted to,—the Sodality of the Sacred Heart of Jesus. This Sodality was introduced into Maynooth College in 1822; and is described by Mr. Kenney, before the Commission of Irish Education, in 1826, as " a pious association " of individuals, Roman Catholics, priests, bishops, laymen, and " women,—any one whatsoever,—having for its object to honour " the Sacred Humanity of Christ, under the symbol of his Sacred " Heart; as the heart is the emblem of the virtues of human " nature." But he, and the other members of the establishment, positively denied that this Sodality has ever been under the direction of the Jesuits, or that it implies the exercise of any influence by that Society over the scheme of education adopted at Maynooth. It would be impossible for us to detail the history of this species of devotion. But if any one is desirous of ascertain‑ ing whether or not it is an institute in the highest estimation with the Order of Jesus, he may satisfy himself by consulting the Life of Scipio Ricci,† Bishop of Pistoia; and, further, by looking into that part of the Eighth Report of the Commission of 1826,

* The Book of Rules for all these societies, and observances, was published in 1832, by Warren, 8, High Street, Dublin, " with approbation of superiors."
† Vie de Scipion de Ricci, Evêque de Pistoie et Prato, &c. &c. Par de Potter, Auteur de l'Esprit de l'Fglise, chap. xiv. tom. i. p. 53, &c. Bruxelles. 1825.

which relates to the system of Maynooth College. We have, before us, several of the offices and exercises in use among the votaries of *Cardiolatry*. Without entering into any discussion of their theological merits or demerits, it may be sufficient to say, that they are such as no sound religious taste could possibly endure. They rankly savour of what may be called a vile sort of Romish Methodism; and this, very frequently, of the most sickening cast. And yet, we can easily imagine, that they might operate, like a luscious dram, upon temperaments weakened and vitiated by the habitual excitements of superstition; and, if so, it would scarcely appear wonderful, if such preparations should be found to have issued copiously from the Laboratory of Jesuitism. A specimen or two may suffice :

HYMN.

" O heart, Love's victim, slain !
　　O Heaven's lasting joy !
　　To whom distressed mortals fly,
Nor fly for help in vain :

" Darling of the Trinity
　　The Holy Ghost is eased,
　　In Thee; th' Almighty is well pleased;
His Son has wedded Thee.

" The Father's only One,
　　Chaste Spouse of Lovers pure,
　　Who canst no rival love endure,
Possess our hearts alone. Amen."

ANTHEM.

" O Sacred Heart of Jesus, the most perfect pattern of purity! make us clean of heart, that we may merit according to thy heart."
Vers. O God of my heart, my heart is ready to do thy will.
Resp. My God! I desire it; and to carry my heart in the midst of thy heart."

&c. &c. &c.!!

Our space forbids us to venture upon a larger exposition of the evidence, which has satisfied us, more potently than ever, that Romanism has in it a power and energy which (humanly speaking) is irrepressible; that it resembles a vegetable seed, which may be buried in a mummy-case for three or four thousand years, and yet, if dropped into the ground, would, incontinently, spring up in vigorous development;—that, what was said of the royal strumpet of Egypt, may almost be said of the Church of Rome,—

" Age cannot wither her, not custom stale
　　Her infinite variety."

Mutable, most undoubtedly, she may be, in her occasional accommodation of herself to " the form and pressure of the age." But nothing, we apprehend, can be more *immutable* than her sleepless ambition, her desire to stamp an image of herself wherever she may find materials at all capable of the impression. We may apply to her the language used by Paley, when speaking of the spine of vertebrated animals, and say, that she has much of " the strength of the oak, and the *sinuosity* of the osier." And, in saying all this, we should perhaps be saying little that would not be to her honour, if her cause were as good, as her main *principles* of action are steady and unchangeable. It might be well for us of the Reformed faith, if, in imitation of her wisdom, there were more converging of our affections to a single point, and more diverging of our activities from that same point, than has ever yet been witnessed since the days of the Reformation. But, be this as it may, we hold it to be unspeakably important that the true genius of Romanism should be distinctly understood; and that we should not be putting an implicit trust in the virtue which is to go forth from merely human knowledge, when we have to do with an adversary who is consummately accomplished in the art of allying herself either with knowledge or with ignorance, as she may find occasion; and of moulding each of them to her necessities and her designs. We are conscious, indeed, that there may appear something preposterously strange, and even ludicrous, in all this urgency of warning, gravely delivered in the nineteenth century, against the influences which are constantly going forth from the Seven Hills. But three centuries have now gone by since this land shook herself from the thraldom of Her that is seated thereon. And, during that period, such changes have come upon the face of society,—such mighty and visible counter-agencies have been at work,—that the ancient predominance of Rome, and her cruel lust for supremacy and power, have well-nigh passed into the regions of fable. At this day, most men think but little more of the faggots of Smithfield, than they do of the gigantic images of wicker-work, into which human holocausts were crowded by the savage priesthood of our painted forefathers. And hence it is that they muffle themselves up in the persuasion that the spirit which dictated these experiments upon mortal credulity and patience is departed from the earth, never to return. Now we, too, are comparatively but little haunted by the " fierce vexation " of those dreams which may agitate the more nervous and hectic students of martyrology. But yet, we are by no means satisfied that there exist at Rome a wax-work Pope, and wax-work Cardinals, and nothing more! On the contrary, our conviction is, that the principle of life is still

active and stirring in the Vatican. And every one must know
that, in Ireland at least, the genius of Rome survives in the plenitude of its original energy; and that, at this moment, it is scatter-
ing dragon's teeth over the soil, which may speedily spring up
into a harvest of anarchy and blood.   And, if this be so, a heavy
spirit of slumber must have fallen upon us, if we can behold the
signs of the coming strife, and yet, " keep the natural ruby on our
cheeks."

That the hopes of the Roman Catholics, throughout the empire, are lofty, and their exultation rampant, is beyond all controversy.   Are not their own words, even now, sounding in our
ears? Their cry is—" Our enemies see the rapid progress which
" our divine religion is making *throughout these islands;* and the
" churches, chapels, colleges, convents and schools, rising up in
" such numbers and magnificence, make them quake for fear.
" And well they may fear! for the arm of the Lord is with us,
" and we defy them, in the name of God, to resist us.   Heresy,
" already grown old, and tottering on its last stage, will soon be
" no more; and these kingdoms will again become faithful por-
" tions of the Church.   Whether we shall live to see this happy,
" this blessed day, we cannot certainly say; but happy and glo-
" rious will he be who contributes to accelerate its arrival."   In
a similar tone, a Roman Catholic priest, very lately, addressed a
gentleman, well known to us, with whom he was conversing on
the efforts made to storm the works of Popery by violence of
preaching. With a smile of triumph, he observed, " *Priests*
" laugh at *preachers,* but they dread *the Church.* They know
" that, in her weakness, lies their strength; *and they love to see*
" *sectarians tear her to pieces from within.* It spares them the
" trouble of assailing her from without. To *our* Church you
" must look for preservation from heresy and schism. *Ours* is
" the only system which *must* ultimately prevail. *I look forward*
" *to the re-establishment of our system, not in Ireland only, but in*
" *England as well.* We shall go over and convert you all there,
" before long. Your Protestant friends have had their day.
" Ours is now advancing." And he added—" Your clergy dare
" not imitate the spirit of unity, which is our great bond of
" strength. They know that if they did, they would merge into
" *our* Church. And, therefore, in order to diverge more widely
" from her, they say but little of their own."

And are not these words of our adversary pregnant with awful
instruction? Is it not appalling to see that Popish Churchmen
rise in their own estimation, just in proportion as they perceive
our Churchmen falling to the level of Dissenters? Preserved by
primitive discipline, our Church might, by the grace of God, bid

defiance to the Infidel, the Romanist, the Dissenter, and the World. But, alas! because the Romanist exalts the authority of his Church to the stars, we, truly, must make proof of our *uncorruptness* and simplicity, by debasing the authority of our Church to the very dust! And thus it is, that while she is acknowledged by us, in words, to be a divinely appointed guardian of truth, we are content that every section of the Protestant world should dispute that honour with her. And thus, too, it is, that while Popery throws a magic veil over her deformities, the ultra-Protestant spirit of the age despises and rejects the sanctities and beauties, which are the appropriate distinctions of the visible Church of Christ. We claim a right to the temples and the endowments which were wrested by our forefathers from Papal domination and rapacity. And, when the secular arm is stretched forth to touch them, we cry out sacrilege, spoliation, robbery! But, just and righteous as this outcry may be, it still is melancholy to find, that, all this while, the voice of our daily services is so often echoed by the bare walls of our glorious cathedrals! The sanctuary is dishonoured by that worst of desecrations, the desertion of the worshippers; and, hence, each man is strongly tempted to erect his own closet into a sort of anti-sanctuary; and to seek the face of God in the prayer-meeting, rather than amidst the assembled congregation; and to make a Pope of his own private judgment; or, at all events, to resort to the lips of the Boanerges of his neighbourhood: till the land is in danger of being parcelled out among a multitude of co-ordinate *Infallibilities!* And all this is just as our enemies would have it. Of course, they prefer to encounter a mob of sects, rather than the compact and massive columns of a *truly* Catholic establishment. And, if a low sectarian spirit should ever deeply and widely penetrate the body of the Church, the fibres of her strength must gradually be loosened from each other. And then will her knees be relaxed, and her hands wax faint; and they who seek her destruction will, at least for a season, be suffered to prevail against her.

This, then, is the lesson we are to learn from the untiring energy of those " posters of the sea and land," the emissaries of Rome. We are to learn that a spirit of unity is not to be successfully encountered by a spirit of division; that the perversion and abuse of Church principles, by one party, can never justify the utter abandonment of Church principles by another party; that if Rome still has, in her, something dangerous, it is our wisdom to fear it,—to fear it, not with abject cowardice, or frantic terror; but with a fear which awakens to repentance for past neglect or error, and which animates to vigorous application, and unsparing self-devotion, for the future. Above all, we have to learn the folly and the mad-

ness of consigning the cause of the Reformed Verity to the protection of refined and highly cultivated Reason.   To rely on the
armoury of Knowledge alone, is to go down to Egypt for help,
and to stay on horses, and to trust in chariots, because they are
many; and in horsemen, because they are very strong.   For, if
we look not to the Holy One of Israel, neither seek the Lord,
mere human knowledge, after all, may prove as the staff of a broken
reed, which pierces the hand of them that lean upon it.   If Knowledge should be strong enough to beat down Popery, it may also
be treacherous enough to build up nothing but a temple to her
own glory upon the ruins.   And, surely, it would be a mad and
desperate game, if we were to offer our backs to the saddle, and
our flanks to the spur, and our jaws to the bridle, of a godless,
heartless, republican, and therefore tyrannical philosophy; and all,
because we once were galled, past endurance, with the burdens
laid upon us by Pontifical ambition! Let us, rather, courageously
look *all* the various perils of our condition in the face.   The
Church of England is, once more, between the upper and the
nether millstone.   The Church of Rome is stretching out her
head, with earnest expectation of her return to supremacy and
dominion; and she is, at the same time, stretching out one hand
to Jacobinism, and another hand to Dissent.   And portentous is
the harmony struck up, for the time, between the high contracting
parties, intent upon the demolition of their common enemy.   And,
all this while, the semi-sadducéan wisdom of the day is looking
on, with the sleepy eye of indifference, or scorn, to see the
issue of this magnanimous and most righteous adventure, —but yet,
with something of secret exultation at the thought, that the various
forms of · *superstition* are, *happily*, engaged in the destruction of
each other.   This, we earnestly believe, is a true and faithful exposition of the present state of things.   But let it not, for one
moment, be imagined that we say this in a temper of craven
despondency, or of fiery exasperation.   There is One who will
have in derision all them that take counsel against the Church, if
her sons be found faithful to Him and to themselves.   Let them be
but true to their privileges and their duties; and then, the pressure
and the crush of the upper and the nether millstone, shall be, as
if the potsherd were striking against the everlasting rock.

ART. II.—*Natural Theology considered with reference to Lord Brougham's Discourse on that Subject.* By Thomas Turton, D.D., Regius Professor of Divinity in the University of Cambridge, and Dean of Peterborough. London. Parker. 1836. 8vo. pp. 354.

It may be recollected by some of our readers, that in our review of Lord Brougham's Preliminary Discourse to Paley's Natural Theology—while we accorded to the noble author the meed of much sound and enlarged philosophy, clothed in a high order of eloquence peculiarly his own—we could not but express our surprise at several extraordinary omissions in his arguments, and much seeming injustice to other writers on the subject. The *first* ground of our complaint referred to the Ethical Department of his Discourse, and his total oversight of the existence of conscience as the basis of our moral constitution. The *second* arose from his untruly arrogating to himself the discovery of the Divine wisdom displayed in our mental structure as a truth in natural theology—thus betraying either an unjustifiable ignorance or suppression of the merits of his predecessors.

In almost any other writer than his lordship we should have visited these grave faults with severity. Some of our contemporary journals have not allowed his right to be an exception. But we felt so gratified that a mind—of whom we had thought such hard things—should come forward with so noble an avowal of attachment both to natural and revealed religion, that we welcomed the incipient buddings, though unhealthy ones, as at least indicative of moral life, and presumptions that a returning spring might be more full of promise. Moreover, common justice demanded peculiar gentleness to such extra-official yet praiseworthy pursuits. Totally forgetting for the time our well-known views of his lordship's public efforts, we felt that the exactitude, and deliberation, and complete logic of the peaceful cloister, could not be expected from the fatigued, feverish chamber of the politician. And if ever we had been driven to look indignantly at some features of his life, we loved to recognize *one* in which our common sympathies could unite. His lordship's sternest foes might at least regard it with affection, as an " oasis " in what they deem a desert.

We are truly glad to find that the amiable and learned Dr. Turton felt the same. Nothing can be more refreshing than to turn from some rabid persecutions of his lordship's performance, to this mild, this dispassionate, this truth-loving little volume. It will be seen hereafter, that on some points we are as much at issue with Dr. Turton as we are on other points with Lord Brougham, but we cannot forbear, at the outset, from thus cordially expressing our approbation. Any reader of his volume— without personal knowledge of the doctor—will draw the true inference of his unaffected learning and amiableness. His literary fault—" a leaning to virtue's side"—is exceeding distrust of the conclusions of his own judgment, arising from a kindly estimate both of the power and honesty of those of others.

It is very evident that Dr. Turton was induced to write this work more from a pious wish to vindicate the fame of some of his favourite authors, than 'to enter the lists of discussion with Lord Brougham. It is true, that in some parts of the volume, he becomes his lordship's antagonist on the abstract merits of a doctrine: this, however, is but seldom. Most generally he is canvassing the noble lord's strictures upon Paley's classifications and omissions, or Clarke's argument *à priori,* or Warburton's paradox. This is a natural and pleasing task. Our affection to our favourite authors is not a cold, passionless approval of their beauties and their truths. We insensibly regard them as living impersonations. We feel towards them as our living friends. We become jealous of their honour: if we hear one of them admired, we look towards the admirer with something more than the response of intellectual assent,—he has with us a *common* friend,—there is a bond of sympathy: or if, on the contrary, we hear one of them impugned, the impugner is not regarded merely as a dissident, he becomes a foe. Now it seems that Dr. Turton has acted under this impression in his answer to Lord Brougham: and he comes forward to vindicate *his* favourites from misrepresentation and oversight. We hardly think that this was necessary: nevertheless, we will not quarrel with Dr. Turton, and since he has, meanwhile, been induced to throw out some valuable correlative sentiments, we give his work our best recommendation.

Happily, our author is not guilty himself of the first fault with which he charges Lord Brougham. One of the great literary sins of the day is the attempt to introduce an aristocracy in style. While some writers are striving to simplify every thing naturally abstruse and scientific, by the adoption of terms and a phraseology the most vernacular,—others, as if they contained within them the elements of repulsion, have started off to the opposite extreme. Philosophers must have no truth exhibited to them in plainness; there *must* be—not only when it is unavoidable but perforce—scientific *language* as well as scientific statement. It is no longer enough that a term is perspicuous, and pure, and elegant, it must be literary—remote from common life—esoteric. Even our moral treatises, our very sermons, have become thus defiled. We quarrel not with that peculiarity of phrase, which—richer and more euphonous than social diction—a constant inter-course with books will make natural. But we abhor from our very souls the forced profundity, and magniloquence which are become so popular. Soon, very soon, Addison and Bolingbroke will be forgotten as too simple, too *unliterary*, for the age—perspicuity will become darkness, and sublimity be seated in the clouds. On this point our author perfectly coincides with us. In his preface he charged Lord Brougham's Discourse with *obscurity*, and in accounting for it he adduces the following admirable observations :—

" It has long been deemed the glory of Socrates, that he brought philosophy from the schools of the learned to the habitations of men—by stripping it of its technicalities, and exhibiting it in the ordinary language of life. There is no one, in modern times, who has possessed this talent to an equal extent with Paley; and we can scarcely conceive any one to have employed it with greater success. The transmutation of metals into gold was the supreme object of the alchymist's aspirations. But Paley had acquired a more enviable power. Knowledge, however abstruse, by passing through his mind, became plain common sense—stamped with the characters which ensured its currency in the world. At present, the tendency is in the opposite direction. The disposition is to dignify almost every thing with the semblance of science. Matters which have long been understood, sufficiently for all practical purposes, are worked up into a system; and the most pliant of ancient languages is ransacked for combinations of syllables, to be employed in the service of the new scheme of classification. To correspond with all this, the infant science is taught to speak in phrases of large import, and to use expressions familiar only to the mathematical philosophers. Now, it is undoubtedly *possible* to give, to many departments of knowledge, the formalities here described; and so, by their aspect at least, to recommend them to men of science; and this appears to have been Lord Brougham's intention with respect to Natural Theology; for he informs us that ' the composition of his Discourse was undertaken in consequence of an observation which he had often made, that scientific men were apt to regard the study of Natural Religion as little connected with philosophical pursuits.' The intention, indeed, is manifest throughout the Discourse; and if I do not mistake, the *obscurity* which has been felt to pervade the work, arises from his Lordship's *manner* of communicating to Natural Theology a more scientific character than, in his opinion, had been previously assigned to it. . . . Beyond doubt, the truth of science may exist with little or nothing of the form; and in that state the great object of inquiry is, after all, the most accessible to inquirers of every order. Such being the case, whoever ventures to invest any portion of human knowledge with a more scientific exterior, ought to take especial care that it do not, from want of clearness or consistency, appear, to those for whom the change is designed, to have the form of science, with little or nothing of the truth."—p. 4—6.

We have said that Dr. Turton is happily exempt from this fault. No *double* meaning—no half meaning, can be assigned to any of his sentences. We should not say that this perspicuity depended so much upon his command of language as on his perspicuity and honesty of mind.

But to pass from the style to the contents of this volume. Its most valuable as well as most original discussions are contained in the last two sections. In some of the notes to his Preliminary Discourse, Lord Brougham had contended that the ancient philosophers held as truths in natural religion the doctrines of " the Immortality of the Soul," and " Future Rewards and Punishments." His lordship, in the body of his work, had argued that these doctrines could be deduced from observations of natural phenomena: and therefore thought it advisable to adduce as a strong confirmatory illustration, that without the aid of revelation, they *had* actually been deduced. And this theory was in such open defiance of the arguments of the celebrated Bishop Warburton, in his " Divine Legation,"—that it was further thought advisable to discuss *them.*

From several expressions in his volume we are inclined to think that Dr. Turton looks very leniently upon the bishop's hypothesis; and as it is certain that this opinion, coming from so influential an individual as the Divinity Professor of one of our Universities will have great weight, we deem it incumbent on us, somewhat fully, to examine into its value. We are quite aware that the stigma of paradox with which the " Divine Legation " was branded, instantly upon its publication, drew upon it " unmerited neglect,"—and that its writer's unconciliatory tone rather armed against than convinced his readers. Nevertheless, abating all this, we are not disposed to think that a more welcome reception would, in the end, have confirmed its positions. We perfectly agree with Lord Brougham: " The merit of the Divine Legation lies in its learning and in its collateral argument; indeed, nearly the whole is collateral and unconnected with the purpose of his reasoning. But much, even of that collateral matter, is fanciful and unsound. . . . . If any one has lent his ear to the theory that the ancients had no belief in a future state of retribution, it can only be from being led away by confident assertion from the examination of facts." Lord Brougham has not entered into any formal proof of these accusations;—neither has Dr. Turton, though he disallows them, undertaken their refutation. We shall therefore endeavour, very briefly, both to revive the work itself to the notice of our readers, and submit our reasons for our opinion respecting it. And if we could but induce the Cambridge Professor to enter on Warburton's vindication, we should hail it as a sure and good accession to our theological literature.

In Bishop Warburton's time it was a popular sceptical objection that the Mosaic economy was seriously defective as a religious system, inasmuch as it revealed nothing of a future state of retribution. The Bishop undertook its refutation, not with the direct reply and proof that the allegation was untrue, but seriously admitting the fact, he denied the inference. The far-fetched nature of his argument would alone be a presumption against its conclusiveness. To avoid the possibility of misrepresentation, we will quote his own outlines:

" In this demonstration, then, which we may suppose very little short of mathematical certainty, and to which nothing but a mere physical possibility of the contrary case can be opposed, we demand only this single *postulatum* that hath all the clearness of self evidence, namely,

" That a skilful lawgiver, establishing a religion and civil policy, acts with certain views and for certain ends; and not capriciously, or without purpose or design.

" This being granted, we erect our demonstration on these three very clear and simple propositions :—

" I. That the inculcating the doctrine of a future state of rewards and punishments, is necessary to the well being of civil society.

" II. That all mankind, especially the most wise and learned nations of antiquity, have concurred in believing and teaching that this doctrine was of such use to civil society.

" III. That the doctrine of a future state of rewards and punishments is not to be found in, nor did make part of the Mosaic dispensation.

" Propositions so clear and evident, that one would think, we might directly proceed to our conclusion.

" That therefore the law of Moses is of divine original. Which one or both of the two following syllogisms will evince.

" I. Whatsoever religion and society have no future state for their support, must be supported by an extraordinary providence.

" The Jewish religion and society had no future state for their support.

" Therefore, the Jewish religion and society were supported by an extraordinary providence.

" And again, II. The ancient lawgivers universally believed that such a religion could be supported only by an extraordinary providence.

" Moses, who instituted such a religion, was an ancient lawgiver.

" Therefore, Moses believed his religion was supported by an extraordinary providence."—*Warburton's Divine Legation*, vol. i. p. 7.

Now it is not our province in this article to enter upon the general argument of the " Divine Legation." Were it so, we should summarily reply that the whole of it was unsound, because it proceeds upon an untruth as to the silence of the Mosaic books upon a future state of retribution: we would simply refer

our readers to the fourth section of the third part of Dean
Graves's invaluable work upon the Pentateuch; or—what in all
honest interpretation would, we think, be sufficient to a believer in
the new Testament—would quote our blessed Lord's own language: " and as touching the dead that *they rise:* have ye not
read in the book of Moses, how in the bush God spake unto him,
saying, ' I am the God of Abraham, and the God of Isaac, and
the God of Jacob.' He is not the God of the dead, but the God
of the living: ye therefore do greatly err." But we say the discussion of this point is not our province, save by showing the
fundamental error of the bishop's work, to justify our dissent from
Dr. Turton's approbation of it. Our object rather is to establish
Lord Brougham's charge in the first place, that most of its
reasonings are collateral; and secondly, that one of those collateral reasonings, namely, that the ancient philosophers did not
believe in a state of future retribution, is inconclusive.

I. The whole of the second Book of the Legation is taken up
with the proposition—that the ancient Philosophers, while they
considered its popular belief essential to the existence of civil society, *regarded the doctrine of future rewards and punishments
nothing but an advantageous fiction.* What relation *this* has to
the argument, is, we confess, beyond our power to discover. It
is an insulated treatise. Whether the doctrine is useful in producing subordination, or is not,—is surely independent on the
degree of credence which a particular body of men thought fit to
attach to it. And herein, therefore, we think Lord Brougham's
critique perfectly substantiated.

II. But the second question is of more general moment. Is it
true that as Bishop Warburton asserts, and as Dr. Turton likewise seems to think, it was only the common people among the
ancients who gravely believed and looked forward to a future
state wherein should be instituted a retributory correspondence
with the present? It is admitted that such acute observers as
the ancient philosophers, must have seen that all the *representations* of a future world, the fields of Elysium and the walls of
Tartarus, and the flames of Phlegethon, the wheel of Ixion, the
stone of Sisyphus, and the Promethean vulture, were creations of
fancy. It is admitted that they regarded the sixth book of Virgil's
Æneid, its Cumæan grot, its " geminæ Somni portæ," with just
as much abstract deference as we regard the " sabbione ardente,"
and " pioggia di fuoco" of Dante, or the
            " Fiery deluge, fed
    With ever-burning sulphur unconsumed,"
of Milton. It is admitted that these poetic accidents of the doctrine had as much weight with thoughtful speculators, as the

mythological details of the wars, the quarrels, the wounds, the lamentations, the incestuousness of the gods.* But are we thence to infer that the unvarnished doctrine itself was similarly esteemed? Because of the scepticism, or rather decided disbelief, of Cicero in the pagan attributes ascribed to their divinities, are we to brand him with Atheism? and may we not ask, with equal justice, because the ancient Philosophers ridiculed the minute specifications of pleasure or torment in a future state which they thought fit to hold out to the unthinking multitude, did they abjure the theory of retribution altogether?

Let us hear Dr. Turton's opinion on this question: " To express my view of the matter in a few words. There is an apparent contradiction between the philosophy and the religion of those ancient times. It ought, then, to be shown, either that the apparent, is not a real contradiction; or that the sages in question fairly abandoned their philosophy and adhered to their religion. Something at least of this kind ought to be done, before any one can justly infer the ' firm and sound belief' of those old philosophers, in a future state."†

We think this is a fair alternative, and we certainly should choose the first; and for this reason—the relation which their philosophy bore to their religion is immaterial. Conduct and opinion may agree or disagree, there is no natural necessity of their correspondence. Now, the religion of these ancient philosophers was more a matter of conduct, of behaviour than of opinion, and their adherence to it, therefore, did not necessitate an abandonment of their philosophy. None can be more disposed than ourselves to insist that the inconstancy, the discrepancies between creed and action, were some of their foulest blemishes. We fully agree with Barrow, " there was few or none of the philosophers, who did not signify his dislike or contempt of the vulgar opinions and practices concerning religion; what Cicero saith of one part, the wiser sort did judge of all: ' Tota res est inventa fallaciis aut ad quæstum, aut ad superstitionem, aut ad errorem,' (The whole business was deceitfully forged either for gain, or out of superstition, or from mistake.) They did indeed,

---

* " Exposui fere (inquit Cicero) non philosophorum judicia sed delirantium somnia: nec enim multo absurdiora sunt ea, quæ poetarum vocibus fusa, ipsâ suavitate nocuerunt: qui et irâ inflammatos, et libidine furentes induxerunt deos: feceruntque, ut eorum bella, pugnas, prælia, vulnera videremus; odia præterea, dissidia, discordias, ortus, interitus, querelas, lamentationes, effusas in omni intemperantiâ libidines, adulteria, vincula, cum humano genere concubitus, mortalesque ex immortali procreatos. Cum poetarum autem errore conjungere licet portenta magorum, Ægyptiorumque in eodem genere dementiam; tum etiam vulgi opiniones, quæ in maximâ inconstantiâ, veritatis ignoratione versantur."—De Nat. Deor. lib. i. sect. 16, Edit. Ernesti.   † Page 296.

most or all of them, in their external behaviour, comply with
common practice, out of a politic discretion, for their safety and
quiet sake: but in their inward thoughts and judgments, they
(as by many passages in their writings doth appear) believed
nothing, nor liked anything in it: they observed those things as
Seneca said, ' tanquam legibus jussa, non tanquam diis grata,'—
(not as acceptable to the gods themselves, but as commanded
by the laws of their country.)"*   Nevertheless as we have
already asked, do these instances of incredulity respecting those
modes in which the religious doctrines of a divinity and a future
state were put forth, prove that they were incredulous respecting
those religious doctrines themselves *in the abstract?*

Now in answering this inquiry we think that too much value
has been given to certain isolated passages extracted from the
tomes of ancient Philosophy.   This we think, though we agree
with Dr. Turton that " it might be distinctly shown by a copious
induction of particulars ; namely, that in the schools of ancient
Philosophy, an opinion very generally prevailed that the human
soul was originally a portion severed from the divine substance,
and therefore by nature immortal—and that it was destined—
after a series of migrations from one body to another—according to Plato for moral purposes, as punishment, reward, and
purification—to constitute, once more, a part of the divine substance—the individual existence being lost in the existence of
the Deity."†   Thus, omitting the mistakes of their Psychology,
the doctrine of retribution enters into the Metempsychosis of the
ancients.   But we say, too much value has been put upon the
induction from particular passages.   We think that if Dr. Turton
had carried out his own admirable principles as to man's *moral
constitution,* he would have been so certain that the ancients *did*
believe in retribution, and so convinced of the danger of a contrary hypothesis, as to have refused his sanction to the arguments
of Warburton.

Speaking of Lord Brougham he says :—

" But the last omission which I shall notice—and by far the most
remarkable of all—is that of the power of *Conscience ;*—the power by
which every man is compelled to pass sentence of approbation or condemnation upon himself, on account of his own conduct.   When, by
means of the Will, the individual is enabled to carry his resolves—the
combined result of his mental faculties —into effect, *who* sees not, and
feels not, the important uses of this reflex operation of the mind, upon
what has been done ? In what manner the Conscience acquires the
power, and vindicates to itself the right, of approbation and condemna-

* Barrow's Sermon on the Impiety and Imposition of Paganism and Mahometanism
† Pp. 281, 282.   ◆

tion, needs not, for the present purpose, to be decided. The fact is sufficient ; and every one becomes, in consequence, a moral agent—an accountable being. Now, consider man apart from conscience, and there is nothing to restrain him from the exercise of his mental and corporeal faculties to the injury of others :—consider him under the controul of conscience, and he becomes *a law unto himself.* It is scarcely too much to assert that there is not, throughout the whole of external nature, a more striking instance of Divine adaptation, and Divine will, than is here presented. But this is not all. If God designed that man should thus become a moral agent, an accountable being—then has God intimated that He is Himself a Moral Governor of his intelligent creatures. In the preceding steps of our inquiry, we were enabled to discern the Natural Attributes of the Deity—as his power and wisdom ; together with his benevolence in providing for the physical happiness of his sentient creatures ; but having now taken into account the moral nature of man, as attested by the supremacy of conscience in the human constitution, we catch a glimpse of God's Moral Attribute of Justice—and of his purpose of finally rendering to every one according to his works." —pp. 84, 85.

Now, Dr. Turton has here asserted that man's moral nature, endowed with *conscience,* furnishes him with the phenomena whence he may as legitimately infer the Divine Justice, as he may from other phenomena infer the Divine Existence. Jeremy Taylor thought so when he wrote, " It was soberly spoken of Tertullian, ' *Conscientia optima testis Divinitatis ;*' our Conscience is the best argument in the world to prove there is a God. For Conscience is God's deputy ; and the inferior must suppose a superior ; and God and our Conscience are like relative terms, it not being imaginable why some persons in some cases should be amazed and troubled in their minds for their having done a secret turpitude or cruelty ; but that Conscience is present with a message from God, and men feel inward causes of fear, when they are secure from without; that is, they are forced to fear God, when they are safe from men."* The doctrine of retribution is thus, in the abstract, as independent of Revelation, as the doctrine of a Divine Existence. Man's Conscience, in all ages, antedates, as it were, a futurity. If man has a moral law within him, that law must have its sanctions. And surely, those sanctions must be drawn, not from this world, where virtue and vice have no inevitable consequents,—but from the other world, where all will be equitably determined. So, we believe, a retributory state is a fact of Natural Religion. True it is, that " life and immortality were brought to light by the Gospel," and by the Gospel alone. That is—its true characteristics, its connection with the present, the means of preparation for its blessedness,—these alone

---

* Ductor Dubitantium, p. 2, fol. 1676.

have come down to us by Revelation. But that there is a state "beyond,"—dark, and shadowy though may be the belief,—is nevertheless inalienable from man's constitution.

Therefore, we contend that Warburton's theory is not only erroneous but dangerous. He traced the belief of the ancients in "rewards and punishments" hereafter, to the legislative wisdom of the philosophers. He did not recollect that though legislative wisdom had thought fit to oppose, instead of cherishing this belief, all their efforts would have been neutralized, until they had eradicated *conscience.*

We have said thus much because it is possible that Dr. Turton's sanction of Warburton might re-introduce that writer's speculations under very favourable auspices; and we have thought it our duty, if possible, to anticipate and obviate, what we honestly conceive would be an evil. The "Divine Legation" will ever be considered a work of extraordinary erudition, and we must add—in agreement with general opinion—a work of extraordinary inefficiency for conviction.

It is very possible that some of our readers will imagine that our foregoing observations concede too much to unassisted reason, and thereby subtract from our obligations to Revelation. This suspicion will, however, we hope, be obviated by recollecting, first, the amount of knowledge respecting a future state, which we contend is ascertainable independently of Christianity, and, secondly, the process by which it is ascertained. We are only arguing that our immortality and attendant retribution are truths as primary as that of the existence of a Deity; and that because —not our intellectual but—our *moral* constitution involves them. We do not say that man solely as a ratiocinative being would find them out,—but we say, that as a *moral* being he has not to find them out, they are "at his right hand." What is Conscience but a bare mental faculty whereby reason can discriminate between certain objects which we intellectually call good, and certain objects which we intellectually call evil,—how can it be called a judge within us,—if it leaves us without the conviction that its decisions will be ratified? What a mock-trial would ever be going on in man's heart,—how fictitious the tribunal,—how useless the adjudicator,—for all *moral* purposes, if to induce a consciousness of merit or demerit was the limit of their power! But fear is the twin-brother of guilt, and hope of virtue,—and both fear and hope live upon *the future.* It is the persuasion that there is a something in the distance which sustains them. Now, such a state of feeling is not a consequent upon Christianity. It existed long before her. It was even in Adam and Eve, immediately upon their transgression, during the moments of their anxious shame, fearfully modifying the threat, " in the day thou eatest, thou shalt *die.*" And after them it was in the darkest days of Paganism, driving men to cry " Shall I give the fruit of my body for the sin of my soul?" It is still among the Heathen. Whence the horrors of Hinduism ; whence the voluntary immolation beneath the wheels of Juggernaut; whence the forecast of the " red man'" as in anticipation of the immortal fields of the " Great Spirit," he pictures to himself forests more trackless,—and prey more noble, in the hunt of which " his faithful dog will bear him company?" Is all this to be attributed to the policy of civil legislation? Or rather, as seems to us irrefragable, to one of those great elements which go to form the ground of man's responsibility?

The theory which would fain assign all this to direct or traditionary Revelation, has been and is adopted from an injudicious but well-meant jealousy for the Scriptures. Some of our readers will be surprised to find the company in which it would place them :

" With respect to the power of man to discover, by the light of nature, the being of God, and the truths of what is called Natural Religion, *Socinus* thought that these principles were above his natural powers, and that the first notices of a Divine Being were derived from Revelation, or immediate communication from God."[*]

Dr. Turton has supplied us in his volume with the following interesting historical statement upon this subject:—

" During the seventeenth century, the opinions of Socinus did not flourish in this country. The seed was sown, but the ground was not quite prepared for it; nor were there, till after the middle of the eighteenth century, any great signs of vegetation. And the fact is remarkable, that with the increase of Unitarian doctrines—while they were avowedly maintained by some, and regarded with complacency by others —there undoubtedly was a tendency to a revival of the opinions of Socinus, touching Natural Religion. Indications of the existence of such a tendency may be traced even in our own times. I do not quote the late Bishop Watson, as a person symbolizing with the Unitarians, but as one who appears to have felt no dissatisfaction at the progress of their tenets ; and we find him thus expressing his sentiments, respecting a future state, in a letter to Mr. Gibbon : ' I have no hope of a future existence except that which is grounded on the truth of Christianity.' The reason subsequently given to THE KING, for such a declaration, is certainly a good one, supposing the doctrine involved to be well founded ; but it leaves that point untouched. ' I had,' he says, ' frequently met with respectable men, who cherished an expectation of a future state, though they rejected Christianity as an imposture, and I thought my publicly declaring that I was of a contrary opinion might perhaps induce

[*] Tombinin's Memoirs of Faustus Socinus, 1777, p. 216.

Mr. Gibbon, and other *such* men, to make a deeper investigation into the truth of religion than they had hitherto done.' The late Mr. Gilbert Wakefield's Unitarian principles are well known; and in the course of his writings, he frequently presents the following views: ' The reason why I never took any pleasure in *moral ethics,* and would not give one penny for all the morality in the world, is because there is no foundation for virtue and immortality, but in Revelation: and therefore I could never see any advantage from moral writings.'.... I do not affirm, nor do I suppose, that such opinions are universally held by Unitarians—although well according with their peculiar views."—p. 208—210.

Our author very philosophically accounts for this disposition, among the Unitarians, to neutralize the value of Natural Religion, upon this principle: the Christianity of the Unitarian, and which he allows to be a Revealed system, differs but little from the system of Natural Religion. Both of them agree very much in their views of the Divine Character and our Moral Obligation: " Is this credible, with regard to a Dispensation (Christianity) promulgated in so wonderful a manner? Now if Natural Religion be an imaginary thing, the difficulty is apparently lessened."

We do not mean to say that this opinion is confined to Unitarianism.

" In the latter part of the seventeenth century—to counteract the mischievous tendency and ill effects, in a practical point of view, of the indiscreet mode in which certain high doctrines had been preached—there were divines of great eminence, who made it their business to impress upon the conscience a serious sense of moral obligation. They dwelt much upon the duties of life. Some of them, unfortunately, called Christianity a Republication of the Law of Nature:—not intending, most assuredly, that Christianity is a *mere* republication, but designing to hold it forth as a Religion abounding in new motives to the observance of all that is required of men in their present state of being. The Adversaries of the Gospel affected to understand what was said, of the ' republication of the law of nature,' in its strictly literal sense; and availed themselves of the opportunity to show, that Christianity is, on that principle, ' as old as the creation.' Controversies arose: in the midst of which appeared certain zealous, but not very prudent, friends of Revelation, whose aim was to prove that there is no such thing as Natural Religion at all. Before the disputes alluded to were closed, a Lay Divine and Religious Philosopher presented to the world some lucubrations which attracted a good deal of notice. ' A very curious and inquisitive person (as Mr. Whiston justly calls him) Mr. HUTCHINSON, thought that, by the light which revelation afforded him, compared with his own observations, he saw farther into the constitution of the universe, and the operations carried on in it, than Sir ISAAC [NEWTON] had done.' Such is the account, given by Bishop Horne, of the philosophy of Hutchinson; who, deriving the principles of ' the constitution of the universe and the operations carried on in it' from Scripture, could scarcely allow that any thing appertaining to *Religion* could be collected from other sources. Accordingly, we are informed that ' he looked upon Natural Religion as Deism in disguise; an engine of the devil, in these latter days, for the overthrow of the Gospel; and therefore boldly called it *the Religion of Satan or Antichrist.*' In such opinions, philosophical and religious, Hutchinson had several followers of great respectability, as the names of Horne, Parkhurst, and Jones, (not to mention others,) will testify; but the Hutchinsonian philosophy was not formed to endure the scrutiny of the eighteenth century—and the inferences from it, as to religion, would have entirely disappeared, had there not been some attempts to evince their correctness by other considerations. By maintaining the senses to be the only natural inlets to knowledge—that is, by discarding ' reflection, on the operations of the mind, as another source of information—Dr. Ellis, the author of a Treatise entitled, *The Knowledge of Divine things from Revelation, not from Reason or Nature,* undertook to prove that neither the being of a God, nor any other principle of religion, could possibly be deduced from the study of the phenomena of the Universe."—p. 211—213.

Now we shall leave it to our readers to determine, for themselves, whether the doctrines of the Hutchinsonians attribute more true glory to Revelation than the few following remarks, with which we must close this article.

St. Paul has, we think, asserted that " the voice of Nature is the voice of God." How otherwise can we interpret his language, " He hath not left himself without a witness, in that he did good and gave us rain from heaven and fruitful seasons, filling our hearts with food and gladness?" Thus certain beneficial natural phenomena are said to be the proclaimers of one of his attributes, namely, his *goodness.* But Revelation likewise proclaims his goodness;—would she be more valuable, or more glorious, if her testimony stood *alone* rather than in harmony with another one?" So too, we contend that certain *moral* phenomena, just as independently of Revelation, are the proclaimers of one of God's attributes, namely, his *justice.* But Revelation likewise proclaims it;—is her testimony, because assisted, less precious? And again, certain *moral* phenomena proclaims a religious doctrine, namely, our obnoxiousness to punishment. But Revelation likewise proclaims it;—is it unnecessary? Now, even if they both uttered the same, and only the same attestations; even if Revealed Religion said so much, but only so much as Natural Religion, " the mouth of *two* witnesses" would be better than that of *one.* But let us mark, that man had, through darkness and sin, misinterpreted the voice of nature, and the gracious voice of Revelation came to correct the misinterpretation: that in proportion as she is understood nature is understood: that as far as they both allude to the same points, both gloriously agree: that, in fine, Revelation supplies the deficiency of her colleague, " what was dark illumines," —brings out, in more blessed definiteness, the lineaments of the Divine love; and in more striking grandeur and awfulness the Almighty's frown;—and with unhesitating minuteness peoples the fear that had been shadowy, and strengthens the hope that had been feeble.

Let us mark, that the Gospel came to pronounce a testimony peculiarly her own,—and as no mean instrument whereby to gain credit to this exclusive attestation she proved her affinity with another testimony that had been credited already. Let a heathen himself decide. Because he had felt God's kindness before and faintly hoped in it,—and because he had felt God's justice before and had trembled at it,—will he the less value that Gospel which accords with both these primary presumptions of his moral nature, and declares the Almighty to be " in Christ" a Deity of Mercy,— but " out of Christ" a Deity of Equitable Vengeance? " Life and immortality were brought *to light* by the Gospel." Does the endangered mariner value the sun less because it brings to light an anchorage which he *knew* was near him, but which he could not master?

Dr. Turton has done much service to the Church in protesting against a theory which, by arrogating too much to Religion, endangers the forfeiture of all. We would unflatteringly tell him, that much importance though we attach to Lord Brougham's Discourse, and likewise to this his notice of it,—yet we think him of too learned and too independent a mind to be merely a commentator. In his Preface, as one of the reasons for his publication, he says, with much modesty, " there probably was no disinclination to leave some permanent foot-marks, on ground over which I had been accustomed to wander from my earliest years." We are not content with these indices of his path; he must give us the full scenery to which it led him.

ART. III.—*Psalms and Hymns adapted to the Services of the Church of England.* London : Wix, 1836.

THE want of uniformity in the congregational Psalmody of the Establishment, and the licence which has been consequently assumed in many of our churches and chapels, constitute a not unimportant matter, which, for some time, has been forcing itself, more and more, upon the public notice. We have, ourselves, expressed our sentiments on more occasions than one : and, in the first instance, we were accused of laxity, even by valued friends, for hinting objections to the two authorized versions of the Psalms of David, and for desiring that official steps should be taken in the business. But the continuance,—or rather the growth—of the evil has at length made men sensible of its effects and patient of its remedy. If there were but one metrical translation of the Psalms, and that one were in universal use, we should have paused long—whatever our private opinion of its merits—before we had ventured even a single word to shake the confidence of others in its favour. But since there are two,—and both of them are confessedly bad,—we can perceive no valid reason, why there should not be a third. Again, since, *because* they are bad, all sorts of collections are smuggled into our places of worship, we can perceive no valid reason, why a *good* collection should not be made and encouraged. At least, whether it be feasible, or not, immediately to fix one uniform practice, there are certain irregular and injurious practices, which ought immediately to be stopped. For some persons are introducing their own hymns into our service, in a manner almost as objectionable, as if they were introducing their own litany and their own prayers. But here we would refer to the words of a Prelate of our Church, who has lately addressed a most judicious and valuable letter to his brethren upon the subject. The existing mischief is pointed out in that brief, but impressive, publication, with calmness and with wisdom, with eloquence and with authority.

The editor of the Christian Remembrancer, or, as we shall say, for the sake of avoiding circumlocution, since we have seen the name specified in a prospectus, Mr. Hall, has brought forward his work, partly, we suppose, with the hope of remedying this lamentable and crying grievance. This compilation, too, comes before us with this adventitious advantage, that it is dedicated, by permission, to the Bishop of London, and published with the sanction, although not exactly under the immediate auspices, of his lordship. The mitre upon the sides of the cover, will, we doubt not, introduce it into many places of worship, to which it might not otherwise have found its way. The object is indeed one in which an indefatigable and sagacious prelate might well take a kind and active interest : nor do we mean to insinuate that the collection itself is unworthy of the patronage which has been bestowed. Mr. Hall, as we have good authority for believing, has devoted to it much labour and much time. He has obviously set about the task, as a man who felt its importance, and was determined to execute it to the best of his ability. There are every where internal evidences of great care, great industry, and very sedulous revision. This new compilation, therefore, of Psalms and Hymns, will be to many Christians, and more especially to many

parochial clergymen, a very welcome and acceptable production.
It is not a failure: yet we can scarcely hail it as an achievement
of very brilliant success. It is the best, perhaps, which we have:
but very far from being the best which we can conceive. It may
be an improvement upon its predecessors: but it certainly does
not preclude, or render hopeless, the attempt of making an improvement upon itself.

The objects and plan of the work may be gathered from the
preface; as also the obligations under which the compiler lies to
different friends, and the degree of responsibility—certainly not
very considerable—which is incurred by the Bishop of London
in affording his encouragement.

"Selections of Psalms and Hymns are already so numerous, that any
addition may perhaps appear superfluous. The compiler of the present
volume has, however, met with none, in his judgment, so fully calculated to promote uniformity in this part of divine worship, as to forbid
the present attempt.

"His leading object has been to select those portions of every Psalm
which best illustrate its general subject, and are calculated to be practically useful; together with such Hymns as, elevating and warming
the heart, without inflaming the imagination or offending the judgment,
may at once, by their expression and sentiment, commend themselves
both to the educated and to the unlettered Christian. Portions of four
verses only have been chosen, in compliance with the custom which has
obtained in most of our churches, except where the unity of the subject
required an addition.

"Besides the *occasional* Hymns, four have been so applied to every
Sunday in the year as to illustrate the subjects and unity of the services
appointed for the day. Thus, the subjects of the Hymns for the first
Sunday in Advent are respectively—'Acknowledgment of Guilt,'—
'Prayer for Santification,'—'The Coming and Reign of Messiah,'—
and 'The Blessings of Christ's Advent.' A reference to the Morning
Lesson, the Epistle, the Evening Lesson, and the Gospel for the day,
will show the connexion. A similar unity will be found in the services
for every Sunday throughout the year, and in the Hymns which are applied to them.

"To each Hymn are prefixed a heading descriptive of its subject, and
a reference to a passage of Scripture in the services for the day. The
name of an appropriate tune is also applied to every Psalm and Hymn.

"The work is published in octavo, 18mo, and 24mo. To the octavo
edition four indexes are added: one, of the first lines of the Psalms and
Hymns; another, to direct the choice of Psalms proper for the different
parts of the service, by classing them, as far as they would allow, according to their respective characters, whether of praise,—penitence and
supplication,—or precept; a third, of the subjects of the Psalms and
Hymns; and a fourth, of the Texts of Scripture illustrated. By this
arrangement, the clergy may be enabled readily to select a Psalm or
Hymn adapted to a particular discourse.

" The editor has now the grateful task of acknowledging his obligations to many friends for their valuable contributions, and especially for
the kindness and judgment with which they examined the successive
sheets. ·To one he owes peculiar thanks—not only for his continued
and friendly assistance during the progress of the work, but also for his
very liberal contribution of original Psalms and Hymns; many of the
latter having been written upon subjects which had hitherto remained
untouched. He is also bound to acknowledge with gratitude the condescension of the distinguished prelate to whom the volume is inscribed,
in permitting the sheets, after they had received all the improvements
which the various criticisms of friends could suggest, to be submitted to
himself for his general opinion; beyond which the editor would not be
understood as claiming the sanction of his lordship's approval.

" The glory of God, exemplified in 'the unsearchable riches of
Christ,' is the great end contemplated in this selection. That in ministering to this object it may promote the comfort and edification of 'the
followers of the Lamb,' is the fervent prayer with which it is affec-
tionately commended to the members of the Church of England."

A regular plan, such as Mr. Hall's, undoubtedly possesses a
very decided advantage over the usual miscellanies: and some
tribute of approbation is due to every man, who makes a fair and
well-digested attempt at enlisting the charms of music and poetry
on the side of religion. This collection, too, possesses the
negative, yet most salutary, merit of rejecting all prurient phrases,
all questionable modes of address to the Being, who is infinite
and eternal, all undue and offensive familiarity with the sacred
name of the Redeemer. Its *positive* value we cannot regard as
being very transcendant. For the misfortune is, that in extract-
ing the nauseous expressions from certain Hymns, which the editor
has inserted in his catalogue, he has sometimes managed to
squeeze out the poetry. The volatile essence of enthusiasm has
been evaporated; and the *residuum* is dull and vapid enough.
The general fault is a stiffness, a cramped hardness, a pervading
want of the gush, and unction, and ardour of holy thought; where
imagination heightens devotion, and yet devotion chastens imagination. Hence this his compilation somewhat resembles a staid,
decorous, respectable person, who will never be guilty of any
solecism in behaviour; but who has scarcely a single particle of
vivacity and fire in his composition: while, now and then, an
effusion occurs, which can only remind us of a versification of a
schoolboy's theme, put into rhyme, by the way, not always the
most harmonious or the most exact.

The reason for this deficiency may be, that, in addition to the
universal and acknowledged difficulties of devotional poetry, Mr.
Hall has fettered himself by limits, even stricter, we should say,
than any trammels which could be essentially necessary to the

nature of his design.   His Psalms and Hymns are confined, almost without an exception, to the dimension of four stanzas, or
sixteen lines; they are lopped to a precise size and shape, as if
they had been made by the square inch; or as if the true canon
of Psalmody was a foot-rule.   We had really thought, that this
Procrustean process had been confined to sonnets and old New-
digate prize poems.   Some boundaries are, of course, requisite;
but more liberty, we think, might have been taken with advantage;
and, perhaps, even a practical utility might have been secured, by
giving portions of two stanzas or of six; so as to equalize rather
than derange the time of service, and form an adjustment to the
different length of Psalms, or Lessons, Epistle and Gospel, or
Sermon.   At any rate, we have our fears, that in cutting the pieces
by so uniform and inflexible a measure, Mr. Hall has reduced
many a production of verdant promise into a kind of " *triste
lignum;*" a dry, hard chip from which all the sap, and juice
and succulence have departed.

A doubt, moreover, may be reasonably entertained, whether the
editor is aware, how much of the glow and current of a poetical
fancy may be made perfectly compatible with the soberness of
genuine piety and the best decencies of public worship.   As a
test of his taste and temperament in such matters, we turned at
once to the hundred and thirty-seventh Psalm.   That most beautiful and affecting of odes stands in his collection as follows:—

" PSALM CXXXVII.

Devoted Love to the Church in her Affliction.

LEDBEUS.   D. L. M.

When Israel sat by Babel's stream,
Their harps were on the willows hung;
Of Sion was their mournful dream,
Sad were their tears, their harps unstrung:
With taunting scorn their haughty foes
Taught them what fate to slaves belongs;
Proud in their power, they mock'd their woes,
And ask'd for Sion's sacred songs.

For Sion's songs? ah thought abhorr'd!
How, Salem, could they sing of thee;
Or tell the praises of the Lord,
While in their sad captivity?
O Sion! to remember thee
Shall ever be thy sons' employ;
Thy woes their heaviest grief shall be,
Thy happiness their highest joy."

The last stanza, more especially the wretched turn, or conceit, in the concluding lines, may raise a strong doubt as to Mr. Hall's capacity for giving us a collection, which will do justice to the sweet Psalmist of Israel; or adequately supply what is so much needed in the congregational services of the Church of England. This compilation, it appears to us, goes upon the principle of partly adopting the authorized versions of the Psalms, and partly altering and curtailing them " *ad libitum.*" We may adduce the first Psalm as a specimen :—

" PSALM I.

The Blessedness of the Righteous.

ST. ANN'S. C. M.

How blest is he who ne'er consents
  By ill advice to walk ;
Nor stands in sinners' ways, nor sits
  Where scorners love to talk.

But makes the perfect law of God
  His study and delight ;
Devoutly reads therein by day,
  And meditates by night.

Like some fair tree, which, fed by streams,
  Its fruit in season bears,
His life shall prosper, and success
  Attend his latest years.

For God approves the just man's ways ;
  To happiness they tend ;
But all the paths that sinners tread
  In sure destruction end."

But the editor is by no means contented with emendations of Messrs. Sternhold and Hopkins, or Messrs. Brady and Tate. Even in the Hymns, and in old and established favourites, there are many alterations, which are certainly not improvements. This is much to be lamented ; for alterations, in such cases, always jar upon the mind, and grate upon the ear ; and, unless it be very decidedly and very palpably for the better, every change runs an imminent hazard of being denounced as a melancholy mutilation. Let us take the Morning and Evening Hymns according to the present version :—

" MORNING.

Holy Resolution and Gratitude.

CAMBERWELL. L. M.

Awake, my soul, and with the sun
Thy daily stage of duty run ;
Shake off dull sloth, and early rise
To pay thy morning sacrifice.

Redeem thy misspent moments past,
And live this day as if thy last;
Thy talents to improve take care ;
For the great day thyself prepare.

Glory to God, who safe has kept,
And has refresh'd me while I slept;
Grant, Lord, that when from death I wake,
I may of endless life partake.

Direct, control, suggest, this day,
All I design, or do, or say;
That all my powers, with all their might,
In thy sole glory may unite."

" EVENING.

Confiding in God's gracious Care.

MAGDALEN.   L. M.

Glory to thee, my God, this night,
For all the blessings of the light ;
Keep me, O keep me, King of kings,
Beneath thy own almighty wings.

Forgive me, Lord, for thy dear Son,
The ill which I this day have done ;
That with the world, myself and thee,
I, ere I sleep, at peace may be.

Teach me to live, that I may dread
The grave as little as my bed ;
Teach me to die, that so I may
With joy behold the judgment-day.

Lord, let my soul for ever share
The bliss of thy paternal care :
'Tis heaven on earth, 'tis heaven above,
To see thy face, and sing thy love.

Praise God, &c."

What can we say for the lines here printed in italics, or who is
responsible for them? There is really something droll in the
idea of Mr. Hall now correcting Bishop Ken, and now making
improvements upon Reginald Heber. Delightful is it, we must
say, in such a compilation as this, to catch a Scriptural image or an
old familiar hymn. How do the well-known odes, the 56th and
57th, for instance, shine out among the novelties, for which we are
indebted to Mr. Hall and his friends! Passing over a good deal
of most unpoetical loyalty, in which the changes are rung upon
" *save the king*," and " *bless our king*," and " *guide our king*," we
would ask, what can be more bald or prosaic than the effusion
which we subjoin, upon the inspiring topic of the

" CONSECRATION OF CHURCHES ?"

" *Sion's promised Glory a Motive to joyful Worship.*

WARWICK. C. M.

Behold the mountain of the Lord
   In latter days shall rise,
Exalted high above the hills,
   And draw the wond'ring eyes.

To this the joyful nations round,
   All tribes and tongues shall flow;
Up to the hill of God, they'll say,
   And to his house we'll go!

The light that shines from Sion's hill
   Shall lighten ev'ry land:
The King who reigns in Sion's towers
   Shall all the world command.

Then come, ye favour'd of the Lord,
   To worship at his shrine;
And, humbly walking in his light,
   With holy beauty shine."

It would, however, be most disingenuous to contend that there is nothing better to be found in this collection. Hymn 298, is a far more favourable specimen.

" FUNERALS.

Reflections on Mortality.

CROWLE. C. M.

Beneath our feet and o'er our head
   Is equal warning given;
Beneath us lie the countless dead,
   Above us is the heaven.

Their names are graven on the stone,
   Their bones are in the clay;
And ere another day is gone,
   Ourselves may be as they.

Turn, mortal, turn! thy danger know;
   Where'er thy foot can tread,
The earth rings hollow from below,
   And warns thee of her dead.

Turn, Christian, turn! thy soul apply
   To truths divinely giv'n;
The bones that underneath thee lie
   Shall live for hell or heaven."

There is power, too, in the 37th hymn, and in the 46th which we proceed to quote:—although, in both, the rhymes might have attained a nicer accuracy.

" *The Hypocrite and Disobedient condemned.*
(Isa. lvii. 12, 13.)

JUDGMENT. P. M.

Jehovah hath spoken! the nations shall hear;
From the east to the west shall his glory appear;
With thunders and tempests to judgment he'll come;
And all men before him shall wait for their doom.

Thou formal professor! thou saint but in name!
Where now wilt thou cover thy guilt and thy shame,
When thy sin long conceal'd shall be blazon'd abroad,
And thy conscience shall echo the sentence of God!

Wo—wo to the sinners! to what shall they trust
In the day of God's vengeance, the holy and just!
How meet all the terrors that flame in his path,
When the mountains shall melt at the glance of his wrath!

O God! ere the day of thy mercy be past,
With trembling our souls on that mercy we cast:
O guide us in wisdom; for aid we implore;
Till, sav'd with thy people, thy grace we adore."

The 44th is an instance of our meaning, when we ventured to
remark, that some of these compositions put us in mind of a short
but serious essay turned into verse, the thoughts being crowded
and indistinct, the expressions flat and feeble.

" *The Christian Character meek and forgiving.*
(Rom. xii. 21.)

BRUNSWICK. L. M.

The holy gospel we profess
Is truth and mercy, peace and love;
Such, let our hearts and lives express;
Such, let our conversation prove.

Whene'er the angry passions rise,
And tempt our thoughts or tongues to strife,
To Jesus let us lift our eyes,
Bright pattern of the christian life.

Dispensing good where'er he came,
The labour of his life was love:
If then we love the Saviour's name,
That love let our obedience prove.

But ah! how blind, how weak we are;
How frail! how apt to turn aside!
Lord, we depend upon thy care,
And seek thy Spirit for our guide."

On the whole, we give Mr. Hall the fullest credit for his excellent intentions; but we cannot think that he has quite reached

the goal of his own ambition; or quite supplied the *desideratum* which by many ministers and members of the Establishment has been long and almost painfully felt. He has engaged, we may repeat, in a work of extreme difficulty; but that difficulty has been rather valiantly met than triumphantly overcome. Some will be of opinion, that we have attached too much importance to his efforts; and others, that we have spoken of them with too great severity. Our own impression, however, is, that a compilation of Psalms and Hymns, which aspires to be generally admitted into the churches and chapels of the Establishment, is a very momentous undertaking; and that it *ought* to be tried by a very high standard, both in a religious and in a poetical point of view. Our wish, we confess, is to see suitable portions, not merely of the Psalms, but of other portions of Scripture—such as parts of the Book of Job, of Isaiah, of the magnificent odes which are scattered through the historical books of the Old Testament, of the affecting passages, which make our hearts thrill in the New, translated and adapted to music by the living authors most competent to the task, such as Southey, Milman, Keble, and many others whom we could name. In the mean time, although the original attempts are not always the happiest; and although there are some perilous experiments at alteration, which could only be justified by complete success, and which have not always that justification; we shall do wrong quite to turn aside from Mr. Hall's compilation. We repeat, that, as far as we know, there is nothing better of the kind *in esse*, although there may be something infinitely better *in posse*. And Mr. Hall may well bid us be thankful to him, at least as a pioneer, and accept his collection with gratitude, at least until we can find one superior to supersede it. He may well think, that, until we can live in " *the best of all possible worlds*," it is idle to wait for the best of all possible Psalms and Hymns. He may well appeal to an objector with the somewhat stale quotation,—

———" Si quid novisti rectius istis,
Candidus imperti ; si non, *his utere* mecum."

It remains to be added, that, besides this compilation, to which the particular circumstances attending its appearance have attracted our especial notice, we see announced a collection of of Psalms and Hymns by the Rev. J. E. Riddle; another has been recently put forth by the Rev. E. Scobell: and a third, we believe,—for " another and another still succeeds,"—is in preparation under the joint superintendence of Messrs. Tomlinson and Dukinfield. Our sincere hope is, that so much competition will lead to excellence; and so in its ultimate effect to uniformity.

Art. IV.—*Kurze Geschichte der Päpste; nebst einem Anhange über den Primat Petri und das Mährchen von der Päpstinn Johanna,* von D. Wilhelm Smets. Dritte Auflage. Köln. 1835.

MOST men, says a well-known Greek historian,* instituting no laborious research after truth, ἐπὶ τὰ ἕτοιμα μᾶλλον τρέπονται. We naturally like to look at things, not as they are, but as it is convenient for us that they should be. We delight in objects ready arranged and prepared to admit of our contemplating them from the most convenient position and with as little trouble as possible. And hence arises within us a constant, though perhaps an unconscious, desire to construct individualities; to bring, in thought, things connected with each other into masses; and then, as it were, to give a personal existence to systems, dynasties, empires, or chains of events; ascribing to the respective unities which we choose to behold in them, broad and general characteristics, deduced, of course, from our impressions respecting the working of these subjects of our speculation in such parts of their fields of operation as have been more immediately brought under our notice.

From some such popular mental process as this has arisen, it is probable, the habit now prevalent among us of viewing as one thing—as an individuality possessing, so to say, an inseparable personal character,—the system of the dominion of the Papacy. What that dominion has been in the times with the history of which we are most conversant,—what it is now, wherever, as in a neighbouring island, it still shows symptoms of life and vigour, —men know, or think they know, by abundant experience. And hence, by bringing that dominion from its infancy to the present hour into one field of view,—by ascribing to it one permanent habit and principle of action rather than that succession of habits and principles which might with greater plausibility be conceived to characterize a power existing through many centuries,—by making of it, in short, an individual object of contemplation, they settle down, unhesitatingly, in the conviction that such as it is now, such, in itself, it always was; and they acquire the custom of predicating fearlessly of its whole historical career the characteristics which they know but as being incidentally connected with its present, or at any rate its recent, phase. Men speak of the papal power as opposed to the diffusion of knowledge and to the enlightenment of mankind; as more especially averse to the study of the Scriptures by lay members of the Church; as friendly

* Thucyd. lib. i. c. 20.

to despotism, and consequently hostile to the reasonable rights and liberties of nations; and as habitually supporting a corrupt system of Christianity in opposition to the true religion of the Gospel. And that this character, if applied to the conduct of the conclave during the last two or three centuries, is, in the main, unjust, we will not undertake to maintain. But two or three centuries form but a small portion of the recorded duration of the papal power; and a careful consideration even of this character, as standing by itself, and without direct reference to the history of remoter times, might suffice to show us how fallacious must be the reasoning which would ascribe it to any long existing system, as a permanent and necessary, rather than as a temporary and accidental definition. We might, even *à priori,* see that many features of such a character exist but in relation to things variable in their nature and foreign to the true internal essence of the system which it is intended to describe. The accuracy, for instance, of the last clause of the description would mainly depend, not on the abstract position, or on the actual temperament of the Papacy, but on the nature of the elements, religious or political, which might at any given period be found to be opposed to it. It would not, as a matter of course, or by a necessary consequence, follow, from the fact of the assertion of a corrupt theology, that the assertor would at all times have to defend it against a purer system. It might certainly be impugned because it was *corrupt;* but it might also be attacked because it was *theology.* It might—and, if amid its corruption it held any great doctrines of the truth, it probably would—find assailants from below—if we may so say—as well as from above; —from the ranks of infidelity as well as from those of pure Christianity. And thus a system, even though itself unchanged, might at one epoch be ·justly described as opposing the truth, and at another designated with equal ·justice the antagonist of error.

Again, with respect to the position of the papal power viewed in relation to the struggles between monarchs and their subjects; this is evidently a position which must at all times have been mainly determined by matters external to that power itself; a position which must have fluctuated with the constant fluctuations of European politics; and which it were clearly an error to incorporate into a definition, intended as a permanent and essential one, of the spirit of Romish ecclesiastical dominion.

We are, in truth, with respect to the Papacy, mainly led into the adoption of the fallacious mode of reasoning above described by the ignorance so generally prevalent among us of one most important fact, namely, that Popery, and by consequence the papal power, underwent, at the epoch of the Reformation, a marked and sudden change of character.

We commonly, but carelessly, acquiesce in the notion—fatal as, were it true, it would prove to the Catholicism of our English Church—that the religion now taught by the Church of Rome, was the religion once spread over Western Europe, our own island included, and that our Protestant doctrines are comparatively new among us. Whereas, the fact is, that the religion of existing Rome, as far as relates to those particulars in which it differs from our own, is, in strictness, a new religion, having its origin with the ever-to-be lamented Council of Trent. The peculiar notions which, according to our current phraseology, stamp on the religion with which they are connected, the title " Popery," had indeed, previously to the date of that Council, extensively prevailed in our own as in other countries. Insensibly had they crept in, some sooner and some later, and imperceptibly had they become amalgamated with the current faith of our people. But the Reformers detected these insidious innovations. As such—as innovations—they embodied against them that series of protests commonly known by the name of the Thirty-nine Articles. At that period* it was that Rome, stung by this rejection of doctrines in which the credit of her existing authorities was involved, adopted the bold—the unprecedented—step of formally incorporating these doctrines so completely with her religion as to make the reception of them a necessary condition for participation in her communion. And this step it is which virtually separates us from that communion at the present hour. We commonly think and speak of our Reformers as though they had separated themselves from the Romish Church and put her to the ban.† But such is not the fact; for aught that they have done we could communicate with her now; but we know that, should we attempt to do so, she would put forth this list of novel dogmas of faith, and call upon us either to subscribe it or to depart from her altars.

---

* The Thirty-nine Articles were adopted by our Church in 1562. The Bull of Pius IV., which promulgated the Tridentine Creed, bore date November, 1564.

† This notion is set forth in a pamphlet lately published by Mr. Bickersteth. He says, " It was this view of Popery which led our Reformers to a decided separation " from the church of Rome. As God commanded the Jews to come out of Babylon of " old, so he explicitly commands those in modern Babylon, by a voice from heaven, " to separate from her. . . . It is not lawful to separate from a pure Church of Christ. " It is a positive duty to go out from the fallen Church of Rome." But let us, against this, set the more historical view of Mr. Dodsworth. " Common as the notion is in our " day, that our Church did so separate, there never was a more groundless notion, " or one more contrary to fact. THE CHURCH OF ENGLAND NEVER SEPARATED " FROM THE CHURCH OF ROME, OR FROM ANY OTHER CHURCH." *Vide* The Church of England a Protester against Romanism and Dissent. No. I.

And though, as we have admitted, these erroneous tenets were held by many—nay, were generally prevalent in the Western Church at the opening of the Reformation,—antecedently, that is, to the date of the Tridentine assembly; yet the admission, by any, of doctrines uncontroverted and unquestioned in their time, —the reception of them, vaguely and undoubtingly, from the influence of habit, example, or education, or upon the broad principle of deference to undisputed authority,—is a very different thing from an adoption of those doctrines when clearly defined, when formally incorporated into a creed, and when asserted in open and notorious opposition to their contradicting verities. Even those, therefore, who were, antecedently to the Council of Trent, the most Popish, if we may so say, in principle, embraced, in adopting the formulary propounded by that council, a religion which was in one sense, and that a most important one, new to them.

Assertors as they were of this novel religion, the position of the successors of St. Peter became also, in some material points, a new one; and the policy, the temper, the moral tone of the Vatican, must needs have undergone considerable remoulding from the change. Even without, therefore, taking into account the general improbability of the maintenance, by a succession of men, through a long series of ages, of what may be called an individual character, we have in our knowledge of this one historical fact sufficient reason to deter us, in the case of the Papacy, from pronouncing decisively our verdict on the past, from the relative, the incidental, the transitory, characteristics of the present.

And the same great change which has thus given to the power in question a new character, has in great measure disqualified us from passing an accurate judgment upon its old one. The reformation of our English Church, necessary, beneficial, blessed, as was the event, was, as a sudden and violent change, necessarily productive of some of those incidental evils by which such changes ever will and must be accompanied. And one of these unfortunate results was, unquestionably, that revulsion of feeling, attendant upon the crisis, which, as it were, wrenched us forcibly from the past; which led us to look on that past with a gaze, not of Christian reverence, but of unchristian suspicion; teaching us that the antiquity of a practice or tenet of religion was rather a reason for shrinking from and abandoning it, than for dutifully receiving or observing it. It is not, of course, our Reformers whom we would blame for the rise of this feeling. Having designated the Reformation necessary, we have already virtually ascribed the evils incidentally connected with the change to the agency of those causes which made that change inevitable. Forced, even for the sake of preserving our Church's purity, to sever the bonds of association which linked our minds to those of our forefathers, our guides almost involuntarily untaught us the duty of tracing up our faith through the annals of other days, and of distinguishing from heretical schemes, the date of whose respective rises could be clearly made out, that system of doctrine " quod semper, quod ubique, quod ab omnibus creditum est ;"* thus to a certain extent imbuing us, even while our orders and discipline yet demonstrated our Catholicity, with the moral tone and temperament of low sectarianism.

Through the influence of some such feelings as this it is that the church history of the long period between the very earliest times of Christianity and the opening of the sixteenth century has become to most of us a blank page. The intervening ages appear dark to us, and such we call them; forgetting, while we do so, that the effect of darkness may be produced either by the want of light upon an object contemplated or by that of visual power in the eye which strives to behold it. And amid this darkness—absolute or relative, or both—some of the few figures which we are able to discern, glare luridly upon us with preternatural proportions; while others, dimly and uncertainly made out from the encompassing vacancy, suggest ideas totally different from those which the sight of the same things, surrounded by their usual accompaniments, and illumined by the radiance of day, would probably occasion.

It is under such disadvantages as these that we ordinarily contemplate the rise and early growth of that extraordinary moral empire which, unsupported by, or rather opposed to, physical power, succeeded during the middle ages to a pre-eminence which had till then been conceded to the iron hand of military force alone. Learning from the history of more modern times what the character of the papal power has recently been,—applying that character to times in which we see of that power no more than the dim outline of its rise,—and in total ignorance of the position in relation to other powers in which, at the period of that rise, it was placed,—we view in it, from its origin, as has been already remarked, a power inimical to purity alike of faith and of manners,—to the rights as well of sovereigns as of their subjects,—to knowledge,—to virtue,—and, in fine, to Christianity itself. We come to regard its whole existence as a devastating phenomenon;—as one of those destructive dispensations

---

* See the Commonitorium of Vincentius Lirinensis. ·This invaluable little treatise should be in the hands of every churchman whose classical attainments will enable him to master some fifty or sixty pages of easy Latinity.

of the Almighty which nothing but a confirmed faith can enable us to regard as compatible either with His revealed or with His discoverable attributes. We fix, as well as we can, what we consider the exact epoch of its appearance, and reckon up from that the years which have since elapsed, as though wondering that the continuance of such a pest through so lengthened a period should have been foredoomed in the councils of Heaven.

And yet, utterly as such an *impassioned* view, so to call it, would seem to disqualify him who entertains it from discharging the duties of a historian, it is to England, and to England alone, that we look with hope for the eventual filling up of that void in the historical literature of Europe, a clear and satisfactory narration of the rise of the papal power. Germany has sons indefatigable in research and profound in thought. Far be it from us to despise or depreciate the exertions of her Schröckhs, her Plancks, her Gieselers. As collectors of intelligence—as accumulators of a great mass of facts, from which all future church historians must derive the most valuable assistance; —they have laboured arduously and well. But Germany, from the line unfortunately adopted by those who conducted her Reformation, contains none who are alike within the pale of the Catholic Church—as that term was understood in early times— and without the pale of Romanism. Her Protestants are formed into communities, each of which, as such, commenced its existence with the great convulsive change of the sixteenth century, branching off and separating itself from that great apostolic Institution which has, by the golden chain of the ministerial succession, been providentially preserved among ourselves. There exists not, therefore, in their case, the possibility of that identification of one's self with the past,—of that habitual and involuntary sympathy with the fortunes of the Church, through all the stages of her history,—which a member of her Anglican branch, if he understand his true position, will necessarily feel; and without which the efforts of the ecclesiastical historian will ever be inadequate suitably to embody the majesty of his subject.

The Romish writers of Germany do not, of course, participate in this particular disqualification. Yet it is not to them that, belonging as we do to a reformed Church, we can look for a satisfactory delineation of any portion of history with which the Papacy is directly concerned. Indeed, the existence of papal power, in its most important features, from the very foundation of the Church, is a portion of the Romanist's creed. The growth, consequently, of that power in the middle ages, he would be the last to describe, or even to examine, in detail.

Dr. Smets, with the title of whose compendious " History of

the Popes" we have headed this Article, belongs to this latter
class of German writers. His work was published in that ancient seat of ecclesiastical authority, the archiepiscopal city of
Cologne. And his object in compiling it appears to have been
to supply his co-religionists with what he conceived an antidote
to the cheap publications which have inundated the German
press, and have fostered in every possible way the light and
irreverent spirit of the age. " To the hostility of that spirit,"
says Dr. Smets, " the clerical office—the ministry of the Catholic Church, in its various grades and orders, is above all things
exposed." A remark in which, we need not say, we fully concur
with him. The experience of our English branch of the Church
Catholic hourly proves the fact. And we much wish to see that
spirit more fully encountered among ourselves by means analogous to those suggested to his fellow Romanists by Dr. Smets;
—by attempts to render familiar to the minds of our countrymen
the history of the Church, and the commission and authority of
her ministers.

But, short as is the work of Dr. Smets altogether, it is, for the
reason above given, as the work of a Romanist, peculiarly brief
and unsatisfactory respecting the point to which we wish at present to direct attention. We have therefore alluded to that work
rather with the view of giving our own views, derived from
general sources, of the subject in question, than of attempting
any direct analysis of the little volume before us. And we have
chosen that volume for the purpose rather than any of the more
elaborate histories with which Germany abounds, because, differing so widely as we do and must in our views from both classes
of her writers, we should—had we undertaken to review any
thing more considerable than a compendium—have been compelled to confuse what we now hope to lay simply and uninter-
ruptedly before our readers, a general account of a most important passage in the Church's history, by digressions on matters
connected with some individual author, or by discussions on
points of controverted principle.

Those who, averting their eyes from the crude and hastily
formed notions to which they are accustomed, could bring themselves calmly and impartially to contemplate the great historical
phenomenon which the rise of the papal domination presents to
our notice, would assuredly find the contemplation fraught with
interest and instruction of no ordinary nature. That in an age
of rudeness, of violence, and of ignorance, an authority should
rise up, based on conscience and supported by spiritual sanctions
alone;—that this authority, led by circumstances to confront that
of the proudest monarchs of the world, should upon trial be

found superior to it, the diadem being abased before the tiara; the sword of empire before the crook of pastoral authority;—that all this should be, of a surety betokens the agency of some higher and more refined principle than is developed in the exaltation of a common earthly empire. And when we recollect, in addition to this, that the power thus strangely rising based its moral energy upon the faith—fearfully corrupted, perhaps, and disfigured—but still upon the faith, the deep conviction of mankind that the Gospel was true, we have unquestionably strong cause for suspecting that the revolution in human affairs by which its elevation was accomplished, was not one fraught with unmitigated evil.

That revolution, like all others of a moral nature, was in truth the gradual work of ages; though its more apparent process, or, in other words, its crisis, took place during the latter portion of the eleventh century, while the councils of the Vatican were guided by the celebrated Hildebrand, who for the last twelve years of his life filled the Papal chair under the name of Gregory the Seventh. This personage, commonly regarded among us as a sort of type or impersonation of the system with the predominance of which he was connected, participates, by a natural consequence, in the odium with which that system itself is habitually regarded. Our ordinary ideas on the subject are, indeed, far too vague to admit of our recognizing, in the agents of a work thus beheld in the mass, individualities separate and distinct from that which we ascribe to the mass itself. And even if, inquiring rather farther than is usual into the subject, we arrive at the knowledge of certain peculiar features of character as having distinguished individual actors in the distant scene, this very knowledge, through the peculiarity of our position, will sometimes mislead and confuse us, rather than guide us in the formation of true judgments or accurate ideas; for the errors, the peculiarities, and the fancies of those times were not only different from, but, if we may so say, contrary to, those of our own age. The violent change of the Reformation did much more than cause the annihilation of certain erroneous modes of thought and systematic prejudices; it established in the Protestant mind a tendency to opposite modes, opposite imaginations. And he, therefore, who, with exclusively Protestant training, looks at the character of a pope of the middle ages, will, it is probable, be startled by much that he sees, not on account of its variance from the true standard of perfection, but on account of the discrepancy between it and a standard fixed by himself—if the expression may be allowed—on the opposite side of the truth. The errors and heresies of our own time are, it is probable, but exaggerations or distorted ex-

pressions of notions in some degree current in our own breasts;
they find within us something which, in a measure at least, responds to them; and, indeed, the very familiarity which, if we move
in the world, we must acquire alike with their theory and their
practice, deadens our minds, if to nothing more, at least to the
strangeness, the apparent unaccountability, of such delusions;
while the faults and follies of ages and states of society widely
different from our own come to us not only unsoftened by any
such palliating influences on the mind, but as it were heightened
by the circumstance of their standing out in contrast with the
habitual tone and current of our thoughts. And thus it is that
the errors in faith and practice of Hildebrand and his contemporary Churchmen,—errors which we by no means wish in themselves to palliate,—the invocation, for instance, of saints,—the
degradation of one of the sacraments by the reception of the doctrine of transubstantiation,—and the abasement of the spiritual
kingdom of the Church by its assimilation to the temporal
monarchies which surrounded it;—these, and such as these, call
forth in us a degree of horror, we do not say absolutely, but relatively misplaced. Nor does it ever occur to us, while openly expressing with regard to them the sentiments which they excite in
us, that Hildebrand and his contemporaries might, perhaps, have
shrunk, with a not less well-founded horror, from other practices
and tenets, which, from their familiarity to ourselves, hardly call
forth from us even a casual sentence of reprehension. What
might not the energetic pontiff of the eleventh century have said
of the general abandonment of public worship on six days out of
the seven? What of the almost universal disregard of Church
authority evinced in the systematic non-observance of festivals?
What of an avowed and legalized system of putting up spiritual
offices to sale? Or what of the cold-hearted denial of the grace
conferred by the holy Sacrament of Baptism, on the ground that
the sacred gift is impalpable to our gross and earthly senses?

These suggestions in favour of the more immediate fabricators
of papal dominion, are, it will be seen, only made, as the phrase
is, *ad homines;* they can but defend these prelates in relation to
ourselves,—not absolutely, or with respect to truth in the abstract. That Hildebrand and his coadjutors professed a theology,
to a fearful extent superstitious and erroneous, is undeniable;
that they felt within, in their souls, and exhibited to the world in
many points of their practice, the evil tendencies of such a dete-
riorated faith, follows from this admission as a necessary inference.
But while we look, as we unquestionably do, on the errors of
our day just alluded to as compatible with a sincere faith in the
Gospel, and with the maintenance, in the main, of a Christian

character, it behoves us seriously to consider the grounds which justify us in excluding in our minds the names of the great churchmen of the eleventh century from the list of true and zealous disciples of our common Master. Amid the corruptions which heresy has ever laboured to introduce, they clung to the great outlines of apostolic doctrine as set forth in the creeds; and it is therefore, under Heaven, to them, in common with the representatives of the Church before and after them, that we owe the possession of these all-important symbols in this our later day.

But the subject which we at present wish to consider is rather the character of the work itself than that of the workmen by whom the structure of papal dominion was consolidated. The materials of that dominion had been, from the earliest age of Christianity, preparing. From the first, and amid the deep and general reverence for Episcopacy which pervaded the primitive times, special honours were attributed to those thrones in which Apostles themselves had sat, and to churches which they had directly benefited by their teaching, or adorned by their exploits or their sufferings. And to such honours Rome had unquestionably a special claim. " How happy," says Tertullian, who states the above fact, " how happy is that Church where Apostles poured forth their whole doctrine with their blood—where Peter was likened in suffering to his Lord ; where Paul was crowned with the martyrdom of John the Baptist; and whence John the Apostle, having been plunged without injury into boiling oil, was exiled to his island."* 'And as Rome was, in historical honours like these, unrivalled by any other city of the Latin Church, the course of events, in separating the Western and the Eastern world from each other, left her prelate standing in this respect single in rank among his fellow-bishops. The political supremacy, too, of Rome, in the first ages of Christianity, tended to establish, on two grounds, the privilege of primacy in her bishop; first, on account of the rule ever observed by the Church, of assimilating her geographical arrangements to those of the civil world around her ; and secondly, because when missionaries were required for the establishment of churches in the newly Christianized portions of the empire, it was from the metropolis of that empire that they would naturally receive their orders and their authority. While, therefore, the frame-work of the Roman empire hung together, the bishops scattered through the various outlying countries of the west, stood, with reference to him who filled the chair of St. Peter, in a position very analogous to that

* Tertullian, De Præscr. Hæret. c. 36.

now occupied by our colonial prelates in relation to the successor of our English Austin. And though, by the breaking up of that colossal machine, this relative position underwent, in one respect, considerable alteration, yet the parental rights, so to speak, of the See of Rome, were unaffected by the change. The city of the Cæsars might cease to be the mistress, but that of St. Peter could not cease to be, in matters ecclesiastical, the mother of the West.

We find, accordingly, that though the territorial empire of Rome had, in the eighth century, been long resolved into its constituent elements, the idea of the general authority of her bishop was still so familiar to the minds of men as to induce a Frankish prince, Pepin, to seek in that authority a plea for the deposition of his Merovingian master, Childeric, and a sanction for his own intrusion into the vacant throne. This sanction was given by Pope Zachary, in 752, and his successor, Stephen II., solemnly placed, at St. Denis, in July, 754, the crown upon the head of the aspiring chieftain and upon those of his two sons. But in the year 800 the alliance between this, the Carlovingian, race of Frankish monarchs, and the See of St. Peter, was yet more closely cemented. On the Christmas day of that year, Charlemagne, having in great measure re-embodied in his own the extinct empire of the West, received, at Rome, the imperial crown from the hands of Leo. III.; thus ratifying and illustrating the theory of Papal primacy to the world, in the most striking manner. Thenceforward, the cause of that primacy became virtually that of the Carlovingian dynasty itself; and the descendants, accordingly, of Charlemagne, however various the positions which they at different times individually occupied with relation to the Pontiffs, were, and must needs have been, on the whole, and by system, the friends and supporters of the Vatican. In honouring, indeed, the Popes, the Carlovingians were honouring the origin and support of their own power; it need not, therefore, surprise us to read that Louis II., one of this race, who had condescended to appear as a spectator at the inauguration of Pope Nicholas I. to his sacred office, should, as the Pope approached on horseback to visit him, leap from his own horse, and lead that of the Pontiff for the distance of a bow-shot. But the most important act of outward homage paid by these princes to the Papal prerogative was the repetition, in the persons of many of them, of the august ceremony of a Roman coronation. This taught the world to realize, if we may so say, the theory that the Church, as represented by her head, the successor to St. Peter, was the great disposer, under heaven, of regal honours and of earthly power. And so completely was this theory admitted by the Carlovingian monarchs themselves, that we find the emperor already named, Louis II., ascribing, in a letter addressed, in 871, to the Grecian monarch, Basilius the Macedonian, his elevation to the dignity which he enjoyed, under heaven, to the imposition of pontifical hands. " Unctione," he says, " et sacratione per summi Pontificis manus impositionem divinitus sumus ad hoc culmen provecti."

But the empire of the Carlovingians passed away. Charles le Gros, the last sovereign of their house, was, in 887, contemptuously expelled the throne. And the imperial title itself, for some time longer the prize of those warlike princes who could successively obtain a pre-eminence over their rivals, and the consequent honours of a Roman coronation, fell, on the death of Berengarius in 924, into disuse: the nations of the West resuming the character of unconnected principalities or kingdoms. Several causes, however, concurred to prevent the ecclesiastical empire, if so we may call it, of the Popes, from sharing in the fall of that founded by their secular sovereigns. Toward the middle of the ninth century—about the precise period in which the effect of Charlemagne's sanction to the papal pretensions, would be most decidedly felt—a collection of decretals, in many respects spurious, saw the light. It contained a number of letters and decrees, professedly emanating from the Bishops of Rome from the very foundation of the See of St. Peter downwards: but many of them—those which gave to the collection its peculiar importance,—were, it is probable, either forged or first published by a deacon of Mentz, in the century just named; though the collection was accredited to the world by the name of Isidore of Seville. Throughout the whole, though a reverence for the episcopal order in general was systematically inculcated, the papal powers and prerogatives were, above all, insisted upon. All privileges which the Roman prelates had claimed or could claim on the grounds already suggested, were, according to the documents now brought forth, no more than had been claimed and exercised by their predecessors from the apostolic age itself. The shadowy theory of their universal and heaven-derived dominion over the Church acquired form and substance ; and, supported in appearance by precedents of incontrovertible authority, was brought forward into open day to challenge the reverence and the submission of mankind.

And yet, singularly as their path to systematic empire over the Church was smoothed by this series of forgeries, the Popes themselves appear to have been by no means instrumental in its fabrication. As has been already intimated, the researches of the learned have led them to trace its origin, or at least its promulgation, to a German city far removed from the immediate controul

of the Vatican. And though the Popes were not, of course, slow
to appeal to the authority of documents so favourable to the
views which circumstances had lèd them to entertain; yet it was
to that authority, as comparatively established, that they did so;
and not, as far as appears, with any direct view of establishing it.
Nicholas I. was, we believe, the first Pontiff by whom (in 865)
the spurious collection was expressly cited; and his citation
was made for the purpose of enforcing inferences drawn from
their contents upon those by whom their authenticity must be
supposed to have been admitted. And eight years before this
pontifical appeal to them, a Frankish monarch, Charles the Bald,
had quoted them with a similar intention.

The fact is, prominently as the papal prerogatives were put
forward in these decretals, it does not seem that the exaltation of
those prerogatives was either the object with which the spurious
parts of the collection were composed, or the main design of
most of those whose reception of them clothed them with authority. The morals of the age, of the clergy as well as of the laity
of the period, had become, through a variety of causes, lax and
unsettled. And to the growing laxity of the former class, the
apostolical constitution of the Church, the gradation of its
orders, and the authority of its bishops, interposed a standing
impediment. Participators as many prelates might be, and
were, in the corruptions of the time, the machinery of episcopal
government, as far as the clergy were concerned, still worked, on
the whole, with tolerable freedom; and fulfilled, in a corresponding degree, the high purposes for which it had been constructed.
The majority, it may be, of the Church's rulers was careless or
worldly, but of those who would act with principle and energy
the hands were unfettered; and, not to speak of the influence
necessarily exerted even by one such bishop over the conduct of
his brethren, the impunity of licentiousness or disorder among
the lower ranks of the clergy was at best dependent in every case
on the continuance of a vicious or indulgent prelate in his see.
That such impunity should be held by a firmer tenure was the
too natural wish of many; and such an end could by no other
means be so readily attained as by the degradation of the episcopal order itself.

Kings, in the civil world, had risen to pre-eminence by the
depression of those with whom they had formerly stood on the
same level as members of an aristocracy. The whole political
system of the world, in the century of Charlemagne, familiarized
men's minds to the idea of one head presiding over a variety of
chieftains, armed in their own respective districts with power of
the same nature with his own. And reasons, in some measure

analogous. to those which in subsequent times taught the commonalties of Europe to seek in the increasing power of the throne a refuge from the more galling, because more immediate, tyranny of haughty nobles, tended, in the age of which we are speaking, to turn the eyes of the discontented clergy of the West toward a power which, too distant to exercise itself over their conduct an effectual controul, might yet be most efficient to balance, and consequently to weaken, the much more dreaded authority of their immediate diocesans. Did the compiler of the decretals of Isidore indeed entertain views like these, he could unquestionably have forwarded them in no more effectual way than by establishing it, as he attempted to do, upon canonical authority, that bishops were in every department of their administration subject to the papal controul; that no national or provincial synods could be held without the Pope's consent or approval ; that his apostolic throne formed a standing court of appeal from the decisions of his brother prelates; and that all causes of greater intricacy than usual should of right be referred to his own immediate jurisdiction.

Those who thus attempted the transference of ecclesiastical power from the episcopal order in general to one king-like prelate, were materially aided in the accomplishment of their design by the influence of a body then of considerable and widely diffused importance in the Church. We allude to the members of the monastic orders, who appear in the strife between episcopal aristocracy and pontifical monarchy to have played a part very analogous to that of the municipal corporations in the contentions between the kings of Europe and their feudal nobles. All institutions of man have some besetting evil tendency or other; and that of religious societies—even when free in their original constitution from the taint of a violation of Church discipline—is, unquestionably, to throw that discipline into the shade; as though the bonds of union thus humanly contrived obscured in men's minds the idea of that more sacred union—our fellowship with each other as members of the one Church—which heaven has appointed for us. And as such evil tendencies are sure, in the long run, to be worked out and to show themselves, it need not surprise us to find that, at the time of which we treat, a jealousy of episcopal interference habitually pervaded the monastery. And a close connection between the conventual houses and the Pope was found the most secure method of setting the legitimate power of the diocesans at defiance. A vast and influential band of men, therefore, throughout Europe, were ready alike to hail the favourable circumstances by which the idea of papal empire over the Church was familiarized to the

world, and to approve of the enunciation of that idea as formally
systematized and set forth in the decretals of Isidore.

. And as the system of Romish ecclesiastical monarchy, thus
supported, gradually acquired consistency and form, further
sanction to it would be given by many even of the best-inten-
tioned of those in opposition to whose legitimate powers its
fabric was reared. It is for the truly Catholic in spirit, and for
them alone, to feel in its full force the obligation of maintaining,
in matters of Church discipline, a line of conduct based upon
principles of permanent and universal utility to the Church, in
opposition to the courses which the welfare of their own immediate generation, were they permitted to look to that alone,
might suggest. The weaker in faith will ever succumb to the
temptation of giving up what they deem the unnecessary niceties
of ecclesiastical regulation for the sake of what they conceive the
instant and manifest advantage of religion. And to many well-
meaning prelates of the time of which we are treating, the tacit
surrender of their rights would appear—what, for the moment, in
fact, it would be—the readiest mode of securing to themselves
the power necessary for the continued discharge of their pastoral
duties. In no age of the world, it is probable, could any national
branch of the Church Catholic continue long in a state of isola-
tion from the rest of that body and yet preserve its strength and
its purity. And in the middle ages, from the comparative pau-
city of the means of inter-national communication, the Churches
of the different kingdoms of the West would, but for the working of some cause singularly and permanently efficient in maintaining their union, have become in effect so many different institutions, each continually modified in character by the genius of
the nation with which it was connected, and each exposed, in a
rude and violent age, to the insults and oppressions of the secular
power; without the possibility of external aid, and without what
perhaps was still more efficacious, the moral force derived to
it, from the recognition by mankind of its Catholic character.
While at the same time, the original intimacy of Christian union
throughout the world having ceased to exist, the degradation of
branches of the one institution of our Lord into national establishments being already a closely impending evil, we can imagine no engine more likely to be promptly efficacious in restoring
to a certain point the interrupted communication, and in supporting each individual branch of the Church by generalizing
the respective energies of all, than that which was in fact resorted
to; the conversion, so to call it, of the ecclesiastical world into
a monarchy. And the idea of such a monarchy had no sooner

been acted upon—the kingly throne of St. Peter had no sooner been, even partially, reared, than its importance, on grounds like these, would be practically manifested. From the haughtiness and licentiousness of irreligious kings and nobles, they, who would otherwise have been the cowed and persecuted pastors of unprotected churches, had thenceforth a court of appeal ever ready and ever disposed, alike by principle and by interest, to maintain their cause. The Roman Patriarch, if permitted to concentrate in himself their spiritual power, could speak, when occasion required it, with the collective voice of all the Churches of the West. The force of the whole Latin ecclesiastical community became consequently disposable, and applicable in its fulness as the antagonist of every partial, we might even say, of every individual assault or corruption. The Church, as she then stood, became apparently stronger, even by the weakening of her appointed pillars. And bishops, the path of whose immediate duty seemed to be made smooth before them by their acquiescence in a system productive of such results, should not, surely, be harshly judged by us, if, thus tempted, they forgot the duty of clinging at all times to the rock upon which the Church is by divine appointment based—the unchanged, the unshaken rock of the apostolical succession and polity.

With our imperfect knowledge of the times, the fact commonly escapes us, that the supremacy of the Pope, as far as the Church herself was concerned, arose not so much from his absolute exaltation, as from the relative importance derived to him from the positive depression of the episcopal order in general. We are apt to identify the principles of his power with what we commonly style high-church principles pushed to their extreme—to regard his autocracy as a sort of exaggerated development of the episcopal polity. Whereas, in truth, it was upon the ruins of that polity;—it was in opposition to it, and upon the general degradation of the prelacy of Western Europe, that was based the usurping throne of pontifical supremacy. The titles with which the Popes arrayed themselves in the plenitude of their power—"Summus Sacerdos"—"Pontifex Maximus" —"Vicarius Christi"—"Papa" itself, were, nearer to the primitive times, the honourable appellation of every bishop;—as " sedes apostolica" was that of the site of every bishop's throne. The ascription of these titles, therefore, to the Pope, only gave to the terms a new force, because that ascription became exclusive; because, that is, the bishops in general were stripped of honours to which their claims were as well founded as those of their Roman brother; who became by the change not so strictly " universal " as " sole " bishop.* The episcopal body retired, as it were, in his favour from the high prerogatives with which it was collectively invested; led, for the above reasons, to acquiesce in a system tending to degrade those who held their spiritual powers immediately—or as the legal phrase is, *in capite*—of the great Head of the Church in Heaven, into mesne or subordinate tenants of those powers, under the universal tenancy in chief of the Romish Prelate. At the Council of Trent,—that ill-omened assembly, by which so many prevalent errors of Popery were incorporated into articles of faith—an attempt was indirectly made to give to this popish heresy among others an official sanction, and to establish by implication the point that the bishops of Christ's universal Church owed their jurisdiction, if not their order, to the pontifical appointment alone. This attempt, thanks to the determined resistance of the Spanish prelates who attended the council, proved abortive; but the fact of its having been made shows the tendency of the papal system, and the feelings of its abettors toward the apostolical discipline and order.†

The working of that system, when the authority of the decretals first became available to its systematic consolidation, was entrusted to able and energetic hands. Nicholas I., already cited as having been the first among the Pontiffs to quote the supposititious collection of Isidore, wielded the powers which the documents therein contained concurred with the popular opinion of his day in ascribing to him, with no vacillating policy. By the threat of excommunication, he compelled Lothair, King of the province since named from him Lotharingia or Lorrain, to put away Waldrada, whom he had disreputably married, and to receive again his injured and repudiated wife, Theutberga. In a synod at Rome he deposed, in 863, Thietgaud and Gunthar, the Archbishops respectively of Treves and Cologne. He compelled,

---

* " Ecclesiæ Catholicæ Episcopus," a style frequently adopted by the Pontiffs in the plenitude of their power—by Pius IV., for instance, in decrees relative to the Council of Trent—was, therefore, an accurate statement of their pretensions.

† The exaltation of the Roman Bishop was resisted, as involving the general degradation of his order, by one not likely to have entertained unreasonable or exaggerated ideas of the evils likely to result from that exaltation—Pope Gregory the Great. " I am," he said in an epistle to the Patriarch of Alexandria, " but a brother of the order. . . . . Nor do I reckon that an honour to myself which is paid me at the expense and prejudice of my brethren. My reputation lies in the honour of the universal Church and in preserving the dignity of the rest of the prelates. . . . Now if your Holiness" (he thus styled the Patriarch) " treats me with the title of Universal Bishop, you exclude yourself from an equality of privilege." And at a much more mature point of the growth of papal pretension—in the eleventh century itself—we find Leo IX. declaring in his epistle to the Grecian Patriarch, Michael, that his predecessor and namesake, to whom the title of Œcumenical Patriarch was offered by the Council of Chalcedon, " superbum refutavit vocabulum penitus, quo videbatur par dignitas subtrahi cunctis per orbem præsulibus, dum uni ex toto arrogaretur."

on the other hand, Hincmar, the sagacious and powerful Archbishop of Rheims, even though that prelate denied the authority
of the decretals, to restore certain persons to their clerical stations whom he had deposed as uncanonically ordained, and to
re-establish in his diocese, Rothad, Bishop of Soissons, who had
appealed to Rome against the decree of the archbishop and his
synod, which deprived him of it.   And the prerogatives of Ni-
chòlas, during these transactions, were so fully admitted by his
contemporary, the Emperor Louis, that when an Archbishop of
Ravenna, who was at variance with the Pontiff, appealed to that
prince, at Pavia, for his support in the quarrel, Louis bade him
lay aside his pride, and humble himself before that great Pope
"before whom," said he, "we and the whole Church bow, and to
whom we show all duty and obedience." While the people of the
town—so thoroughly was the doctrine of the Pope's supremacy
over all other ecclesiastics received into the popular creed—
shrunk not only from receiving the suppliant archbishop into
their houses, but even from holding, in the way of buying or sell-
ing, any intercourse with his attendants.

Thus consolidated and established in the minds of men, the
papal monarchy, as we have already intimated, survived the dissolution of the Carlovingian empire, even though qualities like
those of Nicholas I. were but rarely to be found among his
successors.   In one light, indeed, the extinction of the Imperial
name and power might be regarded as favourable to the prerogatives of these spiritual sovereigns; inasmuch as it taught mankind to view them as standing apart from, and unconnected with,
the shifting constitutions and varying fortunes of secular monarchies.   The independent existence, even of the Pontiff's unauthorized dominion, illustrated the reality of that heaven-derived
authority which he usurpingly presumed to wield.   And he who
could meet the Emperors of the West on the footing rather of
superiority than equality, was left, on their disappearance from
the world, on a throne unapproached in dignity by that of any of
the comparatively petty sovereigns who divided among themselves
the territories of the empire.

That such dignity, howsoever acquired, would in the long run
be abused by its possessors, might as certainly have been pre-
dicted as the tyrannies of monarchs yet unchosen could be described by the prophet Samuel, when in a time strikingly parallel
to that which we are considering,* the Israelites strove to convert
their theocracy into a constitution more nearly resembling that of
earthly monarchies.

* Vide Newman's Parochial Sermons, vol. ii. serm. 21.

A seat so exalted as that of St. Peter now became would of course be often the prize of unworthy occupants; whose conduct when they had succeeded in grasping the crozier would but too well accord with the views with which they had sought it, and with the means by which they had attained it.   Power, kingly in its nature, would, in the hands of persons like these, naturally surround itself with the externals of kingly luxury and magnificence; and of the manners of the earlier successors to the Apostles few traces would be found amid the profusion of a palace and the dissoluteness of a court.

The middle of the tenth century, therefore, presents us with a new phase in the papal history.   Italy, long plunged in anarchy, required that repose which could only be enjoyed under the government of an energetic and powerful monarch; and Otho, the German sovereign, invited across the Alps to assume the crown of her kings, received also, in 962, the imperial diadem from the hands of Pope John XII., thus partially reconstructing the empire of Charlemagne.   But this prince and his successors were led by circumstances to play toward the Roman church a part very different from that of the founder of the Carlovingian imperial line.

Viewed as a whole, the ecclesiastical monarchy still, at the period of Otho's coronation, existed in vigour.   The workings of the system were daily and hourly felt throughout the West. And yet while distant regions tremblingly acknowledged and obeyed the power of the Vatican, that power had become, through the vices of its holders, contemptible at home.   The profligate John XII. had been consecrated at the age of eighteen, and for purposes strictly and avowedly secular, to his sacred office. His demeanour as head of the Roman church was such as might be expected from a beginning like this; and Otho, though invited by himself across the Alps, was soon regarded by him as a strict preceptor, whose presence was irksome as imposing a check upon his irregularities.   The pontiff first intrigued, then rebelled, against his sovereign; and the emperor, who showed toward him, as long as it was possible, the consideration of a kind-hearted man for a wilful boy, was at last induced to drive him from the seat which he disgraced, and to instal thereon in a hasty and rather uncanonical manner John's secretary, Leo VIII. And the headstrong conduct of John was the cause of yet further humiliation to the papacy.   He contrived on Otho's departure from Rome to reinstate himself in his see: while Leo, forced, in his turn, to fly, took refuge in the camp of his imperial patron. And though the profligate pontiff did not himself long enjoy his triumph, as his intemperance, if not a wound received in the prosecution of his intrigues, put an end to his life on the 14th of

May, 964; yet the Romans, to whom the pope imposed on them was odious, elected upon his decease, and in defiance of the imperial will, a cardinal deacon of their church; who assumed the name of Benedict V., and whose election the papal writers still regard as legitimate. Upon which the incensed emperor, entering the city in arms, and having caused this object of their choice to be brought before him, compelled him to divest himself of his robe of state and to deliver his crozier into the hands of Leo, by whose command it was instantly broken into pieces. The successor of Leo, John XIII. (appointed in 965,) was also a virtual nominee of the emperor; whose representatives, the Bishops of Spires and Cremona, attended to sanction the ceremony of his consecration; and whose arms were, in 966, again needed to protect the successor to St. Peter against the unruly nobles and populace of Rome.

It thus appears that Otho, though he, like Charlemagne, accepted the imperial crown in the first instance from the papal hand, was yet far from exhibiting himself to the world, as that monarch had done, as the dutiful son and servant of the Church. Equally well intentioned, it may be, towards her, he was led by circumstances to take upon him the very opposite character of her patron and superior; defending her against her enemies, but asserting over her the right of controul to which this defence of her appeared naturally to entitle him. Through his administration the Church, as represented by her supposed head, became in great measure the vassal of the sovereign; and the more so because the hostility which, in consequence of this their known dependence, the Popes experienced from their Roman subjects, drove them perpetually to cling more and more closely to the protecting arm of the imperial power. And to this, unquestionably, among other causes, must be ascribed the fact that the century which followed Otho's assumption of the title of Charlemagne saw the see of St. Peter, with the exception of some brief intervals, the scene of ever-increasing moral degradation. This painful spectacle reached its climax in the reign of an Emperor of the following, or Franconian, dynasty, Henry III.; when the world beheld in the papal city three worthless claimants of the pontifical dignity—each alike unfit to bear it— contending for superiority: one occupying the Church of Santa Maria Maggiore—one the Lateran—and the third St. Peter's. The scandal of such a state of things was too glaring to permit of its continuance. Henry III. led, in 1046, his army toward Rome: then halting at Sutri, a few miles north of the city, he summoned the rivals before him. One, entertaining some hopes of a decision in his favour, obeyed the summons. But Henry and the bishops, who were his assessors, gave their sentence

against all:—the monarch then selected a German bishop of his
train for the vacant pontificate, and installed him as Clement II.,
receiving himself, on the same day, the imperial crown from his
hand.   And then, in conjunction with the pontiff thus chosen,
Henry laboured zealously, and, as far as the immediate crisis was
concerned, successfully, in the work of purifying the Church.
Simony, the disgraceful system of making spiritual offices the
subjects of bargain and sale, was the object of his most determined hostility.   That system, ever rising anew into vigour as
the spiritual—or in other words the true—notion of the Church's
essence and character fades from the minds of men, had at the
epoch of the council of Sutri, fearfully contaminated Western
Europe.   And it was, undoubtedly, with the honest view of
counteracting this and other evils that Henry was led to take the
whole power of the Church, in a manner, into his own hands.
From the Roman authorities, who had unquestionably shown
themselves, in many instances, unfit to conduct so important a
business as the election of a head of the Western Church, he
exacted an oath that such elections should thenceforward be carried on under the imperial auspices alone: assuming, in effect,
the power of nomination to himself.   And this proceeding may
well represent—as far as the Church was concerned—the general
tenor of his conduct.   He strove to reform her, and in a great
measure, as far as her more visible evils were concerned, succeeded.   But it was in the spirit of a king, rather than of a
churchman, that his reforms were carried on.   He looked more
to the immediate, than to the eventual, working of his amendments; more to the eradication of existing and palpable blemishes
than to the preservation, or rather renovation, of that system in
which alone a permanent corrective of these and other such incidental evils could be found.   Purifying the Church, he enslaved
her,—thus subjecting her, in return for a temporary benefit, to a
lasting evil.   His personal good qualities, on which the benefit
depended for its continuance, could not, in the nature of things,
descend to every inheritor of his throne; while the ecclesiastical
autocracy which he had acquired would as naturally, supposing
no fresh moral revolution to occur, have descended in increased
vigour, to each succeeding generation.   And the evils thus menacing in theory soon showed themselves formidable in practice.
On Henry's death in 1056, the imperial sceptre was at first
weakly swayed by his widow, the empress regent Agnes, and then
by her dissolute and ill-educated son Henry IV.   The advantages which the Church had derived from the energy and integrity
of the deceased monarch's character vanished with himself from
the scene.   His reforming policy was thought of no more; and

the power of which, for the purpose of reformation, he had possessed himself, was employed with intentions the most opposite.
The imperial cabinet allied itself with, and represented, the low,
or lax, party in the Church. Those very abuses which the late
monarch had sought the most honestly to eradicate were patronized
by—and we might almost say incorporated into the system of—his
successor. Irreligion, or at least worldliness, in the church was supported by the whole weight of the imperial power. And considering how completely the Latin Church had, as we have seen, concentrated her authority in the Papacy, and that now that Papacy itself
seemed doomed to become the powerless vassal of the state and
the creature of an arbitrary monarch's will, we are not, perhaps,
asserting too much in saying that never was the Christian church
in so fearful a strait before. An evil infinitely more alarming
than her early persecutions and difficulties threatened—humanly
speaking—irrevocably to overwhelm her. Her proper guardians
had surrendered their rights into the hands of the Roman prelate.
And the emperor, by rendering the latter a mere puppet in his
hands, must have concentrated in himself, unchecked as he would
be by the restraints imposed by ecclesiastical discipline and by
the priestly character, the whole of the sacerdotal power of the
West. Simony, partially checked by the individual efforts of
Henry III., now, as this unnatural system approached its realiza-
tion, flourished anew and extended itself more widely than ever.
Bishoprics, abbeys, and benefices became throughout the empire the subjects of open and unblushing competition by purchase; and the highest bidders for them, receiving investiture
from the monarch with forms nearly similar to those by which his
lay vassals received their fiefs, were regarded as little differing in
position from the other feudatories of his crown. Throughout the West, the sacerdotal was tending to merge itself in
the secular character. The morals of the clergy, high and
low, were in a state of systematic declension; and though their
marriages had long been proscribed by canons to which—whatever we may now think of them—they stood pledged to obedience, they not only habitually slighted this injunction, but abandoned themselves too frequently to irregularities unworthy of the
name, we will not say of a priest, but of a Christian; being little
if at all distinguishable in point of purity from the gross and
profligate laity who surrounded them. Had this state of things
continued, or rather had it, as it must in the ordinary course of
things soon have done, more fully developed itself, the spiritual
character of the Christian religion and of the Christian church
must have altogether disappeared from the dimmed eyes of men.
And the outward form of the ecclesiastical polity, if yet pre-

served, would have stood but as a component part of the system of the empire,—as a machine to be worked, as the heathen religions had been, by the hands of the civil magistrate,—as one element, not more revered or more durable than the others, in the ever-varied and heterogeneous composition of the feudal constitution of Europe.

But a consummation so fearful was, by what we can scarcely forbear to call a marvellous Providence, averted. As the antagonist of this menacing system, the Papacy, which had during the latter years of Henry III. and the minority of his successor, Henry IV., silently snapped several of the chains which bound it in vassalage to the state, suddenly arose in renewed power. The extent of the existing moral evil had in some measure wrought out itself the means of its counteraction. A school of divines, the most conspicuous of whom was the celebrated Hildebrand, had arisen in Rome as the advocates of stricter and purer views in morals and discipline than generally prevailed; and these, having acted in concert with Henry III. in his warfare against simony and impurity, continued their efforts independently after his decease, with the impetus which he had, to a certain extent, assisted in giving. The party of these reformers strengthened itself by its own working. The ascetic purity of its leaders commanded the veneration of mankind, and stood out in bright contrast with the dissoluteness, the corruption, the worldly-mindedness, of that party in the Church which, when the imperial influence came to be arrayed against them, clung to its side; and thus was gradually brought into play a conservative principle capable of coping with and, as the event proved, of withstanding and overmastering the unspiritualizing system, which nothing but such resistance could, it is probable, have prevented from overshadowing the whole Christian, or at any rate the whole Western, world.

The details of the crisis in which the two opposite systems came into collision, and in which, by an unexampled moral revolution, the imperial was crushed before the pontifical power, can scarcely be done justice to within the limits of this article. These, and the character of the principal actor in the eventful drama, Hildebrand, we may probably consider on a future occasion. Suffice it now to say, that of that crisis, happening as it did, the occurrence cannot fairly be ascribed to this or that particular act alone of either party. One event led to another, and the last decisive measure, the excommunication and deposition of Henry IV. by the Pontiff in the council at Rome, was but the reply of the Vatican to the excommunication and deposition of its chief, in the most irregular manner, and upon charges the most absurd and unfounded, by an imperial assembly at Worms. But public opinion, or rather, to use a higher term, public principle, adopted, and gave weight to, the dictum of the Roman assembly alone; and the emperor, gradually deserted by all, was necessitated at length to cross the Alps in the depth of winter, and then to stand barefoot for three successive days in the castle court of Canossa, a suppliant for absolution and restoration to his throne. And from this epoch commenced, in effect, that full dominion of the Papacy, to which all the previous events which we have described had been tending as to a natural conclusion, and which, though commonly regarded among us as fraught with evil alone, should, we think, be looked upon rather in the light of a mysterious dispensation of Providence, in which good and evil were strangely blended. If we look at it in contrast with the government of the Church in the days of her primitive and apostolic purity, it unquestionably presents the appearance of a system of fearful corruption. But if we view it as opposed to the system which, as its contemporary, did in truth oppose it—the system of a general secularization of the Church's polity—it can, whether we consider it with a view to its effect on ecclesiastical discipline, or on the general morals of mankind, be scarcely regarded otherwise than as a blessing. Its theory, lamentably removed in the abstract from that apostolical scheme by which the Church was originally governed, was yet a near approach to that scheme as compared with the irregular and unauthorized domination which it interrupted and succeeded. At the time of its establishment it was, in short, a reformation. It was brought about by the strict, the high party in the Church, in opposition to the efforts of the worldly and the low. It may be contemplated, under a variety of aspects, as the triumph of strictness over impurity, of faith over unbelief, of order over insubordination. And its immediate result was unquestionably manifested in an amendment of manners alike among the clergy and the laity, in an increase of salutary vigour in the discipline of the Church, and in the growth of a deep spirit of popular reverence for the high mysteries of religion.

It may have been observed by our readers, that in tracing, as we have done, the progress of this extraordinary empire, we have said nothing of the doctrinal corruptions with which, according to the current opinion, that progress is to be viewed as essentially connected. This opinion we imagine to arise from that universal, because natural, error in reasoning alluded to at the outset of these remarks: those who have not leisure or inclination to investigate the subject, find it convenient to view the doctrines of Transubstantiation, Purgatory, Image-worship, and the like, as though incorporated with each other, and with the papal dominion, in an essential unity; the Popes being regarded as having been in their official, and, so to say, inherent character, the prime movers in, and principal upholders of, these varied heresies and their dependent errors. Whereas the fact is, that for the origin of most of these abuses the Pontiffs are not in any degree responsible; nor was even their subsequent growth fostered by them in any peculiar, or, if we may use the expression, personal way. The autocratic heads of the Church were of necessity in some measure the representatives and organs of her general feeling; and the papal name has on this account become connected with many pernicious doctrines, which had neither originated in the policy, nor (at least until universally prevalent) been supported by the power of the Vatican.

The doctrine of Purgatory, for instance, whatever hints on the subject might have been given by earlier Fathers, seems first to have assumed a tangible shape in the writings of the celebrated Bishop of Hippo. That of Transubstantiation was moulded by Paschasius Radbertus, a monk of Corbie. Image-worship was adopted from the East. And so far, in the great struggle which preceded the full triumph of the Papacy, was the establishment of these heresies from being associated with the triumph of the Vatican, that a disbelief, or at least a dubious belief, in Transubstantiation, was one of the charges currently brought against Hildebrand by the imperial party, and one of the grounds upon which they attempted to justify the unwarranted sentence against him pronounced by the conciliabule of Worms.

That there existed a sort of mysterious sympathy between the system of errors which, collectively taken, we may style doctrinal Popery, and the elevation of the Roman Patriarch's throne, we will not deny. But it is, perhaps, a more correct view of this connection to regard the two as derived from one common source, than to conceive of the one as having been directly instrumental in the production of the other. As the temper of the times waxed gross, as the vision of spiritual religion faded before men's eyes, both Christianity and the Christian Church became, if the expression may be allowed, materialized; and the conversion of the unearthly system of the apostolic polity into a more worldly, a more tangible, scheme of monarchy, was the fruit of precisely the same mental habits and modes of thought as those which moulded a reverential and mysterious feeling toward the saints departed into an open adoration, and which degraded the holy mystery of the Eucharist into the palpable and more intelligible miracle of Transubstantiation.

Nor that an interested, or, to speak plainly, a corrupt use was made of these doctrinal errors, when once established, by the successors of St. Peter, are we prepared to dispute. But this fact would be more properly cited were we tracing the effects of the false position to which they were elevated in the minds of the Pontiffs, than in an inquiry into the causes by which that position was attained. At the moment of the great struggle in which the Papacy rose to pre-eminence, they and the assertors of their cause participated in the doctrinal corruptions which so generally overspread the world around them; but it was not, generally speaking, either for these corruptions that they fought, or through them that they conquered. Clerical celibacy, indeed, they made subservient to their views; but that system, erroneous as we now conceive it, had, long before the struggle in question commenced, been incorporated into the received code of Christian purity; and we shall have a very faulty view of the question in relation to it, which was really at issue between the Papalists and the Imperialists of the eleventh century, unless we perceive, in the opposition of the latter to the enforcement of this already recognized canon, much of that spirit of hostility to order, to authority, and to strictness of manners, in which, through all ages, the Church and her rulers have found their most persevering antagonist. It will not follow, therefore, that the Popes, in adhering in this respect to established authority, were wrong as against the party of the Emperors, even though we may admit them to have been, in this instance, wrong in the abstract. But the truth is, that this prohibition of the Church was itself but another type of the prevailing mode of thought, and instance of its operation. We are accustomed, after reading St. Paul's sentiments on the subject of celibacy in general, to dismiss them at once from our minds, as though they applied exclusively to the circumstances of the Church in the apostolic age. The Church, in times immediately following that age, unquestionably thought otherwise; and from the high and mysterious impressions of early Christians on the subject, the positive prohibition of clerical marriage might naturally result by a simplifying and unspiritualizing process analogous to that already alluded to, by which a reverence for the dead was converted into an idolatry, and the tenet of the real presence into the doctrine of Transubstantiation.

It was not, then, as the corrupters of religion that the Popes rose to the occupation of the loftiest throne in Europe. Yet that their progress to such power was unaccompanied, necessarily and inherently, by fearful guilt, we cannot affirm; not that we would make that guilt to consist, as many would, in the assumption by a spiritual dignitary of temporal power; for the distinction between spiritual power and temporal is not quite so broad and clear to our eyes as it would appear to be to those of some

among our contemporaries. If by temporal power, as opposed
to spiritual, be meant the power of physical force—the power
which monarchs exercise through their armies, or through the
knowledge of mankind that they are able, if necessary, to compel
obedience by violent means—such temporal power the successors
to St. Peter never either aspired to or possessed. They became, it
is true, the actual sovereigns of a territory in Italy; but this fact is
beside the main question. The strength of their universal empire
lay ever in their controul over the minds, not over the bodies, of
men. And though armies, in the palmy state of Papal Rome,
were undoubtedly brought into the field, and kingdoms overthrown, through her agency, yet the temporal power exerted on
these occasions was in strictness that of her vassals, not her own.
The link of connection between herself and those who were the
more direct agents in these operations, was simply the faith of
mankind in the spiritual prerogatives of the successors of St. Peter.
Her negociations were pastoral letters; her arms, excommunica-
tions; her influence, even over her visible servants, depended on
the belief of men in the unseen world.

Nor if by temporal power, when the Papacy is spoken of, be
meant power applied to temporal purposes, does the charge become much clearer to our apprehension. It appears to us that
every purpose, every end, is in one sense spiritual; and that to
assert the contrary would be to maintain that religion was connected with but a portion, separated and set aside, of the daily
business of life, the remaining parts of the great field of human
enterprize and exertion being without the sphere of her legitimate
influence. Whereas, believing as we do that Christianity is intimately connected with the whole system of social and political
morality, we cannot clearly understand how it can be brought as
a charge against any men, that they exerted its influence in matters
of conduct to which it was irrelevant. The real guilt which
stained the papal cause in its great struggle, and in its triumph,
appears to us to have been but a further development, on the
part of Rome, of the principle by which episcopacy had been
previously debased before her spiritual autocracy. Having forgotten—as led by circumstances to forget—the reverence due to
those who held by succession the apostolic power, the papal
mind was by the natural course of things schooled into irreverence
for another authority, toward which the Church, in the days of
her purity, had ever felt a submissive deference to be a Christian
duty—the authority, we mean, of the secular sovereign. Loyalty
to the chief magistrate, and respect to the divinely commissioned
governors of the Church, are, indeed, kindred virtues, or rather,
strictly speaking, different types and illustrations of the same

moral habit; and they whose episcopal seat had been converted into a solitary throne by the depression of bishops, were, by an almost necessary consequence, regardless of the due prerogatives of kings. Hildebrand and his coadjutors disgraced the quarrel of the Church by sullying it with the crime of rebellion against Cæsar,—by deposing from his royalties, as well as severing from the communion of the faithful, the profligate emperor to whom they were opposed,—by forgetting, in short, while enforcing what was in truth but due reverence for their own authority, the reverence due from them in return to the anointed wielders of the civil sword. Their secular usurpation, therefore, if so it should be styled, was, if the expression may be allowed, rather a negative than a positive one; it was, as in the case of the establishment of pontifical supremacy over the prelacy, wrought out more by the relative degradation of others, than by the positive exaltation of themselves. And by way of extenuating the conduct of the immediate agents in this anti-monarchical revolution, it may be remarked that the line thus adopted by them cannot in fairness be considered as having originated with themselves, inasmuch as it naturally resulted from that closeness of union between the Church and the state to which, certainly with no particular view to the interests of the former, the world had long before their time been accustomed by its rulers. This union having been thoroughly recognized by all,—it having been admitted by all that the ecclesiastical and civil authorities were connected with each other by the links of feudalism, the one holding, in the language of the times, its station of the other,—they are rather to be regarded as modifying a received false notion than as introducing a new error, when they asserted that, of the two, the State was to be considered as the feudatory or vassal of the Church, and not the Church of the State.

With this character, then, and under these circumstances it was, that the papal empire arose to supremacy in the West. And even observers who look not on its fortunes with that deep interest which churchmen must feel in the subject, but who contemplate it as a simple historical phenomenon, have been struck in various ways with the magnificent spectacle presented by its operation;—the spectacle, we mean, of a purely moral power curbing, by the bare expression of its will, the violence of martial monarchs in rude and licentious times,—of old unarmed men, backed by no other force of their own than the faith of mankind in the truth of revealed religion and in the authority of the Church of the Redeemer, acting—by system at least, however often they might have abused their authority—as the dispensers of justice, the protectors of the oppressed, and the avengers of iniquity, in the face of all the kingly authority and military greatness of the world.

But churchmen who, unbiassed by prejudices, can give to the subject of papal dominion their serious attention, may be disposed to attribute to the elevation and continuance of that empire advantages of a higher nature than the mere physical results of such a state of things as this. The Papacy, with all its corruptions, was, to the Latin world, the representative and personification, so to call it, of the Church of the many ages during which it flourished; and the governing power of the Eastern Church, while it yet maintained its position as a rival, was in so many respects similarly circumstanced to it as to feel, as far as the establishment of principles was concerned, a necessary sympathy with its fortunes and its development. In those fortunes therefore, in the struggles and in the successes of the papal party, more was in truth at hazard than the spiritual ascendancy of the Vatican, or the universal monarchy of the successors of St. Peter. Christianity itself, disguised as it might be under a corrupt theology, and subjected to an unauthorized discipline, was in fact at stake in the conflict carried on by Rome against her secular or infidel enemies; and her success in the strife was, as far as human eyes can see, the only means by which the great truths of Revelation, and the blessings derivable from the authorized ministration of the Christian sacraments, could have been handed down to later times. · Revealed religion must, it is probable, as accepted by mankind, be in some degree debased in every age by the low moral tone of those to whom it is proffered, and to whose hands its teaching is confided. The human intellect, we may well suppose, cannot, even under the most favourable circumstances, grasp, as they really are, the great truths presented to it from above; our best and holiest endeavours to grasp them are but approximations; and even the sublime propositions which, upon indisputable authority, we embody in our creeds, true as they are in themselves, and false and impious as would be consequently the denial of them, must be supposed, from the imperfection of our faculties, and from the depravation of our moral nature, to furnish us rather with types and adumbrations of truth than with truth divine itself. Our knowledge, we mean to say, of Christianity, must at best be knowledge in a degree; the purer our minds, the holier our lives, the more we shall know. But we have inspired authority for saying that here we can know but in part. The witnesses for the truth in the purest times of the Church—leaving of course the inspired guides of the apostolic age out of the question—must have all been in some degree defective in their comprehension of the truths of Revelation; and he, therefore, who, in times more generally cor-

rupt, should, with a proportionally corrupt theology, testify to the
truth of religion in general, might be found, upon consideration,
to occupy a position in essentials much more nearly resembling
theirs than would at first sight be apprehended. It is of course
necessary for the accuracy of this resemblance, that the theology
which he should maintain should be opposed in his day by none
purer; but that he should defend and represent views as high as
those entertained by any portion of the Church in his age. But
this condition was, as we have said, in the case of the Papacy,
fulfilled: it was a witness for the truth, not against truth in greater
comparative clearness, but against infidelity and error.

And such it long continued: the monarch who trembled at the
thunders of the Vatican, and the ruffian who quaked at the sight
of a barefooted friar, were alike reminded, by the sentiments of
terror thus excited in their minds, that there was a world " beyond this visible diurnal sphere;" that there was an authority exceeding that which could be founded or supported by violence
and arms. Minds with which the Christian Church, in her true
spiritual garb, would probably never have come into beneficial
contact, were, from the more tangible form which she during the
middle ages assumed,—from her apparent identification with the
palpable system of a powerful monarchy, made to feel her reality,
and to do her reverence. And thus the kingly government, for
so we may call it, to which the Church during these ages committed herself, though as unauthorized in its outset and in its
principle as that of Saul, for which the chosen people of earlier
days had rejected the Theocracy, might be suffered to become, in
some respects, God's favoured instrument of good, as was unquestionably the throne of David, of Hezekiah, and of Josiah.
And even if we were to admit that this good was all of a prospective kind,—that the corruption of Christianity during the period
of papal predominance was such as to make its beneficial influence, as far as that long period was directly concerned, nugatory,—
yet should we of these latter days owe some gratitude to the
power which, while obscuring the great doctrines of the faith from
its contemporaries, preserved them for our more favoured gaze.
For though we may imagine and speculate upon many other conceivable ways by which Christianity might have been kept in
reverence, and the Christian Church and ministry have been pro-
longed from the days of Hildebrand to those of Luther, it is unquestionably true that, as far as Western Europe was concerned,
the dominion of the Papacy *was* the method chosen to effect these
great ends in the councils of Providence: precisely as we may
conceive the monarchical form of Israelitish government to have
been, in the hands of that Providence which ordinarily works by

means, an instrument of ensuring the safety, and of preserving the nationality, of the chosen people, amidst the powerful and war-like monarchies which might otherwise, humanly speaking, have irrecoverably overwhelmed them. The religion of Rome, and of the churches subject to her influence, represented, and that exclusively, when the sixteenth century dawned upon the world, the Christianity of the West.

That the faith once delivered to the saints had, during the ages preceding this last epoch, gradually become obscured,—that the perfect fabric of sound doctrine had been throughout disfigured, and its true proportions concealed, by the unauthorized additions with which ignorance, error, and hypocrisy had encrusted it, is too melancholy a truth. Beneficial as might—as, according to our notions, did—the system of Papal monarchy prove, as far as its immediate and temporary effects were concerned,—important as the part which it played as the conservator of Christianity must prove to the remotest ages, it contained unquestionably within its essence the seeds of deterioration and corruption. In the Pope's first step toward supremacy was involved the debasement, and consequently the enfeebling, of the scriptural guardians of the Church's ordinances, discipline, and faith—the members of the episcopal order; and in proportion as this had been done had the Church forfeited the tenure of that promised and heaven-protected perpetuity which was pledged to her only in connection with the preservation by her members of her Apostolical polity. As far as she had become un-episcopal she had become mortal: her gradual decay, therefore, under the overspreading shadow of the papal autocracy, is not to be traced, as though necessarily depending on them, to any succession of isolated events or accidents; it rather resulted from the fixed constitution of her adopted nature,—it formed, and did not interfere with, the new rule of her existence.

Happily, however, for the best interests of mankind, the frame-work of episcopal polity—the unviolated order of the ministerial succession—was, amid all the errors and all the crimes of papal Rome in the degenerate ages which preceded the Reformation, preserved for the dawning of a brighter day. The doctrine of that succession had, in truth, undergone a fate precisely analogous to—we should perhaps say, sympathetic with—that of the other great doctrines of the Christian Church. It had been obscured and degraded by the submission of the prelacy to the papal autocracy, precisely as Baptism had been by the ascription of the sacramental character to penance, and as the Eucharist had been by being explained away into Transubstantiation. But the reality, alike of the Church Catholic herself, and of these the

means of grace entrusted to her charge, was even by these corruptions preserved in the memories of men, and held up to their
habitual reverence. And thus, when our English reformers at
length arose, their work was wonderfully—or, we would rather
say, providentially—simplified. They were not imperatively
called on to build and to pull down at one and the same time.
The fabric of truth on which they laboured was sound at bottom,
and all that was required was the removal of its disfigurements
to exhibit its great outlines in their pristine beauty. The refutation of the monarchical claims of the Roman Pontiff was calculated, naturally as it were, and without the necessity of any further
process, to restore to its former prerogatives the episcopal order.
The unsacramentizing—if the word may be allowed—of penance,
would, to the thoughtful mind, at once reinvest the holy Sacrament of Regeneration with the fulness of its scriptural glory.
And the exposure of the figment of Transubstantiation was calculated to leave in its purity for the veneration of mankind the
high and mysterious doctrine of the Supper of the Lord.

We do not say that these happy results, or such as these, were
in truth the immediate results of our Reformers' labours. In all
changes in which human agents are concerned, human passions
will mingle; human prejudices will arise; marring and confounding in some degree the highest attempts, and thwarting the
purest intentions. The benefits which we have thus broadly
described could, it is probable, be attained in their fulness, at
any one given time, in theory alone. But an approximation to
such a state of things our English Reformers did, at the Reformation, in truth and in reality, obtain. And as they themselves, by whom that great work was undertaken, may be said to
have arisen out of the papal system—to have acquired in papal
schools their rudimentary knowledge of the great doctrines which
it was permitted to them to illustrate and to clear, as well as to
have acquired from the fact of papal predominance their first
impressions of the reality of the Christian Church, and of the
reverence which was her due,—we may even now, reformed as
we are, owe to the stand against secularity made by the Papacy
of old, and to the influence consequently acquired by it, a deeper
debt of gratitude than most of us have ever imagined, or than
many among us would be at all disposed to defray. For if it be
conceivable that, had the Pontiffs never risen to supremacy,
Christianity would, at the opening of the sixteenth century, have
been found in a purer state than that in which at that period it
was actually found among us—it is equally conceivable, and, as
it appears to us, more historically probable, that, but for their

sway, the very name of Christianity would have disappeared from Western Europe. The very next stage in the process of its secularization under the hands of the German Henries would have been its complete conversion into a state religion, its Church assuming the character of the heathen establishments of old, which were nearly powerless over the morals, and utterly uninfluential over the faith of mankind. And how long, this mutation having been accomplished, its nominal existence would have been continued in the world, is a matter purely problematical, and, we will add, unimportant.

From the date of the Council of Trent, as we have already said, a new era began. Even had no essential change taken place at that epoch in the tenets of the Romish Church herself, that Church would, by the single fact of the occurrence of the Reformation, have been placed in a position not only new, but in some respects even opposite to that which, antecedently to the council in question, she had occupied. When purer Churches, as those of England, Ireland, and Sweden, existed in the West—Churches with which she was in contact, and to which she assumed a permanent attitude of opposition,—the testimony which Rome, as against former opponents, had borne to the truth, would have become, even without intrinsic alteration, a testimony to falsehood,—the partial verity of her creed guiding to the whole truth in the first case, and from it in the second. But the case thus put is not that which actually occurred. By incorporating, at Trent, her prevalent errors into the essence of her faith, Rome underwent, at that important crisis, an absolute change of position in addition to this merely relative one; her Pontiff then officially identifying himself with the establishment, in opposition to purity of faith, and to the authority of legitimate ecclesiastical government, of a system of error, superstition, and usurpation.

In such a position the Papacy has, as far as its own internal character has been concerned, from that period remained. Nor of that position would we—durst we—become the apologists. Our quarrel with it, as it now is, is as deep as can be that of the most fiery champion among the ranks of Protestantism;—though, remembering the Apostle Jude's allusion to the words of Michael, we would not, even in the heat of that quarrel, bring against it a railing accusation. We would say, even of the Roman Church's present condition, in the words of the great Christian poet of our day,—

> " Speak gently of our sister's fall :
> Who knows but gentle love
> May win her at our patient call
> The surer way to prove ?"

And we would not, at any rate, with the view of expiessing our abhorrence of the corruptions of Popery as it is, concede to its advocates the uncalled for—the all-important admission, that those corruptions formed part of the general Christianity of Western Europe for nine hundred years. We would not, for the purpose of strengthening our case against such opponents, declare that all the good and great who during those centuries lived and died " beneath the Church's shade" were on their side in the quarrel between us and them. We would not avow, or glory in the avowal, that our English Reformers were in truth separatists, though they disclaimed the name; or that our English Church was, during the whole of the long interval between Augustine and Cranmer, steeped in all the impurities of post-Tridentine Rome. We would not, we could not, while a spark of the principle of filial duty yet glowed within our breasts, join in the unthinking cry of those who, more familiar with modern prejudices than with ancient facts, seem to feel a positive pleasure while affixing the brand of shame,

> " E'en here, between the chaste unsmirched brows
> Of our true mother."

We would not celebrate, or join those without the pale of our holy Church in celebrating, festivals unauthorized by any legitimate authority, and based upon the assumption of that Church's long apostacy. We would not virtually proclaim to the world, in the teeth of historical facts, and of the declaration of Cranmer himself, that for nine centuries it was the system of that Church to withhold from the people all knowledge of the Scriptures in the vulgar tongue. That there was a period, though it was comparatively a short one, in which, in opposition to her system, her ministers did, first discourage, and then prevent, the study of the sacred records by their flocks, we would, as bound by Christian verity, admit; and over this, as over all other errors and sins of our spiritual parent in her earlier days, we would dutifully mourn; but we would no more acknowledge that those days were altogether dark in the heavens than that these our own days are one unclouded blaze of purity and light.

To that portion of the public which appears to regard a belief in the utter foulness and corruption of Rome, and of all churches which have held communion with her during any portion of the last twelve hundred years, as an essential article of Christian faith, the expression of notions like the above—nay, the very suggestion of them in the way of doubt and with the view of promoting historical inquiry—will savour of heresy—of impiety—nay, worst of all, of Popery itself. But we would, in all good-will and charity, ask of the well-meaning persons who should, on grounds like these, instinctively'exclaim against us, whether, if they have indeed so far incorporated in their minds their own uninspired impressions of historical events and characters with the great doctrines of Revelation as to feel that in an attack on the former is involved an impugnment of the latter, they are not in principle committing the very offence with which they so vehemently charge the Romanists, by adding to the faith once delivered to the saints, and confounding dicta of mere human authority with the sublime system of truths revealed by the Almighty.

If it be Popery to vindicate the past from the charge of fully participating in the corruptions of the present: if it be Popery to declare that the position of the Roman Patriarch, as the systematic opponent of divine truth, is modern as well as unscriptural; that his adherents among ourselves are not, either in doctrine or by succession, the representatives of the churches originally established in our islands, being, on the contrary, the abettors of a recent and intruding sect; and that the proud boast of immutability made by the Church of Rome is a delusion, the difference between her and ourselves consisting in her disregard of, and our reverence for, the voice of Catholic antiquity; if the maintenance of these, and of tenets like these, be Popery, then, unquestionably, we should deserve to be called Papists. But, were it thus explained, we might glory in the title.

Art. V.—*The Life and Character of John Howe, M. A., with an Analysis of his Writings.* By Henry Rogers. London: Ball. 1836. 8vo. pp. 576.

WE learn from Mr. Rogers that all which has been preserved to us of the personal history of John Howe might have been preserved within half the compass of this volume. We are quite of his opinion. Nay, we are, further, satisfied that half the volume might have been amply sufficient for all the purposes of biography, together with a fair allowance for criticism and dissertation. But Mr. Rogers is evidently enamoured with his subject; and, moreover, (as we learn, with sorrow, from his preface,) he has been impelled to seek, in literary toil, for an anodyne against the effects of some great personal calamity. Under these circumstances it might seem ungracious, and almost inhuman, to be out of humour with him for a more than ordinary indulgence in the luxury of diffuseness.

That he should have been captivated with the task of recording the virtues of a man like Howe, is far from surprising; for Howe was one of those rare spirits, in which the elements are so happily combined and blended, as to " give the world assurance" of an almost perfect Christian. It appears that Mr. Rogers has devoted himself to his " labour of love" with a zeal and industry quite worthy of that excellence, the memory of which he delighteth to honour. No source of information has been neglected by him, whether in manuscript or in print; and his diligence has not been without its reward. He has succeeded in rescuing from oblivion some highly interesting letters, and a considerable number of valuable facts, not to be found in the Life of Howe by Calamy.

It is bitterly to be deplored that the voluminous manuscripts of Howe, containing an account of his public and private life, were destroyed, in obedience to his last inexorable injunctions. It would seem as if he recovered his speech, (which he had lost,) very shortly before his death, for the express purpose of commanding this pitiable sacrifice; which has probably deprived the world of a more minute and circumstantial history of religion, in England, during the time of Howe, than can now be hoped for from any existing source. From the scanty materials which yet remain, we learn that John Howe was born at Loughborough, May 17, 1630. His father was minister of that place, by the appointment of Archbishop Laud; but was speedily removed on the ground of non-conformity. We are extremely concerned to find that Mr. Rogers, after having solemnly disclaimed all sectarian bitterness of feeling, has, in this early stage of the narrative, strangely forgotten his pledge, and has broken out into a vast deal of vulgar and ignorant invective against the archbishop,—such as might refresh the spirits of John Prynne himself, and his brother martyrs, if we could suppose that their tempers and principles have followed them into another world. It is, we know, insufferably wearisome to dwell upon these stale and turbid calumnies. But, tedious as it may be, we hold it " very stuff o' the conscience," never to suffer such things to pass without an indignant protest against their foul injustice.

" This excellent man," (the father of Howe,) says Mr. Rogers, " had been appointed to this parish by Archbishop Laud, but was not destined to remain there long. His arrogant patron attached little less importance to the most insignificant ceremonies than to the weightiest articles of the Decalogue. He could see no impropriety in sanctioning the public desecration of the Sabbath, while he was ready to visit the omission of the most trifling rites with relentless severity. As Howe's father, it seems, could not conscientiously comply with those solemn fooleries and minute and frivolous ceremonies, which the zealous archbishop persisted in introducing into public worship, and by which, whether he intended it or not, he was fast assimilating the Church of England to the Church of Rome, it was soon discovered that he was not the man for Loughborough, and he was consequently ejected. This can excite no surprise; what could be expected from Laud—a man apparently so totally destitute of every rational conception of the spirit or essence of religion, and whose whole soul was immersed in pomp and ceremonial; who seemed to think the restoration of broken crucifixes and damaged paintings amongst the most sacred cares of his high office; who busied himself in adjusting the position of altars, in prescribing obeisances and grimaces, in attiring his priesthood in the gaudy fopperies of a childish superstition, and in brushing up the tawdry frippery of the Romish Church, which had lain neglected ever since the Reformation; whose own most solemn acts of public devotion were a tissue of fantastic and ridiculous mummeries; and whose superstition was of so mean and abject a character, that he gravely noted his dreams, regarded the fall of a picture as a serious omen, and rejoiced or trembled as the week or year brought round his lucky or unlucky days? Had the relentless spirit of persecution by which this man was animated been directed, however erroneously, against the gigantic abuses in the Church, he would at least have escaped our contempt, though not our abhorrence. But to see great power abused to such mean purposes, to see a tyrant with the soul of a deputy-master of ceremonies, is surely one of the most ridiculous as well as humiliating of spectacles."—p. 19—21.

Now, in the first place, it is a most outrageous slander to affirm that Laud " saw no impropriety in sanctioning a desecration of the Sabbath." Whether, or not, his views respecting the license which might fitly be allowed to public recreation on the Sabbath-day, were correct or incorrect, is a question totally distinct. But Mr. Rogers *must* know that this whole matter was hotly debated at the time. He *must* have heard of the Sabbatarian controversy; and, therefore, he *must* have been aware, while he was penning these very sentences, that the more indulgent theory was supported, not by Laud alone, but by men who were as incapable of giving encouragement to wilful Sabbath-breaking, as they were of giving utterance to blasphemy. Besides, it is perfectly notorious, and was never denied by his bitterest adversaries, that, in his own person, the Sabbath was always most devoutly honoured by Archbishop Laud. Secondly; to aver that, in Laud's estimation, the weightiest articles of the Decalogue scarcely exceeded in importance the most insignificant ceremonies, is to proclaim a resolute and wilful blindness to the course of a whole life, distinguished by inflexible integrity, by purity which has never been impeached, and by munificence which nobles and princes would do well to emulate. Thirdly; what were the " solemn fooleries" that were to convert Protestant worship into a Popish melodrame? Why, the decent uniformity of clerical habiliments; the restoration of the communion-table to the primitive position, which, at this day, it occupies in all our churches; the deliverance, in short, of the Church of England from the reproach of brutish and slovenly irreverence. But it surpasses all human patience to enlarge, in further detail, upon these miserable shreds and patches of worn-out detraction. Mr. Rogers has really wrought himself up into a fit of almost rabid violence, which. is exceedingly ridiculous. He is evidently in a temper to " enact *Ercles,* or a part to tear a cat in." We hope and trust that a time of better knowledge, and more unclouded candour, may arrive, when he will be heartily ashamed of describing the author of the immortal Conference with Fisher, as " a tyrant, *with the soul of a deputy-master of the ceremonies!* "

But to proceed with the story of John Howe. At the age of seventeen he was removed to Christ's College, Cambridge; and there, it has been surmised, his mind received its " platonic tincture," from his intimacy with an illustrious triumvirate, Cudworth, Henry More, and John Smith. In July, 1652, he proceeded to the degree of M.A., and was soon afterwards *ordained,* at Winwick, in Lancashire, by *Mr. Charles Herle,* who succeeded Dr. Twiss, as Prolocutor of the Westminster Assembly. His ministry commenced at Great Torrington, in Devonshire. What were his views at this period, relative to ecclesiastical polity and discipline, does not appear to be very clearly ascertained. According to Mr. Rogers, he was almost, if not altogether, a *Congregationalist;* but, nevertheless, was passionately desirous of some moderate and catholic scheme of union. That his labours, however, were indefatigable, is manifest from an account which Calamy received from Howe himself. And, if it be correctly reported, it shows that he must, at that time, have combined the ardour of a disembodied spirit, with the lungs of a trumpeter, and the brawn and stamina of a gladiator; a frame of adamant, with a soul of fire.

" He told me," says Calamy, " it was upon those occasions his common way to begin about nine in the morning, with a prayer for about a quarter of an hour, in which he begged a blessing on the work of the day; and afterwards read and expounded a chapter or psalm, in which he spent about three quarters of an hour; then prayed for about an hour, preached for another hour, and prayed for about half an hour. After this he retired and took some little refreshment for about a quarter of an hour or more, (the people singing all the while,) and then came again into the pulpit and prayed for another hour, and gave them another sermon of about an hour's length; and so concluded the service of the day, at about four of the clock in the evening, with about half an hour or more in prayer."—pp. 36, 37.

This is too much for his present biographer, or even for Calamy himself, who confesses that " the above service was one which " few could have gone through, without inexpressible weariness

" both to themselves and their auditors." " Well," says Mr.
Rogers, " might the preachers of that day be called *painful*
" preachers! And surely their auditors were hardly less entitled
" to that unenviable distinction!" Seven mortal hours of preaching, prayer, and exposition, broken only by one brief pause of
fifteen minutes; and that pause, too, allowed only to the minister,
the congregation *singing all the while!*

About the commencement of the year 1657, some important
business brought Howe to London. On the last Sunday of his
stay, (which was accidentally protracted beyond the period fixed
for his return,) curiosity led him to the chapel at Whitehall; and
here, his majestic person and noble countenance attracted the
attention of Cromwell, who, as Calamy tells us, " generally had
" his eyes everywhere." When the service was over, Howe was
greatly surprised by a summons to attend the Protector; and,
with still more astonishment, received from his Highness a request to preach at Whitehall on the Lord's day following. It
was vain for Howe to represent that the good people of Torrington would be sorely grieved, and, perhaps, bitterly displeased, at
his protracted absence. The Protector would hear of no excuse.
He would undertake (he said) himself to procure a proper substitute. Upon this, the preacher found it impossible to stand out
any longer. His first sermon was followed by a pertinacious demand for a second; the second was succeeded by a third; and
the series ended in the settlement of John Howe at Whitehall as
Domestic Chaplain to his Highness, who, after his manner, tram-
pled down all difficulties which were started in the way of the
arrangement. In this situation he remained till some time after
the Protector's death.

We have, in this place, an enormous length of disquisition respecting the motives by which Cromwell was prompted to this
appointment. The eye of Despotism, we all know, is generally
capricious. But the glance of Cromwell was doubtless that of
deep sagacity. In one sense he was (like other men of capacious
and overruling powers) a discerner of spirits. He could look
men through and through. And, if we are to judge by the portrait prefixed to this volume, there was much in the countenance
of Howe which might easily arrest the gaze of a watchful and
restless observer of mankind. There was in his aspect that air of
goodness, before which wickedness is often spell-bound; and
there was, moreover, an air of greatness, in which the usurper
may have recognized the indications of a mind, which stood forth,
like his own, in bold relief, from the quotidian level of human
mediocrity. And this, together with his desire to signalize his

reign by the services of distinguished men, may sufficiently account for this sort of extemporaneous election of a chaplain.

But, whatever may be the true solution of the enigma, if Cromwell expected, in his new spiritual adviser, an obsequious prophet, in whose lips a lying spirit should abide, he was most egregiously mistaken in his man. John Howe proved himself a very Micaiah, always prepared to say, *as the Lord liveth, what the Lord saith unto me, that will I speak.* Of this, one glorious instance is related by Mr. Rogers. It was an opinion, or, at least, a profession, predominant in the Protector's court, that the *special favourites* of heaven were honoured with distinct intimations, not only of the success of their petitions, but of the particular mode in which their desires would be crowned with a prosperous issue. The court of Cromwell, of course, abounded with these *special favourites;* and consequently it required more than ordinary courage and integrity to stand up in the midst of this proud *election,* and to pour in the light upon their refuge of falsehood and absurdity. Yet this was the office which John Howe faithfully and intrepidly performed. He put forth his sentiments in a sermon " on a special faith in prayer," of which some imperfect notes have been preserved by Calamy, and are given by Mr. Rogers in his appendix. While he was delivering this discourse, prognostics of a gathering storm were observed on the countenance of the Lord Protector. He frequently knit his brows—a certain sign 'of his inward displeasure—and manifested other symptoms of impatience and uneasiness. The terrors of his eye, however, seemed to be wholly lost upon the preacher. He proceeded, with his usual sedateness of demeanour and cogency of argument. When he had finished, some person of distinction approached him, and asked him " whether he knew what he had done?" and, at the same time, expressed dismal apprehensions that he had irretrievably lost the esteem and favour of his Highness. John Howe replied, with perfect composure, that he had done what he conceived to be his duty, and could trust the issue with God. The issue, as it happened, was not so formidable as was probably anticipated by the whole court. The tempest, which had apparently been collecting on the brow of the autocrat, never actually burst upon the head of his audacious chaplain, though it often seemed on the point of coming down; for Howe himself told Calamy that his Highness was something more chilly in his manner than before, and looked, at times, as if he was full of the subject, and ready to speak to him upon it. So that he might say, like Trinculo, " yon same black cloud, yon huge one, " looks like a foul bombard that would shed his liquor; it cannot " chuse but fall by pailfuls." But it never did: and Howe was left in unmolested enjoyment of the satisfaction derived from a faithful and intrepid discharge of his conscience.

There are several interesting and important letters recovered by Mr. Rogers from the Baxter manuscripts, in the library at Redcross Street; from which it appears that Howe was reconciled to the occupation of his dangerous and slippery position at Whitehall, by an earnest hope that it might afford him an opportunity, (to use his own words,)—of " setting up the worship and " discipline of Christ" in the Protector's establishment, and of lifting up an honest testimony against the neglects and irregularities of public men. His task, we find, was sufficiently perplexing. Such was the disorderly license of the family, in all matters relating to God's worship, that " it was about" as hopeful a course to preach in a " market, or in any assembly met by chance, as there." It is evident that he would very gladly have retreated from a post, for which he modestly declared himself utterly unqualified. " I am"—he says—" naturally bashful, pu- " sillanimous, easily brow-beaten ; solicitous about the fitness " or unfitness of speech or silence ; afraid (especially having to " do with those who are constant in the *arcana imperii*) of being " accounted uncivil or busy, &c.; and the distemper being na- " tural (most intrinsically) is less curable." He describes himself as " a *raw young man,* not likely to be considerable among *grandees ;*" and complains that his work is little, his success little, and his hopes small. Baxter, however, seems to have known the man better than he knew himself ; and was, manifestly, most anxious that he should remain firm in his arduous position. The result proved that Baxter was right : for Howe emerged from this fiery trial, with an unscorched reputation. The " *raw young man"* contrived to accomplish what has often baffled and defeated the maturest sagacity. He eminently combined discretion with courage, and moderation with integrity. And such was the felicity with which he achieved this triumph of wisdom, that men of all parties were unanimous in his commendation. " Never" —says Calamy—" can I find him so much as charged, even by " those who had been most forward to inveigh against a number " of his contemporaries, with improving his interest in those who " then had the management of affairs in their hands, either to the " enriching himself, or the doing ill offices to others, though of " known different sentiments. He readily embraced every occa- " sion that offered, of serving the interest of religion and learning, " and opposing the errors and designs which, at that time, threat- " ened both."—The testimony of the usurper is still more noble and conclusive : " You have obtained"—said he to Howe—

" many favours for others; I wonder when the time is to come that
" you will solicit any thing for yourself or your family."

It is somewhat remarkable, that honest Richard Baxter, in
this correspondence with Howe, exhibits, on one point, something more of the serpent's wisdom than we, at this day, are
much in the habits of ascribing to him. " I would have you"—
he says—" very tender and *cautelous* in publishing any neglects of
" the governors. A time there is for open and plain dealing.
" But, as long as the case is not palpably desperate and noto-
" rious, and you have leave to speak privately, that may suffice
" you. The welfare of the Church, and the peace of nations, lies
" much on the public reputation of good magistrates; which,
" therefore, we should not diminish, but promote." This prudent counsel is immediately followed by a suggestion, which was
fit to be laid up in cedar, or in cypress, for the use of future
generations.—" I would awaken your jealousy to a very careful,
" but very secret and silent, observance of the *Infidels and Pa-*
" *pists,* who are very high and busy, in several garbs; especially
" of *Seekers, Vanists, Behmenists.* Should they infest our vitals,
" or get into the saddle, where are we then!" We know not
what may be the feelings of our readers : but, to us, it almost
seems as if the spirit of Richard Baxter were, at this moment,
whispering the same caution—(*mutatis nominibus*)—in our own
ears !—" The Lord Protector"—he continues—" is noted as a
" man of a catholic spirit, desirous of the unity and *peace* of all
" the servants of Christ;" (with a reserve, however, we apprehend, very similar to that of the good folks who prayed that,
whatever else might betide, they might, at all events, be delivered
from Popery, *Prelacy,* and Peveril of the Peak !) " We desire
" nothing in the world, at home, so much as the exercise and
" success of such a disposition. But more is to be done for
" union and peace. Would he (his highness) but, 1, take some
" healing principles into his own consideration ; and 2, when he
" is satisfied in them, expose them to one or two leading men
" of each party, (Episcopalian, Presbyterian, Congregational,
" Erastian, Anabaptist,) and privately feel them, and get them to
" a consent; and, 3, then let them be printed, to see how they
" will relish, (with the reasons annexed); and, 4, then let a free-
" chosen assembly be called to agree upon them ;—he would
" exceedingly oblige and endear all the nations to him. And I
" am confident as I live, that, by God's blessing, he may happily
" accomplish so much of his work, if he be willing, as shall settle
" us in much peace, and heal abundance of our dissensions."

We have here the scheme of *comprehension;* that vision of
enchantment, which was incessantly haunting the meditations of

Richard Baxter: a *comprehension* which was to *comprehend*, and
to amalgamate, Episcopalians, Presbyterians, Independents,
Erastians, and Anabaptists! Why, the Protector might have
shaken .these ingredients together, till his giant arm was weary
with the exercise: and, for a time, perhaps, the compound
might have preserved some appearance of a perfect and intimate
admixture. But nothing can well be more certain than the ultimate result. The materials would gradually have separated
themselves; and each would have settled down in its original position and level; much after the fashion which any one may see
exemplified, by shaking vinegar and oil together in the same
bottle. Or, if any thing at all analogous to chemical action
should have commenced between these multifarious elements,
the combination would, doubtless, have turned out, in the end,
a perilously explosive one; to the sore confusion, and possibly
to the grievous damage, of the rash and ignorant experimenter.
We find that John Howe, though of a truly Catholic and *comprehensive* temper, was much less venturesome, or much more
sagacious, than his instructor. It is extremely diverting to observe the manner in which he deals with the proposal. He
quietly asks, whether it might not be as well to begin the experiment with two of the ingredients, instead of tumbling the whole
of them together, in the first instance; and, moreover, to select
those two, between which the principle of repulsion seemed to
be the least violent and dangerous? He submits, in short,
whether it might not be " a more hopeful course, to attempt,
" first, the reconciling only of the two middle parties, the Pres-
" byterian and the Congregational?—inasmuch as the extreme
" parties would be so much startled at the mention of an union
" with one another, (as Anabaptists with Episcopalians, or with
" Presbyterians,) that it might blast the design at the very beginning.
" But if those two parties could be brought together first, en-
" deavours might afterwards be used for drawing in the rest,
" probably with more success: and, therefore, whether accord-
" ingly, it were best to present to his Highness only what might
" serve that end."

But although John Howe was, beyond comparison, less sanguine than his venerated counsellor, and perceived that the *union*,
in Baxter's contemplation, would, eventually, very much resemble
the *union* of the elements, before the Creative Power descended
upon them,—he was yet extremely anxious for the establishment
of a friendly intercourse between ministers of all denominations.
His views and wishes relative to this matter, are expounded in a
document in his own handwriting, which was found by Mr.
Rogers among the Baxter manuscripts; and which appears to

have been the copy of some proclamation, drawn up by him at the command of the Protector, during his residence at Whitehall. In the latter part of that paper, is a clause to the following effect, —"that godly ministers be invited to maintain, as far as possible, "a Christian and brotherly communion with each other. And, "to that end, that they hold frequent meetings together, within "convenient circuits, for amicable debating of all the things "wherein they differ; and the strengthening one another's hands "in the things wherein they agree; the repressing the growing "errors of the times; and carrying on, with as much unanimity "and consent as may be, the great work they are engaged in." This was John Howe's favorite project. It was, doubtless, far less visionary than the scheme of Richard Baxter. But it is very easy to perceive the tendency of the procedure. It must, if widely adopted, have been powerfully instrumental in bringing down the Church to the same dead level, on which the endless multitude of sects were disporting themselves and taking their pastime; a consummation highly acceptable, of course, to all who regarded episcopacy as, at the very best, nothing more than one among the manifold existing varieties of ecclesiastical polity. We have had abundant opportunities, in our own day, of witnessing the result of a long course of experiments, instituted very much in the spirit of John Howe's proposal. For, what are miscellaneous associations of Churchmen and Dissenters, but meetings, in which "circumstantial matters relative to church "order and discipline" are to be forgotten, and men of all persuasions are to enter into a holy alliance against the powers of evil? And how beautiful has been the effect of this *eclectic* process, in diluting the virulence of High Church bigotry; and in neutralizing the pernicious quality of exclusive principles; and of diffusing the blessed and pacific influence of liberal and truly catholic notions!! Truly, the spirit of John Howe might have rejoiced to see the things which we see; and to hear the things which we hear.

And yet,—while we are writing,—we feel somewhat conscience-stricken. We suspect, that, in our haste, we have done injustice to his memory. We do verily believe,—on better reflection,—that there are a great many things, in our time, which John Howe would *not* rejoice to see and hear. He would not rejoice to behold an alliance, "most foul, strange, and unnatural," between the Infidels, and the Papists, and the Dissenters of this age: for the words of Baxter would have still been ringing in his ears—"should the Papists, or the Infidels, infest our "vitals, or get into the saddle, where are we then?" He would not rejoice to see the savage and motley host of radicalism swelled by a furious rush and influx from the ranks of Nonconformity. He would not rejoice to see " the winds untied, to " fight against the Church;" or to hear the voice, which is borne upon the tempest, loudly demanding her destruction. He would not rejoice to see the religion of the land *supported by voluntary contribution;* and the clergy degraded by an abject dependence on the capricious bounty of their congregations. John Howe would *not* rejoice to see, and to hear, such things. He was a loyal and a peaceable man; and, moreover, he was an eminently wise man. And we cannot suppress a strong persuasion, that, if he were living now,—to behold the countenance and the bearing of modern Nonconformity,—he would look, with a yearning heart, upon the Church, which the spirit of the age is labouring to rend to pieces. He would, probably, be impelled to search, once more, into those " seeming virtuous" principles of ultra-Protestant liberality, which are threatening the whole constitution of the Church with ruinous dislocation. And the result might be, that he would find no rest for the sole of his feet, but on the firm ground of primitive antiquity; and be numbered among the faithful sons and champions of the national communion.

We are considerably fortified in this surmise, by the fact, that Howe never ceased to regard the rulers of the Church with respect and reverence. He was, moreover, always ready to do benevolent and generous offices to the distressed Episcopalians. Among many instances of his friendly feeling towards them, one is, more especially, worthy of honourable record. When the celebrated Seth Ward was candidate for the Principalship of Jesus College, Oxford, he solicited the support and interest of Howe. And nobly did the Protector's chaplain justify the confidence which prompted the application. He spoke, in language of the highest admiration, of the worth and learning of the applicant; and even represented to Cromwell that the failure of such a man would be signally discreditable to the government; more particularly, as he had the voice of a majority of the fellows. It so happened, that the promise of the Protector had been given to another man. But, even so, to Cromwell's honour, the suit was not altogether unsuccessful; for he declared to Ward that, on the strength of such recommendations, he was much disposed to give the candidate some token of his regard. He then asked what was the value of the principalship: and, having heard, from the doctor, what it was *computed* to be worth, he promised to make him an annual allowance to the same amount.

After the death of Oliver, Howe remained at Whitehall, until the deposition of Richard Cromwell, for whose integrity and worth he entertained the deepest veneration. By this time, the state of affairs was such as to make a longer residence in London intolerably painful to him. In a letter of his to Baxter, now published for the first time, he says, " such persons as are now " at the head of affairs, will blast religion, if God prevent not. " The design you writ me of, some time since, to introduce infi- " delity and popery, they have opportunity enough to effect. I " know, some leading men are *not Christians. Religion is lost* " *out of England, further than as it may creep into corners.* " Those in power, who are friends to it, will no more suspect " these persons, than their own selves. I am returning to my old " station, being now at liberty beyond dispute. May 21 (1659)." And so, Howe went back to Torrington; hoping to *flee away and be at rest.* But, alas! his *rest* was not long! He was ejected under the Act of Uniformity; and consigned, together with his family, to a long period of indigence and privation. From a conversation held by him with his friend Dr. Wilkins, afterwards Bishop of Chester, it appears that one of his objec- tions against the Establishment was, not so much the peculiar nature of its discipline, as its want of any discipline at all. Ano- ther of his difficulties was, that " he could not recognize, in the " present constitution, those *noble and generous principles of com-* " *munion,* which, he thought, must, sooner or later, characterize " every church of Christ; that, consequently, when that flourish- " ing state of religion should arrive, which he thought he had " sufficient warrant, from the word of God, to expect, a consti- " tution, which rested on such an *exclusive basis,* must fall: that, " believing this to be the case, he was no more willing to exer- " cise his ministry under such a system than he would be to dwell " in a house built on an insecure foundation."

The former of these objections manifestly has reference to the absence of all such ecclesiastical discipline as may effectually con- troul the vices of individuals: an objection, we greatly fear, well- nigh inseparable, not only from all national religious establish- ments, but from all very large religious communities whatever. With regard to the other objection, it would have been particu- larly agreeable and instructive if John Howe had been pleased to mention distinctly those " *noble and generous principles of com- munion,*" which may be reasonably expected to " characterize the Church of Christ." What principles of communion were *noble and generous enough* to satisfy him, it is absolutely vain to conjecture, from any thing which he has here set forth. And, of course, it would be equally vain, to guess the extent of accept- ance, which the same principles would have met with, among the multifarious varieties of Nonconformity. We much suspect that

the standard of *nobleness and generosity* would have been found
most provokingly diverse! It is well known, that the late celebrated Robert Hall was, at one time, a vigorous advocate for
liberal communion: and yet even Robert Hall was, at last, driven
to lament, and to reprobate, the irruption of Socinians into the
orthodox dissenting connections.   Let the line of comprehension
be drawn where it may, there will always be numbers to complain that the boundaries are *ignobly and ungenerously* narrow;
and to clamour against the bigotry which should resist their
further extension.   Again,—we should be very curious to know,
as nearly as possible, what are the precise dimensions of that
basis, upon which the Church is to rest securely, when the palmy
and flourishing state of religion shall arrive?   If it be an *exclusive basis*, we are told the Church must fall.   And yet the basis
can scarcely be so broad, but that something, after all, must be
excluded.   And, if so, how is the charge of *exclusiveness* ever to
be got rid of?   That union and godly concord will " characterize
the Church of Christ," in the days of its perfection, will
scarcely be disputed.   But, of one thing we may be quite certain,
—that the union and the concord of that blessed time, will *not*
be the result of a lax and licentious compromise of principles,—
whether they relate to discipline or to doctrine.   It will rather,
we may reasonably presume, be the result of a more general, and
more perfect knowledge of the truth, together with a more entire
submission of the understanding and the will to the influence of
heavenly things.   In the mean time, how, on earth, are *principles
of communion* to be settled, or the *basis* of the Church to be
measured out, but by consulting the oracles of God, and the
practice of the earliest and purest times, and the unanimous
sense of those holy men, to whom the faith was originally delivered?   It seems evident to us, that the mind of Howe was
peopled with dreams of unity and comprehension, which, like
many other dreams, were infinitely more remarkable for their
brightness than for their distinctness.   At all events, if a pattern
of the tabernacle was revealed unto him, in his mount of vision,
he has left us, here, but scanty means of discerning its outline, or
of tracing clearly its plan and elevation.

That the spectacle of disunion, perpetually before him, must
have been bitterly afflicting to this single-hearted man, it would
be most injurious to question.   He must have perceived that
such a condition of things was in deadly opposition to the spirit
of the Gospel, and to the example of primitive times.   Here was
an endless multiformity of sects, all in a state of incessant and
mortal strife with each other; or, never *at an agreement*, except
when the Church was to be assailed!   And how was all this

stunning discord to be composed? Why, truly, by a cordial harmony in essential matters of doctrine; and by a magnanimous disregard for all subordinate particulars of practice, and of government. Only establish the unity of the *spirit*, and righteousness of life; and then, the hond of peace would, straightway, become indissoluble! The militant Church might wear the most motley variety of uniform, and adopt the most different schemes of tactics and of discipline;—regulars, militia, volunteers, all might follow their own principles of action, in glorious independence of each other;—and, still, all would be well, if the *heart* of this multifarious body were *but* as the heart of one man! All this while, alas! the Lady of the Seven Hills would be looking on with secret exultation. She well knows, that no battle can be fought with her, but by the compact columns of the Protestant Episcopal Church. And hence it is that she hates that Church with a fierce and deadly hatred. And hence it is, that she not only delights to see her baited and worried by the pack of Nonconformity, but is ever ready to *halloo* them on upon the game; and, not only so, but to join with them in the savage sport of the chase. And, still more would she delight to see the Church's sacred strength departing from her; as, most undoubtedly, and most speedily, it would depart, if she should once suffer her ranks to be disturbed, and her movements confounded, by the influx of a miscellaneous and ill-ordered levy. *Unity*, indeed, might be the result of the experiment. But it would be the *unity* of a mob: a *unity* which would be dashed into " ten thousand flaws," on the first argumentative collision with the well-trained battalions of the Papacy.

We shall not attempt to follow Mr. Rogers through his long and somewhat angry *diatribe* on the Act of Uniformity, and the spirit in which it was carried into execution. It is a passage of history, we must honestly confess, which we love not to dwell upon! And we know of no good purpose that can be answered by heating ourselves with a review of those heavy times; seeing that such times never can return. *The danger, now, is from a very different quarter!*

We turn, with pleasure, to the brightest portion of the life of this excellent man. For six years, he had been bearing up, bravely yet meekly, against a sore fight of afflictions. His income had been scanty, and miserably precarious. He had been " steeped in poverty to the very lips." And, as he was now surrounded by a young and numerous family, he tasted the waters of adversity in all their bitterness. The righteous, however, was not forsaken. About the year 1671, he was invited to become domestic chaplain to Lord Massarene, of Antrim Castle;

in Ireland: and the invitation was accompanied with the most liberal and advantageous offers. The proposal was gratefully embraced. .He embarked for Dublin early in the year; and was, shortly'after, joined by his whole family, at the mansion of his noble and generous patron. His journey was distinguished by a striking, but somewhat whimsical occurrence. He was detained at Holyhead, for some considerable time, by adverse winds. The passengers were numerous, and anxious that the period of their detention should not pass without the benefit of Mr. Howe's religious ministrations. While they were in search of a secluded spot on the sea-shore, the clergyman of the parish happened to pass by, attended by his clerk. The clerk, on being interrogated whether his master was to preach on that day, replied that his master never preached at all! He was accustomed only to read prayers. On this, his reverence himself was asked whether he would allow a minister, then in the town, to occupy his pulpit for that day. The parson instantly acceded to the proposal: and John Howe preached, accordingly, in his customary impressive manner. The fame of the morning sermon brought together a very large and attentive congregation in the afternoon. The wind continued foul for another week. And, when the clergyman entered the church on the following Sunday—(" expecting," says Mr. Rogers, " the usual scanty attendance of hearers, to ac-" company him in the usual *frigid* service")—he beheld the place crowded with a prodigious concourse of people. His consternation was unspeakable! Provision he had none, wherewith to satisfy the hungering and thirsting multitude. In this appalling exigency, nothing was to be done but to implore the presence of the same wonder-working man, the rumour of whose spiritual affluence had brought together this exceeding inconvenient assemblage. The clerk was accordingly despatched. He found John Howe sick in bed. His indisposition, however, was, fortunately, not severe enough to disable him from answering the summons. He, afterwards, declared that he had seldom preached with more fervour and energy, and never saw a congregation more attentive or devout. A few days after this, he set sail for Ireland: leaving the incumbent in a predicament, by no means the most enviable that can be imagined. How the sermonless man demeaned himself, under these new and awkward circumstances, we are not informed. But, alas! we fear it must be concluded that he was *molested* no more with overflowing congregations!

The five happiest years of his life were passed by Howe at Antrim Castle. In 1675, he was called from this delightful and peaceable retirement, in which he composed several of his most admired and. useful works,—viz. The Vanity of Man as Mortal;

the treatise on Delighting in God; and the first part of his greatest performance, "The Living Temple." The circumstance which removed him from the household of his noble friend, was an invitation to take charge of a congregation which had recently lost its pastor, Dr. Lazarus Scaman. The deceased, it seems, was one, whose principles of communion were not quite so *noble and generous* as Howe would have desired: for he was a rigorous Presbyterian, and a sturdy champion of the *divine right* of that form of church polity. Nevertheless, Howe was elected to succeed him; though not with a perfectly harmonious call. The " Declaration of Indulgence," which had been put forth during his residence in Ireland, was not then in force. It was revoked by the king in 1673; his majesty being then in need of another subsidy: for which cause,—as Mr. Rogers observes, and as we most potently believe,—he would willingly have repealed the whole Decalogue! But, though the edict itself was annulled, its spirit appeared to survive in sufficient force to mitigate the execution of the laws against Nonconformity; and, under the protection of this comparatively tolerant disposition, John Howe resumed the exercise of his ministry, unvexed by the swarm of scruples which buzzed about the fastidious consciences of many of his Nonconforming brethren. It should never be forgotten that, at this period, he lived on terms of intimacy with many among the most distinguished ornaments of the Established Church; for instance, with Stillingfleet, Tillotson, Sharp, Whichcot, Kidder, Fowler, and Lucas. We further learn from Calamy, that he might, if he had been so pleased, have enjoyed, if not the friendship, at least the protection and the countenance, of an extremely *illustrious* person among the laity—probably, that fantastical " epitome of all mankind," the Duke of Buckingham. It was the pleasure of that nobleman, during the national delirium of the Popish plot, to become, on a sudden, most violently well-affected towards the oppressed sectarians! And it was about this same time, that a certain great man expressed himself desirous of an interview with John Howe. On hearing this, Howe took an opportunity of waiting on the personage in question. In the course of their conference, the duke—(if he were the man)—formally propounded his belief, that, truly, the Nonconformists were much too numerous and powerful to be any longer neglected. They, undoubtedly, were deserving of regard. And, if they were but provided with a friend near the throne, whose influence and counsel might be at their service on all critical emergencies, it must, on every account, be wonderfully to their advantage, &c. &c. &c. The general proposition being laid down, the great man proceeded to intimate, very intelligibly, though indirectly, that he might, himself, be, perhaps, prevailed upon to undertake the office of their advocate and representative at court. This was to spread a net in the very sight of a bird, much too old and sagacious to be caught. Howe replied to the suggestion, with a great appearance of simplicity, that there was one difficulty in the way of this arrangement. The Nonconformists were, avowedly, a religious people. It would, therefore, be of deep importance to their cause that the individual entrusted with the protection of their interests should be one who would not be ashamed of *them*, and of whom they might have no reason to be ashamed. And, he submitted, that it might turn out an extremely difficult matter to find any one who should combine, in his own person, these two indispensable qualifications. By this gentle and quiet *puff*, the project was extinguished, in one instant.

In 1680, John Howe felt himself compelled to enter the lists of controversy against Stillingfleet. Every one has heard of Stillingfleet's sermon on the " Mischief of Separation." On this occasion, it must be confessed, the great divine *took fire into his bosom*, with the usual consequences of such an adventure. In an evil hour, he committed himself to the prodigious averment, that, " although the *really conscientious* Nonconformist is justi- " fied in not worshipping after the prescribed forms of the " Church of England, or rather would be *criminal* if he did so; " yet is he not less *criminal* in setting up a separate assembly." " Such is the pleasant dilemma,"—observes Mr. Rogers,—" to " which, according to this writer, the sensitive consciences of the " Nonconformists had reduced them. An inevitable necessity " of *crime*, was the direct consequence of their scrupulous anxiety " to avoid it." The *dilemma*, indeed, was one of more than usually formidable aspect: for,—according to the following statement of Mr. Rogers, which we profess not to gainsay,—it was armed with *three* murderous horns. " It was at the peril of " the Nonconformists, if they worshipped with the Church of " England. It was at their peril, if they worshipped in the Con- " venticle. And it certainly was not less at their peril, if they " abstained from worship altogether!"

When this discourse was printed, Howe was in the country. He there received a copy of it, together with a letter against it, " from a person of quality;" who was, evidently, as angry and intemperate as the dean himself. John Howe, on the other hand, was one of those who loved an answer, soft enough to turn away wrath, though hard enough to make an impression upon reason. He, accordingly, published a reply, both in de- fence of the Nonconformists, and in palliation of the violence

with which they had been assailed. The reply was in the form
of a letter to his wrathful correspondent: and, undoubtedly, if
nothing else were extant of his writing, this paper alone would
be a monument sufficient to immortalize his meek and patient
wisdom. A few sentences may be sufficient to show the gentleness with which he attempered his unflinching fidelity to the
cause of his brethren. " I would have you"—he says to the
person of quality—" I would have you consider, how great
" reason you have to believe, that this blow came only from the
" somewhat misgoverned hand of a pious and good man . . . . . .
" Believe him, in the substance of what he said, to speak accord-
" ing to his *present* judgment . . . . We ourselves do not know,
" had we been, by our circumstances, led to associate and con-
" verse mostly with men of another judgment, what our own
" would have been . . . . I am highly confident, notwithstand-
" ing what he hath said, that, if it were in his power, we might
" even safely trust him to prescribe us terms; and should receive
" no hard ones from him." It is devoutly to be wished that the
lions of controversy would imitate John Howe; and roar, as he
does here, after the fashion of the nightingale! The world
would be spared a vast deal of harassing dissonance: and the
demon, which walks abroad in troublous times, might then,
perhaps, be tamed, if not expelled, by a cunning like to that
which calmed the tempestuous spirit of Saul.

In the same year, 1680, the temper and the judgment of Howe
were again put on trial, and obtained a signal and most honourable triumph. A sermon had been delivered by Tillotson before
the King; in which he maintained, that " no man is obliged to
" preach against the religion of his country, though it be a false
" one, unless he has the power of working miracles." His Majesty, of course, was fast asleep, during the delivery of this discourse. But, afterwards, when one of the court condoled with
him, for having lost, during his slumbers, the rarest specimen of
Hobbism he had ever heard, he exclaimed, " 'Odsfish, he shall
print it then." And it was printed accordingly; and a copy of
it was sent to Howe by Tillotson himself. Howe instantly drew
up a long letter of earnest expostulation; in which he lamented
that a sermon against Popery should, in effect, " plead the
Popish cause against the Fathers of the Reformation." This
protest, without loss of time, he placed in the hands of Tillotson;
who, having glanced over its contents, proposed an amicable discussion. The scene of this discussion, was the inside of Tillotson's chariot: in which, as they rode together, he enlightened the
preacher with such a fearful exposition of the dangerous nature
of his doctrine, that Tillotson was agitated, even to weeping, and

confessed that this was among the most unfortunate incidents of
his life. He pleaded, however, that he had preached upon an
unexpected summons; that, in his haste, he had fastened on the
terrors of Popery, a subject which then absorbed the public
mind; that the order to print followed immediately after the
sermon had been delivered; and that, consequently, he was deprived of all opportunity of revision. What might have been
the result of a meeting, such as this, between two thunder-
clouds, from opposite regions of the heavens, may easily be
imagined! As it was, the conference showed that the elements
of peace and candour had not wholly perished from the world.

In 1681, the fury of persecution was again let loose upon the
Nonconformists. For the next two years, Howe himself scarcely
dared to appear in the streets. In 1684, the severity was such as
to extort from him a letter of expostulation to Barlow, Bishop of
Lincoln, who had vehemently insisted on the necessity of a rigorous execution of the laws. But still, no venomous *root of bitterness* was found to spring up, among the feelings which were
naturally engendered in his heart by the sufferings of the time.
He concluded his letter with a prayer, that, " if the prelate had
" either *misjudged*, or *misdone* against his judgment, God would
" rectify his error by gentler methods, and by less affliction, than
" he had designed for his brethren." And he concluded with the
expression of his firm belief, that he should " meet him, one day,
" in the place where Luther and Zuinglius are well agreed." In
1685 he gladly accepted the invitation of Philip, Lord Wharton,
to accompany him in his travels on the continent, and so to escape
from the miseries which he could neither avert nor mitigate. With
this nobleman he visited several of the most celebrated cities of
Europe, and enjoyed the society of learned men of various parties. In 1686, he took a large house at Utrecht for the reception
of English lodgers. In 1687, James II. put forth his celebrated
Declaration of Indulgence. John Howe was then in England,
and was foremost among those Nonconformists who saw through
that mystery of iniquity, and looked upon the treacherous gift with
suspicion and contempt. At length the Toleration Act, which
followed speedily in the train of the Revolution, finally cut asunder
those inextricable knots, which had so long been chafing the consciences, and worrying the intellects, of every religious party in
the land. In the proceedings which terminated in this happy
issue, Howe, as might be expected, was prominently engaged.
By him was drawn up " the Case of the Protestant Dissenters,"
in which the whole matter was " represented and argued " with
great ingenuity and power, but, nevertheless, with his customary
command of temper.

The period was now come when the absence of all external force was to make manifest the violence of the repulsive principle which, all this time, had been secretly at work throughout the whole mass of Nonconformity. To use the words of Mr. Rogers— " relieved from the fear of persecution, the Nonconformists began " to quarrel among themselves. Pressure from without had " hitherto kept them together, and its removal was the signal for " internal dissension." Now, let no man suppose that this very natural phenomenon is produced by us for the purpose of vindicating a system of persecution. For any such purpose it is altogether worthless. But it is not worthless when resorted to for the purpose of exposing the extreme complication of the problem which the advocates of *liberal and comprehensive* principles had been eternally proposing to the rulers of the Church. By the adoption of almost *any* scheme of *liberality and comprehension,* the pressure from without would have been as effectually lifted off as it actually was by the system of toleration. And what would have been the result? Why, obviously, this,—that the quarrelling and the dissension would inevitably have been imported into the body of the Church itself, instead of raging without the boundaries of her enclosure. And who can describe the exultation with which the Papists would have contemplated this triumph of confusion? " The first symptoms of dissension," says Mr. Rogers, " betrayed themselves shortly after the publication of the " Heads of *Agreement* (as they were most infelicitously called) by " the *United Ministers.*" And what was the object of the resolutions which were followed by all this discord, but " a *formal* coalition " between the Presbyterians and the Congregationalists;" that is, between those very sections of the Nonconforming body, which, in Cromwell's time, were considered by Howe himself as the most hopeful subjects for an experiment of conciliation! These evils, however, were altogether insignificant, when compared with the fierce agitation of the Antinomian controversy, occasioned by the reprinting of the works of Dr. Crisp—a man whom Mr. Rogers has done what he could to immortalize, by declaring that he " had " a patent for nonsense and folly, which defied successful imita- " tion." Such was the virulence of this conflict, that " the press " teemed with pamphlets on both sides, till party spirit became " inflamed to a pitch of bitterness altogether unprecedented." In vain did Howe attempt to allay the storm by his discourses on " the Carnality of Religious Contention." The voice of reason and of charity was lost in the roar of the tempest. An open rupture was the consequence, which drew forth from Howe a most affecting discourse upon the text,—*There is none that calleth on thy name; that stirreth up himself to take hold of thee. For thou hast hid thy face from us, and hast consumed us, because of our iniquities.*

Of Howe, little more is to be heard for several years, except that he was employed occasionally in the office of negociating marriages between certain honourable and religious families. Early in 1702, the question of " Occasional Conformity" was brought into agitation, and involved him in some " unpleasant controversy." The history of this question may be very briefly stated. From the commencement of the " Great Schism," in 1662, occasional communion with the Church of England had been practised by many of the more moderate Nonconformists, both lay and clerical; and this, *first,* upon the ground that the Church was an *establishment,* under some modification of which they would have been willing to conform, although they were unable to approve its present constitution; and, *secondly,* with a view to the public recognition of the principle, that an essential unity exists among Christians of *all denominations.* This last was the favourite notion of John Howe. The lawfulness of this sort of conformity was a matter to be determined by each man for himself, according to the state of his own individual conscience. The sole question to be settled was, whether such communion could be practised without sin; and this question could be disposed of only by an unfettered exercise of private judgment. Now, private judgment, as every one must be aware, is a hobby by no means remarkable for the steadiness and regularity of its paces. It is very apt to run away with its rider; and to toss the head, and to lift the heel, and to snuff the wind, like the wild ass of the desert, which laugheth at bit or bridle! It has hurried us into a difficulty, out of which we are unable to see our way. We are at a loss to understand how, if constant Conformity were sinful, occasional Conformity could well be otherwise. This, however, is a quagmire which does not appear to have sunk beneath the weight of John Howe; and there was one distinguished member of his congregation equally fortunate. This was Sir John Abney, whose hobby carried him in safety and quiet over this dangerous ground. The ease, however, with which he skimmed across it, occasioned great surprise, and no little suspicion; for, when Sir John became Lord Mayor of London, in 1701, it was shrewdly surmised by some, that his desire to qualify for civil office gave speed and lightness to his movements. The celebrated Daniel De Foe was mounted upon a much more ponderous and un-wieldy steed; and, accordingly, he was scandalized beyond en-durance by the unbecoming agility of his fellow-travellers. His displeasure bristled up in the form of an anonymous pamphlet, the title-page of which he darkened with the following stern *apo-*

siopesis,—" If the Lord be God, follow him; but, if Baal, ——."
In the preface to this publication, he called upon John Howe to
vindicate the practice of occasional Conformity, if he could; or,
if not, to condemn it—a challenge which, notwithstanding his reluctance, Howe felt himself compelled to answer. His reply was
something hotter than the usual temperature of his compositions.
But so much did he abhor debate, that he declared, at the close
of his pamphlet, that nothing should provoke him to resume his
pen. Daniel De Foe, it is well known, had no such abhorrence
of controversy; and, accordingly, he enjoyed the honours of the
last word. But, although Howe redeemed his promise, by abstinence from further publication, a letter on the subject was found
among his papers, after his death, addressed to " A Person of
Honour," in which the whole matter is briefly, but luminously,
stated. The weakness of the case, as here represented by him,
lies obviously in this,—that he complains of the exclusion of the
Nonconformists, as the work of those who " take denominations,
" not from the *intimate essentials* of things, but merely from *loose*
" *and separable accidents;*" not perceiving, or not recollecting,
that some things, which he considered as *loose and separable accidents,* could not in the conscientious judgment of others, be *separated,* without imminent danger to matters of *intimate* and *essential*
importance. But, not to dwell on this, the following passage
may be selected as an indication of the mild and gentle spirit with
which he was accustomed to mitigate the acrimony of disputation.
" Thanks be to God," he says, " we are not so stupid as not to
" apprehend we are under stricter, and much more sacred obli-
" gations, than can be carried under the sound of a name, to ad-
" here to our reverend fathers and brethren of the Established
" Church, who are most united among themselves in duty to God
" and our Redeemer, in loyalty to our sovereign, and in fidelity to
" the Protestant religion; *as with whom, in this dubious state of*
" *things, we are to run all hazards, and to live and die together.*"
There is not more difference between the murmurings of a dove,
and the screams of a ravening eagle, than there is between these
pacific accents of John Howe, and the cry which is constantly
issuing, at the present day, from the throat of modern Nonconformity.

It is curious enough that they who had once complained of the
Nonconforming conscience as too rigid, at length began to reprobate its dangerous elasticity! And it is still more remarkable,
that the *illiberally* scrupulous Bill against occasional Conformity,
after having passed the House of Commons, was rejected by a
decided majority of the House of Lords; but, nevertheless, without any talk of a *collision.* While the matter was pending, a

paper was drawn up by Howe for the purpose of exposing the absurdity of the measure. The merits of the question are there exhibited by him in the form of an hypothetical case. Sir T——— and Sir J——— are two gentlemen of equal estates. Sir T——— is a Churchman, who *seldom*, indeed, goes to church, but *never* to the conventicle. He is, moreover, a person of irregular habits, and a very comfortable laxity of moral principle. Sir J———, on the contrary, is an extremely sober and virtuous individual, who is punctual in the worship of God, but who sometimes frequents the *one sort of assembly*, and sometimes the other. Nevertheless, Sir J——— is declared incapable of any civil or military office; while Sir T——— is made capable of all. Can anything be more monstrous? *&c. &c. &c.!* Now, let the measure in question be as absurd and indefensible as it might, it is quite clear that this mode of attempting the exposure of its folly, is almost equally absurd. It is altogether unworthy of the mind of John Howe. He ought to have seen that the merits of any *general* measure can never be legitimately brought to the test of an extreme and imaginary case, such as the fancy of a zealous advocate may always supply. The proposed law might be villainously bad. But its badness could never be proved merely by showing that there were some vicious men in the ranks of the Church, who might profit by the law; and some worthy men among the occasional Conformists on whom the law might inflict disparagement and injury. The same sort of reasoning would be just as effective for the purpose of demonstrating the absurdity of considering a profession of Christianity (or, at least, the absence of any profession to the contrary) as a needful qualification for office in a Christian country. For instance: A. is a respectable and virtuous Mussulman, punctual in the discharge of his own religious duties, and faithful to all the essential moralities of life. B., on the other hand, calls himself a Christian, but lives in the practice of many things which, virtually, give the lie to his profession. Notwithstanding this, A. is shut out from all hope of public or professional advancement; while the career of honour and emolument is open to a worthless competitor. Can anything be more iniquitous and more absurd!* The writer, however, seems to have been destitute of all con-

---

* If John Howe were now living, he would probably be somewhat startled to find that the principle of his argument had actually been followed out to this full extent. In the short debate which took place in the House of Commons, on Tuesday, May 31, 1836, relative to the expediency of removing the civil disabilities of the Jews, it was distinctly and stoutly contended by several honourable members, that there could be no good reason why Jews, Turks, Heretics, and Infidels should not be admitted to all the rights and privileges of British subjects. And the motion in favour of the Jews was accordingly carried by a majority of 70 to 19. If the Bill should succeed, even the *theory* of a Christian legislature must of course be formally and deliberately abandoned.

sciousness that he was wielding a treacherous fallacy. Nay, he is so full of confidence in the weight and keenness of his weapon, that he flourishes it about with a vehemence somewhat unusual with him.

" Can it be supposed," he exclaims, " that the nation will be always drunk? Or if ever it be sober, will it not be amazed there ever was a time when a few ceremonies, of which the best thing that ever was said was that they were indifferent, have enough in them to outweigh all religion, all morality, all intellectual endowments, natural or acquired, which may happen in some instances to be on the wrong side, (as it must now be reckoned,) when, on the other, is the height of profaneness, and scorn at religion; the depth of debauchery and brutality, with half a wit, hanging between sense and nonsense : only to cast the balance the more creditable way, there is the skill to make a leg, to dance to a fiddle, nimbly to change gestures, and give a loud response, which contain the answer for the villanies of an impure life!"—p. 439.

But the period was now fast approaching, when this benevolent and holy man was to be removed beyond hearing of the tumult and the din of religious or political strife. In 1702 and 1703, the decays of nature began to do their accustomed work upon his bodily frame; though his mind still appeared to be exempt from their deadly influence. At the close of 1704, it was evident to his friends, that his further sojourning in the flesh would be but short. " His constitution had long been crumbling under a complication of maladies." Nevertheless, his decline was so gradual, that, in spite of much feebleness, he was still supported through a partial discharge of his customary duties. As the outward tabernacle was sinking, the spirit within appeared to be rising with greater intensity and vigour,—to be shaking itself from the dust,—and to be *putting on the beautiful garments* of immortality. On one occasion, we are told, that, at the celebration of the communion, he was rapt into such an ecstasy of joy and peace, that his audience expected to see him die, under the strength of his emotions. We shall hardly be suspected of much sympathy with the paroxysms of enthusiasm or fanaticism. But, nevertheless, we should have reason to take shame to ourselves if we were frigidly to suppress our belief that the souls of the righteous may, sometimes, be refreshed with prelibations and *antepasts* of heaven, at the period when they are about to take wing for that region of holiness and felicity. And, if ever there was a spirit upon earth more likely, than another, to be lifted to the mount, from which he might behold the promised land spread out distinctly before him,—so far as human judgment may pronounce, that spirit inhabited the bosom of John Howe.

Among those who came to visit him, towards the last, was

Richard Cromwell; then, like himself, deeply stricken in years. The interview between them was most solemn and affecting. Many tears were shed, on both sides : and much discourse was held, such as becomes those, who feel that, in this world, they have no abiding dwelling-place or city.

We find, however, that, with all his admirable and truly Christian fortitude, John Howe was not wholly exempted from the fears which, in some form or other, will frequently beset our poor and fallen nature. When the surgeon was puncturing the dropsical legs of Samuel Johnson, he called out to him to cut boldly, for that he cared not for bodily pain, but wanted length of days. Not so, John Howe. Length of days he valued not. But he shrunk from the trial of corporeal anguish. When his son, who was a physician, was lancing his gangrened leg, he anxiously demanded what he was doing? And, he added, I am *not* afraid of dying; but I *am* afraid of pain. Thus fearfully, thus wonderfully, and thus *variously*, are we made! And hence may we learn how rash, how presumptuous, and how uncharitable it is, to form hasty judgments, touching the spiritual condition of our brethren, from these varied struggles between the flesh and the spirit—from these " fears of the brave, and follies of the wise." Well may we exclaim, with Jeremy Taylor,

> Odi artus, fragilemque hunc corporis usum,
> Desertorem animi.

But suffering and terror were, at this time, very near their close with John Howe. On the 2nd of April, 1705, he rendered up his spirit, peaceably and without a struggle.

It would be superfluous to attempt a full delineation of the character of this truly admirable servant of God. The foregoing outline of his life, we trust, may be sufficient to show that Howe was one of those men, whom the Lord is pleased, occasionally, to raise up in the world, apparently for the purpose of showing forth His power, and of manifesting the mighty working whereby He is able to subdue all things to himself. A truly honest man, it has been said, is the noblest work of God. But it is a work which, since man fell from his first estate, can only be produced by Redeeming Mercy, and Sanctifying Grace. And, when these have their perfect operation, the spectacle, undoubtedly, is one for men and Angels to look upon with delight and admiration. And seldom, surely, has their operation been more near to its perfection, than in the heart of this sainted Christian. We cannot, indeed, so far abandon or compromise our principles, as to forbear lamenting that he ever was impelled to separate himself from the Church. But, from this one ungraceful line in his portrait—(for such, we must avow, it *is*, in our eyes),—we gladly turn away, to fix our regards on the majesty and beauty of the whole picture. And we scarcely can wish any thing better for the Church, than, that all her members, when they behold his excellence, may be provoked, by the sight, to a holy emulation.

With regard to his intellectual powers, the estimate of his biographer appears to us judicious and correct. His mind was not remarkable for the predominance of any one faculty. It was distinguished, rather, by the harmonious symmetry with which all the faculties were combined. It has frequently been observed, with respect to material and visible objects, that perfect proportions are found to lessen the overpowering effect, which would, otherwise, be produced by extraordinary grandeur of dimensions. And so it is with objects of which the senses take no cognizance. Thus,—all the powers of John Howe were unusually capacious : but yet, he might, perhaps, have more forcibly commanded the eye of posterity, if the light that was in him had been collected into one spot of intense brightness, instead of being diffused, " in serene and solemn lustre," over the whole expanse of his mind.

The writings of Howe are copious; but we apprehend that they are not, now, very generally read. This may partly be owing to the extreme intricacy, if we may so express it, of his rhetorical tactics and evolutions ; a fault extremely common at that period. The sermons, then, were furnished out with an elaborate and complex apparatus of divisions and subdivisions, which must, at all times, have wearied and distracted the mind of the hearer; and which, in the present bustling and feverish age, would be intolerably harassing,—or, irresistibly narcotic! The habit of much circuitous careering, before the preacher, or the writer, begins fairly to grapple with the main body of his subject, is apt to be another cause of grievous irritation, or exhaustion. And, so provokingly immoderate was this sort of preliminary exercitation, in certain of the writings of John Howe, that Mr. Rogers tells us of a good woman who, once upon a time, was quite out of patience with it. She declared that " he was so long laying the cloth, that she always despaired of the dinner !". Another peculiarity of Howe,—which must always have a repulsive influence,—is his want of mastery in the artifices of composition. It is well known that Robert Hall acknowledged the deepest obligations to the works of Howe; but, nevertheless, he observed that " there was in him an innate inaptitude for discerning minute graces and proprieties." His bullion was abundant, and of the purest quality; but the mintage, for the most part, was coarse, unskilful, and inelegant. His diction was poor, and his style rugged. " Such limited powers of expression"—says Mr.

Rogers—" have seldom, if ever, been associated with such
" opulence and grandeur of intellect. He not only dispenses
" with every elegance, but often degrades the noblest thoughts
" by the meanest and most ordinary phraseology."

Our limits forbid us to follow Mr. Rogers through his analysis
of the writings of John Howe. There is one among them, however, which tempts us to a few brief remarks; namely, his Discourse on " the Vanity of Man as Mortal." The admiration of
Robert Hall for this Discourse, was quite enthusiastic. He was,
himself, in the habit of frequently preaching on the same subject,
and from the same text,—*Remember how short my time is.
Wherefore hast thou made all men for nought.* Ps. lxxxix. 47.
When solicited to publish his sermon, he evaded the request, by
candidly avowing, that the whole of it would be found in John
Howe. After the death of Hall, however, an outline of this
sermon appeared, from the notes taken by the Rev. Mr. Grinfield.* The subject, undoubtedly, is one of surpassing interest
and solemnity. It affords ample scope for the highest resources
of sacred oratory. It irresistibly invites the preacher to dwell,
—(as Hall and his prototype have done, with a prodigal application of their powers,)—on the shortness of life—on the depraved
and miserable condition of the world—on the legion of diseases
and infirmities which would *almost* seem to show that the body
was formed to be a receptacle of pain—on the doom, which
consigns by far the larger portion of mankind to a course of
unvaried toil, converting the inheritor of vast capacities and lofty
aspirations into something of little more intelligence than a piece
of mechanism. And then, with what energy and animation will
he, who hopes to be raised with a *spiritual body,* expose the
coarseness and the meanness of merely sensual delight? And,
not only so, but,—in looking forward to the time, when he shall
see no longer, as in a glass, darkly,—how will he set at nought
the baffling, we might almost say the perfidious, quality, even of
intellectual pleasures, which are, generally, sure to break their
promise to our hopes; and, while they swell out the pride of
understanding, leave, after all, a craving void within the heart.
And, then, he will ask, if this life is " the be all, and the end all,"
is *not* man made in vain? Is it not manifest that the destinies
of a being, gifted with such powers, must be left unfinished, in a
world which affords but imperfect satisfaction even to his lowest
faculties, and leaves his highest in a state of frustration and of
mockery? Now, all these, unquestionably, are noble and spirit-
stirring common places; upon which it might be expected that

* Hall's Works, vol. vi. p. 177. Sermon viii.

any man, endowed with much imaginative power, and capable of profound moral emotion, might, for ever, pour out burning words, and breathing thoughts. But, still, they are *but* common places; and we greatly doubt whether they have in them, an anodyne virtue sufficient to charm down that feverish *unrest,* which is the peculiar malady of many a pure and contemplative mind. There, still, is *fixed* before our eyes, a dark and fathomless gulf of mystery, which this argument, precious as it is, can never close up. For, let us now turn to the other supposition. Man is *not* mortal; he is created for eternity,—and, therefore, not *in vain.* And, so long as any one can confine his thoughts to those, who are yearning for the time which is clearly to disclose the councils of Omnipotence, and fully to develope, and to exercise, the deathless capacities of the human soul,—to those who are labouring, day and night, to prepare themselves for that hour of retribution, which shall unveil all hidden things, and make straight all that is oblique to our eye—so long as any man can fix his thoughts on spirits of this stamp, so long will this argument appear bright and impenetrable as the whole armour of God. But, then, unhappily, there will, from time to time, rush in upon the mind, the thought of those innumerable myriads, who approach the gate of death without apparent consciousness of the *vanity* of their condition *here,*—without one desire which points towards any further completion of their destiny,—without the wish, and often without the opportunity, to seize upon the golden chain which the Saviour has suspended from the eternal throne, in order that, thereby, he might draw upwards all men unto himself. And what shall be said of these? Not, most certainly, that they are created *in vain:* for, whatever may be their lot hereafter, it cannot, without impiety, be doubted, that it shall illustrate, before the universe, the wisdom, the goodness, and the righteousness of God. Nevertheless, it must be confessed, that this same argument, which triumphantly rescues the constitution of the world from the imputation of *vanity,* yet leaves a still more fearful shadow hanging over the fate of that vast portion of the human race, of which, we fear, it may be said, *it were good for them, that they never had been born!* That they were not made *in vain,* is a consideration which scarcely can assuage the perplexity, and the anguish, and the terror, with which the anticipation of their future doom must ever weigh down the heart of every one who has " thoughts that wander through eternity!" They are reserved for a state unspeakably more terrible than *vanity.* The blackness of darkness may be their abode for ever.

There is, in truth, something inexpressibly appalling, in the reflection,—*not* that man, through much discipline and tribulation, must enter into the kingdom of heaven,—but, that, in such an overpowering multitude of instances, the discipline and the tribulation, appear to fail of their effect; so that millions upon millions, who, being mortal, would be the heirs of *vanity*, must, in their immortality, be the heirs of perdition! There is room, here, for meditation, even to the verge of madness. And we apprehend that it would have been an office well worthy of a mighty preacher, to have dropped a word or two in season,—(touching a matter so intimately connected with his subject)—such as might soothe the pangs of the trembling and sensitive inquirer,—and still the waverings of them that are in search of rest,—and rebuke the taunting spirit that is ever working in the children of disobedience. It is one thing to show that man, as a creature of this world only, is walking in a vain shadow, and disquieting himself for nought. But it is another, and a far more arduous thing, to grapple with the *searchings of heart*, which must frequently arise, when we are pondering on the fate of those immense numbers who seem content with vanity, and at ease beneath the bondage of corruption.

It is true that we may be faithfully reminded by the preacher, of the *cure* as well as the *cause* of that *vanity*, in subjection to which, " the whole creation groans," together with man. But still, the dreadful *fact* remains,—that the *cure* is, to all appearance, offered in vain to far the greater portion of mankind: and they, who receive it not, must perish in their sins. And when we muse upon these things, we feel almost impelled to break forth into the boldness which, sometimes, Jehovah permitted to his servants the prophets,—and to exclaim, *Righteous art thou, O Lord, when I plead with thee: yet, let me reason with thee of thy judgments!* Why is it, that thy spirit striveth not unconquerably with the wicked, till they become weary of vanity, and are awakened by thy terrors, and subdued by the benignity of Him, who is the power of God, and the wisdom of God? Why is it that thy salvation is, still, like a light that shineth in a dark place? Why is it that,—if thou hast not *made* men in vain,—it should seem as if thou hadst, well-nigh, *redeemed* them in vain? How long, O Lord, holy, and just, and true, dost thou not lead captive the wills and the affections of sinful men, till they follow thy chariot-wheels in joy and triumph! Gird on thy sword, O thou most mighty; and, in thy majesty, ride prosperously forward, till vanity shall be no more, and meekness, and truth, and righteousness, shall inherit the whole earth!

But we must, now, dismiss the work of Mr. Rogers: which we do, with much respect for his abilities, and with a full acknowledgment of the general candour and moderation which pervade the volume. To be sure, we have, here and there, some fiery eruptions, which seem to speak of certain bituminous matters beneath the surface: as, for instance, when he talks of " ferocious bigotry"—and of " tomahawks and scalping-knives" " —and of the tyrant prelate, with the soul of a deputy-master of " the ceremonies." But these little *capriccios* we are willing to forget, in the prevalent tone and spirit of the work. And we have only to add, that we hope he will not be implacably wrathful against us, for having presumed to lift up our testimony, in opposition to his assault upon the memory of Archbishop Laud. We do not quite despair of seeing the day, when, whatever may be his aversion for the principles of that eminent churchman, he may, at least, feel himself constrained to allow, that the primate was a man of unflinching honesty and courage; and that, even if his temperament was somewhat combustible, it was never kindled into flame by the breath of personal interest, or *selfish* lust of power.

Art. VI.—1. *Sermons preached before the University of Cambridge, during the Month of February,* 1836; *to which are added, Two Sermons preached in Great St. Mary's, at the Evening Lecture.* By Henry Melvill, M.A. late Fellow of St. Peter's College. Cambridge: Deighton. London: Rivingtons. 1836. 8vo. pp. 141.

2. *Probation for the Christian Ministry practically considered. Four Discourses, preached before the University of Cambridge in the Month of March,* 1836. By the Rev. Thomas Dale, M.A. (of Corpus Christi College,) Vicar of St. Bride's, Fleet Street. London: Pelham Richardson. 1836. 8vo. pp. 107.

3. *The Unity of the Church in her Communion and Ministry. Two Sermons, preached before the University of Oxford, in March and April,* 1836. By the Rev. Robert Eden, M.A. late Fellow of Corpus Christi College. London: Hatchard & Son. 1836. 8vo. pp. 54.

4. *A Sketch of the Church of the First Two Centuries after Christ, drawn from the Writings of the Fathers down to Clemens Alexandrinus inclusive, in a Course of Sermons preached before the University of Cambridge, in January,* 1836. By the Rev. John J. Blunt, late Fellow of St. John's College. Cambridge: Deightons. London: Rivingtons. 1836. 8vo. pp. 218.

It has long been our pride and boast, that the theological stores of the Church of England are unequalled in any country. Germany is the only rival which can be fairly named; yet, without seeking to depreciate the vast accessions to sacred literature which that land of learning has made, and even being ready to acknowledge that in some peculiar departments it may claim a superiority over England, our divinity, we may safely say, possesses a more useful, applicable, and available character, which invests it, beyond all other, with a practical as well as speculative value. It is an armoury, which has weapons always at hand, to be wielded against the infidel, the Socinian, the Papist, the fanatic, and the sciolist. It is formed of materials, as it were, at once solid and portable,—strong and massive, without being cumbrous or unwieldy. Moreover, from the time of the Reformation, amidst a few exceptions and deviations, by no means numerous enough or formidable enough to invalidate the force of the rule, it has preserved a discretion, and consistency, and moderation, to which German theology can hardly lay pretensions. The Scotch writers, with Dr. Chalmers at their head, however much they may prefer the forms of their own church, and however highly they may rate the pastoral assiduities of their own ministers, have cordially allowed this pre-eminence to the southern over the northern part of Great Britain, and have been glad to gather aid from the exhaustless magazine of our English divinity.

It is clear that this illustrious distinction can only be retained by the same means which originally secured it; namely, by not impoverishing the Church into a kind of literary starvation,—in other words, by leaving opportunities of learned leisure, and dignified posts, in which men of vigorous and cultivated minds may devote not merely the youthful energies, but the matured experience, of their minds to profound erudition and undistracted thought. In this point of view, perhaps, the prospects before us are not bright; but, in other respects, the anticipations which we may form as to the preachers and writers, who are now ascending the horizon, and likely to direct by their light the rising generation, are happier and more favourable, than would be a survey of the immediate present, or a retrospect of much which has very lately past. That survey, that retrospect, we may hereafter be compelled to make; but we now turn to the gratifying task of looking forward.

The Report of the Church Commissioners shows, that attention has been directed to the improvement of clerical education; and that great object may be said to be in the course of attainment, which the Bishop of Gloucester, the Master of the Temple, the Chancellor of the diocese of Chester, and many others, have long urged with untiring and unconquerable zeal. Our hopes here may be expressed by the truism, that the more profoundly and the more systematically theology is studied, the more orthodoxy will prevail. Again, from among similar indications, we may select the encouragement which has been afforded to a knowledge of the original language of the Old Testament:—a knowledge, by the way, which, however much it deserves peculiar encouragement, may soon become too indispensable actually to need it. The pecuniary liberality, and the personal exertions, of men whose names will occur, unmentioned, to our readers, will be productive of wider benefit than the promotion of the cause of Hebrew scholarship. They will impart a stimulus to many collateral acquisitions, and, generally, to depth and comprehensiveness of sacred research.*

We have placed three publications in the front of this article, because they contain sermons preached at those nurseries of our divinity, even more than of our other learning,—the national universities. But, before we proceed to those broad considerations, which the words, Oxford and Cambridge, must suggest, we would despatch our notice of these productions themselves, in the few sentences which we can afford.

Mr. Melvill, here as always, is stirring, fervid, energetic, eloquent. As to the matter of his discourses, the deficiency most observable is a want of spiritual and doctrinal profoundness; as to the manner, an occasional lack of simplicity, calmness, and condensation. Yet passages might be found fraught not merely with glowing imagery, but with simple and admirable force; and certainly Mr. Melvill has, in many portions of this volume, added to the beauty of his style, by somewhat lopping its exuberant and prodigal luxuriance. The following description, which we can extract without violence to the context, is a fair specimen of his present manner: nor the less fair, perhaps, because in its leading idea it reminds us much of Dr. Chalmers; as is the case with a considerable number of other pages, both as to sentiment and expression.

" We all know what a power there is in memory, when made to array before the guilty days and scenes of comparative innocence. It is with an absolutely crushing might that the remembrance of the years and home of his boyhood will come upon the criminal, when brought to a pause in his career of misdoing, and perhaps about to suffer its penalties. If we knew his early history, and it would bear us out in the attempt, we should make it our business to set before him the scenery of his native village, the cottage where he was born, the school to which he

---

* In speaking of Hebrew scholarship and collateral acquirements, it is impossible not to specify the translation of three manuscripts, containing the Book of Enoch, by the Archbishop of Cashel; and also a work lately published by the Rev. Edward Murray, vicar of Stinsford, and chaplain to the Bishop of Rochester. Its title is " Enoch Restitutus, or an Attempt to separate from the Books of Enoch the Book quoted by St. Jude; also a comparison of the Chronology of Enoch with the Hebrew Computation, and with the Periods mentioned in the Book of Daniel, and in the Apocalypse." Rivingtons. 1836.—We hope to take up the subject.

was sent, the Church where he first heard the preached Gospel; and we should call to his recollection the father and the mother, long since gathered to their rest, who made him kneel down night and morning, and who instructed him out of the Bible, and who warned him, even with tears, against evil ways and evil companions. We should remind him how peacefully his days then glided away; with how much of happiness he was blessed in possession, how much of hope in prospect. And he may be now a hardened and desperate man: but we will never believe, that, as his young days were thus passing before him, and the reverend forms of his parents came back from the grave, and the trees that grew round his birth-place waved over him their foliage, and he saw himself once more as he was in early life, when he knew crime but by name, and knew it only to abhor—we will never believe that he could be proof against this mustering of the past—he might be proof against invective, proof against reproach, proof against remonstrance; but when we brought memory to bear upon him, and bade it people itself with all the imagery of youth, we believe that, for the moment at least, the obdurate ·being would be subdued, and a sudden gush of tears prove that we·had opened a long sealed-up fountain."—pp. 71, 72.

In turning back, we see two sentences immediately preceding this citation, which may demonstrate;—the former of them, how powerfully Mr. Melvill can express a moral truth; the latter, how he can still fritter away the impression by some fanciful appendage, and almost spoil his own work, by overdoing what he had already done well.

" The great evil with the mass of men is, that, so far at least as eternity is concerned, they never think at all—once make them think, and you make them anxious; once make them anxious, and they will labour to be saved. When a man considers his ways, angels may be said to prepare their harps, as knowing that they shall soon have to sweep them in exultation at his repentance."—p. 71.

The last sermon, as indeed all the rest, conveys some most impressive warnings in the most striking diction. Its subject adheres closely to the text, " *When I consider*, I am afraid of Him."

" That the fear, or dread, of God is the produce of consideration ; that it does not therefore spring from ignorance, or want of thought ; this is the general truth asserted by the passage, and which, as accurately distinguishing religion from superstition, demands the best of our attention. It is not to be doubted that a superstitious dread of a Supreme Being is to be overcome by consideration; and it is as little to be doubted that a religious dread is to be produced by consideration. The man who has thrown off all fear of God, is the man in whose thoughts God finds little or no place. If you could fasten, for a while, this man's mind to the facts, that there is a God, that he takes cognizance of human actions as moral governor of the universe, and that he will hereafter deal with us by the laws of a most rigid retribution, you would produce something like a dread of the Creator ; and this dread would be superstitious or religious, according to the falseness, or soundness, of principles admitted and inferences deduced. If the produced dread were superstitious, it would give way on a due consideration of these principles and inferences; if religious, such consideration would only deepen and strengthen it.

"We are sure that the absence of consideration is the only account which can be given of the absence of a fear of the Almighty. It is not, and it cannot be, by any process of thought, or mental debate, that the great mass of our fellow-men work themselves into a kind of practical atheism. It is by keeping God out of their thoughts, or allowing him nothing more than the homage of a faint and passing remembrance, that they contrive to preserve that surprising indifference, which would almost seem to argue disbelief of his existence. And there is not one in this assembly, whatever may be his unconcern as to his position relatively to his Maker, and whatever his success in banishing from his mind the consequences of a life of misdoing, in regard of whom we have other than a thorough persuasion, that, if we could make him consider, we should also make him fear.

"It is not that men are ignorant of facts; it is that they will not give their attention to facts. They know a vast deal which they do not consider. You cannot be observant of what passes around you, or within yourselves, and fail to perceive how useless is a large amount of knowledge, and that too simply through want of consideration. To borrow the illustration of a distinguished writer, who has so treated as almost to have exhausted this subject, every one knows that he must die; and yet the certainty of death produces no effect on the bulk of mankind. It is a thing known, it is not a thing considered; and therefore those who are sure that they are mortal, live as though sure they were immortal. Every one of you knows that there is a judgment to come. But may we not fear of numbers amongst you, that they do not consider that there is a judgment to come; and may we not ascribe to their not considering what they know, their persisting in conduct which must unavoidably issue in utter condemnation?"—p. 112—114.

So far the language is as correct as it is animated, but towards the conclusion, Mr. Melvill relapses into a vein, which it is time for him to abandon.

"When I muse on the stupendousness of Creation; when I think of countless worlds built out of nothing by the simple word of Jehovah; my conviction is that God must be irresistible, so that the opposing Him is the opposing Omnipotence. But if I cannot withstand God, I may possibly escape Him. Insignificant as I am, an inconsiderable unit on an inconsiderable globe, may I not be overlooked by this irresistible Being, and thus, as it were, be sheltered by my littleness? If I would answer this question, let me consider Creation in its minutest departments. Let me examine the least insect, the animated thing of a day and an atom. How it glows with Deity! How busy has God been with polishing the joints, and feathering the wings, of this almost imperceptible recipient of life! How carefully has he attended to its every want, supplying profusely whatever can gladden its ephemeral existence! Dare I think this tiny insect overlooked by God? Wonderful in its structure, beautiful in its raiment of the purple and the gold and the crimson, surrounded abundantly by all that is adapted to the cravings of its nature, can I fail to regard it as fashioned by the skill, and watched by the Providence of Him who ' meted out Heaven with a span, and measured the watèrs in the hollow of his hand?' It were as easy to persuade me, when considering, that the archangel, moving in majesty and burning with beauty, is overlooked by God, as that this insect, liveried as it is in splendour and throned in plenty, is unobserved by Him who alone could have formed it.

"And if the least of animated things be thus subject to the inspections of God, who or what shall escape those inspections and be screened by its insignificance ? Till I consider, I may fancy, that occupied with the affairs of an unbounded empire, our Maker can give nothing more than a general attention to the inhabitants of a solitary planet; and that consequently an individual like myself may well hope to escape the severity of His scrutiny. But when I consider, I go from the planet to the atom. I pass from the population of this globe, in the infancy of their immortality, to the breathing particles which must perish in the hour of their birth. And I cannot find that the atom is overlooked. I cannot find that one of its fleeting tenantry is unobserved and uncared for. I consider then; but consideration scatters the idea, that, because I am but the insignificant unit of an insignificant race, ' God will not see, neither will the Holy One of Israel regard.' And thus, by considering the works of creation, I reach the persuasion that nothing can escape God, just as before that nothing can withstand Him. What then will be the feeling which consideration generates in reference to God ? I consider God as revealed by creation ; and he appears before me with a might which can crush every offender, and with a scrutiny which can detect every offence. Oh then, if it be alike impossible to resist God, and to conceal from God, is he not a being of whom to stand in awe ; and shall I not again confess, that, ' when I consider I am afraid of Him ?' "—p. 131—133.

Here, there is much more of effort than of originality; and is it not extraordinary, that, before such an audience as he addressed, Mr. Melvill should employ the word " *atom*," with so strange and careless a mode of usage? We really thought, that in its popular, as well as in its philosophical and etymological signification, an "atom" meant an indivisible particle of matter; one of the first rudiments or component parts of bodies; something infinitely small; assuredly, much smaller than a man or a butter-fly. But here we have " the *fleeting tenantry of an atom;*" " the *animated thing of a day and an atom:*"—a slip or oversight, of which it would be ill-natured to say more.

Mr. Dale's Discourses " on the Probation for the Christian Ministry practically considered," are as a continuation of those, which he delivered in the same place last year. The subject had been almost exhausted ; and there is little that is new in the publication now before us. The style is still, for the most part, upon stilts; and the preacher of March sometimes appears as if he were striving to outshine and outsoar his predecessor of February. This fact is the more to be lamented, because, when he chooses to be simple and natural, few authors of the day can write better than Mr. Dale. The peroration of the third sermon, for instance, is fine and rich in composition, without being over-laboured; and we quote it with the more eagerness, on account of the minister whose awful death it commemorates.

" Christian sympathies are beyond all question of far higher value than mere worldly courtesies. Nor will it be expected that one should be insensible to their value, who has recently assisted in the funeral obsequies of a brother in the ministry*—one who lived with the spirit of the Gospel in his heart, and died with the utterance of it on his lips. We, who attended him to the grave, looked not then upon mere outward trappings of woe—upon a bier followed by unsympathizing mourners, with the cold decencies of a formal aspect, but with hearts unmoved;—we looked upon hundreds, I might say thousands, not only arrayed in the funeral garb, that sometimes masks exultation, and still oftener mocks regret, but dissolved in undissembled grief; all eyes filled with tears—all hearts heavy with sadness—one cry of anguish arising from the thronged and teeming church—from the youthful, ' Alas, my father!'—from the aged, ' Alas, my brother!' The wealth of a thousand kingdoms could not have purchased such a spectacle: hearts are not bought and sold; and I should then have have learned, if I had not known before, that sympathies are strongest upon earth, when the tie of brotherhood has been the hope of heaven, and that those love most truly and most warmly ' who are partakers of like precious faith.'— He of whom I speak was a sure and safe model. He courted not the applause of man: he revolved in no ample orbit, and shed around him no wide-expanding, no conspicuous light: his parish was his family, and his home was his flock. They are about to perpetuate his memory in marble, but his best record is in their hearts. Surely to be thus beloved, thus honoured, thus regretted, thus remembered, on the sole ground of spiritual faithfulness and moral worth, transcends all literary honour, and outshines all worldly fame, while, unlike them, it is within the reach of all. Few can win extended and enduring reputation; but who cannot conciliate love and command esteem? Man, with all his far-gone corruption, has not fallen so low as to have lost all perception of moral excellence. However misconception and misrepresentation may interpose for a season, truth is mighty, and will prevail—fidelity will be appreciated—consistency must be approved. Thus it was with him of whom I spake: those were found, who knew not how they loved till they lost him; and who, having long lightened his labours by their sympathy, paid the last tribute of love when they hallowed his grave with their tears.

" Let us then be stirred up thus to labour and thus to love, if we

* The Rev. Isaac Saunders, M. A., rector of St. Ann's Blackfriars, who expired in the pulpit of his church on New Year's day, 1836, when uttering his text, " Ye are complete in Christ."

would that such grief should attend our departure, and such hearts record our memory; nay, what is of incalculably higher worth, if we would be saved ourselves, and save them that hear us. For the grave is nothing—the funeral pomp is nothing—the marble monument is nothing—the soul is every thing! And, oh! would it not be the few who are lost, and the many who are saved, if the question were asked by the living, to which the dying too often can find no reply, 'What shall a man give in exchange for his soul?' If the blood of Christ was shed for its salvation, what then shall be taken to compensate for its loss? O calculate this, before ye hazard the precious deposit in others, before ye endanger it in yourselves. Rather may ye go hence to do what wisdom counsels, and even what interest would enjoin; to take thought for souls above all beside, because they, and they alone, are the purchase of the 'blood of Christ!'"—p. 74—77.

What, however, of useful or exact knowledge, can be gained by the following mixture of metaphysics and metaphor?

"Man's mind is not coloured by circumstances; it is not like a stream which varies the tint of its waters with the substance of the soil through which it flows. It is like a river, turbid indeed, but made so by a sediment that is deposited in the bed of the channel; and which rolls as black and as troubled through verdant plains and smiling pastures, as between the rifted rocks or along the blasted heath. The channel must be cleansed out, if the stream is to be made pure; and so the χάρισμα must be imparted for the purifying of the heart, before we can expect to witness the purifying of the life."—p. 32.

In such passages, truth of the most sacred and momentous character is disguised, if not sacrificed, for the sake of a comparison. To deny too much is as perilous as to attempt to prove too much. And while we can never agree with Mr. Robert Owen, that man is altogether the creature of circumstances, even that error is less remote from the reality, and less fatal to the progress of the species, than the assertion that man's mind,—whether Mr. Dale means by *mind*, the intellectual or the moral part of his being,—is unaffected, or, as he calls it, *uncoloured* by circumstances.

Mr. Dale seems to have gone to Cambridge as a kind of accredited agent, advocate, and emissary of the *Pastoral Aid Society*:—a society, he tells us in his advertisement,—" of which an account will be found in the appendix to this work,—a society, in the writer's judgment, equally adapted to the exigencies, and consistent with the discipline, of the Church of England."—p. iv. Whether it was quite proper or prudent, that the university pulpit should be turned to such a purpose, we may inquire at another moment. Nor can we here pause to consider what Mr. Dale says, about *the necessity of practical ministers*, or " THE PAROCHIAL SYSTEM INEFFICIENT." But it consists with our present design to transfer to our pages what Mr. Dale calls a "*statement of facts.*"

"Were we describing fictions—were we calling up scenes of imaginary wretchedness—were we grouping images of picturesque horror for the poet's pen or the painter's canvas, we might awaken in our hearers the sympathy of sentiment, and diffuse a pleasing melancholy through the heart, lightly felt, and easily to be forgotten. But we deal in realities—in cold, naked, bitter, stern realities; and if facts cannot penetrate the heart, we will give fiction to the winds. We will speak only what we do know, and testify what we have seen. We have known, and that through the effect of one prolific vice, intemperance—we have known, and we might tell you, of the father and the husband, insensible to the cries of famishing children, and replying but with curses to the prayers of his agonized and outraged wife—we might tell you of the mother, forgetful of her sucking child, and lost to all compassion for the offspring of her womb—of the grey-haired parents, one suffering, one dying, abandoned by their own, their only son, to whom they had given all—of the son, trained by his father's example to live a felon, the daughter, by a mother's connivance, to become that which we will not name; of the noble intellect, that sparkled like a sun among its fellows, going down in thick darkness ere its noon—of the limbs, cast in giant mould, tremulous with premature decay—of the moody maniac, acting unconsciously upon his dying bed the mimicry of the spirit-shop, now, as if raising the glass to his parched lips, now, dashing down the price of the ruin of his soul;—yea, and of the ghastly suicide, first infuriated by jealously, and then maddened by strong drink, pointing the fatal weapon shattering the brain, yet so far foiled in his aim, that ten days of unutterable agony shall intervene between the deadly act and the departure of the imprisoned soul—who dare ask whither? Such are the scenes which will, occasionally at least, present themselves to a pastor's view. He can only avoid them, in a large city, by neglecting his duty and betraying his trust. If they exist, they should be sought out; but why do they exist? It would be falsehood to impeach the premises—it would be folly to resist the conclusion. 'It is *thus* the sheep of Christ perish, because the pastor cannot take heed to ALL the flock.'

"If, then, such are the scenes which ye must occasionally witness, are ye prepared? Will ye be ready, thus summoned, to utter a word of sympathy to the sufferer, of consolation to the mourner, of admonition to the sinner?—And think not that we speak only of one portion of Christ's vineyard; it is to be more than feared, that the metropolis has too many miniatures in all parts of the land; and that in some, it may be, there is an equal depth of darkness, with a less proportion of light, and a similar insolence of profligacy, with a greater comparative inadequacy of the means of grace. Wherever men congregate in numbers, noxious weeds and roots of bitterness will flourish. We must not look, therefore, in this our day and generation, for studious, and abstracted, and contemplative pastors, devoted to pursuits of science, and

emulous of literary fame;—we must not look, exclusively at least, for
the eloquence that captivates, for the imagination that transports, for
the reasoning that carries all, by the very force of its current to anchor
in full conviction. All these, directed to the purposes of the ministry,
and consecrated to the upholding and enlargement of the church, are to
be admired, valued, loved; but that which is essential to win souls,
faithfulness united to diligence, is within the range of ordinary minds.
All ministers of Christ cannot aspire to the model of Paul, haranguing
the Areopagites at Athens, or Peter, confounding the Sanhedrim at
Jerusalem; but who cannot imitate Peter feeding *one by one* the sheep
of Christ, as one who has the oversight thereof;—Paul teaching from
house to house, and warning every one night and day with tears? The
practice of the ministry can alone be the preservative of the flock. It
is a fallacy, too current in the present day, to mix up sentiment with
religion; to clothe in rich and vivid colouring the duties and the delights,
the efforts and the encouragements, the trials and the anticipations of
the Christian minister; to paint him smoothing the way to heaven and
pointing to the skies, with all the accompaniments of striking scenery
and picturesque grouping—the streaming eyes, and uplifted hands—the
deep silence, or the whispered penitence, or the murmur of the broken
sigh, which is the language of the heart. But romance expires on the
threshold of real life, at least in peopled towns and crowded cities—expires in the dwelling of poverty, where there is nothing but desolation
around, and nothing but darkness within,—and where, as too frequently
happens, a thin partition only interposes between the bed of death and
the careless trifler or the reckless drunkard;—and where sounds of revelry or ribaldry disturb the murmured prayer, and shrieks of wild fierce
laughter mingle strangely with the groans of the dying. Think ye this
an exaggerated picture? My own prayers, at the bedside of a dying
man, at an early hour on the Sabbath morning, have been interrupted
by the yells and imprecations of a drunkard, who has reeled home from
the spirit shop, that he might curse himself to sleep."—p. 93—97.

So rhetorical a manner of *" stating facts,"* it has seldom been
our lot to contemplate : and we must add, that this overstrained
style, instead of bearing to our minds the impress of true Christian oratory, rather resembles the scraps of sermons which are
now and then inserted in a lady's novel, where the fair authoress
is ambitious of putting into the mouth of a favourite preacher
something which she intends to be supereminently awakening.

Mr. Eden's Sermons are intituled, " The Unity of the Church
in her Communion and Ministry." The author, although we
dissent from some of his opinions, quite vindicates, in these discourses, his established character as a scholar and a Christian,
and is evidently an able and pious man. His manner, though
Mr. Eden, too, is not without his aspirations, is calmer and more
doctrinal than Mr. Melvill's or Mr. Dale's :—although we regret
to acknowledge that we do not see much, which is definite and

precise;—much, which approximates to any clear information, as to what true union is, or how it is to be attained. We subjoin a single but rather a long specimen :

" With Paul the preacher, ' Christ was All :' not only the *subject-matter*, but the single *subject;* each and all of the truths he laid down, like rays of heavenly light, emanating from, and converging upon, that one glorious and Divine Person. And it is to this point, especially, that we should have regard; on this fix our attentive view—if we would comprehend the meaning, and catch, for our own imitation, the spirit of St. Paul's assertion, that he preached ' Christ Jesus the Lord.' It was not an idea, a notion, a proposition, or even a doctrine (though copious streams of doctrine flowed therefrom) that he primarily preached, but the Word made flesh, and dwelling among men. It was one who had ' gone in and out amongst them,' whom they had heard, and ' seen with their eyes, whom they had looked upon, and their hands had handled,' that this Apostle preached; a living Being, an incarnate God. And it is this exhibition of the *Person* of Christ, which, from the Apostles' age to the present has been the foundation of all effective preaching of Him. Upon this foundation indeed will be reared the whole edifice of truth : upon this platform will be constructed an orderly and complete system of evangelical divinity; but ' other *foundation* can no man lay than that is laid which is Christ Jesus;' ' the Lord from heaven;' ' Christ Jesus the Lord.' When this is habitually done—when the ministrations of religion find their centre, and rallying point, in the reality of Christ's Person, then, all the great doctrines of our faith are intelligently received ; because they are seen, not as abstract propositions, but as lively principles; as the consequences of that work of Christ, which he wrought out for our sake. Of the ministry which is grounded on this reference of all things to the Person of Christ, his proper Deity will of course be the basis ; for, it is the single ground of the glory of that Person. His infinite perfections as ' God, over all, blessed for ever'—equal to the Father, and one with him, are the features which give to the dispensation of the Gospel its unique, its distinguishing excellency. This corner-stone of the future building being firmly set, the whole will rise in grandeur and in strength ; this being unsettled, its solidity and coherence is, at once, destroyed. No labour, therefore, can be deemed superfluous, which is employed in demonstrating this great truth : to impress and reiterate its evidences, will be to make sure work in all subsequent teaching; for here it is that a germinant scepticism, a covert unbelief, first manifests itself. It is here that under the semblance of an expansive philosophy, infidelity creeps beneath the foundations of our faith ; and having corroded the substance on which it stood, leaves us to perish under its ruins. It is here that Rationalism, (libellously calling itself Reason,) first plants its foot; and here, therefore, must we repel its entrance : detecting for ourselves, and exposing to the world, the shallowness of its pretensions ; shewing that the Reason which leads men to confess their natural ignorance upon all other subjects, should pre-eminently so act in this ; and that the finite, in receiving the communications of the infinite mind, has reached its limits when it has listened to the divine voice, and understood the sense of that which Prophets and Apostles have affirmed. Its usurpation of a name derived from ' Reason' must not beguile us; because it adopts this name only to hide from itself its full deformity, its unwillingness to allow those principles, which once granted would compel it to admit the consequences which it hates. Here the minute arguments of verbal sophistry must be defied, as well by the influx of separate testimonies from all parts of the Bible, as from the structure of the scheme of salvation. Not Christ as Divine—in some mitigated sense which all can receive—as possessing a secondary and derivative Divinity; but Christ as absolute God; in whom the Divine attributes, though veiled in the flesh, are not limited, but exist in the fulness of their perfection; at once the image of the invisible God, and the model of unfallen man,—is to be preached, as a truth essential to the Gospel scheme, and with which it is so interwoven, that, if it be touched, the whole edifice must crumble into dust. For this alone is the basis of the Atonement; to which,—when the ' exceeding sinfulness of sin' has been discovered to the conscience,—the Deity of Christ at once conducts. When the mind has arrived at the Atonement through this avenue of conviction of sin, there will be no danger of a false view of that great verity of our faith. None will then imagine that the Atonement is a mere drama enacted by God, to restore to man that self-complacency which sin has disturbed within his breast; whilst God has never been his enemy ; has no attribute of justice to be appeased; has been his friend and continues such still, however sinful he may have been and may remain ; but, (the character of God being unchangeably holy,) that man's iniquities have ' separated between' him and his God ; that an example of his own holiness must precede the example of his mercy; that, by being just alone could he be ' the justifier of him that believeth in Jesus.' To teach that this reconciliation is, on the part of God, complete : and that no ideas of freeness can equal the freeness with which man is invited to be reconciled to God ; that this offer is not only unclogged with conditions, but that its essence is, that it abolishes all conditions; this,—while it will display the effulgent glory of the cross of Christ,—by a law of divine attraction, will kindle a returning love to God ; and will thus evidence that the faith which justifies through the merit of Christ's blood, is intimately and certainly linked with that which sanctifies by his Spirit. And so, in exhibiting the Gospel, we shall find ourselves ' preaching Christ Jesus the Lord;' we shall fulfil the test before laid down, of glorifying his Person, not by any mystic abstractions of mind in contemplating that Person apart from the revelations of Him in the Scriptures, but by understanding the grace of Christ in his gift of himself for us; the pardon of sin through this blood, our union with him, and the consequent communications of his grace for the edification of his members.

" In like manner the privileges and prospects of the church will centre in Christ : the holy Catholic church is ' his body:' the communion of saints ' is with the Father, and with his Son Jesus Christ :' the remission of sins is ' preached among all nations in his name ;' the resurrection of· the body is the work of the Son, whose voice ' all that are in the graves shall hear and shall come forth :' the earnest of the life ever-lasting is ' Christ in us the hope of glory.'

" The promises of God have their stability in him ; being ' in him yea, and in Him Amen, unto the glory of God by us ;' his threatenings are executed by Christ upon ' them that know not God ;' while ' to them that are in Christ Jesus' they bring ' no condemnation.'

" The ordinances of religion have their significancy from him ; for, we are ' buried with Christ in baptism ;' and, in the Eucharist, it is ' the Lord's death,' that we show.

" And, the morals of the Gospel, apostolically taught, will equally be ' the preaching of Christ Jesus the Lord.' Duties civil, relative, and personal, if handled by us as by Paul, will not be rigid precepts· and isolated laws, but animated principles, because grafted upon Christ, the living vine, receiving nourishment from him, and reflecting, by their vigorous operation, the power of that grace which impels to an uncon-strained obedience to his will ; and thus in the display of doctrine and the enforcement, of obligation, · ' the light of the knowledge of the glory of God' will be resplendent ' in the face of Jesus Christ.' By no constraint, but necessarily and naturally, in all our ministrations Christ will be seen riding forth ' conquering, and to conquer :' and like as he is destined ultimately to subdue the whole of his creation to his em-pire, so will he appear in the ministry of those whom he employs as agents to hasten that triumph, subordinating all the departments of his truth to the glory of himself. The life's blood that streams from the cross will thus circulate through the spiritual system, and return to the fountain whence it set out ; the light that irradiates the Redeemer's head will thus shoot its rays around, and encompass the whole body of his truth and carry back the· eye to the glory whence it issued."—p. 37—46.

Amidst all these quotations we may seem to have lost sight of our general topic—the prospects of English Theology. But, in point of fact, nothing can be more pertinent to our subject, than an exhibition of the Sermons which are now preached to our Universities, and the degree of attention with which they are heard. The touching, yet manly strain, in which Mr. Mel-vill takes leave of his audience at Cambridge, may instruct us in both points.

" If we were once deprived of the Gospel ; if the Bible ceased to circulate amongst our people ; if there were no longer the preaching of· Christ in our churches ; if we were left to set up reason instead of Re-velation, to bow the knee to the God of our own imaginations, and to burn unhallowed incense before the idols which the madness of specu-lation would erect—then farewell, a long farewell, to all that has given dignity to our state, and happiness to our homes ; the foundations of true greatness would be all undermined, the bulwarks of real liberty shaken, the springs of peace poisoned, the sources of prosperity dried up ; and a coming generation would have to add our name to those of

countries whose national decline has kept pace with their religious, and
to point to our fate as exhibiting the awful comprehensiveness of the
threat, ' I will còme unto thee quickly, and will remove thy candlestick
out of its place, except thou repent.'

" But we rejoice in pronouncing this a doom, respecting which we
do not augur a likelihood that it will fall on this kingdom.   There may
have been periods in the history of this land, when the upholders of true
religion had cause for gloomy forebodings, and for fears that God would
unchurch our nation.   And some indeed may be disposed to regard the
present as a period when such forebodings and fears might be justly entertained.   They may think that so great is the array of hostility
against the national Church, that the most sanguine can scarce venture
to hope that the candlestick will not be cast down.   We cannot sub-
cribe to this opinion.   We are not indeed blind to the amount of opposition to the national Church ; neither have we the least doubt that the
destruction of this Church would give a fatal blow to the national
Christianity.   We dare not indeed say that God might not preserve
amongst us a pure Christianity, if the national Church were overthrown.
But we are bold to affirm, that hitherto has the Church been the grand
engine in effecting such preservation ; and that we should have no right
to expect, if we dislocated this engine, that results would not follow
disastrous to religion.   I could not contend for the Established Church,
merely because venerable by its antiquity, because hallowed by the
solemn processions of noble thought which have issued from its recesses,
or because the prayers and praises which many generations have
breathed through its services, seem mysteriously to haunt its temples,
that they may be echoed by the tongues of the living.   But as the great
safeguard and propagator of unadulterated Christianity ; the defender, by
her Articles, of what is sound in doctrine, and, by her constitution, of
what is apostolic in government ; the represser by the simple majesty of
her ritual, of all extravagance, the encourager, by its fervour, of an
ardent piety—I can contend for the continuance amongst us of the
Establishment, as I would for the continuance of the Gospel ; I can
deprecate its removal as the removal of our candlestick.   It is not then
because we are blind to the opposition to the national Church, or fail to
identify this Church with the national Christianity, that we share not
the fears of those who would now prophesy evil.   But we feel that
danger is only bringing out the strength of the Church, and that her
efficiency has increased as her existence has been menaced.   The theaten-
ing of our text belongs to the luke-warm and the indolent ; its very
language proves that it ceases to be applicable, if it have fanned the embers and strung the energies.   We believe of an Apostolic Church, that it
can die only by suicide ; and where are our fears of suicide, when enmity
has but produced greater zeal in winning souls to Christ, and hatred
been met by increased efforts to disseminate the religion of love ?

" We might not have ventured to introduce these observations, in
concluding our discourses before this assembly, had we not felt that the
Church stands or falls with the Universities of the land, and that the
present condition of this University more than warrants our belief that

the candlestick is not about to be removed. It is a gratification not to be expressed, to find, after a few years' absence, what a growing attention there has been to those noblest purposes for which colleges were founded; and how the younger part, more especially, of our body, whence are to be draughted the ministers of our parishes, and the most influential of our laity, have advanced in respect for religion, and attention to its duties. One who has been engaged in other scenes may perhaps better judge the advance than those under whose eye it has proceeded; and if testimony may derive worth from its sincerity, when it cannot from the station of the party who gives it, there will be borne strong witness by him who addresses you, that not only is the fire of genius here cherished, and the lamp of philosophy trimmed; but that here the candle, which God hath lighted for a world sitting in darkness, burns brightly, and that, therefore, though enemies may be fierce, the candlestick is firm.

"But suffer me, my younger brethren, to entreat you that you would think more and more of your solemn responsibility. I cannot compute the amount of influence you may wield over the destinies of the Church and the country. In a few years you will be scattered over the land, occupying different stations, and filling different parts in society. And it is because we hope you will go hence with religion in the heart, that we venture to predict good, and not evil. We entreat you to take heed that you disappoint not the hope, and thus defeat the prediction. We could almost dare to say that you have the majesty, and the christianity, of the empire in your keeping; and we beseech you, therefore, to 'flee youthful lusts,' as you would the plots of treason, and to follow the high biddings of godliness, as you would the trumpet-call of patriotism. Your vices, they must shake the candlestick, which God in His mercy hath planted in this land, and with whose stability he has associated the greatness of the state, and the happiness of its families. But your quiet and earnest piety; your submission to the precepts of the Gospel; your faithful discharge of appointed duties; these will help to give fixedness to the candlestick—and there may come the earthquake of political convulsion, or the onset of infidel assault, but Christianity shall not be overthrown; and we shall therefore still know that ' the Lord of Hosts is with us, that the God of Jacob is our refuge.'"—p. 82—86.

Mr. Melvill's testimony to the growing piety of Cambridge, is strong rather than convincing: for he himself is too eloquent and too celebrated a preacher not to have attracted large congregations at any period. The fact, however, is indisputable, that not merely when such men as Dr. Shuttleworth, or Mr. Hook, or Mr. Girdlestone, or Mr. J. Anderson, have been preaching in the one University; or such men as Mr. Benson, or Mr. Rose, or Mr. J. Blunt, have been preaching at the other; but, in the average case, of persons less distinguished; the attendance, particularly of undergraduates, has been lately much more numerous at St. Mary's, than it was some years ago. One cause of this result—there are, of course, many others, indeed too many for present enu-

meration—is the circumstance, fully demonstrated by the extracts which we have adduced, that the cast of discourses has
been of late more exciting and popular, less scholastic and aca-
demic, than heretofore. The preachers have been men accustomed to extensive parishes and mixed congregations; and their
harangues have been of a character brought more immediately
home to the business and bosom of the listener.

Now, this practice, we conceive, to regard it simply in the point
of view which bears upon our immediate topic,—if judiciously
regulated and arranged—if kept in its due place and proportion with reference to a general system, and not inordinately or
exclusively pursued—may be beneficial, in its consequences, to
the theology of a land. For theology, while it is the pro-
foundest and most comprehensive, is also the most practical of
all sciences. Pastoral experience, we are thoroughly convinced,
is indispensable to the maintenance of a good and efficacious
divinity; for, otherwise, there will be no searching and accurate
insight into the human heart—a knowledge, next to a perfect
acquaintance with the Bible, the most useful for a Christian
minister, and absolutely necessary even for a due appreciation
of the Bible itself. Religion—even the theory of religion—
cannot be understood and felt simply amidst the abstractions of
solitary research. Erudition and meditation are, of themselves,
insufficient to teach it. The intensest devotion of the intellectual
faculties, within the rooms of a college, is unable to instil it.
Study, even the severest study, is not enough. A knowledge of
mankind, even in regard to the truths of religion, is almost more
requisite than a knowledge of books. There is—assuredly there
is—many an important lesson of theology, which can best be
learnt amidst the movements and collisions of thousands collected
in society: which, perhaps, can only be gathered from that perpetual commentary on the word of God—that vast school and
seminary of experimental wisdom—the living world: struck out
from the shock of conflicting interests; elicited by the troubles, the
vicissitudes, the reverses, of existence; the frivolities of health,
or the murmurs of sickness; the dissipations of vanity and
wealth, or the terrible evils incident to penury and neglect:
gushing forth amidst the pride of acquirements or the reckless-
ness of ignorance; or flung up from the darkest recesses of the
tempted and shaken spirit. It may well be, that German divinity has suffered considerable damage from the comparatively
secluded position of a *large portion* of its professors: and we
need scarcely say, that the recluse study of a German professor
is a very different thing from the mature and experienced leisure
of an English Prebendary. That position may be expedient

for prosecuting minute and subtle investigation without disturbance, and throwing light upon some separate point of critical disquisition : but on the general character of a national theology its effects may be most injurious. It may generate the abominable distinction between esoteric and exoteric doctrines : or it may lead to a cold and barren rationalism, which the burning wants of the mass will always repudiate and abjure ; a bare, speculative, negative philosophy of religion, which may be said to carry with it in its inefficiency a demonstration of its falsehood. ·

But there is at least as much danger on the other side. The tendency of a scholastic or *professorial* divinity, if there be nothing to counteract its evil, is to become not merely dry, sterile, and uninteresting, but, in sober verity, inapplicable to the moral and spiritual exigencies of living men, amidst the crush of action and the tumult of many passions. But the tendency, again, of *popular* divinity, if left without a counterbalancing power, is to become a thing of quite flimsy and superficial texture ; froth without substance ; a bustle and ferment of superstitious enthusiasm ; a mere *ad captandum* appeal to the senses, the imagination, and the feelings of the multitude. If pastoral experience be essential to the general preservation of good theology in a Church, tranquil inquiry and critical erudition are things of still more direct, and palpable, and indispensable necessity. Hence not only the importance of the divinity, maintained and inculcated at our Universities, is unspeakable and incalculable ; for it involves no less than the question whether the waters of sacredness, which are afterwards to be spread throughout the country, shall be wholesome or polluted at the fountain-head : but let us remember, too, that even pastoral energy, without pure theology, may be a positive mischief ; for it may be, like education without religion, a magnificent power misdirected.

On this account, as on others, we have received and read with very high satisfaction the Cambridge Sermons of the Rev. J. J. Blunt. These discourses, although they were delivered before either of the series already noticed, are of more recent publication. Indeed, they have reached us so late, that we are quite unable to give so full an account of them as we could wish, and as they merit. They form a pleasing interchange with the contemporary and companion publications. There is more stuff in them. They belong to the older style, and from the nature of their design possess a value which is more substantial, and will, perhaps, be more durable than the oratorical displays of Messrs. Melvill and Dale. Much more connected and continuous than the Sermons of the former, much more erudite and historical than those of the latter, they supply most useful and judicious information respecting the institutions, the doctrines, the Liturgies, and the forms of worship of the primitive Church. At the same time, it is doubtful whether Mr. Blunt's plan could by possibility have been adequately executed within the "*iniqua spatia*" to which he was confined; and whether some of his topics could by any mode of treatment have been rendered very impressive from the pulpit. A single specimen may elucidate our meaning. Speaking of the old fathers, of the "*methodical regulations*" which they introduced into the Church, and of the manner in which they exercised their authority, Mr. Blunt says—

" Next they watched with all vigilance against *heresy* and *dissent;* the latter, indeed, in those days being scarcely separable from the other. Nothing can be more striking than the pains they took in this department of their duty. Thus Serapion, Bishop of Antioch, writes to Caricus and Pontius, (a document of the second century, preserved by Eusebius,) warning them against the heresy of Montanus, or the new philosophy, as it was called; and he transmits them not only his own opinion, but that of other bishops, in other parts, which he had been at the trouble to ascertain, to confirm his own. And from the same evidence it may be gathered, that one Sotas, a Bishop of Anchialum, in Thrace, had actually travelled into Phrygia, to observe with his own eyes those novel prophets, as they were named, the Montanists, Phrygia being then their strong hold; and that he came to the conclusion they were persons possessed. A leading object of Ignatius, in his Epistles which he addresses to the several Churches, is to caution them against the two great heresies which had then appeared in the world; the one, that of the *Docetæ*, which went to deny the humanity of Christ, an error which he combats in his Letters to the People of Smyrna and Tralles. The other, that of the *Ebionites*, which went to deny his divinity, an error which he contends against in his Epistles to Polycarp, the Ephesians, the Magnesians, and the Philadelphians. These were the tares that first sprung up, and here were the chief labourers ready at hand to root them out. In process of time heresies multiplied, but still were the spiritual governors of the Church alive to expose and extirpate them; and no stronger proof surely can be afforded of this than the great work of Irenæus, he a bishop, and his book apparently addressed to one of the inferior clergy; the express object of it being to make his friend acquainted with ' the monstrous and deep mysteries,' as he calls them, of the religious speculators of the day, in order that he might again communicate the same to others, and warn them against such ' abysses of folly and blasphemy against Christ.' And truly nothing less than the strongest sense of the duty which his high office laid him under, could have prevailed with him, one may well believe, to unravel the weary web of fanciful visions which these philosophers had weaved for themselves; and the scrutiny to which he submits them, and the diligence with which he replies to them, render that work of Irenæus a conspicuous monument of his patience, and, I must add, a severe trial of our own."—pp. 62—65.

It will be seen that Mr. Blunt's style is peculiar; but briskness and vividness are the first of his peculiarities. It would be unjust to say, that his investigation is superficial; but from the conditions necessary to his task, it could not but be cursory. He asserts, and, as far as time and room would allow him, he establishes, a complete coincidence between the Patristical creed and the doctrines of the Anglican Church. But the summary, which he gives in his concluding lecture, will explain the matter much better than our observations:—

" Thus have I brought before you, in as concise a shape as I could, the leading features of the Primitive Church of Christ, as we gather them from those who are usually termed the Fathers of the first two centuries; and I have made it appear, I trust, that it was not the loose society some would seem to think it, without cohesion of parts, or unity of purpose, but that it had its regular *succession of ministers,* (and those of the *three orders,*) whereby the qualification of the teacher to instruct was secured, duly appointed; its *discipline,* whereby heresy and schism were excluded, duly observed; its *forms of worship,* whereby the rash utterance of unadvised lips was guarded against, duly composed; and yet that it was no Church of mere ritual, but that its *doctrines,* whilst conceived in all soberness, were also those which plain people must understand to be the great doctrines of St. Paul: the *corruption* of our nature, though the degree of it is left undetermined; the need of the *Holy Spirit to restore it,* the Holy Spirit communicated as at other times, so mainly at the *Sacraments;* and the *Incarnation, Cross,* and *Passion* of God's blessed *Son,* whereby this and every other good gift from above was worked out and won for us.

" In all which particulars, the Church of England has no reason to shrink from a comparison with those days. For as I have made my argument tributary to the illustration of our Church as I have proceeded, so would I desire in the end, and upon a general review of my subject, to leave the impression on your minds, more especially in this season of reproach, that our Church is built upon the primitive model, allowance only being made, in common fairness, for such unessential differences as a change of time and circumstance may have dictated. For whatever may be alleged by enthusiasts against the structure and the forms of the Church of England, as restrictive and chilling, they will be found to be no straiter than is necessary to prevent confusion of doctrine and practice, and to secure peace in both; whilst the great evangelical truths of Scripture, no sectary, however ardent, can proclaim more unreservedly and insist on more perseveringly than does she. So that if at any time the preacher, forgetful for a moment of his commission, provide an essay and not a sermon for his flock, the spirit of his Church, as breaking forth in her Homilies, her Articles, her Liturgy, rises up and rebukes him; and thus eventually the pulpit, if for a season it chance to fall under other influence, recovers itself, and is restored to the faithful service of that Gospel, which our reformers made to assert itself in every line that they penned.

" God grant that we her ministers may be only true to her; act up to her spirit; work her theory out; recommend her to the people by presenting her unto them as it were in a sensible shape, (as the internal evidence of all her services proves it was meant to be,) that she may stand confessed before them in all the beauty of activity and life; and sure I am, that so doing, we shall be also true to Christ's Church upon earth; we shall do all things decently and in order; we shall pray with the understanding and heart; we shall rest in a sound and settled faith; not be beaten about by every wind of doctrine; and in our public and private ministrations, in the temple, and in every house, we shall cease not to teach and preach Jesus Christ."—p. 214—218.

On the whole, all they who wish to confirm their attachment to their Church, and their conviction of the purity of its faith, and the soundness of its discipline, will derive instruction, and edification, and delight from this brief volume of Mr. Blunt; and may be led by it to the serious perusal of other and more elaborate disquisitions. Much learning is strikingly presented to us in the compass of a rapid sketch, by the aid of neat arrangement, and dexterous condensation. And if his Sermons exhibit, in some respects, a remarkable contrast to those of the preachers who immediately succeeded him, this may help to show the wide range of topics which our English pulpits admit, and the elastic, comprehensive, catholic spirit of our English divinity. We regard it, indeed, as a most happy indication, that the same hearers could listen with pious gratification to the notices of Barnabas, Hermas, Clemens Romanus, Ignatius, Justin Martyr, Tatianus, Athenagoras, Theophilus, Irenæus, Clemens Alexandrinus; and also to the animating trumpet notes of Mr. Melvill, and the pastoral admonitions of Mr. Dale. And well is it urged by Mr. Blunt in the peroration of his first discourse—

" It is not because I believe that other and higher matters would not be more fitting from this place; or that he who stands before learned men, as I now do, is not called upon to urge them, by all the faculties he has, to save their souls alive, even as he would the poorest and most illiterate congregation, that I have chosen, perhaps hazardously, the topic I have opened to day; but it is because I regard the times such as peculiarly challenge the discussion, and this assembly such as is peculiarly calculated to entertain it; an assembly the like to which no minister can gather together elsewhere; the fountain, beyond every other, from which public opinion flows to every part of our island; and, therefore, offering him the best opportunity of his life to cast in, according to his humble ability, that branch which he thinks may help to sweeten the bitter waters. If I should be the means, by any thing I have said, or shall say, of leading the many future ministers of our Church, whom I see on all sides of me, to ' go round about her, and tell the towers thereof, and mark well her bulwarks,' that they may the better know what they have to defend, where should be their defence, and what weapons they should wield, I shall feel that I have not laboured in vain; confident as I am from some pastoral experience, that the flood of Gospel light, which the Church of England is diffusing over this land, to its most secluded nooks, is vastly greater than many even of her friends suppose; and that spots though she may have upon her disk to tarnish her brightness, they are as nothing compared with the darkness which would follow her eclipse. Let us pray that God will forefend that day, and that having appointed such ministers, it will please Him ' to illuminate all bishops, priests, and deacons; with true knowledge and understanding of his word; and that, both by their preaching and living, they may set it forth, and show it accordingly."— p. 41—43.

We entertain, therefore, high and comfortable hopes. The time, we trust, is at hand when the fervour of pastoral preaching will be associated with that valuable divinity which is embodied, for instance, with few and insignificant exceptions, in the Bampton lectures. Our opinion has ever been, that no system is altogether a mistake in what it says. We mean that men err far more often —save in the desperate cases, when they are mendacious by design —from their omissions, than from their allegations : from putting forth as the whole what is true only as a part. And our attachment is strong to the old orthodoxy of our Church, precisely because we believe that it is the most catholic of theological schemes, and the least exclusive :—preserving the harmony of faith by taking all its ingredients : asserting both the fore-knowledge of God, and the responsible agency of man, without pretending to sound all the depths of that fathomless mystery : fully and freely advocating man's justification by faith, yet advocating also, *for their own sake,* the value and necessity of good works : neither claiming heaven, on the ground of personal merit, nor so distorting truth into Antinomianism as almost to make Christianity itself an indefensible thing.

Our trust is, from the symptoms which are already visible, and from the methods of intellectual and moral discipline which are in progress, that this comprehensive moderation will gain ground. Willingly would we discern every where the traces of some distinctive excellence. *Here* we can admire the child-like docility of evangelical devotion, and the absolute dependence upon the Revelations of Scripture : *there* we can likewise admire the zeal of original inquiry, and the dispassionate exercise of the human understanding. Warm is our gratitude towards men, like Dr. Pusey and Mr. Newman, who have kept alive, and re-invigorated among us, the profound study of historical divinity, the veneration for primitive ordinances, and the habit of ancient reverence for Apostolical forms. On the other side, when confined within those legitimate boundaries assigned by reason herself, we can perceive great use in the bold broad spirit of frank and fearless scrutiny, which is characteristic of Dr. Whately and his friends. We are not afraid of it ;—why should we be ?—we are sure that its eventual effect will be to establish, on yet securer foundations, the principles of English orthodoxy. We are sure, too, that there is no repugnance or incompatibility between candour in investigation, and caution in decision.

Let it be borne in mind, that there is no compromise of truth in avoiding narrowness of conception. On the contrary, whatever is narrow and partial, must, we repeat, in itself, under one aspect, be erroneous, and will be the prolific parent of a whole tribe and family of errors. The materials of a complete theology are now at hand among us, if we can but have them rightly mixed. The one thing needful is their union. It is their union which will consummate the accomplishments of the preacher and the divine; not laying the entire stress upon scholarship, nor yet willing to sacrifice the sobrieties of learning even to the energy of pastoral ministrations. If men will but exercise a little mutual forbearance, and put a charitable construction upon each other's tenets and behaviour; if they can but be induced to think that the truth is to be found in the combination of their systems, and not in the exclusive and angry assertion of any one of them, all will be well. Oh, soon may we behold the glorious spectacle, not of an eclectic school, but of an united, unexclusive, comprehensive Church, blending the ardour of some, with the steadiness of others; mingling the resolute defence of the essential features of Protestantism with a wise and just regard to catholic antiquity; defending the truth, defending every part of the truth; retaining the sameness of a theology, sound, holy, reasonable, scriptural, amidst all the diversities of taste, talent, intellectual constitution and physical power; so that " wisdom may be justified in all her children;" so that " all things may work together for good to them that love God,"—so that fresh oil may be poured into all the lamps and vessels of our religion, until its whole temple shall beam with the effulgence of sanctity, and be filled with the glory of the Lord!

ART. VI.—1. *A Commentary on the Order for the Burial of the Dead, &c.* By the Rev. W. Greswell, M.A. Fellow of Balliol College, Oxford, and Curate of Disley, Cheshire. 2 vols. Oxford: Parker. London: Rivingtons. 1836.

2. *Sir Thomas Browne's Works, including his Life and Correspondence.* Edited by Simon Wilkin, F.L.S. 4 vols. London: Pickering. 1836. (*The Hydriotaphia, or Urn Burial, and the Brampton Urns,* in vol. 3, pp. 449—505.)

SPEAKING of the death and burial of the righteous, it is observed by the great and good Joseph Hall, sometime Bishop of Exeter

and Norwich, that " though the carcase be insensible of any position, yet honest sepulture is a blessing. It is fit the body should
be duly respected on earth, whose soul is glorious in heaven."
And again, in his Occasional Meditations—upon the sight of a
grave digged up—though he calls the earth a great devourer, he
calls it a great preserver too, adding,—

" How safely doth it keep our bodies for the resurrection; we are here
but laid up for custody; balms and cere-cloathes, and leads, cannot do so
much as this lap of our common mother; when all these are dissolved
into her dust, (as being unable to keep themselves from corruption,) she
receives and restores her charge. I can no more withhold my body from
the earth, than the earth can withhold it from my Maker. O God, this
is thy cabinet or shrine, wherein thou pleasest to lay up the precious
relics of thy dear saints, until the jubilee of glory; with what confidence
should I commit myself to this sure reposition, whiles I know thy word
just, thy power infinite ?"

The good, and therefore great bishop, from whose works the
above words are taken, was one whose spirit was quite in unity
with that of the excellent compilers of our Apostolic, and we do
not fear to say unrivalled, Liturgy. And it is very meet and right
that those bodies, which, when alive, were the tabernacles of an
immortal spirit,—and, if the bodies of Christians indeed, were not
only such, but were sanctified also by the presence and inhabitation
of God's holy spirit,—it is very meet and right, we say, that such
tabernacles, when taken down, should be carefully committed to
the dust out of which they were formed, " in sure and certain
hope of the resurrection to eternal life." And such has ever been
the conviction of Christians. From the first establishment of
Christianity till the present time, earth has been decently and in
order committed to earth, ashes to ashes, dust to dust. Nor has
this been the case only under the Christian dispensation; but
from the earliest times, in all countries, and among almost all
people, the shell of the body has never willingly been cast forth
with the burial of an ass. Let the exception prove the rule:—
and for what else we would say, let the lines following from
Wordsworth speak *that*—a poet who has drunk deep of the spirit
of his Bible, and has sent forth its truth to the world, as occasion
called, in a pure stream of " English undefiled."

> " ' And whence that tribute? wherefore these regards?
> Not from the naked *heart* alone of man,
> (Though claiming high distinction upon earth
> As the sole spring and fountain-head of tears,
> His own peculiar utterance for distress
> Or gladness.) No,' the philosophic priest
> Continued, ' 'tis not in the vital seat
> Of feeling to produce them, without aid

From the pure soul—the soul sublime and pure;
With her two faculties of eye and ear,
The one by which a creature, whom his sins
Have rendered prone, can upward look to heaven;
The other that empowers him to perceive
The voice of Deity, on height and plain
Whispering those truths in stillness which the WORD,
To the four quarters of the winds, proclaims.
Not without such assistance could the use
Of these benign observances prevail.
Thus are they born, thus fostered, and maintained;
And by the care prospective of our wise
Forefathers, who, to guard against the shocks,
The fluctuation and decay of things,
Embodied and established these high truths
In solemn institutions.' "*

Well, indeed, may we thank our wise forefathers for their prospective care! Well may we thank the ancient worthies of our
Church, who have taken thought (under God's blessing, from
whom all holy thoughts do come) to provide us with that solemn,
and affecting, and comforting service—THE ORDER FOR THE
BURIAL OF THE DEAD; a service in which our mother Church
—holy in all her Offices, and apostolic in all her Prayers—would
seem even to have outdone herself—for we may surely say, if the
whole Liturgy is *beautiful*, this part of it is " *beautiful exceedingly.*" And if

—— " apt words have power to swage
The tumours of a troubled mind,
And are as balm to fester'd wounds,"†

apter words than those which compose this Office were never put
together. Indeed, we ourselves quite subscribe to the full and
unreserved eulogy of Southey, who says, in his Life of Wesley,
that the Burial Service is " the finest and most affecting ritual
that ever was composed—a service that finds its way to the heart
when the heart stands most in need of such consolation, and is
open to receive it."‡

* See The Excursion, book v. " The Pastor." It were hardly necessary to refer
our readers to the two next books, containing, " The Churchyard among the Mountains."
† Milton, Samson Agonistes, v. 184.
‡ See Life of Wesley, vol. ii. p. 249. The incident which, follows we give in a
note. It is much too valuable to be omitted in these times.
" It was immediately after the happy restoration of King *Charles* the Second, when
together with the rights of the crown, and the English liberties, the Church and the
Liturgy were also newly restored, that a noted ringleader of schism in the former
times was to be buried in one of the principal churches of *London*. The minister of
the parish, being a wise and regular Conformist, and he was afterwards an eminent
bishop in our Church, well knew how averse the friends and relations of the deceased
had always been to the *Common Prayer*, which, by hearing it so often called a *low ru-*

With these impressions in our minds—and, as we trust, in our hearts also, for we are continually called in our ministry to the brink of the grave—we need hardly say that we were glad when we saw advertised, *A Commentary on the Order for the Burial of the Dead, considered as a Manual of Doctrine and Consolation to Christians.* We sent for it—we read it—we were pleased with it—and now we are about to review it. Nor can we doubt for a moment but what Mr. Greswell says in his Address to the Reader is the fact.

" The author has laboured, too, in the due prosecution of his subject, to communicate, if possible, additional point and force to the pathetic allusions of the service; and to place, in a still clearer and more impassive aspect, the truth and propriety of those many confessions of the sinfulness, the misery, the brevity, the transitoriness of human existence, which could scarcely fail to occur in a service like this. To do justice to this part of his subject, he has felt it incumbent upon him to dip his own pen in tears; and to impart to the tone of his commentary, and to the flow and tenor of his reflections, a spirit and character of sadness corresponding to that of the original."—pp. vi. vii.

Altogether the work is a very good one. It is, as it describes itself in the title-page, a Manual both of Doctrine and Consolation. And if there are certain passages (some might call them rhapsodies) in which the language may appear somewhat too harrowing and passionate—let that be set down as in accordance with the above extract—let Mr. Greswell be considered as a " painful minister" of God's Word, feeling deeply every syllable which he reads over a brother's or a sister's grave. Let him be looked upon as one himself endeavouring to die daily, like St. Paul

diment, *a beggarly element,* and *carnal ordinance,* they were brought to contemn to that degree, that they shunned all occasions of being acquainted with it.

" Wherefore, in order to the interment of their friend, in some sort, to their satisfaction, yet so as not to betray his own trust, he used this honest method to undeceive them. Before the day appointed for the funeral, he was at the pains to learn the whole Office of Burial by heart. And then, the time being come, there being a great concourse of men of the same fanatical principles, when the company heard all delivered by him without book, with a free readiness, and profound gravity, and unaffected composure of voice, looks and gestures, and a very powerful emphasis in every part; as indeed his talent was excellent that way; they were strangely surprised and affected. Professing, they had never heard a more suitable exhortation, or a more edifying exercise, even from the very best and most precious men of their own persuasion.

" But they were afterwards much more surprised and confounded, when the same person who had officiated, assured the principal men among them that not one period of all he had spoken was his own; and convinced them, by occular demonstration, how all was taken, word for word, out of the very Office ordained for that purpose, in the poor contemptible Book of *Common Prayer.*

" Whence he most reasonably inferred how much their ill-grounded prejudice, and mistaken zeal, had deluded them, that they should admire the same discourse, when they thought it an unprepared, unpremeditated rapture, which they would have abominated, had they known it to be only a set form prescribed by authority."—*Extract from a Sermon by Bishop Spratt, printed at his Visitation in* 1695.

—as one endeavouring to impress upon the living that this Holy Office is intended as well for their comfort, as for their instruction in righteousness—and in that case, none need wonder that he should describe sin as exceeding sinful, and the end of the righteous as exceeding blessed. At such a time, who need wonder that his heart was big* within him, and that words, powerful as they are in the hand of a ready writer, should, in comparison with the matter in hand, nevertheless appear powerless and paralytic? Be this, however, as it may;—if his thoughts burn, and his words are all a-fire—there is no harm in them—they are all sound doctrine. A child would say (a Christian child, we mean, who knew how to keep himself from idols)—The writer has been to the grave to weep there—he is a man, at least, of godly sincerity!

Thus much as concerns the only possible point to be objected to in these volumes; and when said by us, who hold the wildfire of pretended illuminations in abhorrence, it certainly should not withdraw from the value of the work. But it is not our purpose to dismiss it hastily—but to consider it according to the division of the author. We will therefore proceed to its several chapters, remarking, by the way, that Mr. Greswell is not only a *godly* but a *learned* minister of God's word, as may be seen from the whole of this Treatise, and more particularly from the notes and illustrations appended to the second volume.—(p. 251—353.)

The first chapter is on the propriety of funeral usages generally, and on the motives which make it incumbent on Christians to honour the remains of the dead;—and on this we have scarce any thing to remark, as it has been anticipated in what has been said above. As concerns the Jews, we know from our Bibles that they were particular in the observation of decent funeral rites, insomuch that the lack of them " is recognized by the inspired word of God itself as an aggravation of evil and misfortune, which a contrary treatment would so far have assuaged and prevented." For example, as concerned Jehoiakim, king of Judah, it is said of God, by his prophet Jeremiah, " They shall not lament for him, saying, Ah, my brother! or, Ah, sister! they shall not lament for him, saying, Ah, Lord! or, Ah, his glory! He shall be buried with the burial of an ass, drawn and cast forth beyond the gates of Jerusalem."† Whereas, concerning Abijah, the son of Jero-

---

* Lest our readers should mistake us, we will illustrate what is here said by a remark of the late excellent Bishop Jebb's.—" I don't know whether you have experienced the same kind of sensation ; but, whenever I hear any trait of that kind which you have read to me, I feel my heart swell, as if I could not keep it down ; I can describe it only as a swelling of the heart which affects my breathing."—*Life by Forster*, vol. i. p. 353. Kindred spirit to that of the apostolic Bishop Wilson,—thou art gone to thy rest! *Though dead, he yet speaketh!*

† Jer. xxii. 18, 19.; Cf. ch. xxxvi.

boam, it is said that he was " to come to the grave." And why?
" Because in him there was found some good thing toward the
Lord God of Israel in the house of Jeroboam."* But, on this
point, what need is there to say more?—for the Lord Jehovah, as
it is written in the Book of Deuteronomy, took the matter into
his own hands. " So Moses, the servant of the Lord, died there
in the land of Moab, according to the word of the Lord. And
he buried him in a valley in the land of Moab, over against Beth-
peor: but no man knoweth of his sepulchre unto this day."† As
for Christians,—from the time that the Lord made his sepulchre
with the rich, and Joseph of Arimathea was an instrument in the
hands of Him " by whom all things were made,"—from that time
to this, in the midst as well of perils and persecutions as of peace
and quietness—*sunt illis sua funera*—they have regularly and
devoutly committed to the earth the ruins of these earthly tabernacles, and in so doing they have done that which it was their
duty to do—neither will he do much amiss who shall say of each
one so doing in the words of Naomi, concerning Boaz, " Blessed
be he of the Lord, who hath not left off his kindness to the living
and to the dead."‡ For, to quote the words of Mr. Greswell,

" it is one of the doctrines of the Gospel, that the bodies of Christians,
provided they are Christians indeed, and not in name only, besides being
tabernacles of an immortal spirit, are likewise sanctified by the presence
and inhabitation of God's Holy Spirit. And, as they have thus been
honoured during life, it is only fit and becoming that such marks of
reverence and respect, as suit the worth and dignity of their former occu-
pant, should be paid them after death. Let the reader believe me, when
we consign to the clay-cold ground the remains of a truly good Christian,
it is not ordinary dust that we deposit there: on the contrary, it is the
material fabric of that temple, within which the Holy Spirit of God
dwelt through life. Christian graves of the character were produced in
the soul, which lodged there, far more precious in the sight of God than
jewels of gold and jewels of silver; graces which may well be conceived
to have communicated a corresponding value and sanctity to the body,
within which, as its spiritual attributes, they resided. Such, then, being
the doctrine which Christianity teaches, respecting the sanctification of
these our living bodies, to deny them funeral honours after death, not to
treat them with even more tenderness and regard, for the sake of what
they have been, would be to desecrate and profane the temples of the
living God."§—pp. 8, 9.

The second chapter relates to the " disposal of the body by
interment, and to the funeral ceremonies of the Greeks and Romans." It is here shown that interment is most in unison with

* 1 Kings, xiv. 13.   † Deut. xxxiv. 5, 6.   ‡ Ruth, ch. ii. 30.
§ See the like sentiments in the excellent and striking sermon of Bishop Hall on
Gen. xxiii. 19, 20; Works, vol. iii. p. 97, ed. fol. 1662. Also Sir Thomas Browne's
Hydriotaphia, c. iv.; vol. iii. p. 481, of Wilkin's edition, presently to be noticed.

the Scripture account of the creation of man, and with the sentence pronounced after the Fall,—" In the sweat of thy face shalt thou eat bread, till thou return unto the ground; for out of it wast thou taken: for dust thou art, and unto dust shalt thou return." This accordingly was the way adopted by the Jews, and from them by the Christians. And Mr. Greswell has not thought it beneath his subject to observe, that animals have a care for the decent disposal of their dead;—and that when *in articulo mortis* " wild animals will frequently seek out for themselves some cavity of the earth, which may serve both as a retreat, wherein to expire in peace, and as a resting-place for their bones after death; as if instinct taught even them, that thus to disappear betimes from the earth's surface, and to provide beforehand for the removal of their lifeless remains from view and observation, by secreting and burying themselves, whilst still alive, in hollows and recesses, was the precaution which nature had dictated, for the disposal of themselves before death, with a view to their security after it." We have mentioned this from some curious facts which have come under our own observation, but which we are sorry we have not space to insert. Though, however, this was the earliest, and the most natural mode of sepulture, our knowledge of antiquity will teach us that in very early times it was departed from, and that " the method in use among the Greeks from the earliest times, and subsequently adopted by the Romans,—the method which prevailed in almost every community of the ancient world at the period of the birth of our Saviour, except the Jewish,— was the method of burning, or disposing of the dead body by fire." This leads our author to make a few remarks on the ceremonies used on those occasions, on their monuments, and on the honour and respect shown to what was once " instinct with life," and on their sepulchral urns. For further matter on these points, we beg to refer our readers to the Hydriotaphia,* or Urn Burial of Sir Thomas Browne;—one of the many and curious (not to say elegant) works of that erudite and Christian philosopher. Every lover of the literature of his country must be heartily obliged to Mr. Wilkin for the complete edition of his works just published. But of Sir T. Browne and of this edition in particular we purpose to speak a few words in conclusion. To return for the present to Mr. Greswell.

---

* We refer the scholar to the Laws of the XII. Tables. See Tab. X. *De jure sacro ;* and for a fund of information to the Ed. *Joh. Nicolao Funccio, Marburgensi,* 1744. Sophocles has nothing more beautiful than the impassioned address of Electra, on receiving the urn which contained the ashes (as she supposed) of her dead brother Orestes ; E. v. 1126.

ὦ φιλτάτου μνημεῖον ἀνθρώπων ἐμοὶ,
ψυχῆς 'Ορέστου λοιπὸν, κ. τ. ἑ.

The third chapter is altogether most interesting, and is full of information,—perhaps fuller than any other chapter in the two volumes. It is " On the appropriation of peculiar localities for the reception of the dead; and on the burial places of the Jews, the Romans, the Greeks, and the Christians respectively." Our space will not allow us to follow Mr. Greswell throughout, nor are we called upon in a mere review to dwell upon the customs of the Greeks and Romans, though such a consideration falls in very well with the scope of the work before us. What, therefore, we shall say on this head will be, as it were, incidentally, referring our readers to the work itself for fuller information.

And here there is to be observed a broad distinction between the burial-places of Christians when contrasted with those, whether of the Jews, the Greeks, or the Romans, and this is, " that whereas the former have made their cemeteries contiguous to the places of their public worship, the latter never did so."

" The reason of this distinction," says Mr. Greswell, " among other things, would appear to be principally this; viz. the supposed defilement and uncleanness communicated by the contact or vicinity of dead bodies; the idea of which, whether derived to the Gentiles from the Jews, or the result of an instinctive horror and superstition, which seems natural to the human mind in thinking upon or contemplating death, prevailed among the Gentiles as much as the Jews. By Jew and Gentile alike, a person polluted, through the contact or proximity of a dead body, while the period of such contamination lasted, was conceived to be disqualified for the acceptable worship of that being, or those beings, whom after a stated manner, and with the performance of stated rites, they severally professed to honour."—p. 39.

As concerns the Jews, the first account (and it is the first account in history, either sacred or profane) of the appropriation of a particular spot of ground for the express purpose of the burial of the dead, is that cave of Machpelah, the purchase of which Abraham is said to have made, in Gen. c. xxiii. *The field, and the cave that is therein, were made sure unto Abraham for a possession of a burying place by the sons of Heth.* " The *only* purchase," says Hall, " that we ever find Abraham made; he would be a stranger here below, and neglecting all other assurances, takes only order for graves; those he thinks are the houses he must trust to,"—inasmuch as the grave and gate of death must be passed in the way to heaven. Now the cave at Machpelah we know was an isolated and retired spot. And so again, in later times, we read of the valley of Jehosaphat, on the east of Jerusalem, as the general burying-place in the neighbourhood of that great city,—a valley, in the words of Ezekiel, *which was full of*

bones,—and, behold, there were very many in the open valley; and,
lo, they were very dry.* Through this valley ran the brook Kidron, and it would appear from Jeremiah that *all the fields unto
the brook of Kidron* was but another name for the valley of Jehosaphat, and within it was included the valley of Hinnom, and
Tophet ordained of old. But, not only from these passages, but
from numerous others, relating as well to Jerusalem as other
cities, we find that the place of burial for the Jews, (with the
single exception of their kings,) lay *without the gate,* and not in
the vicinity of the temple, or synagogues. And, that it continued
to be so in later times, we know from the burial of our blessed
Lord;—from the potter's *field* that was bought to bury strangers
in, with the price of blood;—from the account of the corpse of
the widow's son which our Saviour met at the gate of Nain (τῇ
πύλῃ τῆς πόλεως, Luke, vii. 12);—from the raising of Lazarus;—
from the bodies of the saints which slept going *into* the holy city,
and appearing unto many;—and from numerous other instances
which we need not recount.

Concerning the Greeks and the Romans we shall only say that
they also scrupulously avoided burying within the walls. The
sides of their ways, especially on the entrance to their cities, were
lined with the tombs and the busts of their dead; but the cities
themselves were, as they thought, to be kept pure from such a
pollution. As to the Greeks we know from Pausanias that the
wayside from the Piræus to Athens was occupied by many tombs
of the illustrious dead;—and it is natural to conclude that the
burying-places of others were there also, or on the sides of other
ways. The Ceramicus† also,—the burial place for those who
fell in battle,—was itself too exterior to the city. It is needless
to say a word of the Romans, as the "Siste Viator," (so in the
Greek ὁδίτης,) must be familiar to all. We conclude, therefore,
our allusions to them with the following law from the tenth Table.
HEMONEM. MORTVOM. EVDO. VRBED. NEI. SEPELITOD. NEIVE.
VRITOD.‡

Having seen, then, to use the words of Hall, " that it was the
ancientest and best way that sepultures should be without the
gates of the city," both among the Jews, the Greeks, and the

---

* See Ezek. xxxvii. 1, 2; Jer. xxxi. 40.

† The reader of Aristophanes will not fail to call to mind Pisthetærus' hope to be
buried in the Ceramicus—*Westminster Abbey,* as we might say. Nor will the reader of
Thucydides forget the oration of Pericles over those who died in the first summer of
the war.—Lib. ii. c. 35—46. The words of Aristophanes are,

'Ο Κεραμεικὸς δέξεται νώ.

δημόσια γὰρ ἵνα ταφῶμεν, κ. τ. λ. v. 595.

‡ I. e. Cadaverum in urbe sepultura, vel ustio nulla esto. Cf. Funcc. ut supra,
p. 411; Lex iii.

Romans,—moreover that it was made a matter of legal enactment; we shall naturally be led to conclude, that in the earlier
times of Christianity, the Christians' burial-places were without
the city also.   And exactly so we find it to be,—as may be collected from many passages in the early Fathers, and as the reader
will see in Mr. Greswell's work, and more fully in Bingham's
Antiquities of the Christian Church,* a book which no Clergyman, who can afford it, should be without.   It will appear then
to any one who shall make the inquiry, that the Christians were
extremely careful of the burial of their departed brethren, and
that their tombs were to be found on the road sides of their
several cities, and the catacombs, or the subterranean dormitories
mentioned by St. Jerome in the neighbourhood of Rome, are
still visited by the modern traveller.   Such were the early graves
of the disciples of Jesus Christ;—or, if not on the wayside, some
sequestered spot was chosen as a repository for dust and ashes,
and the dead were not forgotten, especially if they had been martyrs and confessors, who rejoiced to lay down their lives for the
Gospel's sake.   So far indeed were they from being forgotten,
that the very place became sacred, and of the funeral harangues,
—the first funeral sermons,—which are delivered down to us in
the works of the early Fathers, " many of them were pronounced
at the sepulchres of their sons who had laid down their lives in
defence of the common faith."   Nor did they *only* pronounce
their funeral harangues here, but in process of time, as the Gospel
went forth conquering and to conquer, on these very spots they
built their churches, and, as Bingham observes, " the first step
towards burying in churches, was the building of churches over
the graves of the martyrs in the country, or else translating their
relics into the city churches."   To quote the words of Mr. Greswell,—

" It is, then, in the still extant orations of this description, that the
allusions are most frequent to those receptacles, in which the early
Christians deposited the deceased professors of their faith.   Chrysostom
speaks of them as θῆκαι μαρτύρων; *memoriæ martyrum* is the name which
Augustine gives them.   They are elsewhere called the κοιμητήρια, or
sepulchra martyrum. Basilicæ martyrum is the name not unfrequently
given to them, when, as was afterwards the case, chapels or oratories
were erected upon the same spots, over their remains.   In Tertullian the
name of *arcæ* is often given to these resting-places of the Christian dead;
as *cryptæ* is the term which, for a similar purpose, occurred in the writings of Jerome.

* Book xxiii. is devoted to the subject "Of Funeral Rites, or the Custom and
Manner of Burying the Dead, observed in the Ancient Church."   The reader is also
referred to the poems of the Christian poet Prudentius,—especially the Περιστεφάνων,
of which Mr. Greswell has made good use.

" But by whatever name characterized in the remains of ecclesiastical antiquity, it was on the spots and in the places thus designated, and in repeated instances consecrated by the remains of the martyrs, that the early Christians buried their dead ; not only such as had finished their course by martyrdom, but such as had died a natural death.   Here they were deposited with that affectionate care and concern with which it was ever usual among Christians to inter the remains of their fellow believers : whether possessing an additional claim upon their sympathies, as those who had suffered for the faith's sake, or not."—p. 86.

Thus we see that at the first the early Christians followed the example both of the Jews, and of the Greeks, and Romans, and were buried without the gate ;—and also, *how* in process of time, and *for what cause*, they came to change this order, and to be buried not only in the neighbourhood of their places of worship any where, but even *within* the city where they dwelt.   It will not suit the space allotted to us in these pages, to follow up at length the various particulars as to the general establishment of churchyards, and, particularly, as to the establishment of them in this country.   Suffice it to say that the first person buried, not *in* the church, but in the *Atrium* or *Church-Porch*,* was Constantine, concerning which privilege, his son Constantius is reported by St. Chrysostom to have said, that he thought he did him great honour to bury him in the Fisherman's Porch.   It was not till the sixth century that the *people* began to be admitted, under certain cases, to be buried (according to the words of the Council of Braga, A. D. 563,) *deforis circa murum basilicæ*, i. e. without the walls of the church,—not *in* the church, nor, as we understand it, even *in* the *atrium*, but in the *churchyard*.   And this the learned Bingham looks upon as the " first authentic evidence of a churchyard, or ground in the neighbourhood of a church, intended or permitted for any such purpose as that of sepulture." But it does not appear that the *general* introduction of churchyards throughout Christendom, that is, of enclosed spaces, adjoining to the churches, and consecrated by the prayers of the Bishop, as the appointed receptacle of the dead, according to the opinions of the learned in ecclesiastical antiquities, bears date earlier than from the end of the ninth, or the beginning of the tenth century.   It would appear that consecrated churchyards became general in England " from the time of Cuthbert,† arch-

---

* Of the Church at Constantinople, which Constantine had himself erected, and dedicated to the twelve Apostles.

† Sir Thomas Browne's words are, " The sensible rhetorick of the dead, to exemplarity of good life, first admitted the bones of pious men and martyrs within church walls, which in succeeding ages crept into promiscuous practice : while Constantine was peculiarly favoured to be admitted into the church-porch ; and the first thus buried in England was in the days of Cuthred." Hydriotaphia, c. iii.   There are several

bishop of Canterbury, about the middle of the eighth century. Godwin," adds Mr. Greswell, " who has written the life of that prelate, informs us, that he came into Britain, both with a commission to regulate the affairs of the Anglican Church, in other respects, and with a general bull or license to consecrate yards for the interment of the dead, in the immediate neighbourhood of churches, whether these were situated in the towns or in the country."—p. 92. With regard to the burial of Emperors and other eminent persons *within* the Church, there is some difficulty to ascertain the date when it began. Justinian in his new code, dropping, says Bingham, the former part of Theodosius's Law, which obliged all people to bury without the city, still retains the latter clause, which forbids men to be buried in the seats of the Martyrs and Apostles. The same prohibition we find also in the Council of Nantes, A. D. 658. But between that date and A. D. 813, when the Council of Mentz was held, certain limitations and exceptions were made in favour of great and eminent persons. The words of the Council are, *Nullus mortuus intra ecclesiam sepeliatur, nisi Episcopi, aut Abbates, aut digni Presbyteri, aut fideles Laici.** However, it is clear from ecclesiastical history that, before this, Bishops and Emperors were buried within the Church, as may be seen in Bingham, book xxiii. c. i. § 8, who adds that after this time the matter was left to the discretion of the Bishops and Presbyters, as to who should, or who should not, be buried in Churches,—and that as to hereditary sepulchres they were not allowed in the ninth century, but were brought in by the Pope's Decretals.† Bingham dates this from about A. D. 1230.

We have thought that the above succinct account might be acceptable to many of our readers;—the substance of it will be found in Mr. Greswell's pages; but, in our capacity of critics, we have taken care to examine what he has said by means of the books which are around us,—" our silent friends." We would now, before we proceed to enumerate the chapters following of the work before us, make a remark or two as to the present mode of sepulture amongst us.

In the first place, then, with such an office as our Burial Service before us, dust cannot be committed to dust but decently

passages which lead us to think that Mr. Greswell could not be ignorant of this remarkable treatise, and yet we do not recollect that he has ever referred to it.

* See Bingham, in loc., who states also that at the Council of Winchester under Lanfranc, Archbishop of Canterbury, A. D. 1076, the clause following was agreed to : " *In Ecclesiis corpora defunctorum non sepeliantur.*"

† We have not space to dwell upon either the avarice of ecclesiastics in general, or in particular on that of the Roman Catholic Church,—though from the mention of the Decretals, full scope is offered for such consideration.

and in order. We should, however, greatly rejoice to find that better accommodations (if we may with sobriety use the expression) were found for the silent tomb. In our great cities we fear,—we know,—it is far otherwise; and although somewhat has of late been done for the enlarging of our churchyards, still, in London especially, the burial grounds are incapacitated to receive those departed this life. And it is for this reason that we could heartily wish to find sacred ground *" without the gate"* bought by parishes and set apart for this very thing, as in the days of the early Christians, and in the old time before them. Those who have *seen* only the churchyards, or more properly, the burial-grounds, in foreign countries, have been delighted with their seclusion, *(" without the gate,")* and with the care which is taken to preserve them from desecration. *We* who have *officiated* at many funerals in a foreign land, and have followed our brethren and our sisters *there* to the *house appointed for all living*, have thought upon such quiet resting-places with an inward joy which we should have been sorry not to have felt. Our own solemn service at such a time seemed doubly impressive,—whether in summer, when all was green and beautiful, and decked with flowers around us,—or in the dreary winter of the north, when the sleet and the snow was twisted by the wind about our bare heads. Nay, more, when we have attended the funerals of others, not our own countrymen, and have sadly missed the comforting words of " The Order for the Burial of the Dead," and have heard in the place of it a mere harangue, we still could not but be alive to the beauty even of a funeral scene, and to the care taken that the receptacles for the dead should show that the dead lived in the hearts of the survivors.[*] Again we repeat that we shall be glad to find a space devoted *by the proper authorities* without *all* our towns as a burial-place for our dead. Sooner or later it must come to pass generally; we rejoice that in some places such a *decent innovation,* or, rather, *such a returning to the old paths,* is already in being.

    . Another point on which we would hazard a remark is on the burial within our churches—a custom we, in general, could willingly see dispensed with, as it renders them unwholesome, and greatly adds to the *crowd* (if we may so say) of a crowded congregation. In former days we see that it was not permitted. Would that it were not so now!—and that all men thought with the good St. Swithin, " who gave charge when he died, that his body should not be laid within the church, but where the drops of rain might wet his grave, and where passengers might walk over it." " But," says

---

[*] In Denmark a trifling sum is paid annually to the curator of the burial-ground (*Kirke-gaard,*) to see that the graves of those *" gone before"* be not forgotten. *" Han er ikke död, Men gaaet forud !"*

Hall, " to speak freely what I think concerning this so common practice, I must needs say I cannot but hold it very unfit and in-convenient, both, first, in respect of the majesty of the place; it is (χυριαχή), the Lord's house; it is (βασιλιχή), the palace of the King of Heaven; and what prince would have his court made a charnel-house?"   And with these sentiments the good and apos-tolic bishop died; and honest Fuller, in his " Worthies of Eng-land," has justly inserted the passage following from his will, at the end of his remarks. " *In the name of God, Amen. I, Joseph Hall, D. D., not worthy to be called the Bishop of Norwich, &c. First, I bequeath my soul, &c.; my body I leave to be interred, without any funeral pomp, at the discretion of my executors, with this only monition, that I do not hold God's house a meet repo-sitory for the dead bodies of the greatest saints.*"*

But to proceed. Chapter the fourth is on " the Passing-Bell," and it is a beautiful chapter, on which we could gladly say much, —*sed non erat his locus,*—and perhaps *the party* might call us Papists, as they have all but done the excellent Mr. Newman, for his Primitive Sermons.   However, we will venture to say thus much,—that, without doubt, we have let go too many of the harmless customs of the olden time, and by stripping off the ancient trappings and ceremonies of devotion,† we have left a cold-hearted set of innovators to rejoice at the cessation of those solemn, though oftentimes superstitious rites, which add many a convert to the Church of Rome.   But there is no need that the Passing-Bell should contravene the eighty-eighth Canon, and be " rung superstitiously,"—no prayers for the dead are wanting,— the rather it is intended to awaken devotion, and to call for the prayers of the living, that so, God who heareth prayer, would not suffer the soul of a dying sister or brother, for any pains of death, to fall from Him.   Yes, reader! instead of running from sermon to sermon so busily as to find no time to be charitable or to do righteousness, Christians of old were fully persuaded of the effi-cacy of prayer; and whenever, or wherever, the Passing-Bell was heard " swinging slow, with solemn roar,"—" it was not unreason-ably, or uncharitably, presumed that such prayers of the living, at that time, might be of service to the dying; or that, in this parti-

* See " Leicestershire," p. 130, ed. folio, 1662, and the Sermon of Bishop Hall's, above quoted, p. 101, where he adds to the above allusions, " Have ye not houses to eat and drink in? saith the Apostle: much more may I say, have ye not church-yards, or other burial places, for the interment of your dead?"

† We would have this understood generally. The mitre and the full dress of the High Priest were not for nothing; and besides this, " Holiness to the Lord" was upon it. It is mere vanity to say that a solemn dress does not give birth to some solemn feelings with the multitude in general ; and as for those who scoff at it, as they do at other things serious, and would down with it and with the wearer to the ground, we say with old Fuller, " *He is no friend to the tree who strips it of its bark !*"

cular district, some one might be found, deserving of the name of Christian, who would not grudge a fellow-Christian, a brother, or a sister in Jesus Christ, while contending with the infirmities of his last sickness, and even then *in articulo mortis*, the benefit of his prayers and intercessions at the throne of Grace."—p. 106. We will conclude these remarks with one of the Occasional Meditations of the good Bishop Hall, so often before quoted in these pages. How well did he consider this solemn sound!

Upon the Tolling of a Passing-Bell.

" How doleful and heavy is this summons of death! This sound is not for our ears, but for our hearts; it calls us not only to our prayers, but to our preparation,—to our prayers for the departing soul,— to our preparation for our own departing. We have never so much need of prayers as in our last combat; then is our great adversary most eager; then are we weakest; then nature is so over-laboured, that it gives us not leisure to make use of gracious motions. There is no preparation so necessary as for this conflict: all our life is little enough to make ready for our last hour. What am I better than my neighbours? How oft hath this bell reported to me the farewell of many more strong and vigorous bodies than my own,—of many more cheerful and lively spirits? And now what doth it but call me to the thought of my parting? Here is no abiding for me: I must away too. Oh thou that art the God of comfort, help thy poor servant that is now struggling with his last enemy. His sad friends stand gazing upon him, and weeping over him, but they cannot succour him; needs must they leave him to do this great work alone; none but Thou, to whom belong the issues of death, canst relieve his distressed and overmatched soul. And for me, let no man die without me, as I die daily, so teach me to die once; acquaint me beforehand with Thy messenger, which I must trust to. Oh! teach me so to number my days, that I may apply my heart to true wisdom."*

The next chapter, which is the last of the introductory ones, is on " the Excesses committed at Funerals, especially those of the Poorer Classes." It is altogether good, and it were devoutly to be wished that these excesses could be put an end to. We would observe by the way, that the *Church-ales* mentioned in the eighty-eighth Canon have no allusion at all to the excesses committed at funerals. These are what the Danish call *Grav-öls*. The *Church-ales* in the Canon, though often riotous and disorderly, were commemoratory of the dedication of the Church. Hence Warton, in his History of English Poetry, is led to observe, perhaps not quite correctly, that *ale*, especially in composition, sometimes

---

* Works, vol. ii. p. 151. See likewise the beautiful remarks of Sir Thomas Browne, in his *Religio Medici*, part ii. § 6, ed. Wilkin, vol. ii. p. 100. In our older poets there are many allusions to the Passing-Bell. Donne says,

——————————————— " Pray'rs ascend
To heaven in troops at a good man's *passing-bell.*"

means a *festival*. By the by, before quitting, this chapter we would ask, are not the words " irreverent and irreligious," in page 134, out of place as applied to brutes? The passage, however, is equivocal.

These introductory chapters ended, Mr. Greswell next proceeds to the *Rubrics* premised to the Order for the Burial of the Dead, observing by the way, that in using this office we are " employing a ceremonial of Christian burial, in its general plan and outline, still the same which the Church has been accustomed to use from the earliest ages." As his authority he refers to Palmer's *Origines Liturgicæ*, c. ix.—a work which we here mention to show the good fruit of the late Bishop Jebb's careful examination of all candidates for holy orders in the diocese of Limerick. The passage following is from his Life by Mr. Forster.*

" Nor did the spirit of inquiry, thus inspired or called forth by the regulations of Bishop Jebb, terminate in the purchase,—it led also to the production of important works. The *Origines Liturgicæ*, a work long a desideratum in English divinity, and for which the Church in these countries is indebted to the learned labours of the Rev. William Palmer, now of Worcester College, Oxon., owes its idea and design to the well-directed workings of the author's mind, when a candidate for orders, preparing for examination at Limerick."

We have not space to make extracts from this chapter,—nor yet to allude to the sensible and feeling remarks on the Absence of Females from Funerals of the Upper Classes, or to the Abridgment of the Burial Service in cases of infection, &c. And we have not space, because we feel it absolutely necessary to give the following long but excellent extract from " Tracts for the Times," a publication which, we think, must do infinite good. The tract is called " The Burial Service," and is quite in unison with Mr. Greswell's views, both upon the first Rubric, and upon that after-passage which is so often objected to.†

" But it will be said, that at least we ought not to read the service over the flagrantly wicked, over those who are a scandal to religion. But this is a very different position. I agree with it entirely. Of course we should not do so, and the Church never meant we should. She never wished we should profess our hope of the salvation of habitual drunkards and swearers, open sinners, blasphemers, and the like; not as daring to despair of their salvation, but thinking it unseemly to honour their memory. Though the Church is not endowed with a power of absolute judgment upon individuals, yet she is directed to decide accord-

* See vol. i. p. 243.

† This extract is from the first volume. Two are already published. But the Tracts may be had separately, either in Oxford or at Messrs. Rivingtons.' The extract has been made because it was exactly to the purpose, and also that we might direct our clerical brethren where to find such suitable Tracts as the exigencies of their parishes may require.

ing to external indications, in order to hold up the *rules* of God's governance, and afford a type of it, and an assistance towards the realizing it.   As she denies to the scandalously wicked the Lord's Supper, so does she deprive them of her other privileges.

" The Church, I say, does not bid us read the service over open sinners.   Hear her own words introducing the service. ' The office ensuing is not to be used for any that die unbaptised, or excommunicated, or have laid violent hands upon themselves.'   There is no room to doubt *whom* she meant to be excommunicated—open sinners.   Those, therefore, who are pained at the general use of the service, should rather strive to restore the practice of excommunication, than to alter the words used in the service.   Surely, if we do not do this, we are clearly defrauding the religious for the sake of keeping close to the wicked.

" Here we see the common course of things in this world;—we omit a duty.   In consequence, our services become inconsistent.   Instead of tracing our steps we alter the service.   What is this but, as it were, to sin upon principle?   While we keep to our principles, our sins are inconsistencies; at length, sensible of the absurdity which inconsistency involves, we accommodate our professions to our practice.   This is ever the way of the world, but it should not be the way of the Church.

" I will join heart and hand with any one who will struggle for a restoration of that ' godly discipline,' the restoration of which our Church publicly professes she considers desirable; but God forbid any one should so depart from her spirit as to mould her formularies to fit the case of deliberate sinners! *   And is not this what we are plainly doing, if we alter the Burial Service as proposed?   Are we not recognizing the right of men to receive Christian burial, about whom we do not like to express a hope?   Why should they have Christian burial at all?"

Alas! we fear we may look in vain for the re-establishment of strict Church discipline.   Even in temporals—as said Hamlet to the grave-digger—" The age is grown so picked, that the toe of the peasant comes so near the heel of the courtier, he galls his kibe;" how much more so in matters concerning the Church! However, we have scrupulously cited the above words, and they, at least, ought to strike the declaimer against ordinances, and the slanderer of the Church Services, dumb.

Chapter VII. relates to the Anthems, or sentences appointed to be said or sung while the minister is preceding the corpse— " a custom," says Mr. Palmer, " of the greatest antiquity, as we learn from the Apostolical Constitutions, from Dionysius Areopagite, Chrysostom, and other sources."   Than these sentences nothing can be well more appropriate,—more affecting,—more true.   The first is what our blessed Lord himself delivered for

---

* We recollect taking the weekly duties for a neighbouring clergyman during his absence, and, to our great surprise, finding the Burial Service *bracketed*,—evidently with the intent to omit this or that passage, according as the life of the deceased might have been,—*sinner*, that is, or *saint*.   What is this but to take the fan into our own hands?   These things ought not to be.

the comfort of the two sisters as he accompanied them to the tomb of their brother Lazarus. They certify the Resurrection of the Dead, and thus, in our Saviour's own words, his ambassadors commence this solemn service, bidding, as it were, the mourners following not to weep as those without hope, inasmuch as the corpse of their dead brother or sister shall again flourish as an herb, *and the earth shall cast out the dead.* We find accordingly that these selfsame words have been used as a part of the burial offices of all Christians. Nor is the next sentence less appropriate, declaring, in the words of the patriarch, Job, the Resurrection of the BODY;* or, as our Church has taken care to express it in the three several Baptismal Services, the Resurrection of the FLESH,—clearly thereby declaring her own Belief. This leads Mr. Greswell to a discussion on the identity of the Resurrection-Body, which is perfectly unobjectionable, and would seem to have been suggested to him by Bishop Butler's Dissertation " Of Personal Identity," which the reader will find at the end of the first volume of the Clarendon edition of his invaluable Works. The last sentence, taken from St. Paul's First Epistle to Timothy, and from the Book of Job, is not less fitting to the occasion than the other two; for what can be more to the purpose, more likely to reach the heart at such a time than the Scripture testimony to the vanity of all worldly possessions? Nothing. So that it has been well said, when we consider all these sentences toge² ther, " Were the happiness of the next world as closely apprehended as the felicities of this, it were a martyrdom to live."

" The Saviour wept—the Saviour wept
  O'er him he loved—corrupting clay!
But then He spake the word, and Death
    Gave up his prey!

A little while—a little while,
  And the dark grave shall yield its trust;
Yea, render every atom up
    Of human dust.

What matters then—what matters then,
  Who earliest lays him down to rest?—
Nay, ' to depart, and be with Christ,'
    Is surely best." †

* See the very remarkable words of Sir Thomas Browne, in his *Religio Medici,* part i. § 48, Wilkin, vol. ii. p. 68. " I believe that our estranged and divided ashes shall unite again, &c." Jeremy Taylor observes in his *own* way, " St. Ignatius, who was buried in the bodies of lions, and St. Polycarp, who was burned to ashes, shall have their bones and their flesh again, with greater comfort than those violent persons who slept among kings, having usurped their thrones when they were alive, and their sepulchres when they were dead."—vol. iv. p. 568.

† From a beautiful little volume of Miss Bowles's, the authoress of " Chapters upon Churchyards." She must have been to the grave to weep there!

Σαφφοῦς παῦρα μὲν, ἀλλὰ ῥόδα !

Chapters VIII. and IX. are on the Proper Psalms and on the Proper Lessons. In this part of the service, as in all other offices, we have followed the custom of antiquity, approaching here, perhaps, nearer to the Eastern than to the Western Churches. In the latter the Eucharist was celebrated at this time, and prayers were made for the happiness of the deceased; but these are both discontinued, the one as a matter of course, because Protestants look upon masses for the dead as " a fond thing, vainly invented, and grounded upon no warranty of Scripture, but rather repugnant to the Word of God," (Art. xxii.); the other probably because, though firm in the faith, the hearts even of those who looked for the appearance of their Saviour, might be bowed down with over-much sorrow for so high a feast, and be ready rather for *the bread of mourners.* Be this as it may, our Burial Service now follows what was observed in the Patriarchate of Constantinople, as we learn from the *Euchologicon sive Rituale Græcorum* of Goar the Dominican, the correspondent of Archbishop Usher. As concerns the Psalms, we may safely refer to what Mr. Greswell says upon them; nor do we see any reason to expunge any part of his remarks, unless it be the last sentence, where the application of ἐδ᾽ ὀνήσιμον to the gift of God can hardly be correct. We mention this, however, merely by the way, because if it be taken connectedly with our author's remarks, there is really nothing objectionable in the words—ἄδωρον δῶρον, ἐδ᾽ ὀνήσιμον.

In turning to the Lesson—a part of 1 Cor. xv.—we cannot but say that it is altogether in unison with the solemn ritual we are treating of. Accordingly we find in Mr. Palmer's *Origines Liturgicæ,* as we might have expected,

" that a part of the Lesson which follows has been used by the English Church for a considerable length of time. It was anciently used in the celebration of the Eucharist, which formerly took place in England, as in other western churches, at this time ; and although the English Church has not continued the custom, but adopted the practice of the Church of Constantinople, the importance of this part of Scripture has caused it be used as the proper Lesson on the present occasion. In the Church of Constantinople they read part of the fourth chapter of St. Paul's Epistle to the Thessalonians, and a Gospel from St. John."

Mr. Greswell, in his Commentary, is led to expatiate on the change of the resurrection-body,—and here, though we cannot say that there is any thing really objectionable, yet we may be allowed to hint at the old adage, *Ne quid nimis.* And, indeed, we think that some few parts do deviate from that chastened and tempered language which should scrupulously be used on so awful a subject. We would instance, particularly, pp. 295, 302. The same remarks may also be applied to vol. ii. p. 124—128, though perhaps the harrowing nature of the subject, in the latter instance, may plead some excuse. Heroic lines, however, in prose, ought to be studiously avoided. They are not natural, and call to our recollection the chapter of Aristotle. (*Rhet.* lib. iii. c. iii.)* Περὶ ψυχρᾶς λέξεως.

"Singula quæque locum teneant sortita decenter."

Having thus far touched upon what we look upon as the only blemish in the volumes before us,—and having before apologized for what some might call rhapsodies,—we shall not refer to the point again,—observing simply, that, if the work should (as we hope) be so popular as to call for a second edition, we trust the author will cut down the "*ambitiosa ornamenta.*"

Other points dwelt upon by Mr. Greswell in this chapter, are, degrees of glory in the resurrection-body, the last trump, the Mediatorial kingdom of Jesus Christ, and that glorious ἐπινίκιον μέλος which occurs at the end of the chapter—"O death! where is thy sting? O grave, where is thy victory?" These are all handled with the pen of a ready writer,—but we have no time to dwell upon them. We will, therefore, end these remarks with the words of Theophylact on those of the Apostle: Ὡσανεὶ γενό-μενα ἰδὼν τὰ πράγματα, ἐνθυσιᾶ, καὶ ἐπινίκιον βοᾷ, καὶ ἀλαλάζει, οἰονεὶ κειμένῳ τῷ θανάτῳ ἐπεμβαίνων. *Operum,* ii. 231. B. (*Notes and Illustrations,* vol. ii. p. 339.)

Chapter X. commences with the Anthems appointed to be saidl or sung while the corpse is made ready to be laid in the eart i.

"The reading of the lesson being ended," observes Mr. Greswell, "that part of the service which is appointed to be solemnized upon entering the church, is over; and the part which is directed to begin and proceed by the grave side, follows next in order. This second and last division of the offices for the interment of the dead, according to the ritual of the Church of England, though, generally speaking, all celebrated without the church, and all by the side of the grave, or sepulchre, which is intended to receive the dead body, consists of three parts: first, that which precedes the commission of the body to the ground: secondly, that which is performed while the interment itself, or consignment of the body to the ground, is taking place; and thirdly, that which is directed to follow when this particular ceremony is over; and, consequently, comprehends what remains of the service to the close of the whole."—vol. ii. p. 1.

And here, in these Anthems, as in the rest of her services, the Church of England follows the order which is found in the ancient rituals of the Eastern and Western Churches. The

* See the Remarks of Archbishop Whately, in his Elements of Rhetoric, p. 212.

whole four of these Anthems, indeed, may be seen in Mr.
Palmer, extracted from the Salisbury Manual,* and they correspond almost word for word. The compilers, however, of our
Liturgy did not, certainly, take the last altogether from that
source. The latter words, at least, of that, are found, as Archbishop Lawrence has observed, in a " German hymn of Luther,
composed as a kind of poetical paraphrase upon another very
ancient one in the offices of the Romish Church. The words of
Luther in the latter part of this hymn are, " Heiliger Herre Gott,
heiliger starker Gott, heiliger barmhertziger Heyland, du ewiger
Gott, lass uns nicht *enfallen von des rechten glaubens trost.*"—
Geistliches Handbuchlein, p. 136. " O holy Lord God, O holy
mighty God, O holy merciful Saviour, thou God eternal, suffer
us not *to fall from the consolation of the true faith.*"† With the
exception of a single passage in page 45, all that Mr. Greswell
says on these Anthems is in unison with the rest of his work.
And even as regards the passage alluded to, we can say, True,
most true! But is it well to rake the charnel-house? Is it not
—(to use the expressive words of John Miller in his excellent
sermons,)—is it not like " ransacking all the depths of iniquity,"
as some do in their sermons? We think so, and should be
glad, therefore, that it were away. We have only further to
remark how studiously our Church avoids all prayer for the dead,
endeavouring to turn all she says to the soul's health of the living;
—and conclude with an extract from Master Hugh Latimer's
Sermons,—that constant martyr of Jesus Christ,—which has an
especial reference to the last Anthem.

" Thirdly, I commend unto you the souls departed this life in the faith
of Christ, that ye remember to give laudes, praise and thanks to Almighty God for his great goodness and mercy showed unto them, in
that great need and conflict against the devil and sin, and that gave
them at the hour of death faith in his Son's death and passion, whereby
they might conquer and overcome, and get the victory. Give thanks, I
say, for this, adding prayers and supplications for yourselves, that it may
please God to give you the like faith and grace, to trust only unto the
death of his dear Son, as he gave unto them. For as they be gone, so
must we; and the devil will be as ready to tempt us, as he was them,
and our sins will light as heavy upon us, as theirs did upon them : and

---

* For the History of the Sarum " Use " see also Mr. Palmer's Origines Liturgicæ,
vol. i. pp. 186, 187. It derives its origin from Osmund, bishop of that see in A. D.
1078, and chancellor of England. It is said to have been adopted in some part of
France, and even in Portugal. The ritual books of York and Hereford have been
printed, but we are not aware that this has.

† See Archbishop Lawrence's Bampton Lectures. Notes on Sermon VIII. p. 448.
He is led to remark on the passage as one, amongst endless others, which proves " the
impossibility of reconciling the doctrine contained in our Liturgy and Homilies with the
Calvinistic predestination."

we are as weak and unable to resist, as were they. Pray, therefore, that we may have grace to die in the same faith of Christ as they did, and at the latter day be raised with Abraham, Isaac, and Jacob, and be partakers with Christ in the kingdom of heaven."*

The XIth Chapter of Mr. Greswell's work is, on the form of words, provided for the interment, which Mr. Palmer considers as peculiar to our Church, as " the rituals of the East and the West appoint some psalm or anthem to be sung or said while the body is placed in the tomb; but the same form nearly has been used in the English Church for many ages, though anciently it followed after the body was covered with earth, and while the earth was placed upon it." As to that part of this formula which others besides sectarians are wont to object to,—there is no need for us to say more about it than what we have already said in the extract given, some pages back, from the " Tracts for the Times." The Church never intended that this office should be read over ungodly sinners,—they, according to the ancient ecclesiastical discipline for which old Latimer called aloud in his sermons before King Edward, would very properly have been excommunicated,—and, could the apostolic Bishop Wilson's words have found a hearing on earth, no sectarians would now have flouted uncharitably, and no sincere churchmen would have been pained by conscientious scruples. But even as it is, the words, perhaps, will bear an easier and a more charitable construction than some are inclined to put upon them, and so all scruple and doubtfulness might be avoided. Let it be observed, then, that they stand thus,—" in sure and certain hope of" (not this one's or that one's, but) " *the* Resurrection to eternal life through our Lord Jesus Christ." In the subsequent parts of the Office, when we thank God that he has been pleased to deliver a brother or a sister out of the " miseries of this sinful world,"—even if he or she were a sinner, still had life been spared, they might have sunk deeper and deeper into the slough of " wretchedness of unclean living," —and so, even in that case, we may charitably thank God with reference to the living also, that they have escaped such a scandal and such a reproach,—and we needs must ask, with faithful Abraham,—" *Shall not the Judge of all the earth do right ?*"† And then, as to the hope in the concluding collect, we have only to say to one and all, let him that is without sin among you, and cares not to make the hearts of his brethren sad, let him, we say, first cast a stone at our *rejoicing in hope*. What is here said,

* See Sermons, p. 91. Ed. 4to. 1575. Black letter. The language in the text is modernized against our will. Our reference was made some years ago,—and not having the copy at hand, we were obliged to write for the extract.

† Gen. c. xviii. 25.

however, is but, as it were, an umpire's or a daysman's word,—
our own sentiments are expressed above, and they will be found
altogether in unison with those of Mr. Greswell, whose remarks
are most excellent.   We conclude with his pious wish, leaving
out the darker side.*

" Oh ! would that every individual Christian, (may the author be ex-
cused for inserting here a wish to that effect,) whose mortal remains may
be brought to be interred according to this Office, thus, as it appears,
provide for one description of the dead only—as the supposed ecclesiastical discipline is now administered in our Christian community,—would,
I say, that every nominal member of the communion of the Church at
present, by the Christian exemplariness of his past existence, might still
warrant, at the time of his death, on the part of the surviving members
of the same communion, the well assured hope of such a resurrection
from the dead, as eventually awaiting him—the hope that his lifeless
body, consigned to the ground amid the tears, the sobs, and groans of
weeping relatives, already sanctified and consecrated for that future glory
by the indwelling of every needful Christian grace—upon the dawning of
that auspicious morn, will awake from the dust, and sing, will start forth
into the plenary enjoyment of its promised crown of excellence and perfection—a star of the resurrection, to illumine the abodes of the blessed
with its peculiar ray of glory for ever."—vol. ii. p. 94.

The XIIth Chapter of the work before us is on the Anthem
appointed to be said or sung next after the interment,—one of
great antiquity, and taken, as is well known, from *Rev.* xiv. 13.
In it, it is said, that the dead which die in the Lord are blessed,
and for this reason, *they rest from their labours.*   Accordingly, it
is a text which may intimate the intermediate state not to be one of
insensibility,—as also do the texts which follow: *Luke,* xvi. 22;
xxiii. 43; *Cor.* v. 6—9; xii. 4; *Phil.* i. 21—24; as well as
others which it is not necessary now to allude to.   On this most
interesting subject Mr. Greswell dwells at large, and those who
have not thought upon this point will find here abundant matter
faithfully and impartially set before them.   But inasmuch as this
is not an essential object of our faith, and many excellent Christians, both in ancient and modern times, have differed as to its
acceptation,—we shall say nothing further on the subject, simply
laying before our readers the following extract from Bishop
Beveridge's works, in which he takes it for granted, as a point

* On reading the last paragraph of this chapter we could not but call to mind the
departure of that good and faithful servant of his Lord,—the late Divinity Professor
in Oxford,—Dr. Edward Burton.   Speaking of the loss of friends, or of gifted men,
who seem, in their day, the earthly support of the Church, Mr. Newman observes, in
his Sermon on the Ascension of our Lord : " For what we know, their removal hence
is as necessary for the furtherance of the objects we have at heart, as was the departure
of our Saviour."—vol. ii. p. 236.

which did not admit of dispute,—and who shall say it is not a comforting point?*

" He adds, ' And if I go and prepare a place for you, I will come again and receive you unto myself.' But what? Will he not receive us before that? Yes, certainly, he will receive our souls, as soon as ever they depart out of our bodies, as we may gather from what he himself said to the thief upon the cross, ' To day shalt thou be with me in paradise.' For, from hence it is evident, that although the penitent body was to be laid in the earth, yet his soul was to be carried the very same day he died directly to Christ, in paradise or heaven, where he then was as God, although his manhood ascended not till some days after. The same appears from St. Paul's ' desire to depart and be with Christ :' which plainly shows that he firmly believed that he should be with Christ so soon as ever he departed out of this life. But the clearest demonstration of this great truth, and that which puts it beyond all doubt, is taken from St. Stephen, who, being just at the point of death, committed his soul into the hands of Christ, saying, ' Lord Jesus, receive my spirit.' Which, questionless, he would not have done, had he not been fully assured by the Holy Ghost, that Christ would, according to his desire, receive his spirit unto himself, at the same moment that it left his body; and so doubtless every soul that ever departed out of this life in the true faith of Christ, is now with him in heaven, his holy angels carrying it, as they did Lazarus, directly thither.

" But what then doth our Lord mean by his coming again and receiving us to himself? His meaning in short is, that although he was now to leave this world, and to go up to heaven, there to continue many years, preparing a place for us; yet at the last day, when the whole number of his elect shall be accomplished, he will come hither again, and then he will receive us altogether, both soul and body, and so our whole man unto himself, that so the same persons who believed in him and served him upon earth, may live with him for evermore in heaven; as he himself hath promised in the following words, saying, ' I will come again and receive you to myself, that where I am, there ye may be also."

The XIIIth and last chapter of these volumes is taken up with the rest of the Office, including the short, or lesser Litany,— the prayer which is headed by the word " Priest,"† the Collect, and the Benediction. Concerning these severally, Mr. Palmer

---

* The subjoined extract is from vol. iv. p. 302, of the 8vo. edition of his works. It is far different, *as to the comfort to be derived from it,* from the statements set forth in Archbishop Whately's Scripture Revelations concerning a Future State,—a work in which so much is *over*-stated, and so much *under*-stated. As to the *doctrinal point,* we said above, that we were not called to dwell upon it further. We remember the words of South, " Nothing can be more irrational than to be dogmatical in things doubtful; and to determine where wise men only dispute."—vol. v. p. 243.

† See the learned note on the word " Collect," p. 196—198. We have nothing to add to it, and the following remark is quite true : " The word Collect, in our Liturgy, is the proper denomination for a general and ordinary, in opposition to a special or occasional form of prayer." " Collecta," in Latin, is probably derived from the Greek σύναξις or συναπτή.

observes, " The ancient manuals of the English Church appointed a similar order to succeed the burial; but the collects which we use in this place are not of great antiquity, though the preface of the first is found in the manual of Salisbury, and in some very ancient monuments of the Western Church." All that Mr. Greswell says on this Litany, on the Lord's Prayer,—which he calls " reverently brief, concisely full, composedly fervent, eloquently simple, and sublimely expressive,"—all that he says, also, on the duty of the Christian mourner,—is quite appropriate, and must be acceptable to the thoughtful and religious mind. Indeed, what he says upon the subject of the Lord's Prayer we could heartily wish were ingrafted in the hearts of those who complain of the length of our services, and would exclude its repetition from the Liturgy.

Mr. Greswell next proceeds to the first of the two Prayers, and having considered the introduction, (which is a paraphrase of our Saviour's words, Luke, xx. 38,) goes on to dwell on that part of it wherein we beseech Almighty God "of His gracious goodness shortly to accomplish the number of His elect and to hasten His kingdom :" in other words, to bring to a close this mysterious dispensation of providence and grace which has been going on from the beginning of the world to the present time, constituting, as it does, the scheme of the state of probation—the condition, for the time being, of the " Church militant upon earth." The consideration of the words " the number of His elect," leads our author to make some remarks on the terms Predestination and Election, and we may say, without fear of contradiction, that no one can read them without acknowledging that they are made discreetly, soberly, and advisedly. For this reason we give the three following lengthy extracts. The two first are, as it were, introductory to the latter,—which is the summing up of what has been said on the point:

" It is supposed then in the above prayer—so much of it, at least, as relates to the consummation in question—that a process of trial or discrimination both has been, and still is, going on among God's moral and responsible creatures upon earth ; the end and effect of which will be, to distinguish that portion of them described by the name of the elect of God, from the rest, whom the event will prove not to be entitled to that name. This process of trial has been going on from the beginning of human existence ; and is not yet brought to an end. The same scheme of moral probation, with the same end in view, and producing the same effects, in discriminating us under the two classes intended to be distinguished thereby, has been in force ever since the Fall—varying only as to the mode or manner of the probation, with the circumstances of the time, and according as the Revelation of the Divine Will, in conformity to which, on points both of faith and of practice, the scheme is regulated, was more or less complete, under the Antediluvian, the Patriarchal, or the Levitical Dispensation respectively, down to the appointed time of the promulgation of the Gospel, when it assumed that last and most definite form, in which it is especially applicable to Christians ; or the nominal members of the visible Church, as established among Christians on earth.

" Since that time, the doctrine and duties of the Gospel revelation, the one in their influence on the understanding, the other on the heart and affections, the life and conversation,—are the touchstone by which this work of discrimination is still carried forward,—the outward criterion by which the nominal professor of the same religion is still distinguished from the real,—the fan by which the wheat is winnowed and separated from the chaff. The elect are those upon whom these doctrines and duties produce the desired effect ; and the non-elect are they upon whom they do not. It would seem also from the language of the prayer in reference to this subject, that the former have beforehand their appointed number, and a number known to God; the filling up of which too to that destined amount, he may either retard or accelerate, according to the purposes of His wisdom and goodness, (which last attribute is here particularly referred to) ; in a word, that Heaven itself (a point, this, to which I have before called the attention of the reader) must ultimately be found to contain a preordained number of inhabitants, and by parity of consequence, Hell its similarly fixed amount of inmates." —Vol. ii. pp. 168, 169.

" With regard, then, to the description of moral agents which require to be understood by the name of the *Elect ;** it appears to the author of these observations, that none are to be supposed designated by it, to whom the name must be considered applicable, because of an absolute ·unconditional decree of Almighty God, in their behalf. The election implied by it, must be understood to denote something which has been the result of foreseen goodness of character. This goodness it is which has rendered the subject meet to be elected by God. The election made him not good,—but the quality of character having been first produced, by the agency of causes properly and strictly moral, (the operation of which, however mysterious to us may be the exercise of that knowledge, —God, as an omniscient Being, foresaw,) the election so made of the subject in question, was the consequence of his previous personal worthiness, or his previous right and Christian use of the means of grace. To be an elected person, according to any other construction of the import of that name, (and equally so, we may add, to be a reprobate or unelected person,) would be to suppose an human agent, in either instance, a mere machine, a passive instrument in bringing about a Divine purpose, affecting the happiness or misery of such and such of its creatures,

---

* Jones of Nayland, of whose works the late excellent Bishop van Mildert thought so highly, says "The true notion of Predestination is to be met with in Ephesians, i. 11, 12, where those are said to be predestinated to the praise of God's glory who *trusted* in Christ. Our attainment of eternal happiness is the *consequence* of our belief in Christ, and the irreversible decree of God is, that those that believe in him should not perish, and this is probably the only sense in which the doctrine of predestination and election can be maintained from Scripture."—Works, vol. iv. p. 39, note.

—over which, in its use and subserviency to that effect,— the agent himself had no control, and with which, except as destined to be affected, in one way or the other, by its consequences, he himself had nothing to do. Such, I say, would be the result,—if we were to look upon election in one of these cases, as the necessary cause of Christian goodness of character, and not as the result of the foreseen existence of it; or reprobation in the other, to be the necessary cause of the contrary description of character, and not simply the consequence of it, as equally foreseen also."—pp. 178, 179.

" Two truths are clearly revealed to us, or clearly ascertainable by us, —both having the testimony of Scripture, and the further evidence of human reason, in their favour. One is, that the foreknowledge of the Deity, even when directed to events of an exclusively contingent description, (the result of the free agency of man,) is absolute and unconditional; the other, that men, notwithstanding, are left themselves in possession of a moral power of choosing how, under the different measures and degrees of natural or spiritual light dispensed to them,—of natural or spiritual facilities and opportunities vouchsafed to them,— they will act.

" Of each of these truths considered apart from the other, we must have the clearest conviction. No truth can be plainer to us than this, that we ourselves are free agents. There needs no argument to convince man of that, of which his own consciousness assures him beyond a doubt, just as much as of his own existence. And yet it is equally certain that God must foresee all things, even the contingent results of our own free agency. Nor in strictness ought these two truths to be considered, except distinctly ; in which point of view it is manifest that neither of them would be liable to doubt or controversy. The free agency of man, considered by itself, and the foreknowledge of the Deity, considered also by itself, could neither of them well be denied or disputed. It is only when they begin to be considered in conjunction, that they begin to create difficulties, and to be liable to objections ; because it is only when regarded in conjunction, that they begin to seem to clash. Man appears a free agent, when considered by himself; but no longer free, when considered as the subject of the foreknowledge of God. And yet it is manifest that we ourselves are concerned with nothing, except what man is, considered in himself; not what he is in reference to another and an independent being. It ought to satisfy us to feel assured that we ourselves are free, without seeking to inquire how that freedom may be compatible with the prescience of God."—pp. 191, 192.

The rest of this chapter is taken up with the contents of the Collect, and with the Benedictory Prayer, from 2 Cor. xiii. 14, in which our author is led to dilate upon the death of sin and life of righteousness,—on the common necessity of dying,— on the last day, with its preceding signs,—on the general Resurrection, and the final acceptance. We have no space, however, to dwell more at length on these interesting subjects. Heartily thanking, therefore, Mr. Greswell for these volumes, the intent of which is excellent, the piety of which is evident, and the ex_ecution, as a whole, good,—we gladly extract, and join in, his final prayer :

" Let the author conclude with a prayer, in which he trusts to have his reader's hearty concurrence—*Esto perpetua.* May Christian faith and hope, Christian * sorrow for the dead, and Christian patience and resignation in the living—continue to be thus expressed, until what time, shall we say ? until the advent of that day, so often alluded to in these commentaries, when the reign of corruption and mortality shall cease, and Christian mourners shall be called upon to bury and lament over deceased friends and relatives no more."—pp. 248, 249.

Thus have we carefully gone through this beautiful and affecting office of our Church, and have severally alluded to the antiquity of its parts, and to the purity of its doctrine. We had a word or two of our own to say more,—but the language of Hooker and of Bishop Horne presented itself to our memory, and though dead, they shall yet speak for us. " The end," says Hooker, "of funeral rites is, first, to show that love towards the party deceased, which nature requireth ; then, to do him that honour which is fit both generally for man, and particularly for the quality of his person ; last of all, to testify the care which the Church hath to comfort the living, and the hope which we all have concerning the resurrection of the dead."† The words of Horne which we would refer to are, " Let not man presume, who withereth like the green herb ; but then, let not man despair, whose nature, with all its infirmities, the Son of God hath taken upon him. The flower which fadeth in Adam, blooms anew in Christ, never to fade again. The mercy of Jehovah in his Messiah is everlasting, and of that everlasting mercy poor frail man is the object. It extendeth to all the generations of the faithful servants of God. Death shall not deprive them of its benefits, nor shall the grave hide them from the efficacious influence of its all enlivening beams, which shall pierce even into those regions of desolation, and awaken the sleepers of six thousand years. Man must pay to justice the temporal penalty of his sins ; but mercy shall raise him again, to receive the eternal

. * Cowper beautifully says " In the case of believers, death has lost his sting, not only with respect to those he takes away, but with respect to survivors also. Nature indeed will always suggest some causes of sorrow, when an amiable and Christian friend departs ; but the Scripture, so many more, and so much more important reasons to rejoice, that on such occasions, perhaps, more remarkably than any other, sorrow is turned into joy."—Vol. iv. p. 275, of Southey's edition,—which may well indeed be called an accession to English literature.

† See Eccles. Polity, book v. §75 ; vol. ii. p. 408 ; and cf. Jer. Taylor, vol. iv. p. 565.—" Of the contingencies and treating our dead." The passage of Bishop Horne is from his Commentary on Psalm ciii. 17, 18.

reward, purchased by his Saviour's righteousness." ·Happy, then, those who are baptized for the dead !

It remains now that we devote the little space we have left to the mention of the beautiful and only complete edition of Sir Thomas Browne's Works which has ever been published. The reason of its being appended to this article is obviously on account of his Hydriotaphia, or Urn Burial,—a treatise in which, amongst much that is curious, and something that is fanciful, almost every thing that could be said has been exhausted,—and, as we hinted before, it seems odd that Mr. Greswell should never have referred to it. We heartily wish it had been in our power to have devoted an article to the works of this remarkable and good man,—his life we could have written *con amore*, as his works, —especially the Vulgar Errors and the Religio Medici,—together with Evelyn's Silva, and old Burton's Anatomie of Melancholie, have ever been amongst our especial favourites. It has, however, become necessary to devote these pages almost exclusively to professed * Theological Works,—for this reason, therefore, the present edition must be appended like a postcript to a letter,— and a postcript, be it remarked, often contains most affectionate regards.

Of this edition we are bound to say that every lover of Sir Thomas Browne's works should be possessed. It has been the labour of twelve years, and (we have heard) no less than 1400*l*. have been expended upon it. We hope a second edition will soon be called for, and then some typographical errors, together with the "additions and corrections" alluded to and inserted in vol. ii. pp. xxi. xxii. may be re-arranged, and the only blemish of the book taken off. In these days of penny-trumpet literature, Mr. Wilkin deserves' the cordial thanks of every scholar, for having had the courage to go through with and to publish, at his own expense, an edition of a work, which, of any other, shows the great talents, the great research, as well as the great piety and charity of its author,—of one who could never hear the toll of a passing bell, though in his mirth, without his prayers and best wishes for the departing spirit,—of one who could not go to view

---

* We cannot avoid remarking here that the letters of Browne are replete with pure and unostentatious piety. Those who will refer to pp. 3, 9, 12, 261, 271, 313, 319, which we have accidentally marked down, will see double beauty in the passage following, from the Religio Medici : " I cannot see one say his prayers, but, instead of imitating him, I fall into supplication for him, who perhaps is no more to me than a common nature : and if God .hath vouchsafed an ear to my supplications, there are surely many happy that never saw me, and enjoy the blessing of mine unknown devotions."—Vol. ii. p. 100. It is needless for us to refer the readers to the Religio Medici, and Christian Morals ; but there are many papers in the fourth volume connected with religious topics, which will probably be new, and show forth the deep thought of this good worthy of the olden time.

the body of a patient, without calling unto God for his soul.—
Religio Medici, part ii. c. vi. The first volume of the edition
before us contains Dr. Johnson's Life of Sir Thomas Browne,
with a Supplementary Memoir by Mr. Wilkin, together also
with the Domestic and Miscellaneous Correspondence—a racy
and interesting collection, whether we look to Sir Thomas Browne
himself, his sons, the goodly Dorothy, or the fascinating urchin
" *litle Tomey*," his grandchild. The second volume contains the
Religio Medici, and part of the Pseudodoxia Epidemica, or Inquiries into Vulgar and Common Errors,—with prefaces by the
editor, containing much information, which may be said also of
the notes at the bottom of the pages in the several volumes. The
third volume contains the remainder of the Pseudodoxia Epidemica,—together with the Garden of Cyrus, Hydriotaphia, and
Brampton Urns. In the editor's preface to the three last-mentioned treatises he observes that he has* "modernized the spelling"
as well of these as of all Browne's other works, but not the
phraseology as characteristic of the author. Of the phraseology
we will say a word presently,—and we could heartily wish that
the original spelling had been left as it was, because that too is
oftentimes characteristic, and we know well that the writings of
the learned and judicious Hooker have suffered from such an
alteration,

" Tantum *elementa* queunt permutato ordine rerum."

Volume the Fourth contains the Repertorium, or the Antiquities of Norwich,—Letter to a Friend, upon the occasion of the
death of his intimate Friend,—Christian Morals,—Miscellany
Tracts, and Unpublished Papers. As connected with the Contents
of the British Critic, we have above alluded to the Christian
Morals and the Religio Medici. We may now refer the reader,
on the same grounds, to Tract i., which contains " *Observations
upon several Plants mentioned in Scripture;*" to Tract iii., on
a question put to him as to the " *Fishes eaten by our Saviour with
his Disciples after his Resurrection from the Dead;*" and to Tract
x. " *Of the Situations of Sodom, Gomorrah, Admah, Zeboim, in
the Dead Sea.*" Besides these, the reader will find many passages relative to Theology in the " Extracts from Common Place
Books," which we have not space to refer to particularly; with
one, however, as it shows the man, we shall conclude, after having said a word on Browne's phraseology, which we will do in
the language of one whom Browne would have loved,—a living
author who has taken a fuller and more comprehensive, as well as
a more exact view of the literature of our own country, than any

* Vol. iii. p. 379.
M 2

one whom we could name,—we mean Mr. Southey, who, in speaking of the style of writing in Charles the Second's time, has the following striking remarks :—

" Three different fashions in writing had prevailed, which were alike faulty. There was the dry, dull, dismal manner of the sober Puritans ; there was a style of overstrained and elaborate wit dealing in affectations of every kind; and there was an ornate style, studded with sesquipedalian Latinisms, Grecisms, Hebraisms, and Arabiaisms, which might frequently send the best scholar to his Lexicons. Indeed, a dictionary was published for enabling some persons to read, and others to write in this refined language. The most remarkable examples of it are found in the poems of Henry More, *and in the works of Sir Thomas Browne* ; to whose peculiar genius, however, this sort of language was so well suited, that it would not have been possible for him to have expressed his thoughts so felicitously, or so naturally, in any other manner. *But it required the knowledge, and the power, and the feeling of such a man to render it tolerable.* Its effect upon inferior writers was to mar good matter, or to render what was worthless intolerable."*

We suppose there is no reader of Browne's works who has not been struck and amazed with the phraseology alluded to,—but we are quite agreed with Mr. Southey in thinking, that in other and weaker, and less cunning hands, it would have been intolerable. That excellent divine, the witty South, was evidently tickled by the peculiarity of Browne's language, in Browne's hands, as the reader may see by turning to his† Sermon on Eccles. vii. 10. *Say not thou, What is the cause that the former days were better than these? for thou dost not inquire wisely concerning this,*—which is totally different, *in style,* from all the rest of his published ones, and concerning which, in a letter lying before us, Southey says, " It is most evidently written in imitation of Sir Thomas Browne, probably as a trial of skill."

We conclude with the following beautiful extract from the Common Place Book above alluded to. It is hardly necessary to say that it was never intended for any other eye than his own.

" To be sure that no day pass, without calling upon God in a solemn-formed prayer, seven times within the compass thereof; that is, in the morning, and at night, and five times between ; taken up long ago from the examples of David and Daniel, and a compunction and shame that I had omitted it so long, when I had fully read of the custom of the Mahometans, to pray five times in the day.

---

* The above will be found in the masterly Paper on Dr. Sayer's Works in the Quarterly Review, No. lxix. pp. 187, 188. The italics are our own.

† This sermon is in vol. v. pp. 232, 249, of the Clarendon Press Edition. By the way we may remark, that the " aphorism of Horace," mentioned in p. 236, is not his but Juvenal's. See Sat. xv. v. 70. The following would seem to be more in South's than in Sir Thomas Browne's style. " The maunderings of discontent are like the voice and behaviour of a swine, who, when he feels it rain, runs grumbling about, and by that indeed discovers his nature, but does not avoid the storm."—p. 245.

" To pray and magnify God in the night, and my dark bed, when I could not sleep; to have short ejaculations whenever I awaked; and when the four o'clock bell awoke me, or my first discovery of the light, to say the collect of our Liturgy;* ' Eternal God, who hath safely brought me to the beginning of this day,' &c.

" To pray in all places where privacy inviteth; in any house, highway, or street; and to know no street or passage in this city which may not witness that I had not forgot God and my Saviour in it; and that no parish or town where I have been, may not say the like.

" To take occasion of praying, upon the sight of any church, which I see or pass by, as I ride about.

" Since the necessities of the sick, and unavoidable diversions of my profession, keep me often from church, yet to take all possible care, that I might never miss sacraments upon their accustomed days.

" To pray daily and particularly for sick patients, and in general for others, whensoever, howsoever, under whose care soever; and at the entrance into the house of the sick, to say, ' The peace and mercy of God be in this place.'

" After a sermon, to make a thanksgiving, and desire a blessing, and to pray for the minister.

" In tempestuous weather, lightning, and thunder, either night or day, to pray for God's merciful protection, and his mercy upon their souls, bodies, and goods.†

" Upon sight of beautiful persons, to bless God in his creatures, to pray for the beauty of their souls, and to enrich them with inward graces to be answerable unto the outward. Upon sight of deformed persons, to send them inward graces, and enrich their souls, and give them the beauty of the resurrection."—vol. iv. pp. 420, 421.

* This is given as written by Sir Thomas Browne. The prayer begins thus, " O Lord, our heavenly Father, Almighty and everlasting God," &c.

† We cannot help giving in a note this sweet passage from Jeremy Taylor, " Venerable Bede reports of St. Chad, that if a great gust of wind suddenly arose, he presently made some holy ejaculations, to beg favour of God for all mankind who might possibly be concerned in the effects of that wind; but, if a storm succeeded, he fell prostrate to the earth, and grew as violent in prayer as the storm was, either at land or sea. But if God added thunder and lightning, he went to the church, and there spent all his time, during the tempest, in reciting litanies, psalms, and other holy prayers, till it pleased God to restore his favour, and to seem to forget his anger. And the good bishop added this reason; because these are the extensions and stretchings forth of God's hand, and yet he did not strike: but he that trembles not, when he sees God's arm held forth to strike us, understands neither God's mercies nor his own danger; he neither knows what those horrors were, which the people saw from Mount Sinai, nor what the glories and amazements shall be at the great day of judgment."—Hist. Gent. Anglor. lib. iii. c. 18. Of the Causes and Manner of Divine Judgments, Works, vol. iii. p. 232.

Art. VIII.—*The Brothers' Controversy, being a genuine Correspondence between a Clergyman of the Church of England and a Layman of Unitarian Opinions.* London. 1835.

THIS small volume consists, in accordance with its title, of a series of letters between a Clergyman and his brother-in-law upon the Trinitarian question, or rather upon those previous questions which the controversy involves, such as the mode of seeking the truth, the use of reason, and the like. It is certainly interesting, but painfully so; and that because it presents the picture of two well-meaning men disputing about sacred subjects on insufficient or mistaken grounds, and so leaving off as they began. In thus speaking we should be grieved indeed to seem to imply that their respective opinions are, in any point of view, to be put on a level, the one not higher nor better than the other. Socinianism is a deadly heresy, full of everlasting evil to its wilful professors, and influential moreover on their moral character; still there is a way of opposing it, which does but seem to justify, and does but confirm them in it. And such in the main is that which is now exhibited in the work before us.

Both the disputants are men of some education and ability. The Clergyman is an orthodox, serious, and amiable man; and there is much of candour and good sense in his Unitarian adversary. The Editor professes to send their correspondence to the press, " giving the whole faithfully without comment, without altering a word or syllable;" and it is but fair to add that " the internal evidence," as he anticipates, is a voucher for the correctness of his representation.

Both parties acquiesce in the fundamental position, that truth of doctrine is to be gained from Scripture by each person for himself; and here lies the πρῶτον ψεῦδος of the controversy, which in consequence becomes a trial of *strength* between the two individuals. The (so-called) Unitarian claims the right of assuming that—

" The Protestant Church says that the Gospel is addressed to *every individual;* and I say that he, who does not use his most serious and powerful understanding in endeavouring rightly to comprehend it, hides his best talent, instead of improving it."—p. 32.

The Clergyman responds as follows :—

" As to the duty of free inquiry, it is impossible for any one to advocate it more entirely than I do, only let Scripture authority be paramount. But, if any one tampers with Scripture, . . . then, be he friend or foe, I will join in reprobating such conduct."—p. 51.

Now these statements are true in one sense, false in another, and in this consists the fallacy of the reasoning. If by " the Gospel" the (so-called) Unitarian means the text of Scripture without note or comment, it is not true that this is " addressed to every individual;" but, unless he assumes this, it does not at all follow that " he, who does not use his most serious and powerful understanding in endeavouring to comprehend it, hides his best talent." Surely " the Gospel" which is " addressed to every individual" is the Gospel as *dispensed by primitive teaching,* as we shall show in the sequel, and this does not require " the powerful understanding" of any one. The true sense of Scripture, *as regards all high theological points,* has been determined by an unerring authority from the beginning. Again, it is a mistake in our clerical controversialist, to " advocate the duty of free inquiry." Those, of course, who are competent to the task may fairly inquire whether the teaching received in the Church from the first is, in matter of fact, Apostolic, as they may inquire whether the New Testament be the writing of Apostles and Evangelists; but *unless* they have first examined and disproved its claim to be so considered, they have so far no duty of free inquiry upon the text of Scripture. It will be observed that, in so saying, we are advancing no pretensions in behalf of the Clergy, as such, to the power of interpreting Scripture more than in behalf of the laity; we subject them both to an existing Apostolical teaching, explanatory of Scripture.

But the " Layman" goes further. Not only does he consider that we have no existing records of Apostolic teaching but those preserved in the Canon, but he seems most preposterously to think that St. Paul *never taught his converts orally,* that he instructed them only through his extant epistles. He takes this strange position for granted, and founds upon it an argument against the doctrine of our Lord's divinity. He asks—

" Can I believe that concerning this Jesus, whom the Apostles so preached" [i. e. as being a man, viz. in the book of Acts] " year after year to Jews and Gentiles, professing their inspiration, and express commission to teach, saying that they had taught all the Gospel, it was afterwards, *for the first time,* revealed, *in a letter written by one of them* to a Church he had established in a heathen country," [alluding to Rom. ix. 5,] " (and in this letter, not by direct declaration of the writer, but incidentally, by way of allusion in a parenthesis,) that He was the very and eternal God ?"—p. 70.

Strange, indeed, that any religionists should be able to satisfy themselves with so unnatural and meagre a view of the actual propagation of the Gospel! Yet it is parallel to an observation of

Mr. Abbot, the American, that our Saviour was under the " dis-advantage" of having " no press," whereby to act upon " the different portions of the community."

Again—

" It is to me inconceivable that the Apostle could possibly, in the winding up of a sentence in an epistle, *intend to reveal* the astonishing doctrine that Christ was God; that He who said to him, ' I am Jesus whom thou persecutest,' should ever have added, ' I am the God of the universe, who took upon myself the form of a created being;' and that the Apostle, having preached Christ crucified and risen, should, *after years of such preaching*, bring out this revelation *in so cursory and elliptical a manner.*"—p. 129.

It is inconceivable, doubtless, and incredible that he should have brought out a new and stupendous truth for the first time " in so cursory and elliptical a manner;" but then there *is* an explanation which the " Layman" overlooks.   Perhaps it was *not* for the first time; this surely is *as* probable as that " God over all" in Rom. ix. 5, does not apply to Christel.   Perhaps whoever converted the Romans had *taught* them this doctrine by word of mouth, as human beings might do now-a-days, and perhaps St. Paul knew it.   Surely oral instruction is not one of modern " advantages," as Mr. Abbot would term them, as well as " the press."

But let us observe how the Clergyman, a sensible and well-instructed man, replies to his opponent.   We do not find that he any where expresses surprise at the unwarrantable assumption above exposed; and in replying to the argument founded thereon he most curiously flutters about what we deem the real state of the case without ever lighting upon or touching it.

Withstood in his criticism, he appeals to the belief of the early Church; and quotes from Irenæus and Tertullian, whose " testimonies are of some authority in showing" the Layman's " notion to be erroneous."—(pp. 95, 96.)   Presently he says, " I have shown by quotations from Irenæus and Tertullian, that the primitive Christians understood it in the sense we attach to it."—(p. 107.)   This is promising—he is now in the right track.   Alas! he raises only to disappoint our hopes.   One should think, before he appealed to the primitive Church, he ought to have ascertained *why* its testimony tells for a certain interpretation of Scripture. The plain reason is this, that it comes close upon the Apostles, and so is more likely to convey their meaning; in other words, it has a certain Apostolic authority in explaining Scripture; and, in consequence, is a source of Christian truth in some sense independent of Scripture, a guide to a certain extent superseding the need of private judgment. If it have not this authority and on this ac-' count, it is no more than the opinion of any other men, and quite irrelevant in the dispute. Almost as reasonably might the Clergyman require his brother to yield to his own interpretation as to Irenæus's, if that Father's proximity to the Apostles has no weight in the question, except indeed that a second opinion corroborates a first. Nevertheless, in spite of all this, he does not fully understand *why* he quoted Irenæus. The Layman boldly says—

" Your quotations from Irenæus and Tertullian prove that the now received construction existed in their time and was received by them; in other words, that they were Trinitarians, and this is all."—p. 130.

The Clergyman, in his reply to this plain avowal, not only misses the true force of his own argument, but suggests a novel basis for it, viz. that *since creeds did not exist in the primitive Church*, (a position running counter both to fact and to the necessities of his argument,) the primitive belief in the doctrine of the Trinity is an evidence of what is the true sense of Scripture, as witnessed by unbiassed and unprejudiced judgments. He says—

" It is difficult to find persons in these times who have never heard of creeds before they read the Bible; but it appears to me, that the most satisfactory way of ascertaining the truth of your remark, will be to observe what doctrines those persons found in the Bible, who certainly *could have their minds prejudiced by no creed*, save that which they received from the mouth of the Apostles, or which they learned from the inspired writings."—p. 195.

In this extract let us observe carefully the clause, " save that which they received from the mouth of the Apostles." The writer not only " burns," he has the truth almost in his hands; yet, as his whole argument plainly evinces, he scarcely has gained it, but he lets it go again. The notion of an apostolical creed authoritatively interpreting Scripture is altogether above him. He continues—

" Let us next see what Clement of Rome believed, *while as yet unschooled by creeds and articles*, &c. . . . Trying Ignatius by the same test, we find him, &c. . . : . As to the *object* I had in view in quoting these passages, since I find that Barnabus, Clement, and Ignatius, *without creed preceding*, arrived at the same *conclusion* that I have, namely, that Christ was God, and also the Creator of the world, I am little inclined to distrust that ' orthodox education' to which you seem to attribute the *inferences* I draw from the study of the Scriptures."—p. 196.

What follows, however, shows he *has* another reason for quoting the Fathers; viz. to make it clear *they cannot be used against him.* Dr. Priestley had pretended to assign the *date* of the first corruptions of the Church's doctrine. " Justin Martyr is the first writer who mentions the miraculous conception."—(*Hist. Early Op:*

vol. iv. p. 107.) Our controversialist meets this assertion; and is employed accordingly, not in showing that the tradition of the Trinity is apostolic, but that it is *not* Justin Martyr's.

His inadequate notion of the primitive creed has already been shown. But one or two extracts in addition will be in point:—

" We say, reason from Scripture, and expound Scripture by comparing it with itself, instead of with *the dogmas of men;* and this is the appeal I wish every where to be made."—p. 115.

" I assert that neither the Church of England nor I have ever required persons to take their creeds for granted, or forbidden the unbiassed comparison of them with the words of Scripture . . . . . The eighth article of our Church says, ' The three creeds ought thoroughly to be received and believed.' And why? because the Church says so? No; but because ' they may be proved by most certain warrant of Holy Scripture.' The word of God is the test by which we pronounce they are to be tried, &c."—p. 185—187.

All this is most true, but not the whole truth. It is most true that Scripture is the sole verification of the creeds, as of all professed Apostolical traditions whatever; but it is as true that the creeds are the legitimate exposition of Scripture doctrine. Revealed truth is guaranteed by the union of the two, the creeds at once appealing to Scripture, and developing it. To take Scripture as the *guide* in matters of doctrine is as much a mistake as to take the Apostolical Tradition as the *rule*. What is written is a safeguard to what is unwritten; what is unwritten is a varied *comment* on a (necessarily) limited *text*. The reason of the Clergyman's misapprehension is obvious. He is hampered by the ultra-Protestantism falsely ascribed to our Articles. At the time they were drawn up, the rights of Scripture, as the test of Tradition, were disparaged; and therefore they contain a protest in its behalf. Were they drawn up now, it would be necessary to introduce a protest in behalf of Tradition, as indeed incidentally occurs even as it is, in the famous clause of the 20th Article, which declares that " the Church," *i. e.* Catholic, " has *authority* in controversies of faith," viz. as being the steward of Apostolical teaching. However, the circumstance that the direct statements of the Articles are mainly in defence of the authority of Scripture, has given specious ground to the school of Ultra-Protestantism to assert that it is a sufficient *guide* as well as an *ultimate appeal,* and that each individual may put what sense he pleases upon it, instead of submitting to that one sense to which the Church has testified from the first, in matter of fact. We see the consequences in the controversy before us. Our orthodox disputant has to argue points which have been ruled in his favour centuries upon centuries ago, as if inquiry was never to have an end. He is obliged to have recourse to grammatical criticism, to consult Dr. Elmsley, in the Bodleian, about the meaning of particles (p. 48), and after all his toil is met with the candid and perplexing admission on the part of his opponent, that he does not think it necessary to rest his faith on any one " certain sentence in a letter written by an Apostle."—(p. 65.) He is obliged to look about for philosophical evidence, and fortifies his scheme or doctrine by the shallow and dangerous argumentations of Mr. Erskine. After all, he refers the reception of the orthodox doctrine to the influence of the Holy Ghost, vouchsafed to the individual student of Scripture; a position which, of course, dispenses with the necessity of any formal proof of the doctrine at all.

At the same time, consistently or inconsistently with this last belief, but in truth betraying a conviction of the insufficiency of his own arguments for the conversion of another, he condemns (though reluctantly) the anathemas of the Athanasian Creed, as investing with undue sanctions mere deductions made by the human intellect from the text of Scripture.

" Nothing that I have advanced upon the subject of the Athanasian Creed is, as I conceive, in the least degree inconsistent with my joining in the sentiment of Tillotson and wishing it removed from our Church service. If I were called upon to give my vote upon the subject, it would be for its omission ; but this would not all imply that I felt less uneasiness as to the future salvation of those who deny the Lord that bought them ; nor do I see how the entertaining such fears necessarily leads to any breach of charity."—p. 108.

We do not set much by this salvo, which seems to us but the protest of true Christian feeling against the latitudinarian conclusions at which the intellect had arrived. Is it indeed possible, —we do not say possible in the way of logical consistency, but is it possible in matter of fact, and in the case of men in general, —to believe that the doctrine of the Trinity is a mere human view of Scripture passages, and yet necessary to be believed in order to salvation? Does not, in consequence, the theory that Scripture only is to be the guide of Protestants, lead for certain to liberalism? We do not, indeed, for an instant suppose that any clear and unprejudiced reasoner could help seeing that the Catholic doctrine really *is* in Scripture, and that, therefore, the denial of it incurs the anathema therein declared against unbelievers; still, while belief in the document is made the first thing, and belief in the doctrine but the second, (as this theory would have it,) it inevitably follows in the case of the multitude, who are not

clear-headed or unprejudiced, that the definition of a Christian
will be made to turn, not on faith in the doctrine, but on faith
in the document, and Unitarianism will come to be thought, not
indeed true, but as if not unreasonable, and not necessarily dangerous. And here we take leave of a work which cannot but give
pain to all who sympathise in our own views, the pain of seeing
one who sincerely holds the truth of the Gospel, so little conscious of the ground on which he holds it as to be unable to instruct a brother in error.

The argument for the existence of a known Apostolical Tradition on the subject of the Trinity, and therefore an unerring interpreter of Scripture so far, which has been taken for granted in
the above remarks, was briefly stated in our January number in a
review of Mr. Blanco White's late work. We then expressed
an intention of treating the subject more fully than our limits
admitted at the time, and we have now a fit opportunity of
redeeming our pledge. That writer, it may be recollected,
entirely dismissed the notion of any existing Apostolical interpretation of the sacred text, and maintained, on the contrary, that
Scripture has no authorized interpreter of any kind, and that
dogmatic statements are not part of the revelation. This is the
ground long ago taken by Chillingworth and Locke; nor would
Mr. Blanco White think we paid a bad compliment to himself to
remark it. He would, of course, maintain that all clear-headed
reasoners on the popular Protestant basis must necessarily proceed onwards to his own latitudinarian conclusions, if they are
but fair to their own minds, and free from the prejudices of education, and the inducements of interest. He would maintain
that what is called " Bible religion" and the imposition of dogmatic confessions were irreconcilable with each other, except in
a system, (if it deserved the name,) which was imposed by the law
and intimately bound up with the security and well-being of the
community. And thus he would account both for the acquiescence of the majority in what is in itself absurd, and the recur-
rence of the same objections and arguments, from time to time,
on the part of men of more independent and enlarged minds. In
consequence, he would rather exult than otherwise in finding
the following passages in Chillingworth and others, anticipating
his recent publication.

" Certainly," says Chillingworth, " if Protestants be faulty in
this matter," (playing the Pope,) " it is for doing it too much,
and not too little. This presumptuous imposing of the senses of
men upon the words of God, the special senses of men upon the

general words of God, and laying them upon men's consciences together, under the equal penalty of death and damnation; this vain conceit, that we can speak of the things of God better than in the words of God; this deifying of our own interpretations, and tyrannous enforcing them upon others; this restraining of the word of God from that latitude and generality, and the understandings of men from that liberty wherein Christ and the Apostles left them, is, and hath been the only fountain of all the schisms of the Church, and that which makes them immortal : the common incendiary of Christendom, and that which (as I said before) tears into pieces, not the coat, but the bowels and members of Christ: ' ridente 'Turcâ nec dolente Judæo.' Take away these walls of separation and all will quickly be one."—*Religion of Protestants*, iv. 17.

In like manner Locke:—

" When they have determined the holy Scriptures to be the only foundation of faith, they nevertheless lay down certain propositions as fundamental, which are not in the Scripture, and because others will not acknowledge these additional opinions of theirs, nor build upon them, as if they were necessary and fundamental, they therefore make a separation in the Church; either by withdrawing themselves from others, or expelling the others from them. Nor does it signify any thing for them to say, that their confessions and symbols are agreeable to Scripture, and to the analogy of faith. For if they be conceived in the express words of Scripture, there can be no question about them ... but if they say that the articles which they require to be professed, are consequences deduced from the Scripture, it is undoubtedly well done of them, who believe and profess such things as seem unto them so agreeable to the rule of faith. But it would be very ill done to obtrude those things upon others, unto whom they do not seem to be the indubitable doctrines of the Scripture. This only I say, that however clearly we may think this or the other doctrine to be deduced from Scripture, we ought not therefore to impose it upon others, as a necessary article of faith, because we believe it to be agreeable to the rule of faith. I cannot but wonder at the extravagant arrogance of those men, who think that they themselves can explain things, necessary to salvation, more clearly than the Holy Ghost, the eternal and infinite wisdom of God."—*Letter concerning Toleration, fin.*

And Hoadly, in his Life of Dr. S. Clarke, speaking of him and his opponents in the Trinitarian question,—

" Let me add this one word more, that since men of such thought and such learning have shown the world in their own example, how widely the most honest inquirers after truth may differ upon such subjects; this, methinks, should a little abate our mutual censures, and a little take off from our positiveness about the necessity of explaining, in this or that one determinate sense, the ancient passages relating to points of so sublime a nature."

The argument contained in these extracts stands thus: "Scripture is the sole informant of religious truth; there is no infallible interpreter of Scripture, therefore every man has a right to interpret it for himself, and no one may impose his own interpretation on another." If it be objected that learning, scholarship, judgment, and the like, conduce to the understanding of this as of any other ancient book, it is replied, that true as this may be, these qualifications are on all sides of the doctrinal controversy, there being no opinion entertained by any party which has not been advocated at one time or another by confessedly learned, scholarlike, judicious, and able men. This being the case, no one has a right to say that his own opinion is important to any one besides himself, but is bound to tolerate all other creeds by virtue of the very principle on which he has leave to form his own. The imposition, therefore, of dogmatic confessions on others by any set of religionists, is inferred to be an encroachment upon the Christian liberty of their brethren, who have in turn a right to their own private judgment upon the meaning of the Scripture text. Such is the latitudinarian argument.

Now we might put it to the common sense and manly understanding of any number of men taken at random, whether this, at first sight, is not a very strange representation, and such as they would never use in any ordinary matter of importance, any business they took an interest in or were earnest about. Surely no one in a confidential situation, on receiving instructions from his principal, which he could not altogether understand, would think himself at liberty to put any sense he pleased on them, without the risk of being called to account for doing so. He would take it for granted, that whether the instructions given were obscure or not, yet that they were intended to have a meaning, that they had one and one only meaning; and in proportion as he considered he had mastered it, he could not but also consider fellow-agents wrong who took a different view of it; and in proportion as he considered the instruction important, would he be distressed and alarmed at witnessing their neglect of his own interpretation. He might, indeed, if it so happened, doubt about the correctness of his own opinion, but he never would think it a matter of indifference whether he was right or wrong, he would never think

thát two persons could go on contentedly and comfortably together who took opposite views of their employer's wishes. Now
all this fairly applies to the Scripture disclosures concerning
matters of faith. First, it is plain, that faith is therein insisted
on as an important condition of salvation; next, it is faith in
certain heavenly and unseen truths; and this faith is expressly
said to be " one," and is guaŕded by an anathema upon those
who reject it. Now let us ask the disciples of Latitudinarianism
how do they understand, in what assignable manner do they fulfil,
the passages in which all this is conveyed? *What* is the doctrine
therein spoken of, and belief in which is pronounced to be necessary for divine favour? Does it not consist of certain mysterious
truths, and these undeniably propounded in the form of dogmas,
(as in the beginning of St. John's Gospel,) so as utterly to preclude the notion of faith being but an acceptable temper of mind
or character? And if so, is it not perfectly wild to imagine that
knowledge of these doctrines is altogether unattainable? Can
we conceive the allwise Governor of man to have made a solemn
declaration of a doctrine which, after all, is so obscurely expressed, that one sense of it is not more obvious and correct than
another? Is it conceivable, that he should have pronounced a
certain faith necessary to salvation, yet that faith should vary with
individual minds, and be in each case only what each person happened to think, so that all that was necessary was to *believe* in his
own *opinion?* These strong arguments in favour of the determi-
nateness and oneness of the doctrinal revelation contained in Scripture, can only be met by appealing to the fact that men do take
different views of it; but this surely proves nothing; no more
than the vicious or secular lives of the majority of men are a
proof that one line of conduct is as pleasing to the Creator as
another. No one denies that the revealed doctrines *may* be
understood variously; but whether this possibility arises from
God's indifference to such variety, or answers the purposes of a
moral probation (which is the Catholic mode of accounting for it),
is not at all decided by the mere fact of its existing.

But here Mr. Blanco White meets us with an objection which
strikes at the root of our entire system. He is not content with
denying the existence of an unerring guide for determining the
theology of Scripture; he boldly advances a step, and maintains
that no form of human language can possibly reveal in one certain
sense those doctrines which we commonly suppose revealed; that
words are necessarily the representatives of things experienced, and
are simply words, and nothing but words, and not the symbols of
definite and appropriate ideas, when used of things belonging to

the next world. Now let it be observed clearly that this objection brings us upon quite a new ground; here it is that this ingenious writer seems to add something to the arguments of his predecessors in the same philosophy. Hitherto the position maintained by latitudinarians has chiefly been, not that Scripture may not possibly reveal to us heavenly truths in any measure, but that we cannot be sure that we individually have correctly ascertained them. The existence of an authorized interpreter, not the possibility of the revelation itself, has been questioned. But Mr. Blanco White denies of unseen truths, as well that they *can* be, as that they *have* been revealed to us under any one determinate view. Under these circumstances we shall claim of the reader the liberty of some little discursiveness, not so much, however, with the view of refuting an evident paradox, as of illustrating the subject itself.

We call it a paradox, for if anything is plain, it is that Scripture does from time to time speak dogmatically on heavenly subjects. The writer in question, tells us that nothing respecting these subjects can be conveyed in language so definitely, as not to admit of the maintenance of the most contradictory theories respecting its meaning. With what *purpose*, then, does St. John, for instance, propose for our belief, " The Word was with God and was God," if nothing definite is gained by saying it, if the matter is left as vague as if he had not said? He cannot but have meant to convey something such, that it could not be anything else; and it is surely a paradox, to use a mild word, to maintain that Scripture attempts that which it cannot possibly accomplish.

It is a paradox for another reason. Would Mr. Blanco White deny that Christians of the English Church at this day, or again, that the Catholics of the fourth and fifth centuries, had embraced one certain view of the doctrine of the Trinity, and not another? We do not say how far definite, complete, consistent; but still, so far forth as they had any view, a view of a certain kind, ascertainable, communicable, capable of being recorded? It seems hard to deny it, yet deny it he must, or else it will follow that human language *is* able to convey, circulate and transmit one certain sense of a mystery—a position which he denies in the abstract.

But this is not all. Human language, he says, cannot stand for *ideas* concerning the Divine Nature, i. e. for definite conceptions such as may be imparted to *us*. Let us, for argument's sake, grant it. Yet even then, at least it may stand for the real objects themselves. Nothing is more common in the usage of the world than what logicians call *words of second intention*, which mean nothing at all to those who are not conversant with the sciences which employ them for their own purposes. Almighty God might surely put His own meaning on human words, if it may be reverently said, and might honour them by making them speak mysteries, though not conveying thereby any notion at all to us. Here then at once we are admitted to the privilege of a dogmatic creed, in spite of Mr. Blanco White. Granting we do not *at all* understand our own words; nor did the Apostles when they were told their Lord should " rise from the dead:" they questioned *what it meant.* Still it is something after all to be intrusted with words which have a precious meaning, which we shall one day know, though we know it not now. Is it nothing to have a pledge of the next world? to have that given us which involves the inten- tion of future revelations on God's part, unless His work is to be left unfinished? We will be bold to say that this is no slight point gained, if nothing else follows; a principle of mysterious- ness, a feeling of deep reverence, of solemn expectation and wait- ing, is at once introduced into our religion. Allow, for argu- ment's sake, that we have no data for disputing about the inter- pretation of the Scripture enunciations; well, then, we have an obligation for that very reason to preserve them jealously, to regard them awfully. Is it nothing that human words have been taken into the dialect of angels, and stand for objects above human thought? Is it nothing that when thus consecrated for a superna- tural purpose, they have been given back to us to know and gaze upon, even though the outward form of them be the same as be- fore? Let all " denominations of Christians" unite as far as this, to set apart and honour the very formulæ contained in Scripture, keeping silence and forbidding all comment upon them, and they will have gone a considerable way towards the adoption of the Catholic *spirit* respecting them.

But again. We are told that human words *cannot* convey to us any idea, one and the same, of heavenly objects. Supposing it; but what then are we to say about the doctrines of natural religion? Has all the world gone wrong for ages in supposing it had a meaning in saying that God is *infinite* and *eternal?* · Yet what known objects do these words stand for? It will be an- swered that they stand only for negative ideas; that we know what is finite, and we say that the Almighty is *not* finite either in His attributes, His essence, or His existence. Truly said; but may not we gain just this from the doctrinal formulæ of the Gospel, whatever else we gain beside, viz. the *exclusion* of certain notions from our idea of the Son and Spirit? · Thus when Christ is said to be the *Son* of God, we conclude thence that He is *not* a crea- ture, *not* of a created essence, *dissimilar* from all created natures. Whether this be the right interpretation of the word *Son,* a fair.

inference from it, is another question; the instance is adduced
here only with a view of exemplifying what is at least the negative
force of the Scripture figures concerning divine objects. So
again, the words " in the bosom of the Father," surely may suffice to exclude from our theology the notion of the Son being distinct in substance and existence from the Almighty Father. We
assert it is possible that human language, as used in Scripture,
should do as much as this,—it may make the truth of doctrine lie in
one direction, not in another, whether there be an unerring arbiter
of controversies or not,—it may have a *legitimate* meaning, so as to
involve readers in guilt if they reject it, and make them amenable
hereafter for not having had an unerring and sufficient judge of
the Scripture text in their own breasts. And let it be observed
that one great portion of the Catholic symbols and expositions
actually is engaged in this department of limitation and admonition. Thus, in the creed of the Nicene Council, the anathema
was attached to those who rejected these negative attributes of
our Lord, viz. His having *no* beginning, being *not* of a created
essence, and being *un*changeable. Again; the following remarks
of a recent writer on the conduct of the Fathers in the controversy
are altogether in point, the more so as being incidentally introduced into his work. " They did not use these [figures] for more
than shadows of sacred truth, symbols *witnessing against* the speculations into which the unbridled intellect fell. Accordingly,
they were for a time inconsistent with each other in the minor
particulars of their doctrinal statements, *being far more bent on
opposing error than forming a theology.*" To the same purpose
are the remarks of Gibbon, who thought he was exposing the
Catholic creed, when he was really illustrating the foundation of
all our doctrine concerning the Divine Nature, whether in natural
or revealed religion. " In every step of the inquiry, we are compelled to feel and acknowledge the immeasurable disproportion
between the size of the object and the capacity of the human
mind. We strive to abstract the notions of time, of space, and of
matter, which so closely adhere to all the preceptions of our experimental knowledge. But as soon as we presume to reason of
infinite substance, of spiritual generation, *as often as we deduce
any positive conclusions from a negative idea*, we are involved in
darkness, perplexity, and inevitable contradiction."—*Gibbon,*
ch. xxi. Yet, strange to say, this very author, who so unhesitatingly blames positive statements concerning the mysterious
essence of God, shortly after indirectly assails the Catholics at
Nicæa for being more eager to denounce the Arians than to explain the formula of the Homousion, and for allowing the Sabel-

lians to shelter themselves under it, so that they would help them in subduing those who denied it. We do not by any means allow the correctness of this charge, but at least it represents the Catholics as doing the very thing which he had shortly before by implication recommended, confining their symbol to the expression of " a negative idea," and excluding from it " any positive conclusions." Gibbon probably was not aware (unless he was too much prejudiced to admit) that the doctrine he puts forward in the above extract with so much pomp and authoritativeness, was a principle taken for granted by the Catholic Fathers, and acted upon in their discussions. St. John Damascene, (e. g.) after speaking of Almighty God as immaterial and spiritual, proceeds, " But even this attribute gives us no conception of His *substance*, (ἀσία,) any more than His eternity, unchangeableness, and the rest; for these declare not what He is, but what He is not; whereas, when we speak of the substance of any being, we have to say what it is, not what it is not. However, as relates to God, *it is impossible to say what He is as to His substance;* and it is rather more to the purpose to contrast Him with all beings (ὄντων) when we speak of Him. . . . . . The Divine Nature, then, is infinite and incomprehensible; all we can know about it is, that it is not to be known; and *whatever positive statements we make concerning God, relate not to His nature,* but to the accompaniments of His nature. For instance, where one calls Him good, just, wise, and so on, one does not speak of His nature, but of what belongs to it."* It is clear, then, that in all their discussions concerning the ἀσία, ὁμοέσιον, and the other subjects of the Trinitarian controversy, the Fathers started with the admission that they were arriving after all at no positive conclusions on the subject, only guarding against the introduction of error.

These observations seem to have carried us as far as this; first, that whereas the New Testament contains dogmatic statements concerning the Divine Nature, proposes them for our acceptance, and guards them with anathemas, it is clearly our duty to put them forth formally, whether we be able in our present state to attach a distinct meaning to them or not, just as the Blessed Virgin pondered our Lord's words, or the Apostles His prophecy of His resurrection, or the Prophets what " the Spirit of Christ signified," without understanding what they received. Next it would appear that these statements, however inadequate to express the divine realities, yet may convey to us at least some negative information about them, whatever else they convey,—in fact, may reveal to us the mysteries of the Trinity and the Incarnation

* De Fid. Orthod. i. 4.

in the same sense in which natural religion teaches us the truths connected with the being and attributes of God; so that we are under no necessity of giving up our interpretations of the Scripture statements, unless we are bound to go further, unless we are to be forced from our notions of religion altogether—forced into Pantheism, or some more avowed form of atheistical speculation.

But we do not mean to stop here, we mean to prove the existence of an authorized interpreter of Scripture, as well as the intrinsic definiteness of its text. The obvious remark on what has hitherto been said, would be, that it justified the use, not the imposition, of extra-scriptural statements; whereas some of the articles of the creed are not simply deduced from Scripture, but are made the terms of Communion, invested with the terrors of the invisible world, and so raised from human comments into the rank of inspired truth. Let us hear Dr. Hampden * on this subject, a writer who is here introduced, not from any wish to come into collision with him, but because it has fallen to his lot to state objections to Catholic Truth in a more distinct shape than they have been found in the works of Churchmen for some time " The real causes of separation," he says, "are to be found in that confusion of theological and moral truth with religion, which is evidenced in the profession of different sects. Opinions on religious matters are regarded as identical with the objects of faith; and the zeal which belongs to dissentients in the latter, is transferred to the guiltless differences of fallible judgments. Whilst we agree in the canon of Scripture, in the very words, for the most part, from which we learn what are the objects of faith, we suffer disunion to spread among us, through the various interpretations suggested by our own reasonings on the admitted facts of Scripture. We introduce theories of the Divine Being and attributes,—theories of human nature and of the universe—principles drawn from the various branches of human philosophy—into the body itself of revealed wisdom. And we then proceed to contend for these unrevealed representations of the wisdom of God, as if it were that very wisdom as it stands forth confessed in his own living oracles. ' The wisdom that is from above' is at once ' pure ' and ' gentle.' Surely it has no resemblance to that dogmatical and sententious wisdom which theological controversy has created."—*Observations on Religious Dissent*, pp. 7, 8.

Now we quote this passage for the sake of meeting it; it contains a fair argument, which ought to be met. If a Christian is pained at it, as he may well be, it is not on account of the argument itself, or the putting it forward, or the necessity of encountering

---

* This article was written before Dr. Hampden's appointment to the Divinity Professorship at Oxford, and has been in type since March last.

it, but to see an author so confident of its correctness as to allow himself in consequence to speak evil of that which others consider as the very word of God. Those who consider that the Creeds are the word of God, as truly, though not in the same sense, as the Scripture, and derived in the same way from transmission from the Apostles, of course will be shocked at finding their expressions treated as a " dogmatical and sententious wisdom." It is surely not modest or becoming in any one, so to connect his own opinions with the truth itself, as to assume that what *he* does not consider as the true view of the case, may be at once treated with contumely; it is, in fact, but a specimen in Dr. H. of the very error which he conceives he has detected in the Church Catholic itself. We suppose he would object to a controversialist who, in arguing against a Calvinist, maintained, that if his opponent's view was the true one, the course of Providence was unjust and tyrannical. He would protest against hazarding the mercy and equity of the Divine dealings on the accident of the correctness of any human reasonings. On somewhat a similar ground we are offended at the above passage; not for the argument itself, which he is at liberty to put forth if he will; but at the lightness (as we view it) of his expressions about what others consider sacred statements, expressions which are not excusable, except a line of argument be true which we think a fallacy. " Let not him that girdeth on his harness, boast himself as he that putteth it off;" and let not the writer now in question assume the very position in debate, lest haply he be found to be scoffing against that very wisdom, which, " dogmatical and sententious " or not, has come by direct transmission independent of Scripture, from the Apostles themselves.

We say, from the Apostles; and thus we advance a claim, which if substantiated, overturns the argument of Mr. Blanco White, Dr. Hampden, Chillingworth, Hoadly, Locke, and the rest from its very foundation. The doctrinal statements of the creeds are not to be viewed as mere deductions from Scripture, any more than the historical statements of those creeds,—the article of the Homousion any more than that of the Resurrection; but as the appropriate expressions and embodying of apostolical teaching, known to be such, and handed down in the Church as such from age to age. If this be so, it is in vain to argue about " various interpretations of Scripture," " pious opinions" and " theories" upon " facts," and of " differences of fallible judgments;" it is equally vain to talk of " hieroglyphics casting shadows" and " metaphors explanatory of metaphors," and so forth. These " interpretations" turn out to be authoritative and original statements; these " opinions" are doctrines; these so-called secondary metaphors are primary symbols given by Apostles or ex-

pressive of their known teaching. Will it be here said that now
in turn we are boasting before our proof? No: we are com-
plaining, and on this score, that this view which we consider
the true one, has not attracted the attention either of Mr. Blanco
White or Dr. Hampden.

This is the more remarkable in the case of the latter of these
two writers, for he approaches the view in question, but strangely
enough in one who has a name for learning, he notices it only to
misunderstand it. He speaks thus of the doctrine of the Church
of Rome. " In the Roman Catholic Church .... the question"
(whether conclusions from Scripture have in themselves the authoritative force of real divine truth) " is formally decided in the affirmative, by the authority assigned to tradition in conjunction with
Scripture; for *tradition is nothing more* than expositions of the
text of Scripture, *reasoned out by the Church* and embodied in a
code of doctrine."—p. 4. This, we confess, is to us information; as we suspect it would be to Bellarmine also or any other
Roman controversialist. We suspect that they would altogether
disavow all claim to impose mere deductions from Scripture, as
divine truths, in spite of their assumed infallibility in matters of
doctrine. Rather it is one of their charges against Protestant
communions, that these do impose, as matters of faith, what after
all they believe only on the assurance of private judgment. They
profess that their traditions exist quite independently of Scripture;
that had Scripture never been written, they would have existed
still, and that they form a collateral not a subordinate source of
information to the Church. We must repeat our utter surprise
at such a statement as the above, from such a quarter, when even
the popular work of Bishop Jebb would have warned Dr. Hampden
of its incorrectness. " The Church of Rome maintains," he
says in his Essay on the Peculiar Character of the English Church,
" not only that there are two rules of belief, but these two rules
are *co-ordinate:* that there is an *unwritten,* no less than a written
word of God; and that the authority of the former is *alike defini-
tive with the authority of the latter.*" Reluctant as we may be
to set before our readers a truth as plain as the fact of the existence of the Roman Church itself,—its maintenance of the *intrinsic*
and *independent* authority of the unwritten Word,—yet we must
insist upon it when writers indulge themselves in so extravagant
a liberty of speculation. Let us turn to the words of Bellarmine.
" Totalis regula fidei," he says, (De Verb. Dei non Script. 12),
est Verbum Dei, sive *revelatio* Dei Ecclesiæ facta, quæ dividitur
in duas regulas partiales, Scripturam et *traditionem.*" And he
has a chapter on the tests by which we ascertain what traditions
are apostolical. Again, among the uses of tradition he places

that of *interpreting* Scripture doctrine. " Sæpissime Scriptura ambigua et perplexa est, ut nisi ab aliquo, qui errare non possit, explicetur, non possit intelligi; igitur sola non sufficit. Exempla sunt plurima: nam æqualitas divinarum personarum, processio Spiritus Sancti à Patre et Filio, ut ab uno principio, peccatum originis, descensus Christi ad inferos, et multa similia *deducuntur quidem ex sacris litteris, sed non adeo facile,* ut si *solis* pugnandum sit Scripturæ testimoniis, *nunquam lites cum protervis finiri possint.* Notandum est enim, duo esse in Scripturâ, voces scriptas, et sensum in eis inclusum..... Ex his duobus primum habetur ab omnibus; quicunque enim novit litteras, potest legere Scripturas: at secundum non habent omnes, nec possumus in plurimis locis certi esse de secundo, *nisi accedat traditio.*—Ibid. 4. In like manner Bossuet, (Exposition, ch. 17, 18,) " Jesus Christ having laid the foundation of his Church by preaching, *the unwritten word was consequently the first rule* of Christianity; and, when the writings of the New Testament were added to it, its *authority was not forfeited on that account;* which makes us receive with *equal veneration all that hath been taught by the Apostles,* whether in writing or by word of mouth .... And a most certain mark that a doctrine *comes from the Apostles,* is, when all Christian Churches embrace it, without its being in the power of any one to show when it had a beginning .... Bound inseparably, as we are, to the authority of the Church, by the Scriptures which we receive from her hand, we learn tradition also from her; and by means of tradition the true sense of the Scriptures. For which reason *the Church openly professes, that she says nothing from herself; that she invents no new doctrine;* she only *declares* the Divine Revelation, by the interior direction of the Holy Ghost, who is given to her as her teacher." Here mention of the third person of the Blessed Trinity is introduced, not as aiding the Church to interpret Scripture, but as guiding her into a right discrimination and application of apostolical tradition. The reader probably is by this time tired of authorities, or we might refer to the words of the Tridentine Decree, upon which the foregoing passages are the comment.* And this matter is perfectly understood by clear-headed men, as Hales and Chillingworth, who, though they deny the fact, yet understand the Roman Church's assumption, that its tradition comes directly from the Apostles, independently of Scripture; whereas Dr. Hampden

---

* Sacro-sancta .... Tridentina Synodus ... omnes libros tam veteris quàm novi Testamenti .... necnon *traditiones* ipsas, tum ad fidem tum ad mores pertinentes, tanquam *vel ore tenus à Christo* vel *à Spiritu Sancto dictatas,* et *continuâ successione in Ecclesiâ Catholicâ conservatas,* pari pietatis affectu ac reverentiâ suscipit et veneratur.— *Sess. quart.*

has ruled it in half a sentence that "tradition is *nothing more* than expositions of the text of Scripture, *reasoned out by the Church,* and embodied in a code of doctrine;" stating what is neither agreeable to the fact nor to the Roman view of it; for no one will say, for instance, that the doctrine of indulgences either is and is professed by the Romanists to be primarily reasoned out from Scripture. Nay the decree of the Council of Trent expressly says "Cum potestas conferendi indulgentias *à Christo Ecclesiæ concessa sit,* atque hujusmodi potestate, divinitus sibi traditâ, *antiquissimis temporibus illa usa fuerit,*" &c., not a word being said of any Scripture sanction for the use of them. Indeed this is the very point of difference between the Romanists and ourselves. The English Church no where denies the existence of apostolical traditions, and their authority in the interpretation of Scripture; so far we do *not* dissent from the Romanists. But what we do deny is the independent and substantive power of tradition in matters of faith, where Scripture is silent,—the right of the Church to impose doctrines on the *mere* authority of tradition, which the Council of Trent has done, for instance, in the above cited decree on indulgences. So that it would seem that Dr. Hampden has not only passed over the question of the apostolicity of the creeds, in which we conceive lies the refutation of his peculiar theory; but he has actually missed that very point in the Roman Church's doctrine, in which she differs from our own.

Here we take leave of Dr. H. for the present, and should feel pleasure if we could be saved the necessity of recurring to him. Other objections will be made to the notion of the authority of the creeds, as a contemporaneous comment upon Scripture, which we must try to clear off as expeditiously as we can. When an educated man of the present day first hears it said that the creeds are the expressions of apostolical traditions, he is at once annoyed, and listens with suspicion. Now why is this? First it is because he has never heard the view stated before, and he feels that doubt which spontaneously rises when the mind is put out of its usual way of thinking. He does not know what the principle may lead to; he does not see how far it may carry him towards popery; he does not see its bearings, its limitations, or its grounds. This is all very natural; yet on second thoughts perhaps he will take heart and be more rational. We say "more rational," for there are certainly fair grounds of reason, prior to evidence, to desire, nay almost to expect, such an informant as we are offering to him about the meaning of Scripture. Such a guide is surely very much wanted. Scripture is not written in a dogmatic form, though there are dogmatic passages in it; it contains the portions and tokens of a theological system, without itself being such. It

promises dogmatic statements without fully supplying them. What
then is so natural as to suppose that Divine Mercy has somewhere
or other supplied this desideratum? and what antecedent improbability is there in the creeds containing the heads and subjects of
the teaching required? It is worth remarking, however, that this
very character of Scripture, which seems by its form and matter
to point at the creeds and the traditionary teaching connected
with them as its due complement, has been paradoxically brought
as an argument for dispensing with them. *Assuming* that in Scripture we have the model and type of all Christian teaching, it has
been decided, that since the creeds, as being dogmatic, are unlike
Scripture, that therefore they are no part of Christianity, which
is about as rational as to conclude (according to St. Paul's illustration) that because the eye is not the hand, therefore it is not
of the body; or because England has a king, therefore its constitution is a development of the monarchical principle; or that because it has popular institutions, therefore it has no king. We must
surely take things as we find them in matter of fact, we must deny
ourselves in theories, (latitudinarian as well as what Dr. Hampden
calls " scholastic,") and use *à priori* reasonings not to prove but
to recommend our conclusions. Moreover, in the present instance,
it is humbly conceived that antecedent probability, as far as it goes,
is for, not against, the apostolical authority of the creeds. Dr.
Hampden came into our minds in this last sentence, because here
too he has indulged in a seeming paradox as on other points. Speaking in depreciation of dogmatic statements, he uses an argument
which tells so fatally against himself, that readers must look over it
twice to be sure that they have not mistaken his meaning. " I ask,"
he says in his Bampton Lectures, in a passage which has been
much quoted of late, " whether it *is likely* that an Apostle would
have adopted the form of an epistolary communication for im-
parting mysterious propositions to disciples with whom he enjoyed the opportunity of personal intercourse, and to whom he
had already ' declared the whole counsel of God?' "—p. 374.
This argument, let it be observed, is to go to prove that Christianity is not dogmatic, because Scripture is not; and we do not
know which most to admire—the boldness of the main position,
or the felicity of a mode of handling it, which oversets the reasoning on which it is founded. It presents a curious contrast to the
reasoning of the present Archbishop of Dublin in his Essay on
Creeds; who advocates the same theory on the ground that there
is no Apostolical teaching now extant, thus failing characteris-
tically, not in the reasoning, which is most intelligible, but in
the matter of fact.

It will serve at once to explain and to defend the position we have taken up against Dr. Hampden, to express ourselves in the language of the learned and soberminded prelate, who is at present in the possession of the see of Lincoln. " If we mistake not the signs of the times," he observes in his work upon Tertullian, " the period is not far distant when the whole controversy between the English and Romish Churches will be revived, and all the points in dispute again brought under review. Of those none is more important than the question respecting tradition; and it is therefore most essential that they who stand forth as the defenders of the Church of England should take a correct and rational view of the subject, the view in short which was taken by our divines at the Reformation. *Nothing was more remote from their intention than indiscriminately to condemn all tradition.* . . . What our reformers opposed was the notion that men must, upon the *mere* authority of tradition, receive, *as necessary to salvation,* doctrines *not contained in Scripture* . . . . With respect to the particular doctrines, in defence of which the Roman Catholics appeal to tradition, our reformers contended that some were directly at variance with Scripture; and that others, far from being supported by an unbroken chain of tradition from the apostolic age, were of very recent origin, and utterly unknown to the early Fathers . . . In this, as in other instances, they wisely adopted a middle course; they neither bowed submissively to the authority of tradition, nor yet rejected it altogether. We at the present day must tread in their footsteps and imitate their moderation, if we intend to combat our Roman Catholic adversaries with success."—p. 297, ed. 1826. In another place he speaks still more explicitly. " Tertullian," he says, as if citing the statement of a writer he was animadverting on, " appeals to apostolical tradition, to a rule of faith, not *originally* deduced from Scripture, but delivered by the Apostles orally to the Churches which they founded, and regularly transmitted from them to his own time. How, I would ask, is this appeal inconsistent with the principles of the Church of England, which declares *only* that Holy Scripture *contains* all things necessary to salvation? Respecting the source, from which the rule of faith was *originally* deduced, our Church is silent."—p. 587.

Granting, however, there was such an apostolical tradition (*e. g.* concerning the doctrine of the Trinity) it may be a question with many persons whether we at this day know for certain what it was. The Creed indeed bids fairest for being reputed such; but though definite in its articles and of primitive antiquity, a question might arise as to its strict apostolicity. On the other hand it might be plausibly asked, if even the Creed be not for certain of apostolic origin, what doctrinal statements can safely be considered as such. It may be right therefore in this place to offer some brief remarks on the *relation* existing between the Creed and apostolical tradition; and here again we encounter at once an observation of Dr. Hampden's. He observes that " it will be said by some advocates of our Church that .... the doctrines expressed in its formularies .... are derived from the confessors and doctors of the primitive ages of the Church—they have descended to us in pure stream from the fountains of orthodoxy, &c." To this he replies; " Is this correct in matter of fact? Are the doctrines *as expressed in our formularies,* (for this is the point at issue, and not whether the divine truths which they are intended to guard, are the same or not,) precisely those which the primitive Church declared? If we look to the course of controversy we must see, I think, that the dogmas have taken their mould and complexion from the discussions of subsequent periods, until they reached a speculative accuracy of expression to which subsequent discussions could not add."—*Obs.* pp. 23, 24.

Not for the sake of interfering with Dr. Hampden, but for the sake of an important question, we will here say a few words in explanation of this subject; are the dogmatic statements of the Creeds, or are they not, of Apostolic origin? the case seems to be as follows:—

It is quite certain from the writings of Irenæus, Tertullian, and Vincent, not to mention other authorities, that from the times of the Apostles, there was a certain body of doctrine in the Church Catholic called the dogma fidei or depositum transmitted from bishop to bishop, and taught to every member of it. It was too vast, too minute, too complicated to be put into writing, at least in times of persecution and proselytism; it was for the most part conveyed orally, and the safeguard against its corruption was, first, the unanimity of the various branches of the Church in declaring it; next the canon of Scripture which acted as a touchstone, not indeed measuring it and limiting it, but coinciding with it in all its greater points and verifying both its outlines and occasionally its details also. As regards its outlines this dogma, or regula fidei, as it was called, was from the first fixed in a set form of words called the Creed, the articles of which were heads and memoranda of the Church's teaching, and as such were rehearsed and accepted by every candidate for baptism by way of avowing his adherence to that entire doctrine which the Church was appointed to dispense. These articles varied somewhat in the different branches of the Church; but, inasmuch as they were but heads and tokens of the Catholic doctrine, and when developed and commented on implied each other, this argued no difference in the tradition of which they were the formal record. This account of the matter, if correct, shows us the mistake of considering, as some have done, that the fact of the Creed being the initiatory confession of the Church, involved a latitudinarian principle in primitive times. This is maintained by Episcopius, who argues as if because the words "Son of God" stood nakedly in some of the early creeds, therefore they might allowably be taken in any sense which the humour of individuals imagined, as well as in that one Catholic interpretation in which the Nicene fathers afterwards developed it.* Bishop Bull shows this was not true as regards that high article of doctrine, and the same might be showed of all the rest; so that if one wished a clear and available definition of heresy, peihaps one could not find a better than this, that it is a wilful rejection of any article of the Creed in that sense in which the early Church understood and taught it. And here, by the bye, we have light cast at once on a question which may, for what we know, perplex us in this day before many years are over. It is notorious there are persons in the Church who wish its recognition of baptismal regeneration to be removed. Now inasmuch as one of the articles of the Nicene Creed witnesses to the "one baptism for the remission of sins," and since any how the doctors of the early Church would so explain the less complete form of words which occurs in the Apostles' Creed, "the forgiveness of sins," it follows, if the above view is correct, that to deny baptismal regeneration is *heresy*, and that a Church which indulged its members in such denial would have forfeited its trust and have done much to deprive it of any claim upon our allegiance. But to return to the subject immediately before us:—it would seem from what has been said that the very articles of the Creed are not Apostolic in such a sense that we can pronounce them to be literally spoken by the Apostles; but they are some among a great multitude of statements of a similar kind, none of which indeed can be identified as literally Apostolic, but which altogether go to convey that view which is Apostolic, and might be ascertained to be Apostolic in the same way in which we become acquainted with each others' views in any matter, not relying on this or that expression, but mastering it from the general bearing and scope of each others' conversation; and this is the view to be taken of certain words, as ὁμοούσιος, θεοτόκος and the like, which at different times were assumed as the criterion of certain doctrines which required the seal of public authority. They are representations, more or less arbitrary, as the case might be, of the Apostolical tradition on

---

* "Symbola certe Ecclesiæ ex ipso Ecclesiæ sensu, non ex hæreticorum cerebello exponenda sunt. Symbola Ecclesiæ non tenet, qui aliter quam Ecclesia intelligit."— Bull. Judicium Eccl. Cath. c. 5, § 10.

the subject of them. They were assumed after a careful consideration and ascertaining of the doctrine which they symbolized. Received opinions were compared together, between the Churches, as they might now-a-days. Bishop compared notes with bishop, and brought out his meaning in the clearest and fullest form. This implied time and accurate thought, freedom of discussion, questioning, reviewing, and all not for the sake of forming a new doctrine, but in order to ascertain the old. The next question was how this one and the same sense in which all parts of the Church were found to agree could be best expressed and perpetuated; and the word or phrase selected for the purpose, and generally from the diction of antiquity, became the expression and representative of the Apostolical tradition, without having any special claim above others to be considered of Apostolical origin itself.*

It has taken a long time indeed to clear our ground; but now at length we hope to proceed without impediment to the *proof* of the doctrine which we have been hitherto explaining. After all, it will be asked, *is* there any ascertainable Apostolical Tradition? Let us see.

First, every one knows that a certain doctrine concerning our Lord's nature is taught *at present* all over the Church, and that this, in matter of fact, was not gained from Scripture in the first instance by the existing generation (though it is fully attested and verified by Scripture), but from the teaching of the generation immediately preceding. This process of transmission and reception has gone on, at least for many centuries; nor is there anything antecedently absurd in the notion, nay it is agreeable to what meets us at first sight, that the process should have been so conducted, independently of Scripture, from the first. Of course, when we come to examine into the course of the history, decisive objections to this supposition may, for what we know, present themselves; but there is nothing in the actual face of things to throw discredit upon it. On the contrary, there is this strong probability *against* the doctrine ever having been strictly *deduced* from Scripture, that it is not sufficiently on the *surface* of the sacred text to force itself as Scriptural upon the observation of men at large. At first sight it is not likely, to say the least, we think no candid man will say it is likely, that the Catholic doctrine, systematized as it is, should be in matter of fact a mere deduction from Scripture, even though it be (as it most surely is) quite consistent with it. To use a familiar illustration, it is like a key to a lock, of independent workmanship, but subordi- +

---

* Vide Vincent. Lerin. Comm. 32 fin.

nate use. We do not say that no acute and subtle mind, no one individual, might not draw it forth and develope it from Scripture as we find it in the Church, nay, add other and more complicated distinctions to it; it is its *general* adoption from so early an age which proves incontrovertibly, that, whether it be by revelation or not, whether it be (as we believe) from the Apostles, or (as others have said) from the Platonists, or Paganism, or in whatever way, it is from sources historically distinct from the written word which is the verification of it. The instances which happen daily of the *differences* of view which take place as to the doctrine, when men, however learned and clearheaded, *do* attempt to deduce from Scripture their "pious opinions," as Dr. Hampden terms them, prove that the knowledge of it which we enjoy does not come from the mere study of Scripture. Let us now approach nearer to this phenomenon and view it at that date, when even heretics will allow it did exist, whatever questions they raise about the earlier centuries, we mean in the fourth century. Assuming that the Church's belief now is the same as its belief then, let us observe what took place in the year 325. At that date, in consequence of a controversy which occurred on the subject of our Lord's Divinity between the bishop of Alexandria and one of his clergy, a council was held of 318 bishops collected from all parts of Christendom. No such general meeting had ever before taken place; no opportunity had before occurred for adjusting their notions one with another. Yet out of this number so collected above 300 agreed in the maintenance of that doctrine which is now known by the title of Orthodox. This is the phenomenon, and on it we make the following remarks.

First, then, let it be observed that no external authority interfered to incline them to the doctrine to which they subscribed. Constantine had originally considered the dispute which led to their meeting as little better than a question of words, and had written to Alexandria to order both parties engaged in it to tolerate each other and keep quiet. On finding however the general opinion before and at the council in favour of orthodoxy, he changed his course, though he abandoned thereby his personal friends, and zealously defended the side professed by the majority. After a few years he gradually changed back again, and exposed the cause of orthodoxy to the revenge of a disappointed faction. Constantius, who succeeded him, took a still more decided part against it. Thus no political influences can be assigned as the cause of the general agreement, such as for instance may be objected to the unanimity at Trent.* On the other hand there

---

* Or again, as at Ariminum, where (A. D. 359) four hundred bishops *under compulsion from Constantius*, signed a formulary short of the Nicene.

were known and long existing rivalries between the separate
Churches which took part in the council. Before this era there
had been serious disputes between Rome and Ephesus, Rome
and Carthage, Rome and Antioch; and if it be said that the bishop
of Rome himself was not at the council, only delegates from him,
in the same proportion as his influence did not act there, is it remarkable that he should have so cordially and zealously co-ope-
rated in the West in carrying its decrees into effect? Further,
there was an old jealousy between Alexandria and Antioch.
Moreover, there was at that time a schismatical communion, called
the Novatian, of about 70 years standing, spreading through Asia
Minor and Africa, as well as Italy; and represented at the council, at Constantine's instance, by one of their bishops. This
communion is known to have held the Homousion as zealously as
the Church Catholic, and to have afterwards suffered persecution
on that account from the Arians. It may be observed that of the
two historians of those times, both of whom were laymen, one of
them belonged, or at least was inclined to this sect.

In the next place, these fathers at Nicæa did not at all profess
to be giving merely their own sense of Scripture; but to be
bearing witness to a simple matter of fact, that they had *received*
their doctrine from the generation before them, and knew of no
other as ever existing in their respective churches. On the contrary, it is observable that the handful of men who advocated
Arianism at the Council, did not make any such appeal to an
uninterrupted tradition. They did but profess to argue from
Scripture; or, if they went further, it was but to say they had
been so taught by a certain Presbyter of Antioch, whose disciples
they avowed themselves to be. Further than this they did not
venture. This contrast is strikingly referred to in one of the
treatises of Athanasius. He remarks, with somewhat of point,
on the circumstance of the Arians dating one of their Confessions
of Faith by the consulate of the current year. " Having composed," he said, " a creed according to their tastes, they headed
it with mention of the consul, and the month, and the day; as if
to suggest to all men of understanding, that now from the time
of Constantius, not before, their faith dates its origin. . . . They
say, ' We publish the Catholic faith,' and then they add consulate, month, and day; that, as the prophets marked the period
of their histories and their ministries by dates," alluding to Isa.
i. 1, and the like, " so they might be accurate in the date of their
faith. Nay, I wish they had confined themselves to speak of
their own faith, for in fact it did then begin, and had let alone
the *Catholic* faith; whereas they wrote, not ' Thus we believe,'
but ' We publish the Catholic faith.' . . . On the other hand [at

Nicæa] many as were the framers of the creed, they ventured nothing such as these three or four men have ventured. They did not care to head it with consulate, month, and day; and, whereas about the Easter feast they said, ' This is the decree,' they did not use ' decree' about the faith, but said, ' Thus believes the Catholic church;' nor had they any delay in stating what they believed, *in proof that their notions were not novel, but aposto-lical.* And what they set down was no discovery of theirs, but the doctrine which was taught by the apostles."* It will be observed, that in this extract the fact (which to scholars is sufficiently notorious) of the contrast between the Catholics as witnesses, and the Arians as inventors, is assumed by the author as so familiar to his readers, that he is able to taunt even the indifferent proceedings of the latter as retaining the savour of it.

Nor must it be supposed that the doctrine thus appealed to by the Catholics was a mere vague and floating opinion; such as may now exist among ourselves, whether true or false, that the Papists keep no faith with heretics, or that the Bible only is the religion of Protestants. On the contrary, it was a fixed and recognized doctrine, as was above noticed, formally committed to the guardianship of every bishop every where, and by him made over to his successor. There is no mistaking about this : we know that such a *depositum* existed, and such a *traditio*, or transmission, was formally observed in and from the apostolic age, and we know what the subject of it was. St. John speaks anxiously concerning the duty of guarding in its purity "'the doctrine of Christ;" St. Paul of the " one faith;" and St. Jude of " contending for" this one " faith once committed." If we would know the matter of it, the fathers who immediately follow, show us; to say nothing of Scripture itself; referring to the creed as containing its outlines. † There can be no doubt, then, that each branch of the Church had its own distinct line of traditionary teaching from the Apostles ;—and that these branches were much, nay obstinately, attached to their respective traditions, and reluctant, on grounds of conscience, to yield them to each other, is proved by such differences in minor matters as occurred before the date of the council. For instance, the above-mentioned dispute between Ephesus and Rome arose from the circumstance, that the tradition of the former about the time of keeping Easter, derived from St. John, differed from that of the latter, derived from St. Peter and St. Paul. Again, sixty years later, the tradition of Rome concerning heretical baptism is represented as differing from that of Asia Minor. In both controversies each

---

* De Synod. 3—5.　　　† Iren. de Hæres. i. 10. Tertull. de Præscr. 15.

party religiously refused to yield to the other. The unanimity, then, in the Council of Nicæa was not a mutual sacrifice, of differences for the sake of peace, it was not merely the decision of a majority, it was simply and plainly the joint testimony of the many branches of the Church, as independent witnesses, to the separate existence in each of them, from time immemorial, of that doctrine in which they found each other to agree.

Perhaps, however, it will be surmised, that this identity of the tradition in various places was the gradual growth of the intermediate period, during which the vague statements of the apostles, similar to those in Scripture, were made accurate and complete. This too is untenable. For, not to mention the existence of the Novatians, who had split off within 150 years of St. John's death, and yet held the Nicene doctrine as precisely as the Catholics, it so happens that in the very age of the apostles a sect arose external to the Church, which at once brought into dispute all those more subtle questions concerning the nature of Christ, which were agitated within the Church during the fourth and fifth centuries. We confidently affirm, that there is not an article in the Athanasian creed concerning the Incarnation, which is not anticipated in the controversy with the Gnostics. There is no question which the Apollinarian or the Nestorian heresy raised, which may not be decided in the words of Irenæus and Tertullian. We are not at this moment determining *which* side in the dispute was taken by the apostles and their immediate disciples,—we only say that the after questions *were* questions then; so that the Catholic doctrine, if not apostolic, is not a mere *addition* to apostolic statements, but a plain going counter to them, in one way or another,—whether, that is, the Apostles be supposed to have shut up these questions in the words of the creed, or to have explained them differently. Thus, on this supposition, we have to account for the phenomenon of this one and the same substitution every where of a new doctrine, in the course of 220 years, in times of persecution, in times of doctrinal controversies, among people of different languages, attachments, and religious attainments, and in spite of the safeguard of episcopal transmission; all this, moreover, altogether silently, without record of the change, or assignable reason why it should be made any where, on tenable reference to any external school or doctrine; lastly, with the unaccountable belief on the part of the fathers in the council, that their own view was that which the apostles had bequeathed them. Still further, it must be recollected, that they had in their different Churches the writings of Christian teachers during the intermediate time, much of which is lost now, but which made them judges, virtually infallible, of the doctrine of

the Church from the first.   Hence too an additional argument
results even at this day; for what remains of these writings serves
the purpose of verifying the correctness of the tradition attested
at Nicæa, just as we might inspect a money account, and, to
satisfy ourselves, here and there cast up a sum, or make a calculation, in a balance sheet, which checks itself without such experiments.   Alexandria, Carthage, Syria, Gaul, and Rome, thus
bear independent witness, during the interval of 200 years, to the
unanimous testimony extant at the end of it.   And what adds.
incalculably to this testimony of the Ante-Nicene writers, is their
stating the Catholic doctrine, not on the sole authority of their
own respective Churches, though that were sufficient, but as the
one doctrine even then preached and confessed all over Christendom.

This, then, is what is meant by Catholic tradition, and thus it
attests the proper divinity of Christ, and anathematizes Socinianism and all other heresy on the subject; not by arguing and
deducing from Scripture, as Dr. Hampden would say, but as
being a separate apostolic information, parallel with Scripture,
verified by, but not subsisting in it.   We know from Scripture
that there was a certain doctrine called " the doctrine of Christ,"
which was enforced by an anathema; we find it contempora-
neously described in the primitive creed by the words the " Son
of God;"—we find it tried, discussed, and sifted by the Gnostics, who arose even in apostolic times;—we find it committed to
the keeping of the bishops of the Church as a perpetual legacy,
and all along in connexion with the creed; at the end of 200
years after the last apostle's death, we find it publicly declared,
still with reference to the creed, and attested by 300 bishops from
various parts of the world, as that which had ever been preached
and taught among them; lastly, we hear of no other doctrine on
the subject, even professing to come from the apostles.   Can we
for an instance doubt, what shadow of pretence have we for
doubting, that the doctrine so declared was that very truth which
the apostles consigned to the Churches as saving?   What cause of
alarm have we, though it be proved by Chillingworth, or Mr.
Blanco White, ever so convincingly, that Protestant communities, as such, have no right to impose articles of faith, or that
uninspired men have no power to add to the metaphorical expressions found in Scripture?   By this review of the case, we are
as certain that the apostles had that definite view which we call
orthodoxy, as we are that we ourselves have it; as certain that
Arians or Socinians do not agree with the apostles, as that they
do not agree with us; as much bound to apply to them the apostolic anathema, as we are sure that there were speculators to
whom the apostles applied it.

And here it occurs to us to notice the obvious mistake of many writers who argue against *Catholic* tradition from the errors of the fathers, whatever they are, in recording, as *individuals*, matters of fact. Thus the notion entertained by Irenæus that our Saviour lived to be near fifty years old, Clement's assertion that St. Paul was married and the like, are urged as if a valid argument against doctrines built, not upon reports or rumours, but on the *agreement* of Christians in all times and places. Even Beausobre is not free from this mistake.

Perhaps the reader may consider enough has been said on this subject; yet, before dismissing it, he must be prevailed on to attend to one or two illustrations of it, which may press on him the *naturalness* of the argument.

First, we take a passage from the work which we have placed at the head of this article. The Clergyman objects to his Unitarian brother, that the mass of men as being unlearned cannot safely decide about the doctrine of the Trinity from reading Scripture, the original of which is in Greek. He is answered in the following words, which *mutatis mutandis* are but a statement of the argument from tradition, which we have been drawing out.

" I have never crossed the Atlantic, and cannot know, but by reading voyages and histories, or by oral communications, that any land exists there; voyagers and historians have often lied or erred; yet I am as much convinced of the existence of a continent there, as I am of the field now before my eyes. Do I then rely upon the testimony of men, who may be deceivers? No, it is not in the nature of things, it is absolutely impossible that such concurrence should take place in the relation of falsehoods. The history of the death and resurrection of Christ was written in a language as unknown to me as are opposite shores of the ocean I have never traversed; *yet the concurrence of translators is as convincing to me as if the account were in my native language, and I do not rely on human authority.*"—p. 155.

Why would not this disputant consider the Fathers *as translators* of Scripture as regards Catholic doctrine? Again, let us refer to Paley's argument for the truth of the received Christian *history*, as contained in the seventh chapter of the first part of his Evidences. It will be found that what he there advances for the *facts* of the religion may be transferred, with little alteration, in proof of its *doctrines*. He begins by asking, " Whether the story which Christians have *now* be the story which Christians had then;" which has been our very question as regards the doctrines of our religion. He answers in the affirmative upon these four considerations:—First, because " there exists no trace or vestige of any other story." " There is not a document, or scrap of account, either contemporary with the commencement of Christianity, or extant within many ages after that commencement, which assigns a history substantially different from ours." Now this is clearly fulfilled as regards doctrine also. It is true there were some few who taught differently from the Catholic faith, but even they did so, not as witnessing an historical fact or from tradition, but as claiming to interpret Scripture for themselves; a ground of argument which does not interfere with the argument from tradition. Or, again, if they appealed to tradition, as the Gnostics did, it was to a secret tradition, known and delivered only by some few of the Apostles, and professedly contrary to their public teaching; a pretence which was evidently adopted to evade the difficulty of their opposition to Catholic tradition, and even grants, in the very form of it, that apostolical tradition was against them. The only real exception which we remember, is the small heretical party at Rome, in the beginning of the third century, which boldly pronounced their heresy to be apostolical; but even these soon abandoned their claim. Paley proceeds:— " the remote, brief and incidental notices of the affair, which are found in heathen writers, so far as they do go, go along with us." The same may be said of the doctrine also; Pliny witnesses to the worship of Christ as a God by His disciples, and Celsus objects it to them. Secondly, " the whole series of Christian writers, from the first age of the institution down to the present, in their discussions, apologies, arguments and controversies, proceed upon the general story which the Scriptures contain, and upon no other. This argument will appear to be of great force when it is known that we are able to trace back the series of writers to a contact with the historical books of the New Testament, and to the age of the first emissaries of the religion, and to deduce it, by an unbroken continuation, from that end of the train to the present." This surely applies word for word to the received doctrine also. He proceeds—" Now that the original story, the story delivered by the first preachers of the institution should have died away so entirely as to have left no record or memorial of its existence, although so many records and memorials of the time and transactions remain; and that another story should have stepped into its place and gained exclusive possession of the belief of all who professed themselves disciples of the institution, is beyond any example of the corruption of even oral tradition, and still less consistent with the experience of written history; and this improbability, which is very great, is rendered still greater by the reflection, that no such change as the oblivion of one story and the substitution of another, took place in any future period of the Christian era." Here Paley even adds a consideration which we had overlooked in the argument. " Thirdly, the religious rites and usages that prevailed amongst the early disciples of Christianity, were such as belonged to and sprung out of the narrative now in our hands; which accordancy shows, that it was the narrative upon which these persons acted, and which they had received from their teachers." The same holds good as regards the doctrines also; Baptism witnesses to the doctrine of the Trinity, and the Eucharist grows out of the doctrines of the Incarnation and Atonement; i. e. these rites arise from doctrines *such as* those which we at this day believe to have been Apostolic. Lastly, " the story was public at the time" the Gospels were written; " the Christian community was already in possession of the substance and principal parts of the narrative. The Gospels were not the original cause of the Christian history being believed, but were themselves among the consequences of that belief." Paley says this to show that the story, coinciding though it did in its details with the Scripture narrative, yet rested on authority wider and other than it. The same may be said of Catholic doctrine also. While no one can deny that at least it is reconcilable with the sacred text, our opponents even contend that it was not the object of that text to enforce it, nor that it is built upon it. Paley concludes by maintaining that " these four circumstances are sufficient to support our assurance that the story which we have now is in general the story which Christians had at the beginning;" meaning by *in general* " in its texture and in its principal facts;" and we can desire nothing more to be granted to us as regards the received doctrines of the Trinity and Incarnation.

Illustrations might be multiplied on this subject without end; one more shall be added as afforded by the universal practice of baptising infants. " Since the proofs drawn by consequences from some places of Scripture, for any one side of this question,", says Wall, in his preface to his well-known work on infant baptism, " are not so plain as to hinder the arguments drawn from other places for the other side from seeming considerable .... it is no wonder that the readers of Scripture, at this distance from the Apostles' times, have fallen into contrary sentiments about the meaning of our Saviour's command, and the practice of the Apostles in reference to this baptizing of infants. When there is in Scripture a plain command to proselyte or make disciples all nations, baptizing them, but the method of doing it is not in all particulars expressly directed, it not being particularly mentioned whether they were to admit into this discipleship and baptism the infants of those that were converted .... or whether they were to proceed in a new way, and baptize only the adult persons themselves, there is nobody that will doubt but that the Apostles knew what was to be done in this case; and, consequently, that the Christian Churches in their time did as they should do in this matter. And since the Apostles lived, some of them, to near the end of the first century, and St. John something beyond it, and had in their own time propagated the Christian faith and practice into so many countries, it can never sink into the head of any considering man, but that, such Christians as were ancient men about 100 or 150 years after that time of the Apostles' death, which is the year of Christ 200 or 250, must easily know whether infant baptism were in use at the time of the Apostles' death or not; because the fathers of some of them, and grandfathers of most of them, were born before that time, and were themselves infants in the Apostles' days, and so were baptized then in their infancy, if that were then the order, or their baptism deferred to adult age, if that were the use then," &c. Thus, it is plain, that those who deny the force of the argument from Catholic tradition in the case of the great gospel doctrines, go far to deprive us of the privilege of administering baptism to our children.

Our discussion has run to an exorbitant length; however, before parting with us, it may interest the reader to observe how the fathers are accustomed to speak of those *private* and *individual* judgments upon the high doctrines of Scripture, which Dr. Hampden benignantly styles "pious opinions," "guiltless differences," "theories of the Divine being and attributes," or, more harshly, as a " dogmatical and sententious wisdom," meaning thereby, if he can, to strike at sacred statements which are happily beyond the reach of scorner or disputant. " Perhaps some one may ask," says Vincent of Lerins, " whether the heretics also do not make use of testimonies from Holy Scripture? Yes, indeed, they do use them, and lay great stress on them, for you may see them ready quoters of each book of God's sacred Law, the books of Moses, of Kings, the Psalms, the Apostles, the Evangelists, the Prophets. Whether, indeed, they are among their own people, or among strangers, in private or in public, discoursing or writing, at convivial meetings or in the open ways, they *never at all advance any of their peculiar positions, without attempting to express it in Scripture language. . . .* If any one of the heretics be asked, how he proves that we ought to abandon the universal and ancient faith of the Church Catholic, he will promptly reply, ' It is written,' and on the spot is ready with a thousand texts and proofs, some from the Law, some from the Psalms, some from the Apostles, some from the Prophets, with the view of precipitating the unhappy soul, by a new and perverse interpretation of them, from the secure pinnacle of Catholicism into the gulf of heresy." And in like manner Tertullian, after repeating the Creed, which he calls the rule or system of faith, and to which it is the Christian's duty to adhere, proceeds to caution us against mere arguing or deducing from Scripture, whether for ourselves or in controversy. " Thy faith," he says, " hath made thee whole," not a troubling of the Scriptures. Faith rests in the rule [*i. e.* the Creed]. You have the Law,—and salvation in the keeping of it. But this cross-examining of Scripture springs from restlessness; having its only glory in the display of skill. Let restlessness yield to faith; glory among men to salvation of the soul . . . As for that person, if there be such, for whose sake you descend to a comparison of Scriptures, to confirm him when in doubt, will he in consequence incline to truth, or rather to heresies? Influenced by the very fact, that he sees you have hitherto gained no ground, and stand even with your adversary in denying this point and defending that, he will undoubtedly leave this level contest in still greater uncertainty, not knowing which side he is to judge to be heresy. For surely nothing can hinder them retorting upon us, if they are minded, the charges we bring against them. Nay, they must, in self-defence, maintain that we rather introduce corruptions of Scripture and false expositions, in order to support their own pretences to the truth. Therefore I do not advise appeal to the Scriptures: it is a ground on which there can be either no victory, or a doubtful one, or one as good as doubtful."—[*Vincent. Comm.* 35; *Tertull. de Præscript.* 14—19.] It would seem, then, that Tertullian and Vincent had not much greater respect for mere deductions from Scripture than Dr. Hampden; differing from him, however, in this,—first, that they called such private interpretations, when Catholic tradition was neglected, not "pious" but "impious opinions;" next, that they did not impute them to the Church Catholic, whose doctrine, though verified by Scripture, is not literally and actually deduced from it. What they would have called Dr. Hampden's own opinions, whether viewed in themselves, or in the mode in which he professes to arrive at them, it does not belong to this place or time to determine.

ART. IX.—1. *Proposals for the creation of a Fund to be applied to the Building and Endowment of Additional Churches in the Metropolis.* By Charles James Lord Bishop of London. London: Fellowes. Rivingtons. Hatchard.

2. *The People of God called upon to build the House of Prayer; a Sermon preached at St. Peter's, Colchester, Essex.* By the Rev. James S. M. Anderson, Chaplain in Ordinary to the Queen. London: Rivingtons.

3. *The Spiritual Claims of the Metropolis, a Sermon.* By the Rev. Baptist Wriothesly Noel. London: Low.

4. *A Sermon in behalf of the Bishop of London's Proposals.* By the Rev. W. Dodsworth. London: Burns.

THE Church of England lies under a fresh debt of gratitude to the Bishop of London for this seasonable and vigorous appeal.

Powerful in its language, and startling in its facts, it has kindled a flame, which, we trust, instead of being extinguished, will burn brightly, and spread wide. Other men have done their duty: nor have our humble efforts been wanting to the cause. But the Bishop's publication, from the precision of its aim, as well as from the authority of the writer, is by far the most effective which the awful subject has called forth. His lordship has put himself at the head of the religious movement, which had for some time been perceptible; and has done what no other person could have done half so well; in fact, what no other person was qualified to do at all. Nor has he merely thrown his own weight into the scale; but, by the announcement of his plan, he has given a definite channel, and a palpable object, in which, and towards which, the exertions of others may be most advantageously directed. If, after what has been accomplished in Cheshire, in Gloucestershire, and in other counties of England,—at Edinburgh, at Glasgow, and in other towns of Scotland,—London cannot actually take the lead, now, at least, let the metropolis set an example to the empire. And the scheme of building fifty new churches at once by voluntary subscription, *is* a noble project, worthy of the first city in the world. Yet, glorious and generous as this subscription is, and much as we rejoice at the Christian liberality of our countrymen and fellow-citizens, let it be kept in remembrance that the Church does not abandon its claim upon the state. For ourselves, we should be glad, even now, if legal provision could be added to voluntary contribution; or if the imperial parliament could be induced to double the money which may be collected from individuals. Hence we have remarked with pleasure the Bishop's concluding suggestion as to a duty on coals; for it is always well to assert a principle, although the attempt to enforce it may be hopeless from the distemper of the times:—just as it is well to demand a debt, which is not likely to be paid, lest the claim should hereafter be called obsolete, and met with a statute of limitations.

The want of new churches in many spots is appalling. The awful *amount* of spiritual destitution in London, and other large towns, may be learnt from the official accounts furnished by the Bishop, and from many other statistical documents, which have been made public again and again. We will not weaken the impression by giving only a portion, where we cannot find room for the whole. Suffice it to say, that there is hardly church-room for one tenth of the population, where there ought, at least, to be church-room for one third. The tremendous evils which must be engendered by this state of things—in all the hideous and abominable shapes of ungodliness, profligacy, intemperance, improvidence, turbulence, filth, riot, sullenness, ferocity, desperation, disease; the unmitigated and intolerable penury which is ever at the heels of vice and low debauchery; the destruction of physical, and mental, and moral, and spiritual health; the murder of soul and body; the atmosphere of pollution spreading and propagating itself without a check;—these frightful evils may, perhaps, be imagined by every man with more force than they can be described, even by the able delineations of Mr. Anderson, Mr. Noel, and Mr. Dodsworth.

A larger supply, then, of churches, and clergymen attached to them, in connection with the Establishment, is emphatically *the* want of our country, and, most of all, of our towns.   Without putting our trust, more than Dr. Chalmers, in any magic of masonry, we may yet say, that the very architecture—the building standing visibly before the eyes of men—must produce its solemn effect.   The edifice of public worship, as it raises its sacred head, has its eloquence and its power.   There is a moral attraction in its walls.   It speaks of the hallowed purposes for· which it is reared.   It is itself a call to holiness, which will not quite be disregarded.   It shines forth a beacon and a monument both of philanthropy and of prayer.

But the church will have its living ministers.   And they are as the salt, which will season, in God's good time, the mass around them, and prevent the progress of corruption.   The church becomes a nucleus, around which all other pious, and charitable, and provident institutions, are most readily and most beneficially formed; and, although such institutions may be started without parochial clergymen, they will seldom be *worked;* although they may be announced with a magnificent conception, they may be almost still-born, or languish and perish in their cradle, unless there are parochial clergymen, who will take the chief trouble of nursing and fostering them.   Let us look, too, at the operation of the scheme, with reference to the different classes of which the community is composed.   First, then, as to the *poor.*   Let it be borne in mind, that, wherever there is very little church-room, the poor will usually have *none.*   The pews will be gradually rented by the richer inhabitants of a district to the exclusion of the less affluent; and the gayer and smarter people will, by degrees, drive even out of the free seats those who are more humbly clad:—not that the latter will be arrogantly dispossessed; but that they will shrink from sitting beside persons who outshine them, and will yield the places from a feeling of modest diffidence or of false shame:—so either absenting themselves altogether from public worship, or going to meeting-houses, where they can be more at ease.   Wherefore, if the poor are objects of Christian solicitude to us, the supply of more adequate accommodation for all classes,

so that none may be betrayed—alas! we had almost said forced
—either into irreligion or into dissent—this, we repeat, is the
very thing which we need.

But, in a somewhat different point of view, the plan of fresh
churches and fresh ministers is necessary for another rank in the
community even more than for the very poor. There are many
ties—long may they continue—between the Church and the aristocracy. There are many ties—long may they continue—between
the Church and the poor. The Church has a firm hold upon the
highest and upon the lowest of the land:—upon the former,
through its dignity—upon the latter, through its charity. The
clergy are allied to the gentry—and, in many cases, to the nobility
—by family connection, and by the habits either of official or
domestic intercourse: they are endeared oftentimes to the multitude by the offices of benevolence, and as the dispensers of temporal, no less than spiritual good. Their influence, unhappily, is
least, just with that class of persons who are now become, through
the process of our legislation, almost omnipotent in the empire.
Among the retail tradesmen, the 30*l.* or 20*l.* or 10*l.* householders,
they appear neither as friends and equals, nor yet as patrons and
benefactors. Where they are brought into contact with them—as
at vestry meetings or parish elections—they are too frequently
brought into collision. They have little share—while in each of
the other ranks of life they have much—in the education of their
children. *Here* they can scarcely be said to exercise a presiding
guardianship over either the present or the rising generation.
The citizens of this grade are estranged from the Church, partly
by temporary circumstances, which soon, we trust, will pass away,
—partly by their relative position in the social scale, and by the
feelings of a proud and sturdy independence which is conscious
of power, and yet, in a certain sense, conscious of inferiority;
which can neither aspire to be quite on the same level with the
clergyman, nor consent to be much beneath it; which can neither
court his personal acquaintance, nor require his pecuniary assistance; which neither seeks to entertain him as a guest, nor wishes
to receive, in another capacity, either himself, or the visitor appointed by him, who comes round to distribute tracts, or to receive
small deposits. They seem placed, as it were, either above or
below many of the parochial ministrations of the established
pastor. On the other hand, the enemies of the Church—we are,
of course, speaking generally, without taking the numerous exceptions into account—find an open door, and a cordial welcome.
The dissenting minister sits at the board, and expounds at the
tea-table: the revolutionary newspaper, or the semi-infidel magazine, has a ready access to the hearth. Moreover, men of this

class, with that fondness for power, which cleaves in every situation to the human bosom, are apt to prefer clergymen whom they have nominated or chosen themselves; hence their bias is usually towards a seceding parson, who is dependent upon their aid; or, within the pale of the Establishment, their favourite is the orator at a proprietary chapel, or the lecturer who has preached them a probationary sermon, and gone round to solicit their suffrages. In fact, they have an affection, very easily understood, for any voluntary system, in which a good deal of canvassing for votes and influence is of necessity and perpetually involved.

And here, let it be observed, the obstacle to more friendly intercourse lies not on the part of the clergyman, but on the part of the citizen such as we have described. Practically, therefore, it is no sufficient answer to say that the minister of the Gospel, the ordained pastor of the parish or district, ought to have *no* social position; that he belongs to all ranks, and ought to have the same relation to all ranks. Clergymen are citizens too: they have their civic place, as well as their ecclesiastical and spiritual character: and, if we would grapple with difficulties to any useful purpose, we must look to human nature and human society as they exist in their actual constitution.

How, then, is this barrier to social improvement—for it is in reality a very formidable barrier—to be removed? Much may be done by subdividing overgrown parishes into manageable districts, where the appointed minister may at length create opportunities of knowing all, and making himself known to all. Much also may be done—as much has been done—by a kind and conciliatory, yet not lax and unspiritual disposition, in clergymen endeavouring to recommend themselves to the lower, as well as the higher department of the middle order in the community; yet careful, at the same time, not to alienate the one class in their attempts to propitiate another. Our present course of observations, however, leads us rather to say, that the class of ministers who will belong to the contemplated churches, together with the peculiar tenure of their appointments, repudiating popular election, yet in a great measure dependent upon public opinion, may be more serviceable than any other could be in gaining over this portion of the community to the Church.

At the same time, we must think also of the rich. Wherefore we would humbly venture to suggest one or two cautions as to the present bias of our ecclesiastical economy; because the perfection of an establishment must be its adaptation to *all* ranks and classes in a kingdom. That three thousand souls are as many as an individual minister can include in his sole spiritual charge, while his regard is also upon their temporal interests, is an allegation which we have no thought of attempting to controvert. But it is one proposition to say that no single minister can undertake the entire pastoral care of a population which extends beyond three thousand persons, and quite another to assert that the whole land ought to be parcelled out into *separate* districts containing three thousand persons each. In many cases it may be advisable, on many accounts, that one clergyman should retain a general superintendence over six thousand, or twelve thousand, or even a larger number; keeping two or more curates in constant employment, and making an *internal sub-division* of his parish, according to the discretion which he exercises under his diocesan. Complete equalization, either of duty, or emolument, or authority, has been, and will, we trust, continue to be, an element quite unknown to our English scheme of ecclesiastical polity. We may take many lessons from the Scottish Establishment: but there are some parts of its economy which we must never imitate: there are some clerical views entertained in Scotland which we never wish to cross the Tweed: and we must observe the differences as well as the agreements. Presbyterianism and Episcopacy cannot be made to rest on the same basis. The Church of Scotland is essentially a system of equality: the Church of England is essentially a system of gradations. Bishops, archdeacons, deans, prebendaries, rectors, or other incumbents of parishes, ministers of districts, and curates, while they all conduce to the symmetry of the fabric, and the solemn uses for which it was ordained, are all necessary, and all necessary alike, if we would reach all the various classes of society—if we would adapt our Church to their several wants and expectations—if we would have our clergy, and the spirit which the presence of the clergy introduces, interfused among them all. It is often said, that Episcopacy suits England, and Presbyterianism suits Scotland. And the objection urged, respectively, against either system, may be, that Episcopacy hardly penetrates the middle, or rather—if we may use the term—the *penultimate* class of a community; and that Presbyterianism hardly mounts to its summit: whence it happens that the shop-keepers in England are so often Dissenters, and that, in Scotland, so enormous a proportion of the highest ranks are Episcopalians. But this disadvantage is, on our side, we believe, an accidental and transient, rather than a constant and necessary result; and we cannot but think—to put the matter for the occasion not upon Scriptural but economical grounds—that a well-organized Episcopacy is far more capable of indefinite expansion and adaptation than a well-organized Presbyterianism, mainly from the gradations which it fosters within itself. Even in listening to Dr. Chalmers, let us not abandon our old and wise, and most salutary reverence for our English Episcopal Church.

The Bishop of London's plan, we may be sure, will be to complete, rather than disturb that system of general and parochial arrangements, which may be said to be coeval and coextensive with the Establishment. And we should apologize for this apparent digression, but that we know a disposition to be entertained in other quarters quite to remodel the parochial system; and, having first laid hands upon the ecclesiastical revenues, to re-distribute them among a certain number of bishops, and an array of district ministers, having each about three thousand souls under their care; the intermediate orders of our clergy being altogether, or very nearly extinguished.

But we return to the subject more immediately before us. Details and all minuter inquiries we shall defer, until the Bishop's complete recovery from his lamented illness shall enable him to put forth his specific proposals. We shall not here drop a word upon the question of patronage; which may, perhaps, create some little difficulty and embarrassment hereafter:—we will only look at the bright side of the picture, and admire its brightness: we entertain a confident hope that the subscription will be very large: we rejoice to see all parties contributing gloriously to this good work, to behold only the sacred emulation of Christian generosity: and we trust that the result will show how vast a proportion of the property and the piety of the land is ranged on the side of the Establishment.

So far, we shall have carried all our readers along with us: and we have rather to apologize for going over the beaten ground of obvious truisms, than to expect the slightest opposition from any friends of the Church. But we must now proceed for a moment to other considerations, as to which many men, entirely zealous and conscientious, although, in our opinion, misjudging—many men whose intentions we altogether respect, and whose motives we must almost venerate—will differ with us both in their theory, and by their practice. Now, we hail the Bishop of London's project, not only for the sake of the good which it must do, but also on account of other plans, on which it may help to put an extinguisher. Some may be startled at this declaration: his lordship himself, we apprehend, will hardly thank us; not, perhaps, having contemplated the effects, which we trust, nevertheless, to see ensue. But a constraining sense of duty urges us to say, that we believe, and are happy to believe, that the erection and endowment of new churches, with clergymen affixed to the districts in which they are built, will arrest, and ultimately supersede the system of home missions, and general visiting societies, and pastoral aid societies, and a hundred other mushroom associations, which would establish quite new centres of influence and authority within the Church of England, and disjoint the frame of its discipline, and thoroughly disturb its local and parochial organization.

The indulgence, however, of an angry tone of controversy, would be here as completely out of place, as, we trust, it is at variance with our own tempers. The work of Christianization must be done. The only question is, *how* is it to be done? We say, as far as human means are concerned, by the maintenance of Episcopal government and parochial ministrations; without the intervention of societies having lay-presidents, lay vice-presidents, lay-treasurers, and committees composed partly of laymen; which either, if they fail, must distract attention from better plans, while they undertake a work which they cannot accomplish,—or, if they succeed, and gather strength, must attain a power, *in direct proportion to their success,* which is sure, in the end, to clash, perilously and violently, with the constituted discipline and the regular action of the Church. We would not disparage the potent, and, in many cases, the wonder-working principle of combination. Yet new associations are dangerous elements, when acting upon a Chnrch, which is itself an association of another kind. The only available plea for more than half these societies is the plea of urgent necessity. But the validity of this plea the erection and endowment of new churches will do away. True it is, as some have in substance objected, that churches are not visitors; that churches are not household ministrations; that churches are not schools, or saving-banks, or lending-libraries, or other parochial institutions, or the living beings by whom those institutions are to be managed. No: but churches will have faithful ministers attached to them; and faithful ministers will bring all these things in their train. Plant but a church, and all the loveliest flowers of Christianity will grow around it. Erect but a house of prayer, and other institutions will arise and shine with their attendant lustre, like satellites about a luminary of the noblest magnitude. Station but a minister, and he will become a guarantee for the rest. He will, almost always, find local visitors, if he needs pastoral aid. Or, if there be a deficiency in some places, and an overplus in others, why may not persons place themselves *generally,* as visitors, at the disposal of the bishop of a diocese, or the incumbent of a large parish, without the intervention of societies; more especially if it be meant, after all, to refer to the bishop, and ask leave of the incumbent? Our chief trust, however, is in the extension and perfection of the parochial system. Even as it is, overtasked, overburdened, almost overwhelmed as many clergymen now are, how vast is the good achieved; and all the other instrumentality which is at work for the moral improvement of the country, what is it in comparison with the ministrations of the working clergy— or, rather, where would it be without them? Yet we ought also to recollect, that too large a sphere of duty may be a fearful temptation to a clergyman. He feels that he cannot fairly be blamed, if weeds are spreading over a district far too wide for his spiritual culture; and, therefore, he may be enticed into sloth, while secure from reprehension. Or he may see that he cannot hope to overtake his work; and so one stimulus to exertion may die within him. He may do almost nothing, because there is too much to be done. He may shrink from the fatigue of visiting from house to house, when so many, after all, must be left un-visited. He may throw up the work in despair; and the sense of responsibleness may be weakened from the felt impossibility of satisfying all its obligations. But how, on the other hand, would the aspect of things be improved, how delightful the prospect and how great the ingathering, if, in the vineyard of the Lord, there were more labourers, and more division of labour!

Then why, it may be asked, reject pastoral aid from Lord Ashley, and Sir Oswald Mosely, and Sir Andrew Agnew, and Mr. Labouchere? Why seek to establish an antagonism between the two schemes? why may they not proceed together and side by side, becoming adjuncts, and auxiliaries, and supplements each to each? Our answer is, for we always leave sorer topics until we are compelled to introduce them—because human means are finite: because there is but a certain quantity of energy and money to be bestowed even upon the promotion of the cause of God and his Gospel. Therefore the two projects for building churches under the Bishop of London or authorized trustees, and of making provision for the spiritual wants of the people by City Missions and Pastoral Aid Societies, must in some measure interfere. Hence comes the vast importance of the inquiry, which plan is the best and safest? We say, with unhesitating confidence, give all possible extent and efficiency to the plan of building and endowing new churches and chapels. Throw *all* the resources into the one channel; do not divert any part of it into the other. You have a certain sum of which you would dispose in religious charity: you are inclined to bestow half upon the erection of churches, and half upon the Pastoral Aid Society, or some similar association; we say, do not divide it; subscribe the whole to the erection of churches. Do not distract your attention, do not dissipate and fritter away your funds, by withdrawing a portion from an unmixed and unquestionable good to the advancement, we will not allege, of a rival, but of a different, scheme, which is at least open to very manifest objections. Build upon the old foundations, which are known to be sound, rather than upon the new, which may at last prove rotten. Do not invert the order of things. Do not have recourse to strange and hazardous expedients, ill adapted to our clerical polity, and out of character with the rest of our ecclesiastical Establishment, before you have tried to the utmost the simpler and the more obvious. The one is a plan which leans upon the unshaken buttresses of former time, and has in its favour the unvarying testimony of many ages, and is in unison with the history, and the constitution, and the practice of the Church; the other is a fresh and uncongenial experiment, which has no certain or calculable futurity more than it has any connection with the past; which *may* introduce strifes and irregularities and disorders; which *may* eventually dislocate and unhinge the entire frame-work of episcopal jurisdiction and parochial management. We do honestly confess that we should rejoice to see some of these multiform societies broken up; their exchequers emptied of their contents, and those contents flung into the treasury of the church-building and church-endowing parties:—in a word, fairly turned over to the bishop's account. To sound the cry of " *more churches and more clergymen*" in the ear of the parliament and of the nation, is to bring a blessing upon the land. To do aught else *may* be to see the distemper, but to mistake the remedy. This is the one safe, legitimate, effectual, consistent mode of removing a dreadful mischief which is quite acknowledged on all hands. It is addition, not subversion;—extension, not change. For we do not require any new-fangled machinery. We want engines of the old description; but in greater number, and of larger power. We must put on more steam.

Let it be our first, our undivided care, to complete that parochial system, from which, under Providence, so many blessings have flowed, and with which so many hallowing and hallowed associations are bound up. Let us see the various ranks of a vicinity linked together by the august solemnities of an united devotion; and summoned, as it were, to all their respective and all their common duties by the same sound of the church-bell.

Art. X.—*The History of the Christian · Church; from the Ascension of Jesus Christ to the Conversion of Constantine.* By the Rev. Edward Burton, D.D.' 1836.

THE unexpected and immature death of the highly accomplished writer of this volume, is one of those events which have tended of late years to change the tone of opinion prevailing in the University to which he belonged, and to introduce into it for good and for evil the characteristics of a new generation. Dr. Burton is the third in succession of Divinity Professors, who have been cut off in the beginning, or in the fulness of their labours and usefulness; men of great consideration in the place, who, doubtless, were they now alive, would take a principal part in the direction of the University in the stormy times seemingly before it. Few men of late years have had the extended influence of Dr. Hodson, or the popularity with junior men of Dr. Lloyd, Bishop of Oxford, both of whom were removed at a time when the Church itself, if not the scene of their previous reputation, seemed likely to feel the impression of their minds. In like manner, the death of Dr. Elmsley took place when he had just entered upon duties to which the careful and silent studies of years had recommended him, and was about to devote to the service of the University the habits of precise thought, the composure of mind, gentleness of bearing, and gifts and attainments of a more striking character, which were discernible by all who knew him ever so little. Professors Mills and Nicoll, are additional instances, in late years, of rising abilities and erudition, cut short in their career by an (humanly speaking) untimely stroke. Such successive losses may, for what we know, be common at all times; but, whether common or not, they cannot happen without changing the character of a place, if there be room for change. And such seems to have been the effect of them in the University in which they have occurred; almost all the distinguished men enumerated were more or less specimens of a school which seems for many years to have had prevalence, or rather supreme sway in the place, so as even to constitute the existing academical body itself. Since quiet days have succeeded in Oxford, to political feuds and parties, from the latter part of the last century almost down to the recent passing of the Emancipation Bills, elegant scholarship and literature have been the main road to distinction, and an abstinence from subjects purely ecclesiastical, or even an indisposition towards them, the characteristic, or at least the accidental property of the gentleman and divine. Some of the most eminent members of the Episcopal Bench at this moment, are instances of the truth of this remark, at the time they were promoted; and what they were in younger days, such were the individuals above-mentioned. They were learned in the languages, they were men of classical attainments, of various accomplishments; they were loved and revered in private; but they either were in no sense theologians, or they added theology to their other attainments, with little concern to ground themselves in it as a science. There was in their day little of political or religious commotion to draw away their minds from criticism and literature, or to make theology much more than a theoretical or amateur pursuit. The Socinian and Predestinarian controversies, and the external evidences, almost exhausted the range of divinity; and though the sagacity of Bishop Lloyd discerned the renewal of hostilities with the Romanists in prospect, and began, in this very Review,* to prepare for defence, he was not allowed time to do much more than direct attention to a conflict of which he himself was to be spared the toil.

If there was any one who might be deemed an exception to these remarks, it was the lamented divine who has led to them. He was unquestionably, not only variously read in classical and modern literature, but deeply versed in the writings of the fathers. Always excepting one venerated individual, whose name will at once suggest itself to Oxford men, he had above all men reputation for patristical learning, a reputation which belonged rather to the seventeenth century than to our own. Yet it may be doubted whether even he was not better acquainted with the writings of Christian antiquity, as historical records, or depositaries of facts, or again in their bearing upon one or two important modern questions, than in themselves, in their great fundamental principles, and their peculiar character and spirit, or what is sometimes called their ἦθος. There was nothing in the circumstances of the day to send him to their works as a revelation of times, feelings and principles gone by; and his study in consequence was far from embracing even an abstract knowledge of their views. While, then, his reading spoke forcibly for the loyalty and devotion of his heart towards those prophets of the ancient truth, and tended much to encourage younger men in the study of them, yet it scarcely separated him in mental characteristics from that classical school to which we have above referred him.

But Dr. Burton's death is remarkable in another point of view. He was not only an University man; he was an active parish priest, and emphatically a religious man. We mean a man who had the heart and the opportunity to evidence sincere and practical

*   *Vide* British Critic for 1825.

religious views; and consequently, abstract and inoperative as . might be his theological reading, he was necessarily forced by his very seriousness and earnestness into the adoption of a definite line of action, at, least during the recent critical position of the University. He might not perhaps make his ecclesiastical learning bear upon his conduct; but a determinate line and a decided conduct he could not forbear adopting; he was too religious to forbear it, and the form of religious opinion which he chose was that which according to all appearances is likely to prevail in the high places of the Church, unless, which is not improbable, some violent convulsion throw all its interests into disorder. As the school of Waterland succeeded to that of Bull, in consequence of the exigencies of the times, which brought into notice men of a more *Protestant* complexion, (if we may be allowed a catechresis in the use of the word); so, according to all appearance, if things go smooth, we shall find a still more modern divinity necessary to harmonize with those secondary systems in religion and education to which the policy of the day is tending. The probability is that the influential places in the Church will be held by men of a widely different stamp from those who have hitherto gone by the designation of high Churchmen. That clear and inflexible adherence to rule and precedent, which is called by its enemies stiffness and narrowness of mind, but which saved the Church during the last century from the gulf of Ultra-Protestantism, is melting away under the influence of feelings which might rightly be called charitable, did they answer in the long run. We are likely to have men in station and authority, not openly latitudinarian, but accessible to all sorts of impressions from without, and deficiently acquainted with the peculiarities and excellences of the system they administer. Unexceptionable in doctrine themselves, except as being tinged with the popular religion of the day, they will give their confidence and their preferment to men inferior to themselves, and as these parties in turn will bestow their own patronage on persons who come short proportionably of themselves, there is danger of the Church being overrun with objectionable principles, while the first authors of it are amiable, and on the whole orthodox men. When we class the late Professor among these, it is not as forgetting the noble stand he made for Christian truth in 1834, when, at the head of the tutorial body, he drew up that distinct and impressive avowal of the dependance of education on religion, which was ultimately subscribed by two thousand members of convocation. Such a man, if indulgent, would certainly be so within limits, beyond which he would be inflexible; still his humility and unaffected simplicity of mind were such, he was so unsuspicious of others,

so liberal and expansive in his feelings, so much better endowed
with candour and generosity than with a clear apprehension of
our ecclesiastical position, that it is easy to see where on the
whole he would have taken his stand, had he been raised to those
higher preferments which were all but his when he died. His
loss is the greatest, perhaps, which his principles could have sustained in Oxford. We think it no disparagement to the talents
and virtues of those who remain as upholders of them, to say that
it is irreparable. His equal or his second cannot be found in the
combined qualifications of extensive reading, unwearied diligence,
promptness and despatch, parochial activity, kindliness of heart,
and general popularity. No man so considerable ever bore his
faculties more meekly. No man descended more entirely to the
level of those with whom he conversed, submitted to their way-
wardness, or sympathized with their peculiarities. No man thought
less of self, laboured less for the appearance of consistency, or
feared less the confession of doubt or error. No man less excited
in others those feelings which tend to jealousy, distance, and disunion. In his death, what may be called the moderate section of
the University, have lost perhaps the only man who was qualified
to head and lead them, or to serve as a restraint on persons
of keener or more eccentric minds. The consequences of it have
been seen sooner than might have been anticipated; his party
have in effect vanished with him, and those who maintained more
and maintained less have come into collision.

If it were not for the hazard of intruding upon subjects beyond
human sagacity, something might be said in connexion with the
above remarks, on the indications which the existing events
furnish of an approaching conflict, sooner or later, between what
are commonly considered extreme opinions. As decks are
cleared before a fight, so in the field of ecclesiastical politics,
those who were hitherto middle men, are either taken out of the
way, or retreat to this or that side in the struggle. The crisis
may be delayed an indefinite time by external events; a foreign
war might call off all our thoughts in another direction; or the
return of the Conservatives to power might partially suspend the
natural operation of the principles at work, and compose the surface of the Church into an apparent calm. Still, whether by a
secret underground influence, or by outward manifestation, what
are called extreme opinions will spread on either side, and sooner
or later will join issue, and find a solution. The highly to be
revered school of divinity, commonly called high Church, has
lately been bereaved of its brightest ornament, in the admirable
Prelate who filled the See of Durham; while it is fast losing
ground in the Christian Knowledge Society. As to the party

who seem to be succeeding to their power, and are full of hope and triumph in consequence, they have no internal consistency, clearness of principle, strength of mind, or weight of ability sufficient to keep the place they may perhaps win. They have the seeds of dissolution in them, and are already breaking into pieces. As Whigs and Tories have disappeared from the stage of politics, so the high Church section of the Establishment, to which we owe so great a debt in years past, is almost broken up, and the Low party has a mortal disease upon it.

It has been thought best to make the above remarks on the present condition and prospects of the Church, in frank, perhaps in blunt language—but it must not be thence supposed that we view the state of things lightly, or range ourselves on neither side of the contest; but we wish to draw our readers' attention simply to our ecclesiastical condition itself, as the first step in their setting about to form a judgment upon it.

The work before us, published under the direction of the Literature Committee attached to the Christian Knowledge Society, is such as might have been anticipated from its lamented author. It presents a luminous and distinct account of the fortunes of the Church during its three first centuries, condensed into a small volume without effort, and abounding in learning without display. It is the composition of one who has full mastery over his materials, and (as it were) got his subject by heart ; and it will doubtless be of the greatest value to those who are already interested in church history, and either desire further information, or a synoptical view of what is familiar to them. These we consider to be its chief merits ; its deficiency on the other hand, if it must be noticed, lies in a want of unity in the history, in the absence of plan or scope, the neglect to interpret the events and facts which occur. This indeed is a very tolerable fault, especially in this age, when scarcely a man can prevail on himself to write without some preconceived theory in his mind, or some striking but peculiar view, which he takes care to herald forth at every pause in the narrative, and to use for the perversion rather than elucidation of its details. As times go, it is a relief and a refreshment to read a work, which is not straining after novelties, and torturing men and things on the Procrustean bed of what the author perhaps calls a "simple principle." As it is pleasant to sit by a smooth river, and gaze upon its stream equably flowing by, so is Dr. Burton's work a balm and solace to those who have busied themselves in many thoughts, and are weary of controversy and speculation. But this very quality which recommends it to the harassed student, is somewhat a disadvantage to it, considered as intended for popular use. It is better indeed to be sound and accurate, than merely amusing; we do. not wish history to be made either a romance or a diatribe, to be poeticized or philosophized: still to interest and to instruct are main objects in its composition, and here we consider Dr. Burton's work, with all its excellence, to be somewhat defective. There is too little of moral and of lesson, we do not mean deduced, but deducible from the course of affairs as he presents them. Yet even in this respect his work is a very considerable advance upon Mosheim's history; which is as dry and sapless as if the Church were some fossil remains of an antediluvian era, lifeless itself and without any practical bearing on ourselves. Nay it is in this respect an advance even on the writings of the present very learned Bishop of Lincoln, who has apparently been led by an accurate taste, critical exactness, and dislike of theory or paradox, into an over-estimation of facts, as such, separated from their meaning and consequences. Dr. Burton had much of this critical accuracy also; yet we should rather attribute this same peculiarity, as far as it is found in this and other of his works, to the cause above indicated, viz. to his having apparently taken up theology without such an accurate grounding in its principles as would enable him to speak confidently as a moralist or divine.

Dr. Burton commences his history from the day of Pentecost, which he conceives to be a truer date for the foundation of the Christian Church, than that of our Lord's public ministry. The transactions of the first century occupy not very far from half the volume, and consist principally of the details of the apostles' own labours. The usual subjects follow; the martyrdom of Ignatius, the spread of Gnosticism, the Paschal controversy, the Persecutions, Montanus, Theodotus and Praxeas, in the second century; and in the third, Tertullian and Origen, the Platonists, Cyprian and the Rebaptizers, Novatus and Novatian, Dionysius of Alexandria, Manicheism, and the gradual victories of the Gospel over the powers of the world. The history ends with the conversion of Constantine. It will be the most respectful course to our author now to put before the reader some passages from his work, with such brief observations of our own as they may suggest. Dr. Burton thus manfully states his view of the tone to be adopted by the ecclesiastical historian.

" I wish, however, distinctly to state, that there are some points upon which the ecclesiastical historian may be allowed to have made up his mind, without being charged with partiality. Thus, he is not required to speak of Christianity as if it was merely one of the numerous forms of religion which had appeared in the world. He is to write as a Christian, addressing himself to Christians; and as he is not called upon to prove

Christianity to be true, so he may assume that his readers are acquainted with its doctrines. In speaking, therefore, of the first propagation of the Gospel, I have said little concerning the nature of those new opinions which were then, for the first time, delivered to the world. A contemporary heathen historian would have thought it necessary to describe them; they would have formed an important feature in the history of the times; but a Christian historian does not feel called upon to explain *the principles of the doctrine of Christ.* He supposes his readers not only to know these principles, but to believe them; and though the differences among Christians form a necessary part of the History of the Church, it is sufficient to say of Christianity itself, as first preached by the apostles, that it is the religion contained in the Bible."—pp. 15, 16.

And he thus forcibly describes that peculiarity in Christianity, which brought upon it persecution from the heathen.

" The Greeks and the Romans had long been acquainted with the Jews; but they looked upon their religion as a foolish superstition, and treated their peculiar customs with contempt. This treatment might be provoking to individual Jews, but it generally ensured for them toleration as a people; and hence they were seldom prevented from establishing a residence in any town within the Roman empire. The Jews repaid this indulgence by taking little pains to make proselytes. In their hearts they felt as much contempt for the superstitions of the heathen, as the latter professed openly for the Jews; but they were content to be allowed to follow their own occupations, and to worship the God of their fathers without molestation. The Christians might have enjoyed the same liberty, if their principles had allowed it; and for some time the heathen could not, or would not, consider them as anything else than a sect of the Jews. But a Christian could not be, sincere without wishing to make proselytes. He could not see religious worship paid to a false God, without trying to convince the worshipper that he was following a delusion. *The Divine Founder of Christianity did not intend it to be tolerated, but to triumph.* It was to be the universal, the only religion; and though the apostles, like the rest of their countrymen, could have borne with personal insults and contempt, they had but one object in view, and that was to plant the cross of Christ upon the ruins of every other religion.

" This could not fail, sooner or later,' to expose the preachers of the Gospel to persecution; for every person who was interested in keeping up the old religions, would look upon the Christians as his personal enemies."—pp. 83, 84.

In this extract we see the same high religious principle avowed by the author, which led to his strenuous effort in favour of dogmatic religion in 1834. In the document then drawn up by him, he carried out the protest, borne in the above passage in favour of Christianity in the general, to a maintenance of the creed of.

orthodoxy in particular. The words to which we allude are as follows:—

" They [the Declarationists] wish to state in the first place, that the University of Oxford has always considered religion to be the founda-tion of all education; and they cannot themselves be parties to any, system of instruction, which does not rest upon this foundation.' They also protest against the notion, that religion can be taught on the vague and comprehensive principle of admitting persons of every creed. When they speak of religion, they mean the doctrines of the Gospel,- as re-vealed in the Bible, and as maintained by the Church of Christ in its' best and purest times," &c.

It has been much the fashion at various times, to speak as if Christianity was becoming better and better understood as time went on, and its professors more enlightened and more virtuous. In saying this, we do not allude to the creed of Montanus, Mani-chee or Mahomet, or of the Gnostics, each of whom professed to be bringing to perfection that system which the apostles began in-deed, but only rudely understood ; nor again of the St. Simonians; nor of those religionists of the sixteenth century and their de-scendants now, who teach that the visible Church was lost in error for an indefinite period, and then emerged into purity and light such as Irenæus himself did not enjoy ;* but of men of the present day, who are considered especially men of the world, well-judging and practical men, and who assume it as an axiom in all their reasonings, or rather as what Aristotle calls an enthy-mematic γνώμη, that the nineteenth century (i. e. *because* the nineteenth) is superior to the first and second. We have been told much of late years about the early receptacles of religious truth having corrupted it by the pagan feelings or heathen learn-ing with which they had been previously filled; or the testimony of the fathers has been considered as the mere *declarations* of indi-vidual *opinion*, not as assertions of the *fact* of certain widely spread and generally received doctrines. Their comments on Scripture, however unanimous in various times and countries, have been considered but glosses and fancies ; as if it were the easiest thing in the world to get Jew and Gentile, bond and free, learned and unlearned, Roman and Alexandrian, to speak the same thing and to be joined together in one judgment,—as if Scripture itself did not give us an instance of the difficulty of making even " two false witnesses" " agree together," in traducing Him whose doctrine it is considered so easy to deface. The fol-

---

* " Like him [Justin] he [Irenæus] is silent, or nearly so, on the election of grace, which from the instructors of his early age he must often have heard, and like him, he defends the Arminian notion of free will and by similar arguments. . His philosophy seems to have had its usual influence on the mind, in darkening some truths of Scrip-ture, and in mixing the doctrine of Christ with human inventions."—*Milner*, vol. i.

lowing admirable remarks are a reply to this gratuitous hypothesis, which, instead of having proved to us, we are unceremoniously called upon to *disprove.*

" There is, perhaps, a difficulty in steering between the opposite extremes of attributing too much or too little value to ecclesiastical antiquity. It is easy to say, on the one hand, that a stream is purest at no great distance from its source; and, on the other, that the world is much more enlightened now than it was eighteen centuries ago. The latter statement, however, may be fully acknowledged to be true, and yet may prove nothing as to the weight which ought to be given to the authority of the earlier ages.

" We do not appeal to the primitive Christians for their knowledge or their opinions of matters upon which the world is now more enlightened; but a question arises, whether the world is really more enlightened upon those points with which the primitive Christians were specially concerned. These points are the doctrines which are essential to be believed as contained in the Gospel, and the method which is most likely to be successful for spreading them through the world. Whether these two points were imperfectly understood by the early Christians, and whether they have received more light from the discoveries of succeeding ages, are questions which it is not difficult to answer, if we rightly understand the nature of the Christian revelation.

" The one word *Revelation* seems not suited to lead us to expect, that the matters which have been revealed would require, or could even admit, successive illustrations and improvements, from the powers of the human mind becoming more developed. If Christianity had been merely a system of moral precepts, which human reason had imagined and arranged, the system might undoubtedly be rendered more and more perfect as the world continued to advance. But, if the scheme of Christian redemption was not only revealed by God, but every part of it was effected by the agency of God, without man knowing anything concerning it until it was thus effected and revealed, it seems impossible that such a system could be modified or improved by later and successive discoveries.

" Now it will not be denied, that the apostles themselves had the fullest and clearest understanding of the doctrines which they preached. It might, perhaps, be said, when their inspiration is taken into the account, that no Christians have had their minds equally enlightened by a knowledge of the Gospel; so that the revelation was, in its very commencement, full and complete; and to say, that we are more enlightened now as to the truths of the Gospel, would be the same as to say, that a ray of light is purer and brighter when it has reached the surface of the earth, than when it was first emitted from the sun. We must also recollect that the doctrine which the apostles preached, namely Justification by Faith in the death of Christ, could not be more or less complete at one period than another. It was complete, when Christ died, or rather when he rose again, and when God consented that faith in his death and resurrection should justify a sinner. The first person who embraced this offer of reconciliation, at the preaching of the apostles, was as fully justified, and as fully admitted into the Christian covenant, as any person from that time to the present, or from now to the end of the world. The terms of salvation are precisely the same now as they were in the infancy of the Gospel. The only written record which we have of this last Revelation was composed by the persons to whom it was made; human reason has added nothing to the letter or the spirit of it: and whoever believes the doctrines which it contains, possesses all the knowledge which can be possessed concerning the salvation of his soul.

" This being the case, it would seem to follow, that we have nothing else to do but to ascertain exactly what the doctrine is which was revealed, and, having ascertained it, to embrace it. This is, in fact, allowed by a vast majority of those persons who call themselves Christians. The notion, that Christianity admits of being improved as the world becomes more enlightened, can hardly be said to be entertained by any persons who really understand the Gospel; and though Christians are unhappily divided upon many fundamental points, they all agree in referring to the Scriptures, as containing the original Revelation; and each sect or party professes to believe its own interpretation of the Scriptures to be the best. It becomes, therefore, of great importance to know which of these conflicting interpretations was adopted by the early Church; and if it can be proved that any doctrine was universally believed in the age immediately following that of the apostles, the persons who hold such a doctrine now would naturally lay great weight upon this confirmation of their opinions.

" It cannot fairly be said, that, in making this appeal to antiquity, we are attaching too much importance to human authority, or that we are lessening that reverence which ought to be paid exclusively to the revealed Word of God. It is because we wish to pay exclusive reverence to the Scriptures, that we endeavour so anxiously to ascertain their meaning; and it is only where our own interpretation differs from that of others, that we make an appeal to some third and impartial witness. We think that we find this witness in the early Christians, in those who lived not long after the time of the apostles; and though we fully allow that they were fallible, like ourselves, and though in sound critical judgment, their age may have been inferior to our own, yet there are many reasons why their testimony should be highly valued.

" In the first place, they lived very near to the first promulgation of the Gospel. Even to a late period in the second century, there must have been many persons living who had conversed with the apostles, or with companions of the apostles. This would make it less likely that any doubts would arise upon points of doctrine, and, at the same time, more difficult for any corruption to be introduced. The simplicity of the Gospel was not in so much danger from the pride of learning and the love of disputation, when Christians were daily exposed to persecution and death, and when the fiery trial purified the Church from insincere or ambitious members. The language in which the New Testament was written made the early Christians better judges of the meaning of any passages than ourselves ; for Greek continued for many centuries to be the language of the learned throughout the greater part of the Roman empire, and the Fathers of the three first centuries wrote much more in Greek than in Latin. These are some of the reasons why an appeal is made to the primitive Christians in matters of faith ; not that we receive any doctrine, merely because this or that Father has delivered it in his writings, but because the persons who lived in those days had the best means of knowing whether any article of faith had been really delivered by the apostles or not. And this testimony of the early Church becomes so much the stronger, if we find, as the following pages will show, that, for at least three centuries, there was a perfect unanimity among all the different churches upon essential points of doctrine."—p. 8—12.

We offer no apology to our readers for this long extract, as they will doubtless be desirous to know the sentiments of a writer of Dr. Burton's views upon the subject. The *principle* on which we consult antiquity is most satisfactorily stated in it ; not less satisfactory is the application of it on the whole, except indeed in one slight respect, which shall be noticed in the sequel, but which does not interfere with the decisiveness of the testimony afforded in it against the Socinianizing spirit of the day, a spirit which in one instance* has proceeded so far as to condemn St. Ignatius for his celebrated Epistles; and next to ascribe to the Apostle Barnabas what the writer calls "a tissue of obscenity and absurdity which would disgrace the Hindoo mythology."

In the following passages we find the like clear and decisive statements on an article of faith, which has of late been much canvassed, that of the Holy Catholic Church.

"The unity of the Church had not as yet (A. D. 200) been broken by any open secession from the whole body of Christians. This body, though consisting of many members, and dispersed throughout the world, was yet one and undivided, if we view it with reference to doctrines, or to the form of ecclesiastical government. Every church had its own spiritual head or bishop, and was independent of every other church, with respect to its own internal regulations and laws. There was, however, a connexion, more or less intimate, between neighbouring churches, which was a consequence, in some degree, of the geographical or civil divisions of the empire. Thus the churches of one province, such as Achaia, Egypt, Cappadocia, &c., formed a kind of union, and the bishop of the capital, particularly if his see happened to be of Apostolic foundation, acquired a precedence in rank and dignity over the rest. This superiority was often increased by the bishop of the capital (who was called in later times, the metropolitan,) having actually planted the church in smaller and more distant places ; so that the Mother Church, as it might literally be termed, continued to feel a natural and parental regard for the churches founded by itself. These churches, however,

---

* *Vide* Mr. Osburn's Primitive Errors, pp. 25, 191; 256—290.

were wholly independent in matters of internal jurisdiction; though it was likely that there would be a resemblance, in points even of slight importance, between churches of the same province. . . . .

" But early in the second century we find proofs of churches, not only in neighbouring provinces, but in distant parts of the world, taking pains to preserve the bond of unity, and to show themselves members of one common head.—The term *Catholic*, or *Universal*, as applied to the Church of Christ, may be traced almost to the time of the apostles; and every person who believed in Christ was a member of the Catholic Church, because he was a member of some particular or national Church, which was in communion with the whole body. We have already seen instances of this communion being preserved or interrupted between the members of different churches : and the anxiety of the early Christians upon this point is shown by the custom of bishops, as soon as they were elected, sending a notification of their appointment to distant churches. When this official announcement had been made, any person who was the bearer of a letter from his bishop, was admitted to communion with the church in any country which he visited : but these *communicatory letters*, as they were called, were certain to be denied him if any suspicion was entertained as to the unsoundness of his faith.—It may be supposed that these precautions were very effectual in preserving the unity of the Church, and in preventing diversity of doctrine. The result was, as has been already observed, that up to the end of the second century no schism had taken place among the great body of believers. There was no church in any country which was not in communion with the Catholic or Universal Church ; and there was no church in any particular town or province which was divided into sects and parties."—pp. 288—291.

The following passage is too important to be omitted, though it retraces in some measure the ground gone over in the last.

" The term *Catholic* was applied to the church, as comprising the whole body of believers throughout the world, as early as the middle of the second century, and perhaps much earlier : and the preceding history has shown us how anxious the heads of the churches felt, in every country, that their members should hold communion with each other, and that this communion should not be extended to any who held sentiments at variance with those of the whole body. During the three first centuries, if a Christian went from any one part of the world to another, from Persia to Spain, or from Pontus to Carthage, he was certain to find his brethren holding exactly the same opinions with himself upon all points which they both considered essential to salvation ; and wherever he travelled he was sure of being admitted to communion : but on the other hand, if the Christians of his own country had put him out of communion for any errors of belief or conduct, he found himself exposed to the same exclusion wherever he went; and so careful were the churches upon this point, that they gave letters or certificates to any of their members, which ensured them an admission to communion with their brethren in other countries.—The first dispute of any moment was that concerning the Paschal festival : but churches which differed upon this point, continued to hold communion with each other; and the bishop of Rome was thought decidedly wrong when he made this difference a cause of refusing communion. So strong a measure was only considered necessary, when the difference involved an essential point of doctrine." . . . . . . " Thus Theodotus, who did not believe the divinity of Christ, was excluded from communion, when he went to Rome. The same church excluded Praxeas for denying the personality of the Son and Holy Ghost : and when a doctrine somewhat similar began to spread in the Alexandrian diocese, the bishop who opposed it was so desirous to know that he was acting in agreement with other churches, that he sent copies of his own letters to Rome." . . . . " It is in this way that we are able to ascertain, at different periods of history, the sentiments entertained by the church, on various points of doctrine. We have also the works of the early Christian writers, which show that the Church maintained the same doctrines during the whole of the period which we have been considering. If we take any particular opinion, Sabellianism for instance, we know for certain that it was not the doctrine of the Catholic Church. Whenever it was brought forward by Praxeas, Noetus, Beryllus, or Sabellius himself, it was uniformly condemned, and that not merely by one writer, or by one church, but by the consentient voice of all the Eastern and Western churches. If we wish to know whether the divinity of Christ was an article of belief at the period which we have been considering, we find no instance of its being denied till the end of the second century, when Theodotus was put out of communion by the Roman Church for denying his belief in it. A few years later, Dionysius of Alexandria was obliged to defend himself from the charge of not believing it : and all the Eastern churches put forth their declaration from Antioch, that not only did they all maintain this article of belief themselves, but that it had been maintained by the Catholic Church from the beginning.—Creeds and confessions of faith were, during this period, and especially the former part of it, short and simple. While there were no heretics, there was no need to guard against heresy. Antidotes are only given to persons who have taken poison, or who are likely to take it : neither do we use precautions against contagion, when no disease is to be caught. The case, however, is altered, when the air has become infected, and thousands are dying all around us. It is then necessary to call in the physician, and guard against danger. The case was the same with the church, when she saw her children in peril from new and erroneous doctrines. When a member wished to be admitted, it was her duty to examine whether he was infected or not. The former tests were no longer sufficient. Words and phrases, which had hitherto borne but one meaning, were now found to admit of several ; and the bishops and clergy were too honest to allow a man to say one thing with his tongue, while in his heart he meant another. It was thus that creeds became lengthened, and clauses were added to meet the presumptuous speculations of human reason. But the fault (if fault it can be called) was with the heretics, not with the church. Her great object from the beginning had been unity."—pp. 424—428.

We have devoted more space to extracts illustrative of Dr.

Burton's ecclesiastical principles than we should have thought advisable, were the author any other than Dr. Burton; but his authority is such that we are not unwilling to produce it in behalf of doctrines which are at the present looked on in some quarters with not a little suspicion. The above passages will serve also to instance, to those who are unacquainted with his writings, the late Professor's perspicuous and easy, or, we might even call it, pleasant way of laying out a view before his readers, without any of that elaborateness or diffuseness of language which is frequently the failing of learned men. · ·

The extract we shall presently give contains Dr. Burton's account of the income of the primitive clergy, and the mode of raising and apportioning it. Nothing is so common with Dissenters at this time as to defend their own Voluntary System by the custom, as they suppose it, of the Primitive Church; yet nothing surely is so unfair. The first ages have nothing in them either of the name or nature of *voluntariness*. No Christian system can be voluntary; except we mean to say, that it ever depends on our free will to receive it or not, and to be judged accordingly. The payments in the early Church were voluntary in that, and that sense only, in which our service to God is such. The word then, as not legitimately bearing this meaning, is an odious one, and becomes those and those only who think they may pass from Church to meeting, as they feel inclined. Nor was there any thing of the nature or the mischief of the Voluntary System of this day in the primitive economy. The mischief of it lies materially in this; that, when it is in operation, a preacher is paid in proportion to his popularity, so that a *bonus* is held out to him for flattering or indulging his audience. But the early Church considered the special gift of a Christian minister to lie, not in preaching, but in ministration of the sacraments, which was one and the same in all who were intrusted with it, and depended for its effect on the *faith* of the recipient, not on the talents of him who exercised it. Here is the true doctrine of salvation by faith, which the very men who make such a clamour about now-a-days, show by their mode of reasoning and teaching they understand least of all mankind. · It is said, " Thy *faith* hath made thee whole," not a running after preachers, not the eloquence, the fervour, or the knowledge of Scripture, or of the human heart, possessed by this or that individual. Nothing is required in the Christian system but God's act and our act; there is no medium interposed such that one man is better than another in his exercise of it. This minister and that minister are but *instruments*, or rather but the *same* instrument, where faith asks, and God answers. This is what the early Church held, and in consequence, did a congregation demand it ever so much, they could not, as they themselves knew, in any way, or by whatever potent bribes, make their minister modify according to their wayward taste, the nature or the quality of that gift which God alone gave and they but passively conveyed, or act in rivalry with his brethren to please them. But not only so; the contributions of the faithful were thrown, as the following passage will show, into a common fund, from which the clergy were paid at the bishop's discretion. Where the bishop had the apportioning of the clergy's incomes, the people could make no discrimination between one of them and another. This is not our usage at this day, nor are we recommending it; but surely it was very different from the Voluntary System. So far, however, we would even go in the way of suggestion; in the noble design under agitation of building additional Churches in the metropolis, might it not be as well that *some such* rule were observed, to hinder those most mischievous inducements to popular preaching which the existing system of chapel building has fostered? Might not, for instance, the pew-rents be thrown into a common fund, to be dispensed by trustees or others, upon equitable and religious principles? Speaking of Natalis, or Natalius, a confessor who had lapsed to heresy, and taken the episcopate in it, at a monthly salary of 120 denarii, Dr. Burton says,—

" The fact of Natalius receiving a monthly payment for his services, may throw some light upon the method which was then established for the maintenance of the clergy: for though Natalius, in consequence of his heresy, was not at this time in communion with the Church, we may suppose that his followers adopted the custom which was then prevalent with the orthodox clergy. The principle had been expressly asserted by St. Paul, as well as supported by the analogy of the Jewish priesthood, and by the reason of the case itself, that the ministers of Christ should be maintained by their flocks. The apostles availed themselves of this privilege; and all those who were ordained to the ministry by the apostles, received their maintenance from the congregation in which they ministered. The common fund, which was collected by subscriptions from the believers, supplied this maintenance; and the poorer members, such as widows, and those who were destitute or afflicted, received relief from the same charitable source. We have no means of ascertaining the proportions in which this common fund was divided between the ministers of the word and the poor: and it appears certain that the distribution must have varied in different churches, according to the amount of sums contributed, and the number of applications for relief.—One fact has been preserved, that the management of the common fund was at the discretion of the bishop, who appointed the presbyters and deacons to their offices, as well as paid to them their stipends. The primitive and apostolic custom was preserved of the money being actually distributed to the poor by the hands of the deacons : but the sums allotted to the respective claimants were settled by the bishop, who was probably. assisted in this work by the presbyters of his church. The bishop himself received his maintenance from this common fund: and we know that in later times a fourth part of the whole was considered to belong to him. But when this fourfold division existed, one of the parts was appropriated to the repairs of the church; an expense which was not required, or in a very small degree, for at least the two first centuries, when the Christians had not been permitted to erect churches, but were in the habit of meeting at private houses. A small sum must always have been necessary for the purposes of congregational worship, even when thus simply and privately conducted: but we may conclude that the remainder of the common stock, after this moderate deduction, was divided between the bishop, his clergy, and the poor: although it does not follow that the proportions were equal, or always invariable. Natalius, as we have seen, a sectarian bishop, residing in Rome, received 120 denarii for a month's salary; and though we cannot suppose that the fund which was raised by a single sect, and that apparently not a large one, was equal to that which belonged to the Church; yet it is not improbable that the supporters of Natalius would be anxious to secure to him as good an income as that which was enjoyed by the bishops of the Church. If this was the case, it follows that the bishops, at the end of the second century, received a payment which equalled 70*l.* a year: or if it be thought that this cannot be taken as an average of the incomes of all bishops, which were certain to vary in different churches, we may at least assume that the income of the bishop of Rome was not less than the amount which has now been mentioned."—pp. 276—279.

As we have above alluded to the project for building additional Churches in London, it may be instructive to contrast with our present liberty of worship the distress and peril in which the early saints met for prayer and praise. We have no obstacle at this moment from without; they had none from within.

" He " [Alexander Severus] " may be said to have expressly tolerated their public worship: for when the keepers of a tavern claimed a piece of ground that had been occupied by the Christians, the emperor adjudged it to the latter, adding the remark, that it was better for God to be worshipped there in any manner, than for the ground to be used for a pothouse.

" The last anecdote might lead to an interesting inquiry into the period when the Christians first began to meet in churches, or at least to have buildings set apart for public worship. They probably acquired this liberty earlier in some countries than in others: but we can hardly doubt that some such buildings were possessed by them in Rome, during the reign of the present emperor. We know that, for many years, they met in each others' houses. Concealment, on such occasions, was absolutely necessary; and we may judge of the perils with which they were beset, as well as of the firmness of their faith, when we know that the excavations in the neighbourhood of Rome, which were formed by the digging of stone, were used for a long time by the Christians, as places of religious meetings. In these dark and dismal catacombs, which may still be seen, and which still bear traces of their former occupants, the early martyrs and confessors poured forth their prayers to God, and thanked their Redeemer, that they were counted worthy to suffer shame for his name. Here also the remains of their dead were interred: and it was long before the intolerance of their enemies allowed the Christians to breathe a healthy air, or enjoy the light of heaven, while they were engaged in their sacred duties. This indulgence appears to have been gained at Rome during the period of comparative peace, which began on the death of Septimius Severus: but since Elagabalus prohibited every kind of public worship, except that of the Sun, we may perhaps conclude, that few, if any, religious buildings had been possessed by the Christians, till the time when Alexander decided the case in their favour.

" At that time, they had a piece of ground belonging to them ; and it appears to have been the property, not of some one individual who was a Christian, but of the whole community. It was probably bought out of the common fund, which has already been mentioned as belonging to the Christians: and the emperor's decision makes it plain, that it had been used for the purposes of public worship. It is not probable that the Christians met in the open air. The spot must, therefore, have been occupied by some building ; which was either a private dwelling converted to this sacred purpose after its purchase by the Christians, or one which had been specially erected for the occasion. The latter conclusion would be the most interesting, as containing the earliest evidence of the building of churches: though it might be thought that the present edifice was rather of an inferior kind, since the opposite party intended to turn it into a tavern."—pp. 316—318.

This transaction took place about A.D. 222—forty years later the See of Antioch had a house attached to it, which was recognized as being so by the Emperor Aurelian. On this account we the more wonder at the following sentence in the author's narrative of the times of Constantine, which seems to sink the primitive Church to the level of the Popish agitators in Ireland in this day.

" It is plain from the terms of this edict, (one of Constantine's) that the Christians had for some time been in possession of property. It speaks of houses and lands which did not belong to individuals, but to the whole body. Their possession of such property could hardly have escaped the notice of the government; but it seems to have been held in direct violation of a law of Diocletian, which prohibited corporate bodies, or associations which were not legally recognised, from acquiring property. The Christians were certainly not a body recognized by law at the beginning of the reign of Diocletian ; and it might almost be thought that this enactment was specially directed against them. But, like other laws which are founded upon tyranny, and are at variance with the first principles of justice, it is probable that this law about corporate property was evaded. We must suppose that the Christians had purchased lands and houses before the law was passed : and their disregard of the prohibition may be taken as another proof that their religion had now gained so firm a footing, that the executors of the laws were obliged to connive at their being broken by so numerous a body."—pp. 418, 419.

As the volume before us is of a popular character, and upon controversial points of the history states but the conclusion to which its author had arrived, and which he has argued at length in his former works, it will not be necessary to notice any of them or examine what may be said for or against them. Every writer has a right to his own opinion in such matters, and a learned man like Dr. Burton, pre-eminently. One of these, however, we are tempted to say a few words upon, because it bears immediately upon the sacred text, and all men, not theologians only, have an interest in it. Dr. Burton considers James the Less, Bishop of Jerusalem, and brother or cousin of our Lord, as a different person from James the son of Alphæus, the Apostle. Without wishing to dogmatize on a point of this nature, we are somewhat surprised that he has been able to acquiesce in that view. In his lectures on the first century, he rests the proof of it on the testimony of antiquity, which he says is certainly in favour of the Bishop of Jerusalem not being one of the Twelve. But in the first place we are by no means sure that the authority of the Fathers in matters of *fact* connected with Scripture history, is greater than that of any one at this day. The personal history of the first propagators of the Gospel seems from the first to have been almost consigned to oblivion; and it is but in accordance with the height and grandeur of the system they administered, that it should be so. Doctrinal truth was carefully guarded, and transmitted; individuals, however illustrious, were passed by. How little is known about the labours and sufferings of the Apostles! while the result of them is clear, the establishment of the Church far and wide. In consequence, the early Christian writers, in attempting to trace the history of Christ and his Apostles, had no other resource than our own, viz. the attempt to glean from the sacred text what slight hints might therein be conveyed about it ; and, having no means of information distinct from ours, they may as fairly be criticised or differed with as if they lived at this day. For instance, Theodoret speaks of St. James and St. Matthew as living together, and Chrysostom of St. James being a publican; can we doubt, under the circumstances, that this belief arose from St. Matthew being called the son of Alphæus as well as St. James ? We have a parallel case in Dionysius's inquiry whether the author of the Apocalypse was the Apostle or another John. He plainly knew no more of the matter than ourselves, and his opinion has no kind of *authority* over our belief. He argues the point critically, and ingeniously, from the structure of the book, and he comes to the conclusion that it is *not* the writing of St. John. As we do not feel bound in this case to adopt Dionysius's opinion, neither are we under any necessity to follow other Fathers, though they even did distinguish between James, Bishop of Jerusalem and James the Apostle. But in the next place the evidence from the Fathers seems not at all so clear, as at first sight might be thought. Dr. Burton refers to Eusebius, Epiphanius, Nyssen, Chrysostom, Theodoret, Jerome, and the author of the Constitutions; but the true reading in Eusebius seems to speak just the reverse. Chrysostom elsewhere strongly implies there were but two, not three, disciples of the name of James; and Jerome thought sometimes one way, somtimes the other. On the other hand various Fathers called James the Less an Apostle, absolutely and without restriction. Thus after all we are cast upon the text of Scripture for our information; and, though it is certain that we read of James the Less in one place, of James the son of Alphæus in another, without any hint in those very places that the names did not belong to separate individuals; yet there is strong reason to conclude from other passages that they were but different designations of the same person. The text in the Galatians would seem decisive in the matter; " *Other of the Apostles* I saw none, *save James the Lord's brother.*" If it be said that the word *Apostle* extended beyond the twelve, being applied to St. Paul himself and St. Barnabas, this cannot be the case in this place, for in that sense St. Paul's declaration does not hold, as he *had* seen St. Barnabas at the season he speaks of. Indeed it seems almost incredible that James the Less should be spoken of as he is, if he were not one of the Twelve. For instance, when St. Paul first came to Jerusalem, St. Barnabas " took him and brought him *to the Apostles;*" that is, as the passage above referred to informs us, to Peter and *James.* It is James who presides at the Council of Jerusalem; it is James before whom St. Paul lays his proceedings on his coming up to Jerusalem after his Apostolic journey; it is as brother of James that the Apostle Jude designates himself, which hardly could be, were James short of an Apostle. Further, if the author of the Catholic Epistle be not an Apostle, it will be the only exception to the rule among the books of the New Testament; the Gospel according to St. Mark and St. Luke, not only being ultimately referable to Apostles, but being a narrative of our Saviour's teaching, not the teaching of the Evangelists themselves.

ι So much stress has been laid of late, in popular divinity, on one or two doctrines of the Gospel, apart from the rest, that it is not wonderful that Dr. Burton, a man of frank, accessible, and un-suspecting mind, and from his parochial habits especially likely to be brought under the influence of the current religion, should have sometimes worded himself in a way which he would be the first to lament, had he discovered whither it was tending. We hear frequent complaints about the evil of seclusion from pastoral labour, of learned leisure, and the like: this counterbalancing good, however, may be expected from it, that the old forms of thought and language will probably be retained in theological teaching, whatever happens in the world. The following passage will explain what we mean.

" The doctrine itself (the ' new and strange doctrine, which was op-posed to the prejudices and passions of mankind,' which the Apostles had to preach,) may be explained in a few words. They were to preach faith in Christ crucified. Men were to be taught to repent of their sins and to believe in Christ, trusting to his merits alone for pardon and salva-tion ; and those who embraced this doctrine were admitted into the Christian covenant by baptism, as a token that they were cleansed from their sins, by faith in the death of Christ : upon which admission they received the gift of the Holy Ghost, enabling them to perform works well-pleasing to God, which they could not have done by their own strength."—pp. 23, 24.

Now, if by this statement it is only meant that the doctrines spe-cified were those elementary portions of the Gospel which in matter-of-fact the Apostles preached to the unconverted as first steps in the Christian faith, it is quite borne out by the book of Acts. Yet we cannot help fearing that most readers, instead of considering it to speak of the first truths put before the minds of those whom the Apostles addressed, will conceive it to specify those which are highest and most sacred, and in such sense the *essence* of the Gospel, that, they being secured, every thing really important is secured with them. They will consider that all other doctrines, however true in themselves, however high in their sub-ject, are but secondary, and only useful as ministering to the for-mer and easily to be dispensed with in individuals, if the former are ascertained. Not that this single passage by itself need con-vey this, but that it seems to do so, interpreted, as it will be, by the mode of thinking and the language of the day. At this mo-ment especially, when the orthodox doctrines of the Trinity, In-carnation, or Atonement, are so lightly treated in quarters where one might have hoped for better things, we regret the *accident*, for it is merely an accident, which makes Dr. Burton appear to put those divine truths in the second place in the Christian scheme, in defence of which no late writer has been more zealous, more energetic, more unwearied than himself in former publications.

It is the same cause, a latent desire, as we conceive, to accommodate the ancient theology to the habits of this day, and to *explain* to his readers, in a manner level to their comprehensions, the abhorrence in which the then existing heresies were held by the early Church, which has led this most amiable and excellent man to *prove* the impiety of the Gnostics, not from their doctrine itself, but from the *consequences* of it. That doctrine *directly* contravenes the Catholic doctrine of the Incarnation; but, as if feeling that the age would respond languidly to any charge of heresy on that score, Dr. Burton observes, what is quite true, but, as we should say, superfluous, that it *indirectly* denied the Atonement. He observes,—

" The name of Christ held a conspicuous place in the system of the Gnostics, but there were parts of their creed which destroyed the *very foundations* of the doctrine of the Gospel. Thus, *while* they believed the body of Jesus to be a phantom, and denied the reality of His crucifixion, they, *in fact*, denied their belief in the death of Christ, *and with it they gave up altogether the doctrine of Atonement.*"—p. 102.

He is not content with observing it once, but repeats it in a subsequent chapter :—

" He (Simon Magus) would not believe that Jesus had a real substantial body; he thought that a divine and heavenly being would never unite himself with what was earthly and material; and having heard of Christ soon after his ascension, before any written accounts of his birth and death were circulated, he formed the absurd and fanciful notion, that the body of Jesus was a mere spirit, or phantom, which only appeared to perform the functions of a man, and that it was not really nailed to the cross. *It has been already observed, that this impiety entirely destroyed the doctrine of the Atonement.*"—p. 154.

Nay, his anxiety on this point leads him to a *third* mention of it, as if he thought that theology must be *recognized* as practical, before it had any claims on the deference of the age.

" He (Basilides) therefore had recourse to the extraordinary notion that Simon of Cyrene was substituted for Jesus ; which may remind the reader of what has been already observed, that Gnosticism entirely destroyed the doctrine of the Atonement : that Jesus Christ suffered death for the sins of the world, did not, and could not, form any part of the religious tenets of Basilides. *We are not, therefore, to be surprised that the heads of the Church took such pains to expose the errors of a system which, though it appears at first unworthy of a serious notice, was fatally subversive of the very foundations of our faith.*"—p. 201, 202.

Were it not that this volume is intended for general circulation under the joint authority of Dr. Burton's respected name and of the Literature Committee, we should not dwell on a point like this. But, considering this very serious circumstance, we think it right to call attention to one or two other passages of a similar complexion, that is, containing expressions, meaning nothing in the work itself, but which the divinity of the day will at once single out, appropriate, and triumph in.

In the first of the passages above quoted, the author speaks of admittance "into the Christian covenant by baptism," "as a *token* that they were cleansed from their sins by faith in the death of Christ." Now if we wished to be critical, we should object first of all to the phrase, "admittance into the Christian *covenant*," not for its own sake, (for it is in itself quite unobjectionable,) but as being a substitute for one which is much more comprehensive, "admittance into the Christian *Church.*" This also is an accommodation in the writer to the temper of the day, which is much more willing to suppose that in baptism we enter into certain *relations* with Almighty God, than that we join a certain *society.* Of course baptism introduces us into a new state, but it does more than this, and we may be quite sure that where there is unwillingness to admit the received *language* of divinity, this is not an accident, a matter of taste, feeling, or habit, but rises from some lurking indisposition towards the *thing* which that language expresses. We have then some light cast upon the declension of this day's divinity from the standard of the Reformation, from the following observable fact, that in the baptismal service, while the expression of "admittance into the covenant" is not once found,—there occur on the other hand those diversified phrases of "received into Christ's holy Church;" "received into the ark of Christ's Church;" "remain in the number of thy faithful and elect children;" "we receive this child into the congregation of Christ's flock;" "grafted into the body of Christ's Church;" "incorporate him into Thy holy Church." It is as clear as words can make it, that our Service contemplates the Church, whatever is meant thereby, (for that is quite a distinct question,) as a *definite instrument* in God's hands, *through* which baptized persons receive the promised blessings. It compares it to the ark of Noah, by which we escape "the waves of this troublesome world," and *in which* we are to be found at the last day, if we are to be "inheritors of God's everlasting kingdom." Substitute *covenant* for Church, as the privilege into which baptism admits us, and an entire doctrine is dropped out of the Christian scheme.

But, after all, it is the word "*token*," in the extract referred to, which makes it necessary to dwell upon it. The author says that admittance by baptism is a *token* that they were cleansed from their sins by faith in the death of Christ. Why not a *means*? Yet this defective expression is used of the sacraments more than once. For instance,—

" They immediately established the custom of meeting in each others' houses, to join in prayer to God, and to receive the bread and wine, *in token* of their belief in the death and resurrection of Christ. . . . Scarcely a day passed in which the converts did not give *this solemn and public attestation* of their resting all their hopes in the death of their Redeemer." —p. 31.

" Whether the dying penitent would have his pardon sealed in heaven or no, was not for man to decide ; but it was not for man to prohibit him from testifying his faith by receiving the symbols of Christ's body and blood."—p. 351.

In a sentence which soon follows, there is indeed an advance towards the higher truth; but not a decisive one. The author speaks of " this solemn rite being considered the privilege, as it was the *blessing and comfort,* of sincere believers only." Once more,—

" If a man did not hold the articles of faith which were taught by the Church, he could not receive the bread and wine *which were taken as a proof of his holding this faith.*"—p. 425.

Surely they were taken as a " blessing and comfort," in the author's own words, or rather as a special channel of heavenly grace, on condition of his faith. Considering what is going on at present in the Christian Knowledge Society on the subject of baptism, we think its Literature Committee should reflect that these passages on the sacraments may be taken in an exclusive sense which the author did not contemplate, and would be the first to disown.

And now having given our readers some insight into Dr. Burton's work, we leave it for the study of those, an increasing number we trust, who think that an acquaintance with the early Church may tend to the edification of their own.

ART. XI.—1. *The National Church Re-adjusted:* A charge
delivered to the Clergy of the County of Nottingham, in June,
1836, at the Annual Visitation of the Venerable Archdeacon
Wilkins, D.D. London. Rivingtons.

2. *Proposals for rendering the Church Establishment Efficient.*
By a Country Clergyman. Hatchard and Son.

3. *A few Words addressed to the Archbishops, Bishops, Deans
and Chapters, and generally to the Members of the Church of
England.* By a Lay Episcopalian. Roake and Varty.

IN mentioning the words Church discipline and Church patronage,
it is impossible not to revert for a moment to the case of Dr.
Hampden. Yet we shall revert to it, not in the way of polemical
debate, but simply as a matter of contemporary history.

The lamentable consequences of that appointment are beginning to be seen and felt. The Convocation, which was stopped
by the Proctors of last year, has been held under other auspices;
and the result has been the overwhelming majority against Dr.
Hampden of 474 to 94, upon a point, which, though apparently
trivial in itself, yet involves an important principle. For if Dr.
Hampden be adjudged unfit to give one vote out of five in the
appointment of select preachers in the University, how is he fit to
teach and train, by his sole instructions, the candidates for Holy
Orders, who will occupy the pulpits throughout the country in a
few years?

Our object is to take the case of Dr. Hampden as an illustration of a departure from discipline arising from the misuse of
patronage. For here is an appointment—not the result of a bare
majority after the struggle of a disputed election;—not flowing
from any inferior source of authority;—but issuing from the Crown
itself as the great fountain of dignity and honour. Yet against
this appointment a cry of sorrow, or indignation, or alarm, has
sounded from the Clergy of the land. Nor have they been content
with mere expressions of censure and distrust; but an actual resistance has been set on foot; an actual mark of disapprobation
has been stamped: and the event may be, that the appointment
will be virtually rescinded; and that the professor, made by the
King as Head of the Church, will soon vacate the Chair in the
University of Oxford. And by whom has this opposition been
organized? Not by the Bishop, not by the Heads of Houses, but
by an assemblage of men for the most part under forty years of
age. Now, it is plain, that a disrespect has been thrown, from
one quarter or another, upon the prerogative of the Crown; the
King has been ill-treated either by the members of Convocation,

or by his own responsible advisers. The Majesty of England ought not have been placed in such a position. It is plain, too, that the whole proceeding, though not against law, not against precedent, has been a kind of democratical movement in the Church; a movement, as the leaders in the opposition to the appointment have invariably felt, which could only be justified by the occurrence of a very urgent emergency.

And what is the actual, present, undeniable position of the matter? It is a most serious and painful one to all well-wishers of the Church. As far as things can be in a state of schism, they are. There is one College at Oxford reported to signify an intention of recognizing, only or almost exclusively, the lectures of Dr. Faussett. On the other hand, one, if not two Bishops, have announced their purpose of taking none but the certificates of Dr. Hampden. Again, other two Bishops have declared that they will not take his certificates. Besides, how lamentable, how almost indecent is it, that two Divinity Professors should be reading lectures against each other, as has been the case during the last term. Now, the true friends of the Establishment will do well to look at all this mischief as a fact, without reference to the question which side is right, and which wrong. Such a state of things cannot last, if the Church is to be preserved from disorder and disorganization. And Dr. Hampden's removal may really become a measure of imperative necessity, unless the interests of the Church are to be altogether abandoned; unless schism is to creep up even into the Bench, and be enthroned in the high places of the Establishment.

Into the recent pamphlets, which contend either for or against Dr. Hampden, we have no spirits to enter. Alas! the waters of strife are already turbid enough, without being stirred. Wherefore, we forbear to notice the clever *conspectus* of Mr. Miller, the calm and logical letter of Mr. Woodgate; or to commend other efforts which well deserve our commendation. On the other side, we are happy to think that there can be no necessity for commenting on the taunts or the invectives, which, under the strange pretence of justifying Dr. Hampden, have been levelled against some as sincere, pious, and conscientious men, as any University in the wide world can boast. Many, indeed, of these pamphlets are filled with local *historiettes*, and personal matters, which are calculated to have wonderfully small currency or influence beyond Magdalen-bridge; and in which it can hardly be expected that Oxford and the rest of the empire should have much sympathy with each other. Still less can we perceive the use of such a publication as the one intituled " *Oxford Persecution* in 1836: Extracts from the Public Journals." As a report or synopsis of the whole case, these extracts are quite valueless; they are all on one side. But for what other purpose could it be worth while to scrape together the rubbish of anonymous contributors to obscure newspapers, or rake the worthless embers into a heap so as to keep alive the fire of irritation? *One* end, however, this compilation, as well as other things, may serve. It may show the different tone which has been adopted by the opponents and the supporters of Dr. Hampden. It may show on which side are the real virulence, the real persecution, the real intolerance;—the black and out-poured venom of calumnious attack and sneering ribaldry. We allude chiefly, of course, to the nameless slanderers; not to the clergymen or laymen who have openly taken part in the contest. For the rest, we are anxious *not* to quarrel with Mr. Baden Powell: and we have left some of his former statements, in which he has misrepresented and probably misunderstood our meaning, unan-swered on this account.* Still less are we inclined to turn an inch out of our way for the purpose of replying to the somewhat childish innuendo of Mr. Grinfield. We ought, perhaps, in com-mon compassion, to be silent about the Article in the Edinburgh Review, and its presumed author, Dr. Arnold, a man, whom we did not expect to find writing in such a temper, and whose name we grieve to see made notoriously public in the business, whether by inordinate vanity or lamentable indiscretion. Besides, the matter has fallen into good hands. A very just and powerful castigation has been administered by Mr. Churton, who has given us, as the last, so one of the very ablest productions, which this unhappy controversy has called forth.

Of that Article, however, we shall just say, what we happen to know. It has been more injurious to the cause of Dr. Hampden than any thing else, which has been written on either side of the question. It has, in several cases, decided the doubtful, and con-firmed the wavering, making them vote against a man, in whose be-half such arguments and such expressions could be deemed requi-site. Its title and its contents have done him equal mischief. Many, who feared that it would seem want of charity to press hard upon the Regius Professor, felt that it would now be want of prin-ciple not to range themselves on the side of his opponents. Even private regard for the individual gave way to the necessity of openly proclaiming an affectionate reverence for the Church, now ma-ligned, insulted, and calumniated in the persons of its staunchest defenders. Such defenders, it was seen, were to be defamed,

---

* As a specimen, however, of the random way in which Mr. Powell flings about his reproofs, we may remark that he accuses us of blundering about the word "*facts*," because we have not read Butler:—when it happens, that the very passage in Butler which bears most upon the point at issue was appended to that very inaugural Lecture of Dr. Hampden on which we were passing our comments.

traduced, and persecuted in a manner the most extraordinary and the most wanton: and the very emotions, so to speak, of gallantry and honour, which might otherwise have prevented men from bearing down Dr. Hampden, now hurried them to the support of Mr. V. Thomas, Dr. Pusey, and Mr. Newman. For these, we suppose, are *the malignants!* And we might just ask, what one *malignant* has done in furtherance of the Bishop of London's project for building and endowing new Churches—or what is the private character and the ministerial conduct of another " *malignant;*" or how the " *malignants*" in general have upheld the Establishment, not by empty phrases, but by substantial deeds, and unwearied labours, and the bright lustre of their living examples? Would to heaven, that we could all of us become such *malignants!*

. One great argument, indeed, for the weakness of Dr. Hampden's cause is, we cannot but think, the manner in which it has been conducted. The chief effort has been to make a diversion in his favour,. by carrying a fierce attack into the quarters of his adversaries. But this course, although it may be justifiable and prudent in many cases, seems quite inapplicable to the present. Dr. Hampden has been appointed Regius Professor of Divinity at Oxford. The question is about the propriety of that appointment. It, therefore, turns altogether upon the opinions and qualifications of Dr. Hampden, not upon the opinions and qualifications of other men. A. is nominated to a very important trust: an objection is urged to certain sentiments delivered, printed, and published, which are supposed likely to vitiate the character of his theological instructions: and the objection is met by the assertion of opposite errors on the part of C. and D. We need not say to persons who can reason, that this mode of proceeding is either arrant trifling, or disingenuous artifice. Every *argumentum ad homines,* every specimen of the " *tu quoque,*" every recriminatory charge, made with whatever force and dexterity— how does it bear upon Dr. Hampden's principles, or the effect of his teaching with reference to the youth of the University and the rising generation of divines? How could a confutation of Dr. Pusey or Mr. Newman be a vindication of Dr. Hampden's mistakes? The notion is preposterous. If the advocates of the Regius Professor could prove their heaviest imputations upon the soundness of other men's theology, still the strictest demonstration would be *nihil ad rem.* But they cannot prove a particle of them. They must indeed undertake to prove that the tenets of all the clergymen of the Church of England, with the exception of a really minute fraction, are erroneous and heterodox. For Churchmen of all shades of doctrine flocked up with a simultaneous spontaneity, to oppose Dr. Hampden. But the principal shafts are aimed against a few distinguished " *malignants.*" To them are addressed the serious rebukes and the ironical praises, the Encyclical Letters, and the Pastoral Epistles, from his Holiness the Pope. As if their aim was to abet Popery, instead of placing the refutation of it upon the right grounds; so that the cause of truth may not be abandoned to the well-intentioned but weak-minded zealots, who, if left to themselves, would soon manage, on several momentous points, by a most unfortunate ingenuity, to put Protestantism in the wrong.

But the Oxford malignants need not our defence. Faction—party-spirit—selfish interest—political venality—even these motives have been imputed to them; although the charges can only attest the folly as well as injustice of their accusers. In these respects, at least, their high-souled independence and disinterestedness must be beyond the reach of impeachment, and even calumny. In these respects, at least, Oxford may glory in her sons, and England may be proud of her University. And England is proud. We may thank God, that, even in these days of cowardice and vacillation, and that wretched short-sightedness, which is miscalled expediency, England knows how to value the solid steadiness of purpose, the unswerving devotion to a sense of right, the depth and consistency of religious principle, which ennoble her seats of learning, and bear the best witness to the sterling nature of the education which they confer. For these are the things which bind around their brows a crown of more august and sacred grandeur than the most illustrious conquests of war and even of science could ever gain. We are not asking, it will be observed, whether the leading men of Oxford and Cambridge have been always correct in their views and anticipations. On some points, we may have held, and we may hold, opinions not quite in unison with theirs. But we still feel, that we cannot be too thankful to them for the moral greatness of their conduct; or pay too large a tribute of admiration and gratitude to the firm and inflexible sincerity, the unalterable fidelity to perhaps a sinking and unpopular cause, the utter disregard of personal consequences, not to be awed by the menaces of power, not to be intoxicated by the incense of adulation. We may almost borrow, with a slight change, the fine old hyperbole, which has helped to immortalize the memory of the Roman, and say that it were easier to move the sun from his course, than to shake the column of their unbending integrity. And this sturdy attachment to a supposed duty,—how far has it been from a blind and bigoted partizanship ! When the Duke of Wellington and Sir Robert Peel were in the zenith of their strength, Oxford had her hundreds who would rather have forfeited every hope of human advancement, than have made, or countenanced, concessions, which, as they regarded them, savoured of apostacy. And the same men, or men of the same stamp as they, then held persons in honour, but reverenced principles more than persons; so now they have wished for peace, but they love religion more than peace.

But our feelings are here leading us away; and we may be losing sight of our general inquiry, even in the particular matter by which we would illustrate it. That matter is now before us simply by way of *instance.* For ourselves, we have not the honour of any acquaintance with Dr. Hampden: but we can feel for the situation, into which rash and injudicious patrons have thrust him, to his almost torturing annoyance. We most sincerely regret that a man, whose personal qualities have secured the warmest affection and respect of all who know him, should have been placed in a position which has compelled other men, as esteemed, as learned, as amiable as himself, to visit him with censure, and carry against him, by an enormous majority, a vote which implies want of confidence.

We would put the questions—not in the name of the Church, for in the name of the Church we can have no right to put them, but in the name of ourselves, and of those who may think with us; can any possible good arise from Dr. Hampden's appointment at all commensurate with the actual mischief, which it has already caused?—Is the system of such appointments to be continued? Is it worth while for Ministers, either as friends to the Church, and such a friendship they profess, or as friends to their own interests, and such a friendship they must undoubtedly entertain, to unite against them those two great sections of the establishment, which, on other points, may be only too ready to differ between themselves? Is it worth their while to place an appearance of disagreement between the body of the Church and the temporal head of the Church? Is it worth their while, to proceed with offensive nominations in defiance of at least nine-tenths of the English Clergy? We say, at least nine-tenths; for many even of those, who voted on a late occasion in Dr. Hampden's favour, ranged themselves on his side, not because they participated in his opinions, or thought his published theology unexceptionable; but because they had a keen perception of the inconveniences which might accrue, from resisting an appointment, when absolutely settled by the Crown. Yet we cannot be blind to indications, and deaf to rumours, which seem to render a perseverance in obnoxious appointments, on the part of his Majesty's advisers, more than probable. We would, therefore, pursue our inquiries upon a hypothetical case: and we are anxious to pursue it, while the case *is* hypothetical, and before we are again reduced to the wretched and distressing necessity of making personal objections to a particular individual, whose private character may command attachment and esteem. We would pursue it quite frankly and freely; because we feel that we can pursue it with a clear conscience, which acquits us altogether of malignant motives. Our constant aim has been to hold ourselves aloof from the mere ferment of parties; and to examine the great questions which affect our Christian interests, as if standing calmly on the bank, without being sucked into the whirlpool of factious rivalries. We cannot fairly be charged with political hostility. The accusation against us has been urged, and is more plausible, that we have exhibited too little warmth on subjects, where a man's politics become a part of his religion.* We speak, therefore, not as the adherents or the foes of any set of statesmen; but as men who would bitterly lament that an established and aggravated enmity should exist between the government of the country and the Church of the country, whether Episcopal or Presbyterian.

The inquiry, which we would institute, is about the principle on which Church-patronage is to be bestowed; or, to state it in another form, the class of persons who are to be elevated among our hierarchy. There may be a disposition to take the masters of our principal schools, *on account of their preceptorship;* as if the task of ordering boys was the best preparation for the task of managing mankind. But, although there have been, and are, and, we dare say, will be, some splendid exceptions, our belief is, that there is no real parity between the government of a school and the administration of a Diocese; and that the most successful pedagogue is not likely, as such, to be the most judicious Bishop; both from the experience which he must want, and the habits with which he has been conversant. There may be an inclination, again, to exalt into spiritual peers men, whose views as to creeds and articles, the regulation and polity, and even the theoretical constitution of a Church, must create a radical difference of sentiment between themselves and almost all with whom they will have to come in contact. But we will not imagine—for it is a spectacle which, happily, we have not hitherto been called to behold—the soreness and irritation, half-vented and half-smothered, which must rumble, with a scarcely subterranean current, through

---

* Upon that most important and somewhat confused question, the connection between politics and religion, we would refer to an admirable discourse in Mr. Newman's third volume; and also to a volume of Sermons recently published by the Rev. W. Gresley—a volume sensible, practical, and valuable, both on this and other accounts. It is intituled " *Sermons on some of the Social and Political Duties of a Christian, with a Preface on the Usefulness of Preaching on such Subjects.*"

a diocese, where the Bishop should be an object of suspicion; the utter absence of that kind and almost paternal relation, in which a Prelate ought to stand towards his Clergy; the sense of disliked authority on the one part, and the lack of cheerful obedience on the other.

A correspondent has requested us to remonstrate against the prevalent system of putting very important trusts upon very young shoulders. And certainly, a damage must thus be inflicted both upon the country at large, to which the prudence of middle age existing among its sons might be in a measure lost; and upon the persons themselves, of shining talents and vast future capabilities, who should be invested with the most laborious and responsible charges too early in life; before they could have enjoyed the fittest preparation for command in the school of obedience; before their character would be formed and all its elements harmonized; before that moral stability could be consolidated in the mind and heart, which, next to the divine influences of religion, can best prevent men from being too lowly or too aspiring—too self-distrusting, or too self-confident. Hereafter we may return to this subject as a not uninteresting or trifling question in social economy; but, although the two matters have clearly their connexion, our present argument has reference to the qualifications, rather than to the age, of the parties who may be exalted to the highest stations of the Church of England.

In that work of so much performance and so much promise, " *The History of England, from the Peace of Utrecht,*" there is a passage full of warning, which may become applicable to our times, although we thank God, in all sincerity, that things have not yet come to such a pass as to make it applicable now. Lord Mahon writes; " The Earl of Nottingham concluded an eloquent speech with a bitter and impressive allusion to Swift, whose favour with the ministers was now firmly established and generally known. ' My Lords,' he said, ' I have many children, and I know not whether God Almighty will vouchsafe to let me live to give them the education I could wish they had. Therefore, my Lords, I own I tremble when I think that a certain divine, who is hardly suspected of being a Christian, is in a fair way of being a bishop, and may one day give licences to those who shall be intrusted with the education of youth.' "

Now, we repeat, in order to prevent all possible misconstruction, that things *have* not come—we trust, they never *will* come —to such a pass as this. But we would look to a wide principle, to the tendencies of a system, and to the probabilities of the future. We can at least conceive Ministers of the Crown who would heap all their patronage upon clergymen, if they could find them, of one peculiar party in politics—and that one peculiar party, the party hostile to the constitution of the empire. We can conceive a profligate, flagitious, and traitorous administration, endeavouring, even wantonly and by design, to bring Episcopacy, as an order, into disgrace and contempt, by exalting unworthy persons to the Episcopal dignity; and striving to throw ridicule upon the theory of apostolical succession, by preferring, one after another, a race of unapostolical men. If ever such an administration should arise, there would be no terms of indignant rebuke, of burning and withering execration, in the whole vocabulary of the English language, too strong or too explicit for brands of infamy upon their conduct. We should not then shrink from the performance of a fearful duty: but we should cry out for the impeachment of those ministers with as austere a determination as the most vehement zealot in the kingdom. In the mean time, however, there seems danger of another kind, which may be scarcely less disastrous in its ultimate consequences.

A bishop should now be a guide and umpire, ruling with a firm and delicate hand, amidst a variety of conflicting opinions and conflicting practices. What will happen, if men should step upon the bench, with their own experience so slight, their own sentiments so unsettled, that they hardly care which is which, or know one from the other? The nation needs some men in the high places of her Church who are not only versed in parochial details, but have exhibited skill, and temper, and Christian discretion in the government of parishes: men who are acquainted, not merely with the truths of theology, but with the application of theology to the people: who practically understand the state of national feeling and education: who have taken their share in the conduct of the great Christian Societies of the land: who have had clerical and ecclesiastical affairs to manage, and who have succeeded in their management. What must happen, if a school, or a college, is to be the only antechamber to the House of Peers; or if the main requisite for a bishopric is to be a mastery of the differential calculus, or an addiction to oryctological research?

But let us not be mistaken. The pestilent notion that extraneous knowledge is injurious or useless to a clergyman, is at the very antipodes of our belief. A clergyman, we hold, cannot possess too large a variety of general information, provided it be made consistent with his professional avocations; and the one needful study be not neglected for the adjuncts and embellishments. In fact, if he is behind his age: if, in any region of inquiry or intelligence, he exhibits a marked and palpable deficiency, he must risk—he will probably forfeit—some portion of his clerical influence and power. At a period, also, when much may turn upon right views of material phenomena, he who can blunt the edge of every weapon forged against Christianity in the armoury of physical science ; he who can render geological and mineralogical pursuits auxiliaries, as Dr. Buckland and Mr. Conybeare have rendered them, to the cause of religion, does us an eminent service, and may well ask our fervent gratitude as its return. We are impressed with the conviction, that arguments for or against revelation will be drawn, more and more, from the entire compass of the universe, the whole encyclopædia which treats *de omni scibili.* Too many attainments of knowledge, too many accomplishments of literature, cannot, therefore, be clustered around the theological learning and the pastoral employments of a minister of the Gospel. But, nevertheless, this learning, these employments, must continue to be his primary, and paramount, and central aim; and other things are to be subordinated to them, and regarded as their auxiliaries, and cultivated chiefly for their sake.

Our admissions, therefore, do not go one step to prove, that the highest prizes in the Church ought to be bestowed on account of recommendations altogether *extra-professional;* or, in other words, upon persons who are distinguished by their scientific character, but have, properly, no clerical or theological reputation. We may even say, that scientific acquirements ought, in many cases, to be an additional weight in the balance of desert, and allowed, *cæteris paribus*, to turn the scale of favour : we may be glad, that the Bench of Bishops should represent, as it were, all the claims which the Clergy of England have upon the respect and admiration of their country-men :—but we still remain impregnably intrenched in our general position.

That general position is, that, while we rejoice to have Clergy who possess enlarged and liberalized minds, and who have expanded their views through the circle of many sciences, still we need men in our hierarchy who have mounted through the clerical offices step by step ; and have occupied a space in the eyes of their brethren, being known and reverenced in a theological or ministerial capacity. The assumption of a dignity will exert no magical influence to change the man who is invested with it. It will not make that man a good divine, who has never studied divinity : nor that man competent to superintend the exertions of a body of clergy, who is himself destitute of all pastoral experience ; who has, perhaps, been less conversant with his living fellow-creatures, than with the gigantic lizards of a pre-Adamite world; who may have examined into the stratification of earths, rather than into the succession of human emotions ; who may have dived into the caves of the sea-shore, more than into the recesses of his own spirit; who may be more disposed to break the stone on the mountain, than to soften what has been called the granite of the soul; and more able to ascertain the bones of a mammoth, than to deal with feelings which are not fossilized, and passions which are not petrifactions. Of such a man it may be true; he gathers to himself an European fame. Let him enjoy it. He acquires wealth and reputation by honourable and lucrative employment in the tuition of youth. He deserves it all. He is engaged in some of the noblest and most elevating contemplations which can occupy the mind of man. That sublime satisfaction who shall grudge him? But to lift a man to the topmost pinnacles of the Ecclesiastical Establishment, *because* he is a good geologist, or *because* he is a good astronomer; or even *because* he is a good classical or mathematical tutor; *because* he has measured the distances of the stars, or devised a physical theory of the globe which we inhabit, is a practical *non sequitur* of the most awful kind. It confounds all things, that a man should be eminent in *one* way, and, *therefore*, rewarded in another. And the system might, in fairness and consistency, be extended beyond the inquirer, whose talk is of marl and schist, and to whose mind plesiosauri and ichthyosauri are familiar images, to another, if the alliterations may be allowed us, who is learned in Linnæus, and whose life has been busied about butterflies.

The Church is a profession. And the rewards and honours of the profession ought to be given to men the most distinguished for professional superiority. Celebrity in extraneous endowments and pursuits ought not to be the passport to its most exalted stations. Nothing can be so fatal to the well-being of a profession as to confer the foremost places in it upon persons known, solely or chiefly, upon other grounds. You thus degrade it of necessity. You impair the stimulus to regular exertion in it. You induce the ablest and most energetic men to take a bye-path as the shortest and surest road to its distinctions. Most of all, you degrade the Church. You debase divinity as a thing secondary and subservient to the acquisitions, which should be its supplements and its ornaments;—but not its substitutes.

We say then, *first*, that the most dangerous and baneful of all precedents is to assign the highest honours of a profession to men who have not made that profession their leading study; but who have subordinated their professional to their general pursuits. Some such experiments have been made, once or twice, in the law; but they are not considered to have been remarkably successful. We say, that *any* profession must be degraded, if men in power award its first prizes for merits—even transcendent merits—other than professional. For, by the same rule, they might give a field-marshal's baton to the soldier, who should be most expert in chemical manipulations; or they might make Serjeant Talfourd a judge, because he has written a good tragedy, or exalt a man far less distinguished than Serjeant Talfourd, because he has furnished some smart papers on general politics. In fact, there is no end to the anomalies and mischiefs, which must grow out of such a system.

But we say, *secondly,* that, in the sacred profession of the Church, the mischiefs of such a course are aggravated, beyond all power, not merely of expression, but of conception. No other depart-ment of human life can afford a just measure of the guilt of en-trusting the general direction of men, on whose labours thousands of souls may depend for life or ruin, to one who is a Clergyman merely from the accident of being the Tutor or Fellow of a Col-lege :—or one, who is quite out of the stream of clerical habits and ministerial pursuits :—or one, who knows more about pieces of rock than knotty points of divinity, and has had a hammer in his hand more often than his Bible.

Under these circumstances, we call upon the ministers to pause and beware what they are doing. If they pursue a head-long course of making obnoxious appointments, one after ano-ther, they will convert into stern and inexorable enemies, not merely the political parsons, who canvass at elections; not merely the declaimers, who seek a public notoriety at Exeter Hall; not merely the few inflammable rhetoricians, who thunder out eloquent speeches after dinner at a tavern, or in a theatre; but the whole body of the Church of England,—her consistent dignitaries,—her vigilant pastors,—her accomplished writers,—her profound divines. They will raise against them, not a passing tempest, but a majestic and enduring element, of serious, solemn, high-princi-pled, Christian opposition, which no government can resist; or, if it does resist, can resist only by the aid of revolutionary allies, who will erect a wild democracy upon the prostrate fragments of the British constitution.

Another and a momentous consideration is the consideration of *time.* It must be recollected that the prerogative of the bishops is now to be stretched; that a larger jurisdiction, and more sum-mary means of correcting the delinquencies of the subordinate clergy, are to be placed within their grasp. Hence, in the first application of a new system, it will be essential to the well-being of the Establishment, that the authority should be vested in per-sons, in whose hands it will be regarded with a cordial respect, rather than with any emotions of fear or misgiving. The conse-quences may be most painful, if the screws of authority should be tightened at the same moment that the sentiments of affection and reverence hang loose; if there should be at once a tension of the legal power, and a diminution of the moral: For thus the very increase in the strictness of discipline might help to tear and shatter the edifice of the Church, like an iron roof expanding or contracting more than the stone-work, and the brick-work, and the woodwork would admit.

That uneasiness is felt and manifested it were idle to deny. Nor, perhaps, is it altogether without reason. On the one part, Dr. Wilkins, an archdeacon delivering a charge to the clergy, talks of the *readjustment* of the Church; talks of the Church being *renovated* and *remodelled* by a board of commissioners, whose determinations, according to the archdeacon, are to be final and absolute, the legislature having little more to do than register their edicts, and the clergy nothing but to obey them. On the other part, the inferior clergy, as a mass, begin to be startled, if not alarmed. They see that the internal regulation of the Church, and the internal distribution of its property, are to be definitively arranged, without even the form of asking their concurrence. Hence they demand a convocation. They complain that everything is to be done *for* them and suffered *by* them; that they are to be made the perpetual objects, or victims, of legislation; but that they are to have no share in it, and almost no voice. And, although we have very distinct apprehensions of the difficulties and the probable mischiefs which must attend a revival of Convocation, we hardly know how the request of the clergy is to be resisted, if agitation on the subject is once seriously and strenuously set on foot; and really agitation, of all kinds, and in all places, has now become so profitable a business, that our wonder is, why every body does not take it up. Many of the clergy—perhaps very many—are anxious for some authorized mode of expressing their sentiments, and consulting with one another. For ourselves, we do not want a convocation; but we do want an ecclesiastical synod, which may decide certain points of doctrine and discipline, more important to our minds than even the settlement of tithes,— far more important than the exact size and shape of a parish, or the task of rounding off the corners of a diocese.

However, our present purpose is neither to dogmatize, nor to conjecture, nor to argue disputed points. It is simply to show the actual tendency of the state of our ecclesiastical affairs. Now, they tend, as it appears to us, to despotism on the one side, and to democracy on the other. And the danger is, lest the Establishment should be pulled to pieces between the opposite impulses. By a despotism, be it understood, we do not mean the tyranny of any particular prelates, but the kind of summary and domineering legislation which is inflicted upon the Church and

clergy. By a democracy, we mean partly a not unnatural re-
action against this despotism, and partly an exhibition, perhaps
an unconscious one, even among the clergy, of the popular spirit
of the times, by which unauthorized individuals would take matters into their own hands, and make the will of the majority a law
which allows of no appeal. Certain it is, in our opinion, that, in
some respects, the cords of discipline are strangely loosened; in
others, the assumptions of authority are pushed much too far.

Our humble advice to the clergy has been, that, almost to the
extremity of Christian endurance, they should bear and forbear.
It has been our uniform endeavour to soothe acerbities and to
prevent violence. But it is our fate, from the nature of our position, to hear notions put forth in conversation, and see them promulgated in print, which could hardly have found countenance in
a happier and healthier state of things. Thus we hear and see a
severance from the legislature recommended, upon the model of
the Episcopal Church in Scotland and America. For men begin to
deem it better that there should be no connection between Church
and State, than that the Church should recognize an affinity where
the State is only as a step-mother, ready to despoil and harass,
but unwilling to support and uphold. In this case, even more
than in the case of convocations, we would earnestly deprecate all
extreme and unadvised proceedings; but we are taught what
others think of the disease, when they can talk of having recourse
to these desperate remedies.

By way of verifying our statements, we would merely refer to
the published sentiments of Mr. Kempthorne, Mr. Willis, and
Mr. Close; and extract one or two brief extracts from the charge
of Archdeacon Wilkins; as also from the other pages, which,
straws as they are, may yet show the direction of the wind.

Dr. Wilkins says,—

" The present time constitutes an æra in the Church, second only in
importance to the period of the Reformation, when the national religion, after various convulsions, settled down into that solid form,
which, as far as doctrine is concerned, it has preserved in purity to this
day; and which, being based on the rock of Scripture, it is calculated
to preserve as long as we continue a Church and nation."—p. 3.

" In this period of returning calm, our government has wisely determined to employ a dispassionate and enlightened commission, consisting
of the highest officers of Church and State, to remodel the Establishment,
and to diffuse its limited resources over as wide a space as they can be
spread."—p. 7.

" I feel a conviction that it is not only for our benefit as a body, but
that it is for our very existence as an Establishment, that this reform be
received in the spirit in which it is made; that it is our wisdom, as it
will become our duty, to co-operate with its provisions to the utmost in

our power, and that we show a ready and a cheerful compliance with all its enforcements. In a measure of this important nature we must lay aside all our own fancies and schemes of improvement, and acquiesce in the judgment of those who are actuated by the purest motives, in whose friendly feelings as well as in whose mature wisdom we may confide, and who, having every necessary particular, and the result of every inquiry fully placed before them, are alone qualified, upon a calm investigation of them, to decide upon whatever is best calculated to uphold the venerable structure and to quicken it with life and energy." —pp. 7, 8.

" The bishops will be empowered to require, at their discretion, two full services in every parish in their respective dioceses, whatever may be the value of the benefice, or the extent of population. And in every case where the benefice amounts to £150, and the population to 400, it will be imperative on the bishop to insist upon the same. These alterations will necessarily require the intervention of additional curates, all of whose future salaries, graduated in amount by the existing scale of population, are to be fully secured to them without collusion by either of the contracting parties."—pp. 16, 17.

" With respect to the matters of discipline which the next part of the general Report of the Commissioners may be expected to recommend, provision will assuredly be made for the future adjudication of clerical delinquencies, by bringing all charges of that nature under Episcopal jurisdiction. Here will be an additional and painful duty imposed upon the diocesans ; but as it is essential to our character and constitution that good government should be preserved, and that justice should be administered by those who bear lawful rule over us, a power must be given to the bishops to take cognizance, and to impose summary restraints and penalties upon those whose misconduct disgraces their profession, and to withhold from such the exercise of public ministration." —p. 19.

".What further means beyond these are to be adopted for the maintenance of public ministration, or for due controul and superintendence over the clergy and their churches, will shortly be developed, upon bringing up that part of the report to which I have alluded. *That their several recommendations, with little or no variation, will be carried into immediate effect, there can be no doubt ;* and for the security and well-being of the Establishment, and the advantage of the public, it is desirable that there be as little delay as is compatible with sufficient and calm deliberation."—pp. 20, 21.

" And now, my reverend brethren, with all the outward aids to which I have alluded ;—with our establishment renovated, and all its various machinery improved ;—with the countenance and support of the well-informed and well-conducted orders of society ;—and, let us hope, with the returning confidence of others who have been opposed or indifferent to us,—be it our earnest endeavour to discharge our relative duties with all the zeal and energy, the devotion and ardour, that it becomes the ministers of Christ to manifest in the great and mighty cause of the

Gospel; that Gospel which opens the only way to heaven to fallen, sinful man."—pp. 26, 27.

Now, we concur, in the main, with the Archdeacon's admonitions: and they may save us from examining more deeply, at the present moment, into the Reports of the Commissioners. At the same time, a quotation from the Lay-Episcopalian may convince Dr. Wilkins and many others, that no *re-adjustment* of the Church will be successful, and that no "*patent renovator*" is to be found; unless the members of the Church at large shall be satisfied with the hands, to which an increased power is committed : for that otherwise they will not be pleased or acquiescent more than an army will move with alacrity and zeal, when it can place no reliance in its superior officers. The "*Country Clergyman*" favours us with a scheme for "*rendering* the Church *efficient;*" and the Lay-Episcopalian contends :

"As the British Magazine says, if heretical doctrines prevail in the Church, there will be a great schism, 'a resolute separation of the healthy from the unhealthy portion;' if those who are constituted the guardians of our Christianity, will not defend, but will betray it; *then* we must, at whatever cost, take care of it for ourselves, and in my own name and in that of thousands of others, of all the adherents to our Liturgy and Articles, I may, I doubt not, declare that we will not accept any change whatever in that Liturgy, or in those Articles, which is not sanctioned by persons in whom we can place confidence, who by their preaching and writings are known to be firm adherents to our fundamental doctrines ; that we will accept no new religion which sceptical professors or bishops may attempt to impose upon us, and that we will neither frequent churches nor listen to preachers where either such new religion is celebrated, or where the articles of our creed are either denied, or not fully and faithfully upheld ; we will at whatever cost ' come out and be separate, and touch not the unclean thing,' always remembering that ' purity of faith is more precious to the Christian than unity itself.' See British Magazine for March, 1836, p. 239. And we will form among ourselves, as the Episcopalians of Scotland did when Presbyterianism became the established religion of that country, an Episcopal Church unconnected with the state, in all respects the same as the Episcopal Church in Scotland."—pp. 10, 11.

The subjoined note, again, is curious.

"An appeal has lately been made to every Christian to promote the erection of new churches; but, in the name of common prudence, let Christians pause, and, before they do this, obtain *something like a rational assurance* that *Christianity*, and not Socinianism, Rationalism, or Latitudinarianism, is to be taught and inculcated in those churches; let them either obtain this guarantee, or let them refuse to contribute one single farthing, for they will have to build orthodox churches and chapels *for themselves,* unconnected with an establishment which has forsaken the true and pure religion of the Gospel.—*Ibid.* p. 10.

It is melancholy to find any members of the Church giving utterance to language such as this: for what can ensure the Church from demolition, but the strong unflinching attachment of the mass of the clergy, and that part of the lay-population among which the influence of the clergy is predominant? Without this attachment, the *re-adjustments* which improve the harmony of its proportions may yet behold it, not a living, breathing, actuating thing, but simply a more beautiful and shapely corpse. Again, if clergymen see raised over their heads, those who have not, or are imagined not to have, a fixed, abiding, habitual reverence for the Church, as it is, wrought into the texture of their minds; or men either comparatively unknown, or known for qualifications other than theological and ecclesiastical; or men either distinguished but obnoxious, or unobnoxious because undistinguished, Episcopacy itself may be brought into some jeopardy. One despotic bishop, exalted but unacceptable to the clergy, clothed with extraordinary authority, yet not in a position to render that authority beloved, might go far to ruin the whole order, by raising up, not so much a valid argument, as a keen feeling against it. Episcopacy is now a kind, gentle, almost patriarchal rule, which it is felt a glory and a pleasure to obey. Let this rule be exchanged for a harsh, imperious, arbitrary dominion: or this unforced but reverential obedience be exchanged for distrust and dread: make enlarged power simultaneous and side by side with unpopular appointments,—elevate persons, who are regarded with misgiving over others quite equal to them in talents and learning and education, more than equal in experience and judgment,—

> " Older in practice, abler than themselves
> To make conditions,—"

and who shall then answer for the consequences, who shall say how soon we must bid adieu to the well being and the stability of the Church of England?

Here, however, as elsewhere, we are determined, while we can to look at the brighter aspect of men and things. Here, as elsewhere, we would repeat that the great fount of mischief is a partial, circumscribed, and, therefore, erroneous view; and that the one great corrective must be a calm comprehensiveness of vision. Our hope is that our theology will go right, provided men can consent to be directed by all that has been given them for a guide, and not attempt to make a clear and consistent scheme of the Gospel by the strange process of leaving out one half of it. Our hope is, that the future ministrations of our clergy will even excel the past, provided they will embrace the whole compass of religious inquiry, and have respect to all the religious wants of man, both in his individual capacity and his social state. Our hope is, that God will prosper by his blessing what Dr. Wilkins calls the readjustment of the Church, provided men will abstain from an exclusive and inordinate devotion to some one favourite principle ; but will regard both the basis on which the Church has been founded, and also the habits and exigencies of the present time. But there. is, we urgently reiterate, there is one thing more of imperative necessity. We mean a distribution of Church-patronage which shall be without taint and without suspicion. . Otherwise the reports of Commissioners may be in vain : the effects of legislation may be vain : the whole paper-and-parchment apparatus of Church-Reform and Church "*renovation,*" may be vain. . The re-adjusted system cannot be successfully worked by persons in whom the clergy shall have no confidence. But the wheels even of change. may proceed with smoothness and ease, if the chief appointments in the establishment shall be filled up with Christian prudence and Christian integrity. .There may be danger from without; but Providence may in mercy overrule it into good; and the storms, if they burst, may purify without destroying. There may be a crisis within; but, if the meekness of wisdom be at all infused, even the agitating discussions and the searching controversies of the day may lead to doctrinal truth and practical advantage.

ECCLESIASTICAL RECORD.

THEOLOGY.

In the present, as in previous numbers of this Review, we have taken our stand between Popery and Ultra-Protestantism. For this, we conceive, is the legitimate position of the Church of England. There is neither truth nor safety in any other course. The many excellent and moderate men who compose what is called the Evangelical section of the Church will soon find, if they have not found already, that an extreme position is a false, a perilous, and an untenable position. As yet, we have only been enabled to put forth parts and fragments of the case. The rest of the argument, together with those qualifications and explanations which its nicety and intricacy must in many respects demand, we reserve until we can examine in detail the various works which are poured out upon the controversy; such as " *Dr. Wiseman's Lectures ;*" " *The Comparative View of the Tenets of the Anglican and Roman Churches, from the earliest Period, by a Clergyman of the Church of England ;*" " *Villers on the Reformation of Luther, abridged by the Rev. W. Marsh ;*" and " *The Lectures on Popery, delivered in Glasgow, at the request of the Glasgow Protestant Association.*" In the mean time, our readers, we are confident, will feel neither surprise nor apprehension, if we have not fulminated the bolts of wrath or censure with quite so indiscriminate and unmeasured a profusion as others, who have been moved to a perhaps not unnatural warmth, not only by religious considerations, but by the political circumstances of the day, as well as the language held and the attitude assumed by the leaders of the Irish—it is far otherwise with the *English*—papists. The country holds no stauncher friends than ourselves to the Reformation and the true principles of the Reformation; but we know that the cause of Church-of-England Protestantism will be most—nay, can be solely—endangered by a rash, crude, unlettered, unreflecting advocacy.

The matter, we conceive, has very seldom, if ever, been put upon its right grounds. In fact, all these questions require to be discussed in a far more profound, and searching, and dispassionate, and comprehensive spirit than the temper which has usually encountered them. One favourite plan of the day is the scheme of *defending the Church of England* by leaguing the whole of Protestantism in a common crusade against Popery. And the only danger apprehended and sought to be averted, is the rise of a Papal, upon the ruins of the existing, *Establishment.* Yet our own opinions are quite unchanged. If we look to England and Scotland, this peril, we are sure, is entirely and altogether visionary. If we look to *Ireland*, it may be a reasonable fear, that, should the Union between the sister-islands be repealed; should Ireland have again the blessing, or the curse, of a domestic legislature, *then* an attempt may be made to establish the system of the Papacy as the national Church. The question in that case comes, what conduct, on our part, is likely to accelerate the repeal of the Union? We confidently answer, as we have answered before, every thing that tends to create a kind of *national* antipathy between England and Ireland;—all the truculent harangues, all the exasperating statements, which are as remote from manly statesmanship and fair opposition as light from darkness; and which, in the endeavour to kindle the zeal of Protestants into a blaze, insult, without enfeebling, the adherents of another faith. But, *unless* the Union be repealed, we do *not* fear the national establishment of Popery even in Ireland. On such a question there must be, sooner or later, a complete *division* and disunion of the component elements of the majority in the British House of Commons. Here the philosophical revolutionists of England, the Grotes, the Molesworths, the Humes, the Roebucks, the Whittle Harveys, have no sympathy, no real fellow-feeling, with the Irish Priests and their nominees in the Imperial Parliament. Mr. O'Connell perfectly understands this fact; and, therefore, advocates the *voluntary principle in religion*. The actual danger is *there.* Mr. O'Connell is well aware that, in one sense of the word, the most pliant, the most flexible, the most accommodating of all systems is Popery. Mr. O'Connell is right in saying, that it is not *essential* either to the theory or the practice of Popery, that it should be linked in any intimate alliance with the forms of civil authority; and he brings forward the instances of France, and Belgium, and Hungary. In fact, one of the most remarkable phenomena connected with Popery is the Proteus-like slipperiness of its multiform devices amidst all its pretensions to a fixed immutability. Without question, Popery is always ready to put out its *feelers* in quest of secular aggrandisement; to strengthen itself with the *fasces* and all the *insignia* of temporal dominion. Without question, Popery is always ready to ally itself with the state for its own purposes. It would make an instrument and lever of the state. But its glory is, as Mr. O'Connell himself intimates, " *not to be maintained under, but to gain an ascendancy over, the state.*" We, who in the head of the state, recognize also the temporal head of the Church, we, who see Church and State included as to their secular organization under one co-extensive and conterminous authority, *we* can hardly conceive our English Episcopal system otherwise than as a national Establishment. But the Papacy aspires to be, in its *visible* unity of character, not a *national*, but an *universal* Church. The sovereignty over that Church it would fix in the person of the Pope of Rome; and hence it is, that the argument of " *divided allegiance"* derived in other days its weight and legitimacy. Yet it by no means follows from these premises, that a conscientious Papist may not uphold the voluntary principle, may not deprecate a *State-Church* in any particular kingdom; since the genius of his religion may sometimes acquiesce in being *less* than a state-church, even because it is intent upon being *more*. We might rather regard it *à priori* as a reasonable presumption, even if we had not the special evidence before our eyes, that Roman Catholics would assert and vindicate the voluntary principle under their existing circumstances in the British empire; and if Popery *should* be erected into the dominant, the *state-religion* of Ireland, we venture to prophecy that, without the repeal of the Union, it will be so erected through the triumph of the voluntary principle in the first instance. What, then, is it but sheer madness, if Churchmen band, and amalgamate, and identify themselves with Dissenters, and act *upon* the voluntary principle and the principle of the equality and fraternization of all Protestant denominations, for the sake of opposing Popery; when their *friends* will turn round upon " *Prelacy, the ape of Popery,*" at the very first favourable opportunity, which they can discover or create? What is it but to play the very game of the Papists, if Churchmen rush into a headlong career of blind and frantic vehemence, practically nullifying and stultifying their own system, and trampling Church principles into the dust at every step? But these topics may seem to belong not so much to theology, as to the other head of

ECCLESIASTICAL POLITY.

Here we may almost continue the foregoing train of thought. During this session of parliament, Church questions, as usual, have been in the front of state legislation. His majesty's ministers have urged their Irish Bill with its *appropriation* clauses, even against Lord Stanley's amendments, which certainly were not wanting in the ingredients of Church Reform. What must we say? The time is arrived when every man, if he is honest, must take his side. It is the part but of cowards and traitors to stand aloof. Now, there are three sides which may be taken. It may be contended, either that there ought to be a Protestant Establishment in Ireland; or that there ought to be a Popish Establishment; or that there ought to be no Establishment at all. But our present business is not with the republican theorist, or with the Roman Catholic priest. Yet, compelled as we are by reason and conscience to oppose them; believing that an Ecclesiastical Establishment has been, and is, most beneficial to the British empire; believing, too, that the opinion of the majority in a single quarter of the empire for the time being cannot be the *only* element in determining its character; because, in that case, it would be absurd to talk of the uses of an Establishment, in preserving the purity, the integrity, and the sobriety of faith ; compelled, therefore, to oppose them, we can yet understand their arguments, and sympathize with many of their feelings. The sentiments of the speculative Utilitarian, and, still more, perhaps, the sentiments of the Irish Papist, may be honestly, consistently, powerfully supported. But what are we to think of men, who take the premises of one party, and rush to the conclusions of the other? Here we address ourselves to the Ministers of the Crown, and the *Whig* members of the House of Commons. They tell us, that a Protestant Establishment is to be, not subverted in Ireland, but upheld ; — they tell us, at least until within this last month they have told us, that they desire to see neither the Establishment demolished altogether, nor a Popish Establishment supplanting the Protestant. This is their avowed, we assume it to be their real, creed; for, otherwise, the hollow insincerity of their professions, or, rather, the indelible infamy of their falsehood, must degrade them into a class of persons with whom we should be sorry to hold any discussion. The question, then, with them, as with us, is not *whether* the Protestant Establishment shall be preserved, but simply *how*? Yet are they fit to direct the destinies of a mighty kingdom, if they are so shallow as to imagine, or so disingenuous as to pretend, that they can support Protestantism in Ireland by echoing, or, if not echoing, at least not resisting the cry of Messrs. O'Connell and Shèil, about the folly and the wickedness of attempting to maintain a State Religion which is not conformed to the faith of the numerical majority of the population—the majority, that is, of *one* portion of an empire which has not yet been dismembered? Mr. Daniel Whittle Harvey at least puts forward an argument which will hold together; whatever may be the motives for his secession from the ministerial ranks.

These discussions, however, are worn so thread-bare, that we leave them. For, in very truth, projects are agitated again and again, as if to fan the flames of party-spirit, without ever being brought to a conclusion. We see and hear of Irish Church Bills—English Tithe Bills—of which far the best explanation will be found in the elucidatory pamphlet of Professor Jones—Marriage and Registration Bills—Parish Vestry Bills, *cum multis aliis*, hawked and paraded about, until they seem almost like the same wild beasts carried round the country, year after year, in the same caravan, and announced by the showman with the same marvellous descriptions. It is probable that hardly one of these bills will pass the legislature in its present shape ; yet the *animus* with which they are concocted, seems to cause disquietude to the ministers and well-wishers of the Church. If *some* of them *should* pass in their present shape, the immediate confusion which they must create is inconceivable; while, in the case of Marriage, the still more serious objection will lie, that, if it is to be a merely civil contract between two human parties, then at the will of those same contracting parties it may soon be dissoluble; but that it is only the solemn intervention of a third party, even the God of the Universe, in whose name the engagement is sealed, and to whom a vow is made and registered in heaven, that can render Marriage that sacred and inviolable rite, which the nature of its institution, and the habits of a Christian country, and the best interests of society, alike demand it to be. We shall not stop to insist upon the pecuniary loss which must be suffered by the Clergy; although it might reasonably be represented as a grievance, that they should be disburdened of their fees on Marriage by one statute, and disencumbered of their fees on Baptism by another, and "relieved"— for *that*, it appears, is the proper and fashionable term— "*relieved*" of their fees on Burial, by a multitude, of Cemetery. Companies, of which, as we understand, seven new schemes have been lately issued, with a flaming prospectus a-piece.

If the loss sustained by the Clergy could be a gain to all beside, they would cheerfully acquiesce. If the measures proposed had been well digested; and maturely weighed ; if they could constitute a panacea for our national maladies; if they could satisfy the Dissenters, and pacify the Roman Catholics; if they could still the waves of religious discord, and introduce a golden perpetuity of harmony, and order, and prosperity, God forbid, that one voice should be lifted up against them. But, alas, quack doctors in other matters, besides civil and ecclesiastical polity, have taught us, long ago, the difference between theory and practice, promise and performance. Otherwise, we should indeed wonder, how any man, or any woman, in this nineteenth century, could fail to have a luxuriant forest of curling hair, the colour at discretion ; and teeth stronger than iron, and whiter than ivory ; and a head incapable of aches ; and a stomach of imperturbable digestion. We should indeed wonder how any person could consent to a pimple, or a freckle, or a wrinkle, when the clearest, smoothest, most brilliant complexion can be had for half-a-crown ; or be weak enough to submit to the encroachments of old age, when all human ailments, and infirmities, and inconvenlences can be removed by a box of pills ; or be foolish enough to die, when it is so easy to be made immortal by an infallible elixir at thirteen pence halfpenny the bottle. And yet men and women do grow old ; and the coffin-maker is as busy as the vender of patent medicines. And so it may be, we fear, in the case of other specifics with which the body politic and ecclesiastic is concerned.

The Sabbath Bill of Sir Andrew Agnew has been again thrown out. With regard to what is called the Sabbath-cause, as with regard to what is called the Temperance-cause, some mischief and much delay, as we apprehend, may arise from the extreme measures of zealous but injudicious reformers. As to the observance of Sunday, let men always bear in mind the distinction, which the Bishop of London and others have drawn between restrictive or coercive legislation on the one hand, and protective legislation on the other. England will now endure little of restrictive, and still less of coercive legislation: but that protective legislation must be secure from cavil, which would guard the conscientious and the religious tradesman from the unfair competition of the rapacious and unscrupulous; and which would afford to all the opportunity and the power of devoting the Lord's day to Christian and holy purposes.

In speaking of the Sabbath, we would just allude to the outcry which has been raised against the determination of the Poor Law Commissioners, that the paupers in the workhouse shall receive religious instruction within its walls: but shall not be allowed to attend divine service in the parish church. Their argument is forcible and well put: yet, as this may be regarded as a matter not merely of reason, but of feeling, we do hope that the decision will be reconsidered. It does look like a painful hardship, that, while all others may go up to the House of God *as friends*, the poorest should be cut off from the privilege and the blessing of public and united worship in company with their fellow creatures. There are some two or three features in the new system which we have never been able to approve, however ruinous might be the evils of the old: but we have earnestly desired that it should have a smooth and favourable trial: and we have particularly rejoiced at that general and almost unprecedented demand for labour, which may well be reckoned providential at the crisis of its introduction. Deep, therefore, would be our regret, that any odium should be attached to it on religious grounds. The Poor Law Commissioners deserve the thanks of the country, as on other accounts, so for their late printed explanation and recommendation of the institution of Sick Clubs:—an insurance against sickness being one essential ingredient in the formation of provident habits.

Some communications, we may here say, have reached us respecting the plans of a Church report, and also, if it be practicable, a synoptical view of Ecclesiastical Literature:—the work, whatever its scale, to be, of course, confined to a statement of facts as distinguished from opinions. We are perfectly assured that good statistics must be the only basis either of sound legislation, or of any individual judgment which is worth a farthing: but we have here neither time nor space to speak in detail. Let us just throw out the suggestion, that a *Church report,* perhaps, might be accomplished on that *mutual principle,* which is merely a new shape of the principle of association or combination, and on which even daily newspapers are to be set on foot. We mean that a certain number of persons, say 2,000 or 3,000, should each subscribe a small sum in the first instance, say ten shillings,—or else should make themselves jointly responsible for the expense of one number of the work; should appoint a committee, or an editor to conduct it; should sell the copies at an appointed price to non-subscribers: while themselves should either have their copy *gratis,* if they had originally subscribed; or at a price, which should be found proper, and, if the thing succeeded, would be most extremely cheap, after the expenses of publication had been deducted. The plan would, of course, require much care in its actual development: but it seems calculated for works, which could not involve difference of sentiments, but would be exclusively confined to the collection and distribution of positive information. As to its *general* application to *cheap literature,* there may be strong doubts: but the matter will be well worthy of consideration, when we come, as we hope soon to come, to a broad inquiry into the means of " *social improvement in connection with the Church.*" On this most interesting and animating question we are now collecting materials: and for any authentic accounts of intellectual movements, and philanthropic projects, friendly in their spirit to the religion of the land, we shall be peculiarly thankful.

All human amelioration, it is our solemn belief, must be bound up with that divine system which alone can explain man's nature, or correct it; which holds out the mirror of his degradation and corruption, and at the same time developes his noblest capacities, and carries him onward towards the highest perfection of his being.

Our whole inquiry, then, would proceed upon the principles that the Clergy of civilized lands must be the chief instruments in all social improvement; and that the whole problem of human happiness must depend upon the solution of the previous questions;

1. What is the best and purest form of Christianity?

2. By what machinery and what constitution of things can the work of Christianization be best performed; so that the letter and the spirit, the doctrine and the practice, of the Gospel shall be diffused throughout a community, and ultimately throughout the habitable globe?

3. How these two elements, the purest forms of Christianity, and the best machinery for diffusing it, ought to be connected with all other means and processes of human improvement?

Many collateral problems are also involved; as, for instance, how far these questions·are of universal solution, and· how·far they admit of modifications, as being variable with local and temporary circumstances.

RELIGIOUS SOCIETIES.

The platform season has just closed. The interval has arrived, during which the actors separate, and the system of Christian *agitation*,—we would use the word in a good and not an offensive sense,—is hushed and lulled. Far be it from us to denounce this system altogether; seeing, as we must see, how vast an impetus is communicated by it to pious benevolence; and feeling, as we must feel, how necessary it may be in this imperfect world, to put to some spiritual interest that love of excitement which scrupulous persons could not gratify so well in any other way, that love of celebrity which is so powerful an incentive to action in many minds; to take advantage, in fact, of human nature as it is, to turn even its vanities to account, and make its very weakness conduce to the spread of virtue and religion. Yet, while we quite abstain from any sweeping condemnation in the gross, while we must acknowledge that Associations, and speeches, and public meetings, have their potency, and very often their use, we cannot think that all the elements and all the details of the system will be found ultimately subservient to the cause of social improvement; that is, if social improvement is connected with the integrity of the Church.

There is before us a Statement, printed for the use of persons of decided piety, which contains a list of no less than *sixty-six* "*Public Meetings*" which were to take place from the 27th April to 14th June, both inclusive, in the year 1836. It specifies, in parallel columns, the name of the society, the occasion, the *place* of meeting, the *day*, the *hour*, and the *preacher* or *chairman;* and it is really a very curious document, of which, with some other more valuable papers, we hope hereafter to make use. There appear to be some omissions from inadvertence; but, of course, we could not feel surprise that such poor and insignificant societies as the Society for Promoting Christian Knowledge, the Society for the Propagation of the Gospel in Foreign Parts, and the National Society for the Education of, the Poor, were left out of a catalogue which could only find room for the *Wesleyan Missionary Society, the Christian Instruction Society, the British Reformation Society, the City Mission Society, the Established Church Society, the Church Pastoral Aid Society, the Protestant Association,* and the like. We must say, however, that it is some proof of the *buoyancy* of the Establishment, to find the " *Episcopal Floating Church*" among the number.

But let us say, in serious earnest, that there are many *foreign* objects for which Associations are absolutely required; there are some home objects for which Associations are most desirable; but still, as we have already hinted more than once, there are certain rules, which must be binding at least upon Churchmen: certain axioms of which *they* at least will hardly deny the truth or the importance. Three only of such canons would we now venture to lay down, and they are truisms so self-evident, that we should have been ashamed to have enunciated them, if we had not seen them so often, in practice, forgotten, or overlooked, or even outraged.

1. Fresh associations are not to be encouraged by Churchmen, where they are likely materially to interfere, and even clash in a kind of hostile collision, with organized Church societies already established and working well.

2. Societies are not to be encouraged by Churchmen, where they have for their bond of union any principle at variance with the theory or practice of a national Church, as distinguished from the multitude of independent sects.

And 3. Societies are not to be encouraged by Churchmen where they infringe upon the authority which the Church exercises through her prelates; or disturb the regular local or parochial action which she exercises through her ordained pastors and ministers.

NOTICES OF BOOKS.

From the throng before us we can now only select two publications:—the first being the collected " *Works of Dr. Chalmers,*" carefully revised by himself and published by William Collins at Glasgow, of which two volumes have reached us, containing and concluding the treatise on Natural Theology. An elaborate criticism would here be out of place; because we have already reviewed the main substance of the present production—although it is now much enlarged and in some parts quite remodelled,—when it appeared as one of the Bridgwater Treatises: and because a more fit opportunity will offer itself hereafter for giving a general survey of the genius and the labours of Dr. Chalmers, Yet we cannot refrain from saying that this essay is an almost exhaustless mine of intellectual wealth: and we doubt not that many and many a young author will dive into its treasures and spread some of its precious ore over the surface of his own pages. The prominent excellencies are a vast fecundity of thought; a glowing richness of diction; a moral tone lofty, noble, impassioned and animating: a copiousness which leaves nothing unexamined and unexplained; a searching spirit of an analysis, and yet a glorious power of combination. The faults are, for this admirable writer is not without his faults, the iteration of the same conceptions under different, and sometimes *scarcely* different aspects, until their repetition almost wearies and confuses the mind; the redundancies of a style too diffusive, too gorgeous, too metaphorical, for the austere and simple chasteness of philosophy; the introduction of some topics, which disturb the unity of design, and which, if not altogether unconnected with natural theology have yet no more peculiar relevancy than a crowd of kindred topics in ethical, or political, or economical science; the occasional display of rhetorical mannerism; and the use of a few neologisms in expression, which sound strangely and harshly at least in English ears. This enumeration may be ungracious, where use and beauty have so entire a preponderance over defects: but we have made it, because a literature is never corrupted by little men; whereas the faults of great writers are sure to be imitated by their successors and exaggerated by those who never reach or even appreciate, their excellencies.

The other work of great value and importance, to which we have alluded, is the New Edition of Cowper's Works, with the " Life " by the Poet Laureat, published by Messrs. Baldwin & Cradock. Four volumes have already come out in a type such as it is a pleasure to look upon : all enriched with new matter of the highest interest ; and full of beautiful embellishments, intellectual as well as pictorial. The delineation of the strength and the weakness, the piety, and, alas, the madness of the unhappy Cowper, is as forcible and impressive, as remarkable for pathetic truth and unaffected vigour, as any thing which it has ever been our fortune to read. No lesson can be more admonitory either to the philosopher or to the Christian. Yet it is almost awful to see the curtain drawn away from before the struggles and the terrors of such a mind. It were idle to quote from a work, which is in every body's hands. Nor can it be needful to say, that, in point of style, Southey's Memoir is quite worthy to introduce Cowper's Letters. Both are unrivalled and inimitable in their way. Southey stands foremost among the biographers with as unquestioned a pre-eminence as Cowper among the epistolary writers of our land and language.

For the rest, in speaking of the works of which we might have been anxious to present some account to our readers, we must begin with mentioning that the long forthcoming Bridgwater Treatise of Dr. Buckland has not yet been published. The delay, we believe, has arisen from the careful labour which has been bestowed; more especially from the number and novelty of the illustrations, and the very few persons in London who are competent to their mechanical and typographical execution. We have been allowed some opportunities of forming a judgment ; but it might not be deemed fair either to author or publisher to give another explanatory review before the appearance of the production itself. At the same time, it is but just to ourselves to state our reasons for not yet doing what we have more than once promised to do.

The want of space must be an excuse for now omitting an analysis of other publications; reviews of some of which have been already either completed or in preparation. We may specify "The *Physical Theory of Another Life ;*" Gilbert's " *Lectures on the Atonement ;*" and the work of Dr. Whitley on the same subject, intituled " *The Doctrine of Atonement and Sacrifice ;*" " *The Religion of the Universe, by Dr. Fellowes ;*" and " *The Abridgement of Jeremy Taylor on Prayer,*" by the Rev. W. H. Hale. Among productions which may be styled controversial, we beg to recommend, on many accounts, " *The Scriptural Vindication of Church Establishments,*" by the Rev. George Holden ; and there are many volumes of general importance, which we can now only announce, although to some of them at least we shall recur hereafter ;—as, for instance, "The Remains of Knox," and " The Life of Bishop Jebb ;" " The Christian *Theology* of John Howe ;" "The Edition of Paley's Natural Theology," with notes by Lord Brougham and Sir Charles Bell ; Mr. Irons " *On Final Causes ;*" " *A Dissertation on Philosophy and Theology,*" by Daniel Chapman ; the miscellaneous works of Dr. Clarke, " *Faber on Primitive Election,*" " *Calvinism scripturally examined and refuted,"* by William Houghton ; and " *The History of Episcopacy in the United States, beginning with Virginia,"* by Dr. Hawke. Perhaps the most interesting Biography before us is " *The Memoirs of Dr. Carey ;"* and from books of travels we cannot but single out " *The Journey to Mount Sinai and Petra,"* by M. Léon de Laborde. Of this great work a very cheap and useful English edition, with quite a multitude of illustrations, has been ᚃ published by Mr. Murray, who deserves our thanks for presenting, in an accessible form, a publication which must be of extreme value and interest to every Christian reader, and which affords fresh proofs, how the face of the globe bears testimony to the truths of the Bible. The account of China, in the Edinburgh Cabinet Library, is also most worthy of perusal both on religious and general grounds. Nor can we help mentioning that altogether beautiful book, as classical in style as in subject, breathing throughout the spirit of elegant taste and varied scholarship, " *Athens and Attica: Journal of a Residence there,"* by the Rev. C. Wordsworth, Head Master of Harrow School. Of Sermons—one by the Master of Trinity College, Cambridge, we see announced—we can only allude to the recent labours of the excellent and indefatigable Mr. Girdlestone ; to the *Sermons on Association,* by the Rev. G. A. Poole ; and to the Lent Lectures of the Rev. R. C. Coxe, intituled " *Death disarmed of his Terrors."* The pamphlets of the day are too many even for enumeration. Their prevailing tone, however, with regard to Church matters is, we must say, either apprehensive complaint or indignant remonstrance. One *brochure* is called " *The Church in Danger,* an Address to the Members of the Established Church," and the anonymous author writes on the fly-leaf to inform us, "This pamphlet is intended to show that an apostacy of the National Church must be the inevitable consequence sooner or later of the present system of Church Patronage, founded as it is on the statute 25 Hen. VIII. ; and, therefore, that we ought to petition against it—see page 21 ; and *if that petition be disregarded, then* to take measures for the preservation of our faith among ourselves."

We looked, accordingly, at p. 21, and there we found the *measures* proposed to be, that we should separate the Church from the State altogether; or, if we fail in doing this, *separate ourselves* from the Church, and form a new communion." Such things as these, and the similar outbreaks already exhibited, sometimes cause us to feel, that only divine Providence can save the Church amidst the insidiousness of its enemies, and the wild panic-stricken imprudence of its friends. Yet even these things may, at least, indicate the fever of uneasiness which is now burning in many bosoms, and our statesmen will do well not wantonly to disregard them.—Mr. Fielden's Pamphlet, the *Cause of the Factory* System, may afford matter for future discussion.

Mr. Place, and the Rev. Mr. Owen, two apostles of Irvingism, have been calling. we believe, on almost all the clergymen in the metropolis, and favouring them, like ourselves, with a long rhapsody of a pamphlet, in the shape of an appeal to the Archbishops, Bishops, and Ministers of the Church, in support of their delusions. Would that we could sometimes take a lesson from the activity of enthusiasm. In other respects these gentlemen can hardly be thought fit models for imitation; though Mr. Owen, at least, as having been a Clergyman of the Establishment, really calls for our intense compassion. They too, we perceive, affect a prodigious attachment to Episcopal authority, and to the Church of England, even while they are building Chapels in opposition to both as fast as they can find means. The whole system of these unhappy Irvingites is to our minds only another demonstration that religion, when no longer submitted to the fair exercise of the understanding, when once unmoored from reason, must and will drift about on a tumbling sea of fanaticism and folly.

The Illustrative Works seem to realize the poet's description of Cleopatra; they are still full of beauty and freshness; nor can even " custom stale their infinite variety."

INDEX OF BOOKS REVIEWED,

OR

NOTICED IN THE ECCLESIASTICAL RECORD.

———◆———

*** *For Remarkable Passages in the Criticisms, Extracts, and Ecclesiastical Record, see the Index at the end of the Volume.*

———

THE

BRITISH CRITIC,

QUARTERLY

THEOLOGICAL REVIEW,

AND

Ecclesiastical Record.

VOLUME XIX.

LONDON:

PRINTED FOR J. G. & F. RIVINGTON,

ST. PAUL'S CHURCH-YARD, AND WATERLOO-PLACE, PALL-MALL;

AND

SOLD BY BELL AND BRADFUTE, EDINBURGH; AND
MILLIKEN, DUBLIN.

1836.

LONDON:
PRINTED BY C. ROWORTH AND SONS, BELL YARD,
FLEET STREET.

INDEX

OF THE

REMARKABLE PASSAGES

IN THE

CRITICISMS, EXTRACTS, AND ECCLESIASTICAL RECORD.

N.

LONDON:

C. ROWORTH AND SONS, BELL YARD,
TEMPLE BAR.

This day is published, in 8vo. price 9s. in cloth boards,

THE FIRST PART

OF THE

OLD TESTAMENT.

WITH A

COMMENTARY

CONSISTING OF

SHORT LECTURES FOR THE DAILY USE OF FAMILIES,

BY THE

REV. CHARLES GIRDLESTONE, M.A.

VICAR OF SEDGLEY, STAFFORDSHIRE.

CONTENTS:

GENESIS & EXODUS.

In this Edition of the BIBLE it has been one chief object to supply Families with an Exposition for daily reading. The Scripture is divided into paragraphs of convenient length ; and the explanatory and practical matter is digested, under each portion, into one continuous Lecture, so as to require no previous examination on the part of those who read it to their families. At the same time it is hoped, that the pains which have been taken to explain all obvious difficulties, and to derive from each passage its appropriate lesson, whether of doctrine or of duty, will render the work no less useful to those who study the word of God in private.

In Eight Parts, forming Four Volumes.

LONDON:

PRINTED FOR J. G. & F. RIVINGTON,

ST. PAUL'S CHURCH YARD, AND WATERLOO PLACE, PALL MALL;

SOLD BY J. H. PARKER, OXFORD ; H. C. LANGBRIDGE, BIRMINGHAM ;

AND ALL OTHER BOOKSELLERS.

[See Specimen over leaf.]

Jacob journeyeth to Bethel.

1 And God said unto Jacob, Arise, go up to Beth-el, and dwell there: and make there an altar unto God, that appeared unto thee when thou fleddest from the face of Esau thy brother.

2 Then Jacob said unto his household, and to all that *were* with him, Put away the strange gods that *are* among you, and be clean, and change your garments:

3 And let us arise, and go up to Beth-el; and I will make there an altar unto God, who answered me in the day of my distress, and was with me in the way which I went.

4 And they gave unto Jacob all the strange gods which *were* in their hand, and *all their* earrings which *were* in their ears; and Jacob hid them under the oak which *was* by Shechem.

5 And they journeyed: and the terror of God was upon the cities that *were* round about them, and they did not pursue after the sons of Jacob.

6 So Jacob came to Luz, which *is* in the land of Canaan, that *is*, Beth-el, he and all the people that *were* with him.

7 And he built there an altar, and called the place El-beth-el: because there God appeared unto him, when he fled from the face of his brother.

8 But Deborah Rebekah's nurse died, and she was buried beneath Beth-el under an oak : and the name of it was called Allon-bachuth.

9 And God appeared unto Jacob again, when he came out of Padan-aram, and blessed him.

10 And God said unto him, Thy name *is* Jacob : thy name shall not be called any more Jacob, but Israel shall be thy name : and he called his name Israel.

11 And God said unto him, I *am* God Almighty : be fruitful and multiply ; a nation and a company of nations shall be of thee, and kings shall come out of thy loins ;

12 And the land which I gave Abraham and Isaac, to thee I will give it, and to thy seed after thee will I give the land.

13 And God went up from him in the place where he talked with him.

14 And Jacob set up a pillar in the place where he talked with him, *even* a pillar of stone : and he poured a drink offering thereon, and he poured oil thereon.

15 And Jacob called the name of the place where God spake with him, Beth-el.

LECTURE 71.

How often God repeats his mercies.

" Pay that which thou hast vowed," says the Preacher. Eccl. 5. 4. " Arise, go up to Bethel," said God to Jacob ; reminding him of the vow which he had made, when he fled from the face of Esau. Vows must not hastily be made. But vows like this, once made, must most carefully be kept. Let us remember, that we also have a vow. We are bound by promise to be holy to the Lord. And as Jacob, before he set off for Bethel, would have his household put away the strange gods that were among

them, and be clean, and change their garments; so must we
order our families according to God's will, and be cleansed by
the purifying blood of Christ, and change " the garment spotted
by the flesh," Jude 23, for white linen, which is " the righteousness of saints." Rev. 19. 8. Are we surprised to find that such
a family as that of Jacob, should harbour any strange gods at all,
and wear such superstitious ornaments as the earrings here mentioned? We may suppose that they were what were brought
from Padan-aram. Or they might be the gods of the captive
Shechemites. In either case we cannot doubt, that they who had
them were much attached to them. In either case we ought to
note for imitation, the readiness with which the household obeyed
the master, and put away their abominations. Oh that we may all
learn from this example, the advantage of submitting ourselves
one to another, in the fear of the Lord! See Eph. 5. 21.

What a happy commencement of their journey was this; a
whole family in subjection to the head, each surrendering his own
will to the will of him that had authority! And what a safeguard
was this that God provided; " the terror of God was upon the
cities that were round about them, and they did not pursue after
the sons of Jacob." Truly God was dealing with this family, as
He still kindly deals with us, overcoming evil with good, giving
them abundantly more than they deserved or expected; peace
when they must have looked to be pursued, and life when they
deserved to die. Thus they arrived safe at Bethel, and there
Jacob built an altar according to his vow. And there it appears
that Deborah Rebekah's nurse was buried; whose death is here
mentioned in connexion with the place, though in all probability
she both lived and died in the family of Isaac and Rebekah.
" And she was buried beneath Beth-el under an oak : and the
name of it was called Allon-bachuth." This name means, the
oak of weeping. And this name given to the nurse's grave, and
this notice taken of her death and burial place, seem to say to us,
that a faithful and devout servant is of no small esteem, in the
eyes of God's people, and in the sight of God.

In the same Beth-el where God had appeared to Jacob before,
He appeared now again, after his return from Padan-aram; repeating his promises, and confirming the change of Jacob's name
to Israel. Thus He had oftentimes renewed his covenant with
Abraham. Thus He has in many ways confirmed his covenant
with us. We have his word, and we have his oath. We have
the sacrifice of his Son, and the gift of his Holy Spirit. Let us
observe that when God appeared, Jacob set up a lasting monument of his mercy. Could we but do something more for God,
as often as He repeats his benefits to us, what spot in all the
world would be without its pillar, in what grace of all the Gospel
should we be wanting to our Lord?

WORKS

BY THE REV. CHARLES GIRDLESTONE, M.A.

VICAR OF SEDGLEY, STAFFORDSHIRE.

1. The NEW TESTAMENT, with a COMMENTARY. (Arranged, and printed, uniformly with this COMMENTARY on the OLD TESTAMENT.) *Third Edition.* In 2 vols. 8vo. price 36s. in cloth boards, gilt lettered : or in Four Parts (sold separately), price 9s. each. Part I. contains St. Matthew and St. Mark.—Part II. St. Luke and St. John.—Part III. Acts to Corin. thians.—Part IV. Galatians to Revelation.

2. A COURSE of SERMONS for each SUNDAY in the YEAR. 2 vols. 12mo. 14s.

3. TWENTY PAROCHIAL SERMONS. FIRST SERIES. With an Appendix of Parochial Papers. *Second Edition.* 12mo. 5s.

4. TWENTY PAROCHIAL SERMONS. SECOND SERIES. For the Use of Families. With an Appendix of Family Prayers. *Second Edition.* 12mo. 5s.

5. SEVEN SERMONS on CHRISTIAN LIFE. *Third Edition, revised.* 12mo. 2s. 6d.

6. SEVEN SERMONS on SOCIAL CONDUCT. *Third Edition, revised.* 12mo. 2s. 6d.

7. SEVEN SERMONS in the time of CHOLERA. *Second Edition.* 12mo. 2s. 6d.

8. SEVEN SERMONS on the LORD'S SUPPER. 12mo. 2s. 6d.

9. DEVOTIONS for PRIVATE USE. 16mo. 2s.

10. DEVOTIONS for FAMILY USE. 16mo. 2s.

11. A COLLECTION of HYMNS, in Two Parts, for Private and Public Use. 16mo. 2s. *(Each Part may be had separately, in 24mo. at 6d.)*

12. A CONCORDANCE to the PRAYER BOOK TRANSLATION of the PSALMS. 16mo. 4s. 6d.

13. A BROKEN CATECHISM. *Third Edition.* 12mo. 3d. or 2s. 6d. the dozen.

14. THREE LETTERS on CHURCH REFORM. 1s. 6d.

In the Press.

TWENTY PAROCHIAL SERMONS for PARTICULAR OCCASIONS. 12mo.

THE BOOK OF PSALMS, according to the two authorized Translations of the HOLY BIBLE and COMMON PRAYER, in parallel columns. 16mo.

LONDON:

RIVINGTONS, ST. PAUL'S CHURCH YARD & WATERLOO PLACE.

WORKS

PUBLISHED BY

OLIVER & BOYD, EDINBURGH:

SOLD ALSO BY

SIMPKIN, MARSHALL, & CO., LONDON; W. CURRY, JUN. & CO.,

DUBLIN; AND DAVID ROBERTSON, GLASGOW.

PRINCIPLES of the LAW of SCOTLAND. By GEORGE JOSEPH BELL, Esq., Advocate, Professor of the Law of Scotland in the University of Edinburgh. Third Edition. One large volume 8vo. 21s. cloth boards.

OUTLINES of PHILOSOPHICAL EDUCATION, illustrated by the Method of Teaching the LOGIC CLASS in the University of Glasgow; together with Observations on the Expediency of extending the Practical System to other Academical Establishments, and on the Propriety of making certain additions to the Course of Philosophical Education in Universities. By GEORGE JARDINE, A. M., F. R. S. E., late Professor of Logic and Rhetoric in that University. Second Edition, enlarged. Post 8vo. 10s. 6d.

" It is the production of an experienced teacher, as well as of a sensible and conscientious man; and contains much valuable matter, in the nature of remarks on the present mode of teaching in our universities, with suggestions towards a reform. We would gladly have analyzed it for the benefit of our readers; but as it is not a long work, while it is written in a plain sensible manner, and in an agreeable style, we shall rather recommend it to their own perusal."—*Westminster Review.*

" Independent of the merits of this work, as combining an excellent system of education, it includes some admirable and well-written essays on the science of the human mind, the origin and progress of written language, the improvement of the memory, the culture of the imagination, the elements of taste, and a variety of other subjects."—*Literary Chronicle.*

THE MORNING and EVENING SACRIFICE; or, PRAYERS for PRIVATE PERSONS and FAMILIES. Eighth Edition. Handsomely printed in 12mo. 5s. 6d.

" This is a work," says the *Evangelical Magazine,* " whose commendation is almost in all the churches. We wish it all possible success. It ranks equally high in its intellectual and spiritual character; but it is eminently fitted to bind up the broken in heart."—The *Edinburgh Theological Magazine* " most cordially recommends it to all individuals and to all families, as peculiarly fitted to promote their highest and most lasting interests."—The *Scottish Episcopal Review and Magazine* remarks, that " the language of these Prayers is pure, and much more simple and becoming than that of any similar work which has yet fallen under their eye." The *New Monthly Magazine* pronounces it to be " admirable for its plan, and charming for the beauty and simplicity of its style;" while, according to the *Athenæum,* " it is in many parts very strongly imbued with the purest and most sublime Christian doctrine."

ALSO, BY THE SAME AUTHOR,

THE LAST SUPPER; or, CHRIST's DEATH KEPT IN REMEMBRANCE. Third Edition. 12mo. 7s. 6d.

The *Caledonian Mercury* observes, that " the dignity, the beauty, the prevailing energy of true religion, breaks out from every word that he (the author) utters, and possesses him evidently to a degree for which he cannot find expression."—" We cannot," says the *Evangelical Magazine,* " but regard ' The Last Supper' as an important accession to the library of the closet, and an acceptable aid in the all-important work of cultivating the religion of the heart."

FAREWELL to TIME; or, LAST VIEWS of LIFE, and PROSPECTS of IMMORTALITY; including Devotional Exercises, a great variety of which are in the Language of Scripture. To be used by the Sick, or by those who minister to them. Third Edition. 12mo. 7s. 6d.

" This book," remarks the *Monthly Review,* " is pervaded, indeed, by a spirit of rational and beautiful piety, which we should think it impossible for any heart to resist, and to the influences of which no heart, we are sure, would resign itself, without being made both wiser, and better, and happier."—" The devotion of this book," says the *Evangelical Magazine,* " is mild and solemn, the sentiments are tender and solacing, and the style is characterized in a superior degree by elegance and beauty."

THE TESTIMONY of NATURE and REVELATION to the
BEING, PERFECTIONS, and GOVERNMENT of GOD. By the Rev. HENRY
FERGUS, Dunfermline.   Post 8vo. 7s. 6d.

" This is a work," remarks the *Evangelical Magazine*, " of great research and great talent. It does equal
credit to the head and heart of the author, and we sincerely wish it success."—The *New Monthly Magazine*
characterizes it as " a very seasonable and valuable work. Its philosophy is unimpeachable, and its theology
pure and elevated."—" We hope," says the *Athenæum*, " that this work will be extensively used in the education of youth; it is admirably calculated to stimulate students to scientific research and the observation of nature: it suggests subjects of contemplation by which the mind must be both delighted and instructed."—The
Dublin University Magazine observes, " We feel strongly impressed in favour of this work as one of more than
ordinary merit. We have read the volume with an awakened and increasing interest, and we now close it
with the conviction that it is the production of a scholar and a Christian,—of one who, while he is possessed of
genuine taste and extensive knowledge, has applied them to their only true and estimable uses, his own honour
and the happiness of others—the advancement of religion, and the glory of God."

A DISSERTATION on the REASONABLENESS of CHRIS-
TIANITY. By the Rev. JOHN WILSON, A. M., Minister of Irvine.   Small 8vo. 4s.

" This is a work of no ordinary description. The author of it has lighted on a vein of virgin gold, and he
has wrought it nobly. It is the following out of one of the most precious books in our language—Bishop Butler's ' Analogy.' A more able, dispassionate work, it has seldom been our happiness to peruse. The style is
elegant and perspicuous, and remarkably suited to the philosophic view taken of the most important subjects
that can occupy the thoughts of man. We scruple not to recommend it to the hoary Divine; for there are
few Divines who may not be profited by the perusal of it. We would cordially recommend it to Parents and
other Guardians of the young. It is well calculated to establish those who are already favourably disposed;
and where the enemy has sown tares, the good that it may do is incalculable."—*Scottish Guardian.*

" This work, we think, will be popular; we, at least, have perused it with much pleasure; and the author
has our cordial thanks for presenting us with a well-written volume and well-sustained argument on a subject
of infinite importance to the everlasting interests of man."—*Church of Scotland Magazine.*

D ISCOURSES on some important POINTS of CHRISTIAN
DOCTRINE and DUTY. By the Rev. ALEXANDER STEWART, Minister of Douglas.
8vo. 10s. 6d.

" With more energy of language, and greater practical power than the *Sermons* of Blair, they possess much
of the finished elegance of Logan, and a great portion of the fervent piety to be found in the excellent Discourses of Walker."—*Scots Times.*

A GUIDE to the LORD'S TABLE, in the Catechetical Form; to
which are added, An ADDRESS to Applicants for admission to it, and some Meditations to aid
their Devotions. By HENRY BELFRAGE, D. D. Second Edition, improved. 18mo. Price only 6d.

" By the publication of the ' Guide to the Lord's Supper, in the Catechetical Form,' Dr B. has added
another to his numerous and powerful claims on public gratitude. We heartily recommend Dr B.'s work to
our readers, as at once an affectionate and faithful guide. He has certainly succeeded in no common degree
in his avowed objects."—*Christian Monitor.*

" We offer our sincere thanks to Dr B. for his ' Guide to the Lord's Table;' it is worthy both of his talents
and piety, and furnishes a most comprehensive and scriptural view of the solemn ordinance to which it relates."
—*Evangelical Magazine.*

R EADINGS for SUNDAY EVENINGS.   Post 8vo. 6s. 6d.

⁎ The object of this Volume is to present for the use of Families a series of short Discourses, selected from
the most eminent English and Scottish Divines, combining variety with excellence, and fitted, by their
elegance of thought and simplicity of style, to render attractive the duties of the Christian Life.

THE SCRAP BOOK; a Collection of Amusing and Striking
Pieces, in Prose and Verse. With an Introduction, and Occasional Remarks and Contributions. By JOHN M'DIARMID. Seventh Edition.   In one thick vol. post 8vo. 6s. 6d.

⁎ In recalling attention to this work, of which a *Seventh Edition* now appears, the Publishers are actuated as well by a desire to do justice to an acknowledged favourite, as by a wish to place within the reach of
every reader of taste a repertory of popular literature, which it may be safely asserted stands still unrivalled in
its line, whether for the school-room, the family, or the library. It is unnecessary now to enter into any
statement as to the merits of a work so well known and generally appreciated. On its first appearance it was
greeted on all hands with the highest eulogiums of the Reviewers; successive editions were rapidly called for;
and imitations of various kinds, *Musical Scrap Books*, *Poetical Scrap Books*, and numerous other collections
formed on the same plan, sprung up in different quarters. Amidst this competition the Original Work,—comprising the most interesting specimens of the best publications of the age, enriched with the occasional Remarks
of the Editor, exhibiting the styles of almost all the popular authors of the day, and embodying the most striking parts of their works, if estimated according to its power in forming the taste and improving the mind,
remains still unapproached. The success of the work has enabled the Publishers now to reduce the price
to 6s. 6d.,—a rate which, viewed in reference to its interest, the quantity of the matter contained in it, and the
style in which it is got up, may be pronounced greatly below that of the cheapest periodicals at present in
circulation.

ETYMONS of ENGLISH WORDS. By John Thomson, M.R.I. and M. A. S., late Private Secretary to the Marquis of Hastings, Governor-General of India. Uniformly printed with Dr Todd's Edition of Johnson's Dictionary. 4to. 18s.

The object of this work is to trace the descent of English words; their affinity with the different dialects of Gothic spoken in Europe; and the connexion between our own and some other tongues both of Europe and Asia,—without introducing any remarks where the general meaning is obvious.

THE COOK and HOUSEWIFE'S MANUAL: A Practical System of Modern Domestic Cookery and Family Management. Containing a Compendium of French Cookery, and of Fashionable Confectionary, Preparations for Invalids, a Selection of Cheap Dishes, and numerous useful Miscellaneous Receipts in the various Branches of Domestic Economy. By Mistress Margaret Dods, of the Cleikum Inn, St Ronan's. Fifth Edition, considerably enlarged, and, from its great and increasing circulation, much reduced in Price. 12mo. 6s. 6d.

The New Monthly Magazine says, "There cannot be too many editions of Meg's precepts," especially as, observes the Literary Gazette, "French Cookery is particularly expounded; and it is one of the best oracles extant for gastronomical consultation;" while a younger namesake of this journal adds, "The mingling of the modern French with the old English kitchen renders this a perfect work."—"As a curiosity the work is unrivalled," states the Atlas; "its author is the personage of a novel, and the scene of its experiments the invention of a poet. But this is only the garnishing. Take stewpan in hand and try."—It is the opinion of Blackwood, that "The individual who has ingeniously personated Meg Dods is evidently no ordinary writer," and that "the book is really most excellent miscellaneous reading."—The Morning Chronicle declares, that "The rapidity with which Meg Dods has run to a second (now a fifth) edition is in no small degree owing to its literary talent."—It contains all that the most exquisite epicure could desire to know," remarks the New Scots Magazine, "and what will make it supersede every other work."—The Courant pronounces it "A valuable compendium of culinary knowledge;" and, according to the Scotsman, it "well deserves to be in the hands of every housewife in the kingdom."—But, greater than all, Sir Walter Scott, in his Notes to the new edition of St Ronan's Well, records, that "Mistress Dods has preserved the recipes of certain excellent old dishes, which we would be loath should fall into oblivion in our day."

OBSERVATIONS on the ADVANTAGES of CLASSICAL LEARNING, viewed as the Means of cultivating the Youthful Mind, and more especially as compared with the Studies which it has been proposed to substitute in its stead. Delivered at the Lecture founded by the late Dr Bell, by the Rev M. Russell, LL.D. Second Edition. 8vo. 1s. 6d.

MATHEMATICAL and ASTRONOMICAL TABLES, for the Use of Students in Mathematics, Practical Astronomers, Surveyors, Engineers, and Navigators; preceded by an Introduction, containing the Construction of Logarithmic and Trigonometrical Tables, Plane and Spherical Trigonometry, their Application to Navigation, Astronomy, Surveying, and Geodetical Operations; with an Explanation of the Tables; illustrated by numerous Problems and Examples. By William Galbraith, M. A., Teacher of Mathematics, Edinburgh. Second Edition, greatly enlarged and improved. 8vo. 9s.

"A valuable work of real practical utility, in which the compiler has kept the medium course, avoiding the two extremes of bulk and too great compression; so that his tables are available for all readers, and within the reach of all. The method pursued in the work, the judicious selection of the materials, and the care and accuracy with which the tables are drawn up and printed, cannot fail to recommend Mr Galbraith's book, and introduce it into very general use."—Asiatic Journal.

"These tables will be found very useful to practical mathematicians, but especially to those engaged in the naval service. The formulæ of calculation have been very skilfully selected, while none of the improvements of modern science have been neglected; and the compiler has generally chosen those rules which will be found most easy to reduce to practice."—Athenæum.

"By far the best selection of tables, much improved in their use and construction, accompanied with more valuable matter than any other work of the same size and price with which we are acquainted; and as such confidently recommend it to the notice of the public."—Quarterly Journal of Agriculture.

MATHEMATICAL ESSAYS. By the late William Spence, Esq. Edited by John (now Sir John) F. W. Herschel; with a brief Memoir of the Author. 4to. 36s.

AN EPITOME of the GAME of WHIST; consisting of an Introduction to the Mode of Playing and Scoring; the Laws of the Game essentially Reformed; and Maxims for Playing, arranged on a new and simple Plan, calculated to give rapid Proficiency to a Player of the dullest Perception and worst Memory: With Definitions and a Table of Odds. By E. M. Arnaud. 18mo. 2s. 6d.

"It is written in a more popular and agreeable style than Hoyle's Treatise, and contains many instructions which Hoyle has omitted."—Edinburgh Literary Journal.

MEMOIRS of REAR-ADMIRAL PAUL JONES, Chevalier of the Military Order of Merit, and of the Russian Order of St Anne, &c. &c.—Now first compiled from his original Journals and Correspondence: Including an Account of his Services under Prince Potemkin, prepared for Publication by himself.   2 vols small 8vo.   14s.

*** The scenes in which this celebrated character was personally engaged in America and Europe, and the distinguished or remarkable individuals with whom he was connected or in correspondence, must give his papers great interest with the general reader; while the incidental lights which they throw upon the secret policy and intrigues of the several European courts, and the events of the American revolution, render them not less important to the historian and politician.

A TOUR through NORTH AMERICA; together with a comprehensive View of the CANADAS and UNITED STATES, as adapted for Agricultural Emigration. By FATRICK SHIRREFF, Farmer.   8vo.   12s.

HISTORICAL SKETCHES of the NATIVE IRISH and their DESCENDANTS: Illustrative of their Past and Present State with regard to Literature, Education, and Oral Instruction. By CHRISTOPHER ANDERSON. Second Edition, enlarged.   12mo.   7s.

" The mass of information that is concentrated in this small volume renders it a most valuable memorial, and does high credit to the author's diligence and research."—Eclectic Review.

" Mr Anderson's book cannot fail to make a deep, and, we trust, a practical impression, wherever it is read. Its perusal has afforded us more than ordinary pleasure."—New Baptist Miscellany.

" We confess we scarcely know any work we are so anxious to recommend to all who take an interest in the genuine welfare of Ireland, as this work of Mr Anderson's."—Christian Examiner.

ALSO, BY THE SAME AUTHOR,

IRELAND, but still without the MINISTRY of the WORD in her own NATIVE LANGUAGE.   18mo.   1s.

OLIVER & BOYD'S NEW TRAVELLING MAP of SCOTLAND, carefully corrected to the present Time, and beautifully engraved and coloured. In a Case, or neatly half-bound, forming a small Pocket Volume, 9s.

*** This Map is constructed on an improved plan, with the distances on the great roads, by which any place or route may be traced with ease by the traveller, either in a carriage or on horseback, without the inconvenience to which he must submit by unfolding Maps on the ordinary construction.

OLIVER & BOYD'S NEW TRAVELLING MAP of ENGLAND and WALES, carefully corrected to the present Time, and exhibiting the different Counties, Towns, Villages, Stages, Principal and Cross Roads, Hills, Rivers, Canals, &c.; constructed and drawn with the greatest care. By JOHN BELL, Land-Surveyor.
In a Case, 7s. 6d.; on Rollers, 9s.

SURENNE'S NEW FRENCH MANUAL, and TRAVELLER'S COMPANION: containing an Introduction to French Pronunciation; a copious Vocabulary; a Selection of Phrases; a Series of Conversations, on a Tour to Paris by Four different Routes, through France, Holland, Germany, and Switzerland; with a Description of the Public Buildings, Institutions, Curiosities, Manners, and Amusements, of the French Capital, &c.; also Models of Epistolary Correspondence, and Directions to Travellers. To which are added, the Statistics of Paris, and Tables of French and British Monies, Weights, and Measures. Illustrated by Three Maps. Fifth Edition, revised and enlarged.   Royal 18mo.   4s. half-bound.

BEAUTIFUL POCKET EDITION OF THE

FRENCH NEW TESTAMENT, printed on a NEW DIAMOND TYPE (uniform with the King's Printers' small English Testament).
24mo.   3s.; with English Psalms, &c. 3s. 6d.

*** This Diamond French Testament, executed in the first style of elegance and accuracy, forms a most excellent and appropriate present for Young Persons, and may be had richly bound, embossed covers and gilt edges, 4s. 6d.; morocco, 6s.

STORIES from the HISTORY of SCOTLAND, in the Manner of
Stories selected from the History of England. By the Rev. ALEXANDER STEWART, Author of
The History of Scotland, &c. Second Edition, greatly enlarged. With a Frontispiece.
18mo. 4s. half-bound.

" Mr Stewart has rejected every thing in the Scottish annals that holds a doubtful place betwixt history
and fable, and by judiciously avoiding long details, he has succeeded in bringing his interesting performance
within the limits of one volume, forming an admirable companion to Mr Croker's ' Stories from the History
of England.' "—*New Monthly Magazine.*

" This is a very amusing and instructive little book for a juvenile present. The stories in it are well
chosen, and abridged with care. It deserves to be preferred to scores of other works intended to awaken a love
of reading in the young scholar, and furnish him with materials for thinking. We recommend it to persons
engaged in tuition, as a very useful little volume."—*Athenæum.*

THE TOUR of the HOLY LAND; in a Series of Conversations:
with an Appendix, containing Extracts from a MS. Journal of Travels in Syria. By the
Rev. ROBERT MOREHEAD, D. D., F. R. S. E., &c. With a Map of Palestine. 18mo. 3s. 6d.

" " The pious and learned author of these dialogues, having had his attention called to Palestine, turned
over a variety of books on the subject, and with a praiseworthy regard to the wants of the rising generation,
arranged the most interesting facts and descriptions that occurred to him in the course of this voluminous
reading, into the form of a series of conversations, intermixed with reflections of a grave and religious
character. The execution of the work is worthy the design; and the result is a little volume, which parents
and guardians of youth will do well to present to their charges."—*Atlas.*

" In this brief but spirited compilation, the reverend editor has collected together some of the most touching
descriptions that can be found in our literature, of all those scenes and places in the Holy Land, which are
endeared to our memories by associations of the deepest and most durable interest."—*Monthly Review.*

SPECIMENS of the LYRICAL, DESCRIPTIVE, and NARRA-
TIVE POETS of GREAT BRITAIN, from CHAUCER to the Present Day: with a Preli-
minary Sketch of the History of Early English Poetry, and Biographical and Critical Notices. By
JOHN JOHNSTONE, Editor of " Specimens of Sacred and Serious Poetry." With Frontispiece and
Vignette, engraved by Horsburgh, from Paintings by Thomas Stothard, Esq. R. A. 24mo. 5s. 6d.

" In fine, this is a little volume which seems to us calculated to diffuse much both of enjoyment and of
refinement of feeling among the families of our land, with the rising portion of whose members especially we
have no doubt it will soon become a favourite manual."—*Monthly Review.*

. " Not only has Mr Johnstone selected well and amply, but he has accompanied his selections with brief
biographical and critical notices, replete with just observation and the fruits of vigilant research. We are not
acquainted with any publication so admirably calculated to awaken a true zest for genuine English lore, nor
do we think that the larger and more costly compilations possess half the merit of this unassuming little
volume."—*Atlas.*

. " In intrinsic value the volume is literally worth a great deal more than its weight in gold, for it contains
the most precious portion of the most precious literature in existence."—*Athenæum.*

POEMS, by WILLIAM COWPER, of the Inner Temple, Esq.; to which
is prefixed, a Memoir of the Author; also Critical Remarks on his Poems. By JOHN
M'DIARMID. New Edition, revised and extended. *Nearly ready.*

" The kindred warmth with which the biographer enters into all the feelings of his author; the animation
of his style, kindling not unfrequently into poetical fervour; and the good sense and acuteness that characterize his observations, cannot fail to render his narrative highly acceptable to the admirers of this amiable
and eminent poet.—But it is in his Critical Remarks that the abilities and taste of the editor are chiefly
displayed. On this part of his task he enters with all the ardour of a kindred spirit; and, while he estimates
the characteristic qualities of Cowper's various works with great acuteness and accuracy of discrimination, he
appreciates the efforts, the feelings, the inspirations of the poet, with a truth and fulness of sympathy which a
poet only could feel."—*Edinburgh Magazine.*

GOLDSMITH'S VICAR of WAKEFIELD, ESSAYS, & POEMS;
with Prefatory Remarks by JOHN M'DIARMID.   24mo. 5s.

PAUL and VIRGINIA, from the French of ST PIERRE; and
ELIZABETH, from the French of Madame COTTIN. New Translations; with Prefatory
Remarks by JOHN M'DIARMID.   24mo. 3s.

" This New Translation of the two most beautiful and interesting tales in the French language is executed
in a style of elegance, sweetness, and simplicity of diction, that renders it a valuable addition to the library
of the man of taste and the lover of whatever is pathetic in story or sentimental in feeling. From the translator's Prefatory Observations, he would seem to possess a soul as ductile and susceptible of all the finer impulses
of our nature as St Pierre himself."—*European Magazine.*

THE POEMS of OSSIAN, translated by JAMES MACPHERSON,
Esq.; with the Translator's Dissertations on the Era and Poems of Ossian; Dr Blair's Cri-
tical Dissertation; and an Inquiry into the Genuineness of these Poems, *written expressly for this
Edition.* By the Rev. ALEXANDER STEWART.   24mo. 5s.

POEMS and SONGS, by ROBERT BURNS.   With a Memoir of the
Author, written expressly for this Edition ; and a Glossary, Vignette, and Frontispiece.
24mo.   2s. 6d.

MY EARLY DAYS.   With a fine Frontispiece.   Third Edition,
improved.   18mo.   2s. 6d.

" This is really one of the best little volumes of its class which we have ever met with."—*Literary Gazette.*

" This is a pretty domestic tale, narrating with much truth to nature the events of early life, and pointing out their influence in forming the human character at mature age.—The story is interesting, and the moral it inculcates excellent."—*Literary Chronicle.*

" It is an excellent book to put into the hands of children."—*Gentleman's Magazine.*

" It is beautifully written ; and were we to speak of it as warmly as we felt disposed to do under the fresh impression of the perusal, we might be suspected of partiality or extravagance."—*Eclectic Review.*

" The principles it inculcates are directly conducive to the cultivation of filial piety, reverence for the Sabbath, and a watchful regard to the dictates of conscience in the formation of early habits. A higher degree of talent in the delineation of character is evinced in this volume, than in most of the publications of this order."—*Congregational Magazine.*

DIVERSIONS of HOLLYCOT ; or, The Mother's Art of Thinking.
By the Author of Clan Albin, Elizabeth de Bruce, Nights of the Round Table, &c.
18mo.   3s. 6d. neatly half-bound.

Contents.—Introduction. Quizzing—The Boast of Knowledge—Rational Reading. The Nutting Excursion. Saturday Night at Hollycot. Memoir of Grisell Baillie. Sunday at Hollycot. Lights and Shadows of Juvenile Life. Style and Vulgarity—Courage and Humanity. The Ship Launch. True Charity—Instinct of Birds. Punctuality—Visit to a Cottage. The Juvenile Debate—Beauty or Utility. Infirmity of Purpose—Philosophy of Daily Life. The Geysers—The Cuttle-fish—Knowledge is Power—Young Casa Bianca. Christmas—A Home—Holidays.

" This is a very delightful production in that most difficult branch of writing—juvenile literature.—The story is interesting, but made subservient to instruction ;—little Anecdotes of Natural History are admirably introduced, and the children are drawn as so few can draw them—clever, well-disposed, but still children. The moral lessons conveyed are not less simple than striking."—*Literary Gazette.*

NIGHTS of the ROUND TABLE ; or, Stories of Aunt Jane and
her Friends.   FIRST SERIES.   By the Author of Diversions of Hollycot, &c.   Small 8vo. 5s.

Contents.—When I was a little Girl—Miss Harding's Tale. The Spittalfields Widow. The Royal Chapel of Windsor. The Magic Lantern—The Three Westminster Boys. The Curate's Tale ; or, Practical Joking. The Magic Lantern—Fashion and Personal Ornament. Miss Harding's Tale concluded—High Life.

" The narratives are very well executed : stories of grave and gay succeed each other in pleasing alternation —and over the whole is thrown that charm of graceful simplicity, in which we at once recognise the instinctive power of the female heart."—*Monthly Review.*

" This is a very handsome volume, and, what is far better, a very valuable one. It consists of seven instructive stories, which the young will read with pleasure and profit : nor are we sure that they would be thrown away upon the old and the wise. They are very characteristic, and worthy of the accomplished authoress ; good sense and good feeling every where abound ; there is much knowledge of human nature, and that practical wisdom which seeks to be useful and elegant. We have seldom met with a work, aiming only at instruction, in which there are so many attractions. The writer unites the affection of a mother, the vigilance of an aunt, and the skill of a governess, with the grace and elegance of a well-bred lady."—*Athenæum.*

NIGHTS of the ROUND TABLE ; or, Stories of Aunt Jane and
her Friends.   SECOND and CONCLUDING SERIES.   Small 8vo. 5s.

Contents.—The Quaker Family. The Two Scotch Williams. The Little Ferryman.

" The Second Series of these ' Nights of the Round Table' is quite equal to the former. The Tales are written with the same moral purpose, and delineate life and manners, and general nature, with great truth and feeling."—*New Monthly Magazine.*

" With many graces of style, and felicities of thought, Mrs Johnstone excels in the delineation of character. Her ideal personages are painted with so much individual truth, that they live in the memory, as if they were our familiar and long-known acquaintances. '—*Scotsman.*

LETTERS from a LADY to her NIECE ; containing Practical
Hints, intended to direct the Female Mind in the Pursuit of Attainments conducive to Virtue and Happiness.   With a Frontispiece, designed by Uwins and engraved by Horsburgh.   Third Edition.   18mo. 2s.

" The anonymous writer of Letters from a Lady to her Niece is more justly entitled to the praise of the judicious critic, and the thanks of her own sex, than many others who have been eager to avow their claim to their productions. The style is easy and elegant ; the maxims inculcated are those of sound prudence and sincere virtue ; and, to any female entering into life, the perusal of this little volume will be attended with manifold advantages, in strengthening the intellectual powers, and indicating the most eligible path to the attainment of tranquillity of mind and true happiness."—*Monthly Magazine.*

EDINBURGH CABINET LIBRARY.

THE primary object of this undertaking was to construct, from the varied and costly materials that have been accumulating for ages, a popular Work, appearing in successive volumes, and comprising all that is really valuable in those branches of knowledge which most happily combine amusement with instruction. A scheme so comprehensive necessarily embraced a wide range of subjects; all of which, however, though treated by separate writers, were designed to form component parts of one uniform system. To record the principal events and the prominent changes and revolutions in the history of nations;—to describe their social condition, political institutions, and domestic habits, with their natural history, productions, and resources, their literature, antiquities, and physical appearance;—to follow the progress of inland and maritime discovery, embodying the researches of those fearless adventurers who have traversed stormy oceans, or penetrated into the interior of barbarous kingdoms;—to mark the steps by which the sciences and arts that refine and improve human nature have arrived at their present stage of advancement;—in short, to exhibit, under all their variety of circumstances and forms, Man and the objects by which he is surrounded,—are among the leading features in the design of the EDINBURGH CABINET LIBRARY.

Its reception hitherto has exceeded the most sanguine anticipations of the Proprietors; and they need only refer to the favourable notices in almost every journal in the British empire, for evidence that it is now established in the estimation of the public as a Work of acknowledged merit. It has also been reviewed with much commendation in numerous foreign periodicals; on the Continent, translations of it continue to be executed from time to time; and in America, the volumes as they appear are regularly stereotyped.

The following valuable Works have already appeared, beautifully printed in small 8vo ; with Maps expressly constructed for the several subjects, Portraits, and numerous appropriate Engravings by the most Eminent Artists : Price of each Volume, in Cloth Boards, 5s.

I.

NARRATIVE of DISCOVERY and ADVENTURE in the POLAR SEAS and REGIONS: With Illustrations of their Climate, Geology, and Natural History; and an Account of the WHALE-FISHERY. By Sir JOHN LESLIE, PROFESSOR JAMESON, and HUGH MURRAY, Esq., F.R.S.E. Fourth Edition, revised and enlarged.

II.

NARRATIVE of DISCOVERY and ADVENTURE in AFRICA, from the Earliest Ages to the Present Time: With Illustrations of the Geology, Mineralogy, and Zoology. By HUGH MURRAY, Esq., F.R.S.E.; PROFESSOR JAMESON; and JAMES WILSON, Esq., F.R.S.E. & M.W.S. Second Edition.

III.

VIEW of ANCIENT and MODERN EGYPT: With an Outline of its Natural History. By the Rev. MICHAEL RUSSELL, LL.D. Second Edition.

IV.

PALESTINE, or the HOLY LAND; from the Earliest Period to the Present Time. By the Rev. MICHAEL RUSSELL, LL.D., Author of "View of Ancient and Modern Egypt." Third Edition.

V.

LIVES and VOYAGES of DRAKE, CAVENDISH, and DAM-PIER: Including a View of the HISTORY of the BUCCANEERS. Third Edition.

VI. VII. VIII.

HISTORICAL and DESCRIPTIVE ACCOUNT of BRITISH INDIA, from the most Remote Period to the Present Time: Including a Narrative of the Early Portuguese and English Voyages, the Revolutions in the Mogul Empire, and the Origin, Progress, and Establishment of the British Power: With Illustrations of the Zoology—Botany—Climate, Geology, and Mineralogy:—Also Medical Observations,—an Account of the Hindoo Astronomy—the Trigonometrical Surveys—and the Navigation of the Indian Seas. By HUGH MURRAY, Esq., F.R.S.E.; JAMES WILSON, Esq., F.R.S.E. & M.W.S.; R. K. GREVILLE, LL.D.; PROFESSOR JAMESON; Sir WHITELAW AINSLIE, M.D., M.R.A.S., late of the Medical Staff of Southern India; PROFESSOR WALLACE; and Captain CLARENCE DALRYMPLE, Master-Attendant at Madras. Second Edition.—In Three Volumes.

IX.

HISTORICAL VIEW of the PROGRESS of DISCOVERY on the more NORTHERN COASTS of AMERICA, from the Earliest Period to the Present Time. By PATRICK FRASER TYTLER, Esq., F.R.S. & F.S.A. With DESCRIPTIVE SKETCHES of the NATURAL HISTORY of the NORTH AMERICAN REGIONS. By JAMES WILSON, Esq., F. R. S. E. & M.W. S. To which is added, an APPENDIX, containing Remarks on a late Memoir of Sebastian Cabot, with a Vindication of Richard Hakluyt. Second Edition.

X.

THE TRAVELS and RESEARCHES of ALEXANDER VON HUMBOLDT: Being a condensed Narrative of his Journeys in the Equinoctial Regions of America, and in Asiatic Russia; together with Analyses of his more important Investigations. By WILLIAM MACGILLIVRAY, A.M., F.R.S.E., Conservator of the Museums of the Royal College of Surgeons of Edinburgh, Member of the Natural History Societies of Edinburgh and Philadelphia, &c. Second Edition.

XI.

LIFE of SIR WALTER RALEIGH: Founded on Authentic and Original Documents, some of them never before published: Including a View of the most important Transactions in the Reigns of Elizabeth and James I.; Sketches of Burleigh, Essex, Secretary Cecil, Sidney, Spenser, and other Eminent Contemporaries: With a Vindication of his Character from the Attacks of Hume and other Writers. By PATRICK FRASER TYTLER, Esq., F.R.S. & F.S.A. Second Edition.

XII.

NUBIA and ABYSSINIA: Comprehending their Civil History, Antiquities, Arts, Religion, Literature, and Natural History. By the Rev. MICHAEL RUSSELL, LL.D., Author of " View of Ancient and Modern Egypt," " Palestine, or the Holy Land," &c. Second Edition.

XIII. XIV.

HISTORY of ARABIA, Ancient and Modern: Containing a De-scription of the Country—an Account of its Inhabitants, Antiquities, Political Condition, and Early Commerce—the Life and Religion of Mohammed—the Conquests, Arts, and Literature of the Saracens—the Caliphs of Damascus, Bagdad, Africa, and Spain—the Civil Government and Religious Ceremonies of the Modern Arabs—Origin and Suppression of the Wahabees—the Institutions, Character, Manners, and Customs of the Bedouins; and a comprehensive View of its Natural History. By ANDREW CRICHTON. Second Edition.—In Two Volumes.

XV.

AN HISTORICAL and DESCRIPTIVE ACCOUNT of PERSIA, from the Earliest Ages to the Present Time: With a detailed View of its Resources, Government, Population, Natural History, and the Character of its Inhabitants, particularly of the Wandering Tribes; including a Description of Afghanistan and Beloochistan. By JAMES B. FRASER, Esq., Author of " Travels in Khorasan," " A Tour through the Himala," &c. Second Edition.

XVI.

LIVES of EMINENT ZOOLOGISTS, from ARISTOTLE to LIN-NÆUS inclusive: With Introductory Remarks on the Study of Natural History, and Occasional Observations on the Progress of Zoology. By W. MACGILLIVRAY, A.M., F.R.S.E., &c., Author of " A Narrative of the Travels and Researches of Alexander Von Humboldt."

XVII.

HISTORY and PRESENT CONDITION of the BARBARY STATES: Comprehending a View of their Civil Institutions, Antiquities, Arts, Religion, Literature, Commerce, Agriculture, and Natural Productions. By the Rev. MICHAEL RUSSELL, LL.D., Author of " View of Ancient and Modern Egypt," " Palestine, or the Holy Land," " Nubia and Abyssinia," &c.

XVIII. XIX. XX.

AN HISTORICAL and DESCRIPTIVE ACCOUNT of CHINA; Its Ancient and Modern History, Language, Literature, Religion, Government, Industry, Manners, and Social State; Intercourse with Europe from the Earliest Ages; Missions and Embassies to the Imperial Court; British and Foreign Commerce; Directions to Navigators; State of Mathematics and Astronomy; Survey of its Geography, Geology, Botany, and Zoology. By HUGH MURRAY, F.R.S.E.; JOHN CRAWFURD, Esq.; PETER GORDON, Esq.; Captain THOMAS LYNN; WILLIAM WALLACE, F.R.S.E., Professor of Mathematics in the University of Edinburgh; and GILBERT BURNETT, Esq., late Professor of Botany, King's College, London.—In Three Volumes.

₊ For Works nearly ready for publication see last page of this List.

WORKS ON EDUCATION.

The high character which many of the Schoolbooks contained in the following List have acquired, in every part of the United Kingdom, and in America, has induced the Publishers to spare no exertion in still further improving them, both with respect to matter and style. The preparation of such Manuals as appeared to be *desiderata* in the great business of Education was committed to individuals not only of established reputation as authors, but whose experience also in teaching fitted them to produce. works which could not fail to be highly useful. Although the Class-books thus furnished were from the first arranged according to the most approved methods, the Publishers have nevertheless at all times kept steadily in view the possibility of improvement; and while no means for that purpose have been neglected, the suggestions of practical men especially have invariably met with the most attentive consideration. The works now revised have been carefully adapted to the advanced state of knowledge and the improved system of teaching; the most authentic sources have been examined; and no change has been admitted which is not stamped with undoubted accuracy. While acting under these impressions, the Publishers have at the same time preserved such a neat and correct style of typography, as will at once gratify the Teacher, and be of no little advantage to the Learner.

English Reading, Grammar, &c.

A MANUAL of ENGLISH GRAMMAR, Philosophical and Practical; with Exercises; adapted to the Analytical Mode of Tuition. For the Use of Schools, or Private Students. By the Rev. J. M. M'CUL-LOCH, A. M., Minister of Kelso, formerly Head-Master of Circus Place School, Edinburgh. New Edition, greatly improved. 18mo. 1s. 6d. bound.

*** The sale of a large impression in the short space of a few months, is the most gratifying proof of the general approbation with which this Manual has been received, and has stimulated the Author to render it still more deserving of public favour.

" No schoolbook," says the *Presbyterian Review*, " has of late been more wanted than a Manual of English Grammar, adapted to the improved methods of teaching, and treating the subject not as an art but as a science. It was therefore with the greatest pleasure that we saw the announcement of this little work by Mr M'Culloch, whose experience as a public teacher, success as a compiler of schoolbooks, and varied and extensive learning, were the surest pledges that he would bring to the composition of it the necessary practical and philological knowledge. We regard this Manual of English Grammar as decidedly the best book of the kind in the language; and if we are not greatly mistaken, we shall soon see it supersede the defective and inaccurate abridgments at present used in our schools."—According to the *Liverpool Journal*, " It is full of valuable information, conveyed in such plain terms as to render it of *practical* utility to teachers and learners."—The *Atlas* adds, " We are glad to see a second and enlarged edition of a schoolbook, which on its first appearance we felt inclined to hail as a very great improvement on the elementary Works on Grammar by which it was preceded. Mr M'Culloch's *Course of Elementary Reading*, and his *Lessons in Prose and Verse*, have already distinguished him among the teachers of the rising generation. We have no less reason to be satisfied with the little work before us than with those of which we have long since expressed a favourable opinion."

M'CULLOCH's SERIES of LESSONS in PROSE and VERSE, progressively arranged; intended as an Introduction to the " COURSE of ELEMENTARY READING in SCIENCE and LITERATURE." To which is added, a List of Prefixes, Affixes, and Latin and Greek Primitives, which enter into the Composition of the Words occurring in the Lessons. Fifth Edition. 12mo. 2s. 6d. bound.

This little work, in common with the author's " Course of Elementary Reading,"—to which it is meant to be introductory,—has been prepared in adaptation to the Improved System of Teaching which has of late years been so generally introduced into our initiatory schools. Being intended for seminaries where the preceptor makes it his business to instruct his pupils in the *meaning* of what is read, as well as in the *art of reading*, such lessons only have been introduced as appeared well fitted to stimulate youthful curiosity, and enrich the mind with the knowledge of useful and interesting facts. Simple extracts, relating to Natural History, Elementary Science, Religion, and the Duties of the Young, have been preferred to Dramatic Scenes, impassioned Poetry, and Parliamentary Orations. And, while no pieces have been admitted but such as seemed likely to inform and entertain, care has been taken to abridge and otherwise alter them, so as to adapt their style as well as their sentiments to the juvenile capacity.—It may be mentioned as new features in this work, that the extracts are progressively arranged according to their simplicity,—that each Section is preceded by Exercises on the more difficult words that occur in it,—and that, besides the ordinary selections, there is a series of Elliptical Lessons, or what have been termed, by the ingenious author of the " Diversions of Hollycot," *Rational Readings*. The list of Prefixes, Affixes, and Latin and Greek Primitives, given in the Appendix, is, since the publication of the author's "Course of Elementary Reading," no longer a novelty in works of this description.

M'CULLOCH's COURSE of ELE-MENTARY READING in SCIENCE and LITERATURE; to which is added, a copious List of the Latin and Greek Primitives which enter into the Composition of the English Language. Fifth Edition. 12mo. 3s. 6d. bound.

The compiler has admitted into his pages only such lessons as he considered fitted to stimulate juvenile curiosity, and enrich the mind with useful knowledge. Great space has been allotted to Natural Philosophy and Natural History; but not more, he feels assured, than the claims of these sciences and the taste of the present age justify. Those who have not attended to the subject, can have no idea of the delight with which children listen to details of natural history and explanations of common phenomena; and it is surely impossible too early to introduce young persons to studies which tend more than any other to form habits of observation and reflection, and to inspire admiration of the power and wisdom manifested in every part of creation.

P REFIXES and AFFIXES of the ENGLISH LANGUAGE, with Examples. To be committed to Memory. Extracted chiefly from Mr M'Culloch's " Manual of English Grammar." New Edition. 18mo. 2d. sd.

MR WOOD'S BOOKS.

OLIVER & BOYD beg to intimate, that they have recently become the Publishers of the following Popular Works connected with Education, as taught in that justly-celebrated Institution—the Edinburgh Sessional School :—

L

ACCOUNT of the EDINBURGH SESSIONAL SCHOOL, and the other Parochial Institutions for Education, established in that City in the Year 1812; with Strictures on Education in general. By JOHN WOON, Esq.

" Ignorance is the curse of God ;
Knowledge the wing wherewith we fly to heaven."
Shakspeare.

Fourth Edition. 12mo. 5s. boards.

This well-known Work, which has been reprinted in America, not only contains an account of the celebrated Seminary, which for years past has given the tone to elementary education in our own country, and excited much attention abroad, but also embraces a wide field of inquiry relative to education in general ; discussing, among other topics, every important question regarding the instruction of the lower orders—The benefits to be derived from Sunday Schools, Evening Schools, and Infant Schools—The method of conducting, and advantages to be derived from the Explanatory, or what is now called the Intellectual System—Tuition by Monitors—Qualifications of Teachers—Effects of Emulation, Places, and Prizes—Modes of Punishment—Public Examinations, Holidays, &c. &c.

II.

EDINBURGH SESSIONAL SCHOOL FIRST BOOK. Thirteenth Edition. 18mo. 3d. sewed.

- It is the peculiarity of this Primer, that the pupil, instead of being detained with unmeaning sounds, is at once, after learning the Alphabet, introduced to short significant words of two letters, and begins the Explanatory System in its simplest form, as exhibited in the "Account of the Edinburgh Sessional School." He is thence gradually led on to words of three and four letters, when he is presented with instructive Lessons principally taken from incidents in Sacred History, or such as inculcate moral duties.

III.

EDINBURGH SESSIONAL SCHOOL SECOND BOOK. Ninth Edition. 18mo. 1s. half-bound.

This Book, besides carrying the child forward in Scripture reading, supplies him with much interesting and useful instruction in Natural History ; such as, accounts of the Dog, Horse, Sheep, Cow, Hog, Swallow, Pigeon, Herring, Salmon, Oyster and particularly the Pearl Oyster, Bee, Caterpillar, Oak, Fir, Corn, Cotton, Flax, Hemp ; the various Metals, with their different uses ; also simple descriptions of the Manufactures of Cloth, Pins, Glass, &c., and other Miscellaneous Instruction.

IV.

SESSIONAL SCHOOL COLLECTION. Ninth Edition. 12mo. 3s. bound.

- This Compilation consists of Religious and Moral Instruction, both in Prose and Verse, a Selection of Fables, Descriptions of Animals, Places, Manners, Historical Passages, and other useful information interesting to youth.

V.

INSTRUCTIVE EXTRACTS. Fourth Edition. 12mo. 3s. 6d. bound.

This Book also comprises Religious and Moral Instruction, Natural History, Elementary Science, Accounts of Remarkable Persons, Places, Manners, Arts, and Incidents, with a Selection from the British Poets.

VI.

HELPS to the ORTHOGRAPHY of the ENGLISH LANGUAGE. 18mo. 4d. sewed.

This little Manual contains twenty-six Rules for Spelling, relating principally to the niceties of Orthography ; such as, the occasions for doubling letters, employing silent *E*, and changing *Y* into *I*.

VII.

ETYMOLOGICAL GUIDE to the ENGLISH LANGUAGE. Second Edition. 18mo. 2s. 6d. bound.

This is a Collection, alphabetically arranged, of the principal Roots, Affixes, and Prefixes, with their Derivatives and Compounds. For example, from the Latin word "animus" the mind, are shown to be derived *magnanimity, pusillanimity, equanimity, unanimity, animadversion.*

VIII.

OLD TESTAMENT BIOGRAPHY, in the Form of Questions, with References to Scripture for the Answers. Seventh Edition. 18mo. 6d. sewed.

IX.

NEW TESTAMENT BIOGRAPHY, on the same Plan. Stereotype Edition. 18mo. 6d. sewed.

X.

A CONCISE and FAMILIAR EXPOSITION of the PROPHECIES regarding MESSIAH, which have already been fulfilled ; intended as a Manual for Young Persons. Second Edition, 18mo. 4d. sewed.

XI.

EXPOSITION of the DUTIES and SINS pertaining to Men in their various Relations of Superiors, Inferiors, and Equals. 12mo. 6d. sewed.

XII.

SACRED HISTORY, in the Form of Letters. In Seven Volumes 18mo. 3s. each ; neatly half-bound.

This Work has received the very highest commendation, not only in the Religious Periodicals and Newspapers of the day, but also from the most distinguished Clergymen of all persuasions, both in England and Scotland, as being well calculated to communicate the most valuable instruction to persons of all ages. It comprises the whole period from the Creation to the destruction of Jerusalem ; and hence, besides elucidating the Scriptures of the Old and New Testament, it puts the reader in possession of the little-known but deeply-interesting History of the Jews, both during the intervening and subsequent periods ; thus supplying what was formerly a great *desideratum* in the historical instruction of youth.

THE ENGLISH LEARNER; or, a Selection of Lessons in Prose and Verse, adapted to the Capacity of the Younger Classes of Readers. By THOMAS EWING, Teacher of Elocution, Geography, History, &c. Edinburgh. Tenth Edition. 12mo. 2s. bound.

EWING's PRINCIPLES of ELO- CUTION; containing numerous Rules, Observations, and Exercises, on Pronunciation, Pauses, Inflections, Accent, and Emphasis; also, copious Extracts in Prose and Poetry; calculated to assist the Teacher, and to improve the Pupil in Reading and Recitation. Nineteenth Edition. 12mo. 4s. 6d. bound.

EWING's RHETORICAL EX- ERCISES; being a Sequel to the *Prin- ciples of Elocution*, and intended for Pupils, who have made considerable Progress in Reading and Recitation. Second Edition. 12mo. 3s. 6d. bd.

LESSONS in READING and SPEAKING; being an Improvement of *Scott's Lessons in Elocution*. By WILLIAM SOOTT, the original Compiler. Twenty-eighth Edition, enlarged. To which is prefixed, An Outline of the Elements of Elocution, illustrated by numerous Rules and Examples, directing the proper Application of Rhetorical Pauses and In- flections of the Voice. By J. JOHNSTONE. 12mo. 3s. bound.

SCOTT's BEAUTIES of EMI- NENT WRITERS (Oliver & Boyd's im- proved Edition); containing an Outline of the Elements of Elocution, illustrated by numerous Rules and Examples, directing the proper Appli- cation of Rhetorical Pauses, and the Inflections of the Voice; with Biographical Notices of all the Authors from whose works Scott's Beauties are selected, and a variety of Striking Passages from the most celebrated Modern Poets, adapted for Recitation. By J. JOHNSTONE. In 2 vols 12mo. Vol. I. 2s. 6d.; Vol. II. 2s.; or both vo- lumes bound together, 4s.

A PRONOUNCING SPELLING- BOOK, with Reading Lessons in Prose and Verse. By G. FULTON and G. KNIGHT. Six- teenth Edition. 12mo. 1s. 6d. bound.

FULTON's PRONOUNCING VOCABULARY; with Lessons in Prose and Verse, and a few Grammatical Exercises. Second Edition. 12mo. 2s. bound.

FULTON's improved and enlarged Edition of JOHNSON's DICTIONARY, in Miniature: To which are subjoined, Vocabu- laries of Classical and Scriptural Proper Names; a concise Account of the Heathen Deities; a Col- lection of Quotations and Phrases from the La- tin, French, Italian, and Spanish Languages; a Chronological Table of Remarkable Events from the Creation of the World till the present Time; and a List of Men of Genius and Learning; with a Portrait of Dr Johnson. Sixteenth Edition. 18mo. Price only 3s. bound.

DR HARDIE's EXTRACTS, for the Use of Parish Schools. Eleventh Edition. 12mo. 2s. 6d. bound.

ANALYSIS of the SEVEN PARTS of SPEECH of the ENGLISH LAN- GUAGE, with a view to fix their Character, and furnish simple Rules for ascertaining them; as also to elucidate and facilitate the Method of Parsing. By the Rev. CHARLES J. LYON, M.A., late of Trinity College, Cambridge. 12mo. 3s. boards.

Geography and History.

STEWART's COMPENDIUM of MODERN GEOGRAPHY; with Remarks on the Physical Peculiarities, Productions, Com- merce, and Government of the various Coun- tries; Questions for Examination at the end of each Division; and Descriptive Tables, in which are given the Pronunciation, and a concise Ac- count of every Place of importance throughout the World. Fifth Edition, thoroughly revised and considerably enlarged. Illustrated by Ten New Maps constructed for the Work, and an Engraving showing the Heights of the principal Mountains on the Globe. 18mo. 3s. 6d. bound.

*** In preparing the present Edition of this Compen- dium for the press, neither labour nor expense has been spared to render it still more deserving of the prefer- ence which has been given to it both by teachers and by the public. Every part of it has been minutely and carefully revised, and the utmost attention has been bestowed on the facts and descriptions, with the view of maintaining its character for accuracy of detail. Besides various improvements throughout, this im- pression will be found to embrace a great deal of va- luable geographical knowledge, derived from the most recent and authentic sources, Foreign as well as Bri- tish; the extent of which can only be fully appreciated by an examination of the work itself. The Descriptive Tables are considerably enlarged, and to all the more important cities, seaports, capes, &c., the latitude and longitude have been added. The description of the American Continent, besides being enriched with much additional information, is now rendered more conform- able to the general plan. An accurate set of Maps has been prepared, strictly adapted to the text, and includ- ing all the latest discoveries. Upon the whole, this Edition is sent forth in the confident expectation, that it will be found still more entitled than any of its pre- decessors to the high degree of popular favour with which the work has been every where received.

AN OUTLINE of SACRED GEO- GRAPHY; with References to the Pas- sages of Scripture in which the most remarkable Places are mentioned; and Notes, chiefly histori- cal and descriptive. For the Use of Schools. By ALEXANDER REID, A. M., Rector of Circus Place School, Edinburgh. New Edition, im- proved; with a Map of the Holy Land. 18mo. 6d. sewed.

EWING's SYSTEM of GEOGRA- PHY, from the latest and best Authorities; including also the Elements of Astronomy, an Account of the Solar System, a variety of Pro- blems to be solved by the Terrestrial and Celestial Globes, and a Pronouncing Vocabulary contain- ing all the Names of Places which occur in the Text. Fourteenth Edition, carefully revised and enlarged. 12mo. 4s. 6d. bound; or with Nine Maps, 5s. 6d.

EWING's NEW GENERAL AT-
LAS; containing distinct Maps of all the
principal States and Kingdoms throughout the
World, in which the most recent Geographical
Discoveries are accurately delineated. *An en-
tirely new Set of Plates, and Price much reduced.*
In royal 4to, 14s. half-bound; coloured outlines,
16s. ; or, full coloured, 18s.

⁎ The encouragement which these two distinct
but closely-allied works have uniformly received, has
induced the author and publishers to spare neither
trouble nor expense in bringing them to the utmost
possible perfection. In revising the *System of Geography* for a *fourteenth edition*, every care has been
bestowed to introduce such additions and improvements as might sustain its established reputation.
The *Maps* have been *re-engraved;* and it is hoped,
that, for beauty of execution and distinctness of delineation, they may challenge a comparison with the
most esteemed and costly productions of the present
day. With these improvements, the *Atlas* still pre-
serves unimpaired the peculiar feature which has rendered the work so popular from the beginning,—that
as an accompaniment to the *Geography*, it can be
used with the greatest advantage, since the name of
every place, mountain, river, lake, bay, cape, &c.,
mentioned in that work, is to be found in it; while,
as a *Consulting Atlas*, it is equally well adapted for
the library, or for general reference.

STEWART's HISTORY of SCOT-
LAND, from the Roman Invasion till the
Suppression of the Rebellion in 1745 ; with Exor-
cises; for the Use of Schools or of Private Students.   In one thick vol. 12mo. 5s. bound.

STEWART's improved Edition of
Dr GOLDSMITH's Abridgment of the
HISTORY of ENGLAND; from the Invasion
of Julius Cæsar to the Death of George II. ; with
a CONTINUATION to the Commencement of
the Reign of George IV. To which are subjoined, copious Exercises. Eighth Edition.
In one thick vol. 12mo. 5s. bound.

SIMPSON's HISTORY of SCOT-
LAND, from the Earliest Period to the
Accession of William IV. To which is prefixed,
an Outline of the British Constitution; with
Questions for Examination at the end of each
Section. For the Use of Schools or Private Stu-
dents. Twentieth Edition. 12mo. 3s. 6d. bound.

SIMPSON's improved Edition of
Dr GOLDSMITH's HISTORY of ENG-
LAND, from the Invasion of Julius Cæsar to the
Death of George II. ; with a CONTINUATION
to the Accession of William IV.; and Questions
for Examination at the end of each Section. To
which is added, a Chapter on the British Constitution. Twelfth Edition. 12mo. 3s. 6d. bound.

SIMPSON's improved Edition of
Dr GOLDSMITH's HISTORY of ROME;
with Questions for Examination at the end of
each Section. To which are prefixed, Outlines
of the Geography of Ancient Italy, and Introductory Chapters on Roman Antiquities, containing
an Account of the Origin, Progress, Institutions,
Manners, Customs, Government, Laws, and Military and Naval Affairs of the Romans; and a
Vocabulary of Proper Names accented. With a
Map of Ancient Italy. Tenth Edition.
12mo. 3s. 6d. bound.

SIMPSON's improved Edition of Dr
GOLDSMITH's HISTORY of GREECE ;
and Questions for Examination at the end of
each Section ; with Introductory Chapters on
the Geography, Manners and Customs, Religious
Institutions, and Military and Naval Affairs of
the Greeks ; and a Vocabulary of Proper Names
accented. Illustrated by a Map of Ancient Greece.
Sixth Edition.   12mo. 3s. 6d. bound.

Penmanship.

BUTTERWORTH's COPY
LINES, or SLIPS. all the different kinds,
35 Sorts.   Each 6d. sewed.

BUTTERWORTH's YOUNG
WRITER's INSTRUCTOR; containing
his Method of Teaching, by which one half of the
Paper is saved and the Pupil greatly benefited ;
with a variety of Specimens, calculated to inspire
a true Taste for useful and elegant Writing.
Done up in a neat printed cover.   4to. 7s. 6d.

BUTTERWORTH's YOUNG
ARITHMETICIAN's INSTRUCTOR;
combining accurate Writing, correct Figures, and
judicious Arrangement: designed for the Use of
Schools and Private Families. Done up in a neat
printed cover.   4to. 5s.

INTRODUCTION to PENMAN-
SHIP; or, First Book for Children. By J.
WEIR.   0d. sewed.

RANKINE's ROUND TEXT
SPECIMENS of WRITING. 9d. sewed.

RANKINE's SMALL HAND
SPECIMENS of WRITING. 6d. sewed.

FINDLAY's COPY LINES, or
SLIPS, Round and Small Hand, 3 Sorts.
6d. each, sewed.

Arithmetic and Mathematics.

LESSONS in ARITHMETIC for
Junior Classes; with Tables of Money,
Weights, and Measures, according to the Imperial Standards. By JAMES TROTTER, of the Scottish Naval and Military Academy, &c.; Author
of " A Key to Ingram's Mathematics," &c. A
New Edition, revised.   18mo. 6d. sewed.

⁎ This little work was originally composed for
the use of the Author's Junior Classes, and is now
submitted to the public in the hope that it will be
found worthy of being introduced into Public Schools
and Academies, and that, from the number and variety of the Exercises, it may prove a useful auxiliary
to Governesses and Private Families.

ALSO,

A KEY to LESSONS in ARITH-
METIC. By the same Author. 18mo. 6d sd.

THE PRINCIPLES of ARITH-
METIC and their Application to Business
explained in a popular Manner, and clearly illustrated by simple Rules and numerous Examples:
to which are prefixed, Tables of Monies, Weights,
and Measures, according to the Imperial Standards. By ALEX. INGRAM, Author of "A Concise
System of Mathematics," &c. Seventeenth Edition, thoroughly revised and considerably enlarged. 18mo. *Price only One Shilling bound.*

ALSO,

A KEY to this Work; containing
Solutions of all the Questions performed at length.
By the same Author. 18mo. 2s. 6d. bound.

ELEMENTS of ARITHMETIC;
with an Appendix on Weights and Measures. By ELIAS JOHNSTON, Editor of an improved Edition of "Hamilton's Merchandise,"
&c. 18mo. 2s. bound.

MELROSE'S CONCISE SYSTEM
of PRACTICAL ARITHMETIC; con-
taining the Fundamental Rules and their Application to Mercantile Calculations; Vulgar and
Decimal Fractions; Exchanges; Involution and
Evolution; Progressions; Annuities, certain and
contingent; Artificers' Measuring, &c. Revised,
greatly enlarged, and better adapted to Modern
Practice. By ALEX. INGRAM. Fourteenth Edition. 18mo. 2s. bound.

ALSO,

A KEY to the above Work. By
ALEX. INGRAM. 18mo. 4s. 6d. bound.

A CONCISE SYSTEM of MA-
THEMATICS, in Theory and Practice,
for the Use of Schools, Private Students, and
Practical Men; comprehending Algebra, Elements of Geometry, Practical Geometry, Plane
and Spherical Trigonometry, with their Practical
Applications; Mensuration of Surfaces and So-
lids, Conic Sections, Surveying, Gauging, Specific
Gravity, Practical Gunnery, Mensuration of Artificers' Works, Strength of Materials. With an
Appendix, containing the more difficult Demon-
strations of the Rules in the Body of the Work.
The Third Edition, thoroughly revised, with many
important Additions and Improvements; besides,
an accurate Set of *Stereotyped Tables*, comprising Logarithms of Numbers; Logarithmic Sines
and Tangents; Natural Sines and Tangents;
Areas of Circular Segments; Squares, Cubes,
Square Roots, Cube Roots; &c. By ALEXANDER
INGRAM, Author of "Principles of Arithmetic,"
"Elements of Euclid," &c. *Illustrated by upwards of 300 wood-cuts.* 12mo. 7s. 6d. bound.

ALSO,

A KEY to INGRAM's CONCISE
SYSTEM of MATHEMATICS; containing
Solutions of all the Questions prescribed in that
Work. With an Appendix on Gunnery. By
JAMES TROTTER, of the Scottish Naval and Mi-
litary Academy, &c. 12mo. 8s. 6d. bound.

HUTTON's COMPLETE TREA-
TISE on PRACTICAL ARITHMETIC
and BOOK-KEEPING. Edited by ALEXANDER
INGRAM. A New Edition, with many important
Improvements and Additions; to which are
added, New Sets of Books both by Single and
Double Entry, exemplifying the Modern Practice
of Book-keeping. By JAMES TROTTER, of the
Scottish Naval and Military Academy, &c.
12mo. 3s. bound.

ALSO,

A KEY to HUTTON's ARITH-
METIC; containing Solutions at full length of
all the Questions proposed in that Work.
12mo. 4s. 6d. bound.

SIMSON's ELEMENTS of EU-
CLID. A New Edition, carefully revised
and corrected; to which are annexed, Elements
of Plane and Spherical Trigonometry, by JOHN
DAVIDSON, A. M., &c. 8vo. 8s. boards.

AN ELEMENTARY TREATISE
on ASTRONOMY; or, an Easy Introduction to a Knowledge of the Heavens; with Four
Maps of the Constellations, and a Plate of Figures
illustrative of the Work. By A. MYLNE, D. D.
Second Edition, corrected and improved.
8vo. 9s. boards.

Latin and Greek.

EDINBURGH ACADEMY LA-
TIN RUDIMENTS. Fourth Edition.
12mo. 2s. bound.

EDINBURGH ACADEMY LA-
TIN DELECTUS; with a copious Voca-
bulary, containing an Explanation of every difficult Expression which occurs in the Book. Second Edition, enlarged and improved.
12mo. 3s. bound.

"This is a great improvement," remarks the *Asiatic Journal,* "on the common *Delectus* in respect to
arrangement, as well as the number and selection of
the examples. The excellent Vocabulary, or rather
Dictionary, adapted to the *Delectus,* is a very useful
auxiliary to the learner." The *Edinburgh Weekly
Journal,* in reviewing the work, thus closes a comparison between Dr Valpy's Delectus and that of the
Edinburgh Academy:—"When we take into consideration that the sentences are more equally progres-
sive and better selected, and present us at the same
time with a choice collection of the beauties of the
Roman Authors, we cannot hesitate to affirm, that
the Editor of the Edinburgh Academy Latin Delectus
has given to the public an initiatory schoolbook infinitely superior to that of Dr Valpy, and calculated to
imbue the youthful mind with a love of classical
learning; while it removes altogether the obstacles
which have hitherto rendered the attainment of that
elegant accomplishment difficult and repulsive."

EDINBURGH ACADEMY
GREEK RUDIMENTS. Third Edition.
12mo. 4s. bound.

EDINBURGH ACADEMY
GREEK EXTRACTS, chiefly from the
Attic Writers; with a copious Vocabulary. Se-
cond Edition. 12mo. 3s. 6d. bound.

EDINBURGH ACADEMY EDITION of the GRAMMATICAL EXERCISES. Carefully revised and improved; with Notes, and a Vocabulary containing all the Words that occur in the Work. By GEORGE FERGUSON, A. M., of the Edinburgh Academy. Second Edition.   18mo. 2s. bound.

CORDERII COLLOQUIA; a New Edition, carefully corrected, with the Quantities marked; and containing a Vocabulary *of all the Words that occur in the Text.* By the Rev. GEO. MILLIGAN.   18mo. 2s. bound.

MAIR's INTRODUCTION to LATIN SYNTAX. A New Edition; with improved English Readings, Additional Notes, an English and Latin Vocabulary, and a Vocabulary of Proper Names. By the Rev. ALEX. STEWART.   18mo. 3s. bound.

STEWART's improved Edition of CORNELIUS NEPOS; with Marginal Notes, a Chronological Table, and Roman Calendar; a Vocabulary, containing all the Words that occur in the Work, with their various Significations, and an accurate Reference to the Passages in which any Peculiarity of Translation is required; and an Index of Proper Names. Twelfth Edition.   18mo. 3s. bound.

MAIR's TYRO's DICTIONARY, Latin and English; comprehending the more usual Primitives of the Latin Tongue, together with their Derivatives and Compounds. Eleventh Edition.   12mo. 6s. bound.

AINSWORTH's LATIN DICTIONARY, abridged for the Use of Schools by THOMAS MORELL, D.D. New Stereotype Edition, carefully revised and corrected from the best Authorities, by JAMES ROSS, LL. D.   8vo. 15s. bound.

RUDDIMAN's LATIN GRAMMAR; edited by JOHN HUNTER, LL.D., Principal of the United College of St Salvator and St Leonard, formerly Professor of Humanity in the University of St Andrews. 12mo. 4s. bd.

DR HUNTER's VIRGIL; carefully revised according to the best Readings, and illustrated by English Notes. Fourth Edition, improved.   18mo. 3s. 6d. bound.

DR HUNTER's LIVY, Book XXI. to XXV.; with Notes, critical and explanatory. Fourth Edition, improved.   12mo. 4s. 6d. bound.

DYMOCK's improved Edition of SALLUST; with copious Marginal Notes, and an Historical and Geographical Index. Fifth Edition.   18mo. 2s. 6d. bound.

DYMOCK's CÆSAR; with English Notes, and an Historical and Geographical Index. Eleventh Edition.   12mo. 4s.

DYMOCK's LIVY, First Five Books. New Edition, revised by W. M. GUNN; and illustrated by English Notes, and an Historical and Geographical Index.   12mo. 4s. 6d. bound.

French.

SURENNE's NEW PRONOUNCING FRENCH PRIMER; or, First Step to the French Language : containing a Vocabulary of Easy and Familiar Words, arranged under Distinct Heads; and a Selection of Phrases on Subjects of the most frequent Occurrence. The whole intended as an Introduction to " The New French Manual." Fourth Edition, revised.   Royal 18mo. 1s. 6d.

A FRENCH, ENGLISH, and LATIN VOCABULARY; intended to facilitate the Acquisition of these Languages, and to show how essentially a Knowledge of Latin and French conduces towards a correct Understanding of English. By T. A. GIBSON.   12mo. 2s. bound.

" This is a very ingenious little work, well calculated to sow the seeds of etymological science in young minds. It exhibits the gender and declension of nouns, the nouns themselves, adjectives, verbs, &c., arranged so as to show at once their respective affinities in French, English, Latin, and occasionally the Greek languages. It is a manual which will be useful even to the adult scholar."—*Asiatic Journal.*

BUQUET's NOUVEAU COURS de LITTERATURE; ou, Répertoire des Chefs-d'Œuvre de Corneille, Racine, Voltaire, Molière, La Fontaine, Fénélon, &c. ; suivi des Commentaires de La Harpe, et précédé d'un choix des plus beaux Morceaux, en Prose et en Vers, des plus célèbres Ecrivains Français, &c. A l'Usage de l'Académie d'Edimbourg. Third Edition, revised and considerably enlarged.   12mo. 7s. bound.

" This is another of those works most admirably calculated for the use of young people. Considerable judgment has been displayed in the choice of pieces; and from this many advantages are derived. Not only is a knowledge of the language gained, but the taste is cultivated, and ideas as well as words acquired. It is a most useful volume to all students of a language now almost absolutely necessary."—*Literary Gazette.*

SCOT's FRENCH RECUEIL. Twelfth Edition, improved, by G. WELLS and L. DURIEZ.   12mo. 5s. bound.

CORNILLON's PETIT DICTIONNAIRE des DIFFICULTES de la LANGUE FRANCAISE. Second Edition.   18mo. 3s. 6d. half-bound.

THREE LECTURES on the proper OBJECTS and METHODS of EDUCATION, in reference to the different Orders of Society; and on the relative Utility of Classical Instruction. Delivered in the University of Edinburgh, November 1835. By JAMES PILLANS, M.A.,F.R.S.E., Professor of Humanity in that University.   8vo. 2s.

NEW EDITIONS JUST READY.

DISCOURSES · by the late REV. JAMES MARTIN, A. M., Minister of St George's Church, Edinburgh ; and part of an Intended Series of Letters on Prayer, written by him while at Nice. To which is prefixed, a Memoir of the Author. Second Edition, with a Portrait. 8vo. 10s. 6d. boards.

Extracts from Reviews of the FIRST EDITION of this Work.

" This publication is a monument to the memory of an exemplary minister of the Church of Scotland, cut off in the prime of manhood. Few will read these remains without feeling that, had his life been spared, he would have ranked with the first theologians of our day."—*Athenæum.*

" In a word, the Sermons are of a very high order, and, altogether independent of the circumstances which attach a peculiar interest to the volume, it is one which will long continue to occupy an honourable place in our theological literature. The Memoir prefixed to the Sermons is a beautiful composition."—*Edinburgh Christian Instructor.*

A GRAMMAR of the FRENCH LANGUAGE : In which its Principles are explained in such a manner as to be within the reach of the most com mon Capacity. By M. HALLARD. New Edition, 12mo. From the increasing circulation of this popular work, it is now reduced in price from 5s. to 4s. bound.

Among the numerous French Grammars published in this country, that of Hallard deservedly holds a high rank. This is evinced by its increasing sale, and the preference given to it in the most respectable seminaries, and by distinguished teachers, who are the best qualified to appreciate its merits.—The Author, himself an eminent scholar and practical instructor, has succeeded in producing an elementary treatise on his native language which is at once simple in its plan and judicious in its arrangement, comprehending a series of well-chosen Exercises, adapted to the purposes of tuition, both public and private.

ALSO,

A KEY to HALLARD's FRENCH GRAMMAR. 12mo. 4s. bound.

WORKS IN THE PRESS.

DISCOURSES by the late REV. JOHN B. PATTERSON, A. M.; Minister of Falkirk, Author of the Essay " On the National Character of the Athenians," to which was awarded the Prize proposed by the Royal Commissioners for visiting the Universities of Scotland. To which is prefixed, a Memoir of his Life ; including Select Literary and Religious Remains. 2 vols post 8vo. With a Portrait of the Author.

HISTORICAL ACCOUNT of the CIRCUMNAVIGATION of the GLOBE, and of the PROGRESS of DISCOVERY in the PACIFIC OCEAN, from the Voyage of MAGELLAN to the Death of COOK. With a Portrait of Captain Cook, engraved by Horsburgh, after Dance ; a Fac-simile of his Observations of the Transit of Venus in 1769 ; and Twenty-one highly-finished Engravings in Wood, by Jackson. Forming No. XXI. of the EDINBURGH CABINET LIBRARY.

This volume exhibits the history of maritime enterprise in one of the most interesting regions of the world, during a period of more than two centuries and a half. It contains, besides many others, Narratives of the Voyages and Adventures of Vasco Nunez de Balboa, the discoverer of the South Sea—Magellan—Quiros— Schouten and Le Maire—Tasman—Commodore Anson—Byron—Wallis—Carteret, and Bougainville. The Account of Captain Cook's Voyages is ample and comprehensive, and is very fully illustrated from the Works of recent English and French Navigators; and in the Memoir of his Life is embodied some valuable informa tion, for which the Publishers are indebted to the Relatives of his Family.

LIFE of HENRY the EIGHTH, founded on Authentic and Ori ginal Documents (some of them not before published) : Including an Historical View of his Reign ; with Biographical Sketches of Wolsey, More, Erasmus, Cromwell, Cranmer; and other Eminent Contemporaries. By PATRICK FRASER TYTLER, Esq., F. S. A. With a Portrait of Henry, beautifully engraved by Horsburgh, from Houbraken after Holbein. This work will form No. XXII. of the EDINBURGH CABINET LIBRARY.

RUDIMENTS of ENGLISH GRAMMAR ; for the Use of Junior Classes. By ALEXANDER REID, A. M., Head-Master of Circus Place School, Edinburgh ; Author of " An Outline of Sacred Geography," &c.

RUDIMENTS of MODERN GEOGRAPHY ; for the Use of Junior Classes. By ALEXANDER REID, A. M.

AN INTRODUCTORY ATLAS of MODERN GEOGRAPHY, with an Index containing the Names, and the Latitude and Longitude, of all the Places laid down in the Maps. By ALEXANDER REID, A. M.

Published Monthly, price 2s. 6d.　　　　　[MAY, 1836.]

THE

DUBLIN UNIVERSITY MAGAZINE,

A Literary and Political Journal.

THE attention of the Conservative party in England and Scotland is invited to the DUBLIN UNIVERSITY MAGAZINE, a Monthly Journal, which, in addition to its literary merits, so amply acknowledged by the Press in all parts of the Empire, contains political essays by many of the most distinguished of the Irish Conservatives.　Upon important subjects connected with the best interests of the Empire, the Conductors of the UNIVERSITY MAGAZINE offer *authentic information.* The recent Numbers contain—

I. What is an Orangeman? with the Ritual for the admission of Members, the real Principles of Orangeism, together with a brief history of the causes which led to the formation of the Institution.—II. The Irish Church Question, with authentic letters from Clergymen in distress, Tables of the present state of Church Property, and other documents furnished by authority.— III. Causes of the Failure of the Reformation in Ireland.—IV. Church Reform.—V. The Protestant Deputation to England.—VI. Emigration of the Protestants of Ireland.—VII. How ought Ireland to be Governed?

To BOOK SOCIETIES and NEWS ROOMS the University Magazine will also be found a valuable and agreeable Miscellany, containing LITERARY ARTICLES by the most distinguished writers of the day.

Among the Contributors to the Volumes already published, are—

JOHN ANSTER, LL.D. Translator of "Faust."

Mr. MAXWELL, Author of "Stories of Waterloo," &c. &c.

Mr. CARLETON, Author of "Traits and Stories of the Irish Peasantry."

Mr. LOVER, Author of "Legends and Stories of Ireland."

The late lamented Mrs. HEMANS.

Mrs. S. C. HALL.

The six Volumes for the years 1833, 1834, 1835, may be had bound in cloth, lettered, price 16s. each, or any Single Number at 2s. 6d.

Underneath is a selection of the Literary Articles which have appeared in the Volumes already published—

CHAPTERS OF COLLEGE ROMANCE.

1. Reading for Honours.	4. The Billiard Table.
2. The Murdered Fellow.	3. The Sizar—Arthur Johns.

Series to be continued.

HIBERNIAN NIGHTS' ENTERTAINMENTS,
A SERIES OF IRISH HISTORICAL TALES.

1. The Children of Usnach.	4. Corby Mac Gillmore.
2. The Captive of Killeshin.	5. Rosabel of Ross.
3. The Rebellion of Silken Thomas.	

Series to be continued.

BY MR. CARLETON,
Author of "Traits and Stories of the Irish Peasantry."

1. Stories of Second Sight and Apparition.	3. The Resurrections of Barney Bradley.
2. The Dead Boxer—an Irish Legend.	4. Lha Dhu, or the Dark Day.

BY MR. LOVER,
Author of "Legends and Stories of Ireland."

1. Barny O'Reirdon the Navigator.	2. Little Fairley.

SCENES FROM THE LIFE OF EDWARD LASCELLES, GENT.

Chapter	Chapter	Chapter
1. Boyish Days.	8. Algoa Bay.	16. An Uninvited Guest.
2. My First Cruize.	9. Episodical but pertinent.	17. Homeward Bound.
3. St. Helena—Tender Reminiscences.	10. A Chase.	18. An Affair of the Heart.
	11. The Painted Petrel.	19. Joining the Flag Ship.
4. Cruizing to Windward.	12. Capture of the Camilla.	20. Off Algiers.
5. Cabo Tormentoso.	13. L'Isle d'Alphonse.	21. Malta.
6. Retribution.	14. The Duel	22. Naples.
7. Unexpected Meeting.	15 Flat Island.	23. Naples.

Series to be continued.

BY MR. MAXWELL,

Author of "Stories of Waterloo," "Wild Sports of the West," "My Life," &c. &c.

1. The Unknown.
2. The Condemned Soldier.
3. My First Steeple Chase.

4. Rambling Recollections—Mr. M'Dermott's Story.
5. Leaves from a Game Book.
6. Love against Law, or My Aunt Botherem.

BIOGRAPHICAL ESSAYS.

George Joye the Reformer.—The late Dr. Edward Walsh. (*With a Portrait.*)—Sir Charles L. M. Von Giesecke.—Earl Grey.—Schiller.—Sir James Mackintosh.—Coleridge.

GALLERY OF ILLUSTRIOUS IRISHMEN.

1. Goldsmith, with a Preface to the Series.—2. Grattan.—3. Bishop Berkeley.—4. Boyle.—Flood, Sterne, Burke, Swift, and others, will shortly appear.

◆ **ADVENTURES IN SOUTH AMERICA.**

1. The Elopement.—2. The Dolphin.—3. The Nunnery.—4. The Prize.

MISCELLANEOUS TALES.

1. Mary Gray and Bessy Bell.
2. Perils of the Irish Poor.
3. Love and Loyalty—a Leaf from the Old Almanack.
4. Village Annals.
5. Reading for Honours.
6. An Old Man's Story.
7. The Court Martial—a Tale of Portugal.
8. The Rivals.
9. The Lawyer's Last Brief.
10. The Flibustier—a Tale of the Seventeenth Century.
11. The History of Pierce Bodkin.
12. My Uncle's Manuscripts.
13. The Haunted Grange.
14. Maitre Cornelius.

15. Vicissitudes.
16. The Red Inn of Andernach.
17. The Invisible Gentleman
18. Axel — a Tale of the Thirty Years' War
19. Illustrations of the English— the Old School and the New.
20. The Tartar Princess—a Tale of 1241.
21. The Spectre of the Log Hut.
22. The Choice and the Minister's Annie, by the Ettrick Shepherd
23. The Red Cross of Burgundy.
24. Walter Martem, or the Three Cups of Weimar.
25. Sympathies of Illness.

26. The Mad Officer.
27. Memoir of the late Sir Chippin Forrage.
28. A Strange Adventure, by Terence O'Ruark.
The Vault of L——.
29. A Gambler's Luck.
31. A Tale of Ten Years Ago.
32. Leaves from the Journal of a Deceased Pluralist.
The Black Monday of the Glens.
. Terence Ryley's Adventures, by Mrs. S. C. Hall.
. The Jew and the Beggarman— a Tale of Oriental Swindling.
. Shawn Lauv Dhearg.
38. The Black Mask.

MISCELLANEOUS SKETCHES.

1. The Bores of My Acquaintance.
2. Annoyances of a Poet.
3. Raptures of Riding.
4. My Opinion of Sportsmen.
5. Life and Opinions of Gregory Greedy, Gent.
6. Delights of a Dirty Man.
7. The Horrors of Harmony.

8. Mishaps of a Short-sighted Man, or the Adventures of Bartholomew Buzzard, Esq.
9. The Saunters of Castle Saunter.
10 Sentimental Journey through London and Westminster
11. Passages from the Diary of Terence O'Ruark.
12. Historic Doubts relative to the Archbishop of Dublin.

NOTICES.

ADVERTISEMENTS AND BILLS

ARE INSERTED ON THE FOLLOWING TERMS:

Ten lines and under	£0 6 0	Half a page	£0 12 0
Ten to fifteen	0 7 6	A page	1 4 0
Fifteen to twenty	0 9 0	Bill stitched	1 1 0

Bills and Advertisements to be left with the Publishers in London and Edinburgh by the 8th; or in Dublin, by the 18th of each month.

Dublin: Printed for WILLIAM CURRY, JUN. AND Co. 9, Upper Sackville-street; SIMPKIN, MARSHALL, AND Co. London; and FRASER AND Co. Edinburgh; to whom all Communications and Advertisements are to be addressed. It may also be procured *by order* from any respectable Bookseller in Great Britain or the Colonies. Annual Subscription, 1*l.* 10*s.*

WORKS

PUBLISHED BY

WILLIAM CURRY, JUN. AND COMPANY,

9, UPPER SACKVILLE-STREET, DUBLIN;

SOLD BY

SIMPKIN, MARSHALL, AND COMPANY, LONDON; FRASER AND COMPANY,
EDINBURGH; AND ALL OTHER BOOKSELLERS.

TALES OF IRELAND,

BY WILLIAM CARLETON,

Author of ' Traits and Stories of the Irish Peasantry,' small 8vo, with 6 Etchings by W. H. BROOKE, 7s. 6d. cloth.

CONTENTS.

1. DEATH OF A DEVOTEE.	5. THE ILLICIT DISTILLER.
2. PRIEST'S FUNERAL.	6. THE DREAM OF A BROKEN HEART.
3. NEAL MALONE.	7. LACHLIN MURRAY AND THE BLESSED
4. THE BROTHERS.	CANDLE.

"'The Death of a Devotee,' and 'The Priest's Funeral,' are pictures of Irish life, whose graphic fidelity will be immediately recognised by every one who is in the slightest degree conversant with the subject; but it is in the beautifully instructive tale of ' The Brothers,' that the influence of priestly domination, working upon contracted bigotry, is exhibited in all its dark, but unhappily, not fictitious colouring. The prison scene, in which the two brothers, their broken-hearted mother, and the father—Dan Gallagher, are the actors, is one which no reader can possibly forget—it is the very soul of natural pathos itself, while the moral conveyed by it is irresistible."—*Belfast News-Letter.*
"We cannot bestow too much praise on this volume, whether we regard its object or execution."—*Brighton Gazette.*
"The Irish press is now taking high ground, both as to the character of the works it produces, as

well as the elegant style in which they are brought out. This is a work of decided talent, being from the pen of a writer, now celebrated for his portraiture of Irish character. * * * The etchings are in Brooke's best style."—*Edinburgh Weekly Chronicle.*
"The volume before us is a genuine emanation of the spirit which produced 'Traits and Stories of the Irish Peasantry,' which are popular throughout the empire."—*Edinburgh Evening Post.*
"One of the most amusing and spirited publications of the season."—*Aberdeen Observer.*
"It is decidedly one of the most interesting publications we have ever read."—*Derry Sentinel.*
"What tale more abounds in real Irish fun than ' Neal Malone,' and where will we find a more touching narrative than ' The Dream of a Broken Heart.' "—*Scots Times.*
"Long after the strong frame,

that is not without its own meed of athletic renown, shall have turned into the clay of the church-yard, the memory of the author of ' Traits and Stories of the Irish Peasantry,' will be cherished by instructed and grateful generations of his countrymen."—*Dublin University Magazine.*
"We do not know that we were ever more interested in reading any thing regarding Ireland, than we have been in perusing this volume. Mr. Carleton, the highly-gifted author, has our best wishes and highest commendations. We have no opportunity of knowing in what estimation he is held in the sister kingdom; but of this he may be assured, that on this side of the water his genius is appreciated; and he has only to write as he has hitherto done, to ensure universal popularity. Brooke's illustrations are good, and add materially to the value of the volume."—*Greenock Intelligencer.*

By the same Author. 18mo, 3s 6d. cloth.

FATHER BUTLER AND THE LOUGH DERG PILGRIM.

WORKS BY MRS. HEMANS.

NATIONAL LYRICS AND SONGS FOR MUSIC.

Small 8vo, 8s 6d cloth. Containing one hundred and twelve pieces, and among others the following:

SONGS OF A GUARDIAN SPIRIT.	SONGS FOR SUMMER HOURS.	MISCELLANEOUS POEMS,
SONGS OF SPAIN.	SONGS OF CAPTIVITY.	ETC.

"We have derived great delight from the perusal of this Volume"—*Sheffield Iris.*
"We could point out many poems which have proceeded from her gifted pen, which have few equals in the lyrical poetry of England. The present volume contains many such pieces."—*Edinburgh Evening Post*
"In this delightful volume are collected the many

beautiful ballads and other poetical pieces which have lately enriched the pages of our principal periodicals; some of them are exquisitely beautiful."—*Brighton Gazette*
"It fully equals her former productions, and still further exalts her as one of the foremost, or rather, the foremost poetess of the day."—*Edinburgh Weekly Chronicle.*

HYMNS FOR CHILDHOOD.

24mo, 2s. 6d. cloth lettered, or 3s. silk.

"The book itself is a very pretty book; and what is much more important, the contents, both in feeling and expression, worthy of the highly gifted author."—*Literary Gazette.*
"We cordially recommend this small volume, (which Messrs. Curry and Co. have got up in a style of first-

rate elegance,) to all who have the young under their charge."—*Scotsman.*
"We have been much delighted with the perusal of this elegant little volume."—*Edinburgh Weekly Chronicle.*

MARTIN DOYLE'S WORKS.

I.
ADDRESS TO LANDLORDS,

On Subjects connected with the Improvement of their Estates, and the Melioration of the Lower Classes. New Edition, enlarged. 12mo, 2s. 6d. cloth, or 2s. sewed.

II.
COMMON SENSE FOR COMMON PEOPLE ;
CHIEFLY ADDRESSED TO THE PEASANTRY.
12mo. One Shilling sewed.

" A most interesting little publication."—*Kilkenny Moderator.*
" Landlords especially should aid its circulation, and | we hope that it will be purchased by many of them for distribution among their tenantry."—*Derry Sentinel.*

III.
HINTS TO SMALL FARMERS.

This little manual has been found most extensively useful, and this perhaps is best proved by the fact that already 22,000 copies have been sold.   New Edition, 12mo. One Shilling, sewed.

IV.
THE KITCHEN GARDEN.

New Edition, improved. 12mo. One Shilling and Six-pence, sewed.

V.
THE FLOWER GARDEN.
12mo. Two Shillings, sewed.

" Another excellent little work by our good friend Martin Doyle."—*Brighton Gazette.*
" In this little work we have the same spirit of practical utility, the same straightforward plainness, | as we find in the other tracts of Mr. Doyle."—*Tyne Mercury.*
" Destined, like Martin's other works, to be highly popular."—*Scots Times.*

VI.
IRISH COTTAGERS.
12mo. New Edition, enlarged. One Shilling, sewed.

" We sincerely wish that we had it in our power to place a copy of this work in *every Cottage in Ireland*, and to prevail upon its occupants, male and female, either to read or have it read to them two or three times a year. It would be impossible for them, we | think, to become acquainted with the simple precepts, the practical and interesting lessons which it embraces, without deriving from them immediate and extensive benefit."—*Monthly Review.*

VII.
HINTS ON PLANTING, CATTLE, POULTRY, FISHERIES,
PLOUGHS, HARROWS, FLAX, &c.
New Edition, 12mo. One Shilling sewed.

VIII.
HINTS ON SUBJECTS CONNECTED WITH HEALTH, TEMPE-
RANCE, AND MORALS.
New Edition, 12mo. One Shilling, sewed.

" We have not for a long time met with a more *useful* writer than Martin Doyle, two of whose little works are now before us."—*Carlisle Patriot.*
" We can conscientiously say, that they are most meritorious productions, that instruction and amusement are in them most happily blended, that from | their homely style they are calculated for the meanest understandings, that the information they contain is of the most useful description, and that, we should be glad to see them in every Cottage, not alone in Ireland, but in England and Scotland."—*Aberdeen Observer.*

IX.
HINTS ON EMIGRATION TO UPPER CANADA,

Especially addressed to the Lower Orders in Great Britain and Ireland.
With a Map of Upper Canada. Third Edition, 12mo. One Shilling, sewed.

" It is a capital digest of all we know or can learn of Upper Canada, mixed with much practical advice."—*Inverness Courier.*
" Altogether it comprises such a fund of information | on the subject, that we know of no treatise to which we could more safely give our recommendation, or with more propriety style, ' The Emigrant's best Companion.' "—*Aberdeen Observer.*

X.
THE WORKS OF MARTIN DOYLE COLLECTED.
2 vols. 12mo. Twelve Shillings, cloth.

" The Works of Martin Doyle are calculated to do more good to Ireland, than the folio works of other and prouder authors."—*National Magazine.*
" We cannot bestow too much praise on these little Works."—*Quarterly Journal of Agriculture.*

M'KAY'S IRISH FLORA.

FLORA HIBERNICA, Comprising the Flowering Plants, Ferns, Characeæ, Musci, Hepaticæ, Lichenes, and Algae of Ireland, arranged according to the Natural System, with a Synopsis of the Genera, according to the Linnæan System.

By JAMES TOWNSEND M'KAY, M.R.I.A. Associate of the Linnæan Society, &c. &c. 8vo. 16s.

MR BLACKER'S AGRICULTURAL ESSAYS.

I.

AN ESSAY ON THE IMPROVEMENT TO BE MADE IN THE
CULTIVATION OF SMALL FARMS,

By the introduction of Green Crops and House-Feeding the Stock thereon. 8vo. One Shilling, sewed.

II.

A PRIZE ESSAY,

Addressed to the Agricultural Committee of the Royal Dublin Society, On the Management of Landed Property, the Consolidation of Small Farms, Employment of the Poor, &c. &c. 8vo, One Shilling, sewed.

III.

THE CLAIM OF THE LANDED INTEREST TO LEGISLATIVE
PROTECTION,

Founded on a Review of the Manner in which the Manufacturing, Commercial, and Agricultural Classes contribute to the National Wealth and Prosperity, and a Practical Mode of Relief pointed out. Addressed to the Central Agricultural Society of Great Britain and Ireland. 8vo. 6s. 6d

THE IRISH FARMER'S AND GARDENER'S MAGAZINE,

November 1833, to December 1835, inclusive.

Two large Volumes, 8vo, £1 8s. bound in cloth and lettered,

The Work continues to be published in Monthly Numbers, at One Shilling each.

"This valuable miscellany is always welcome to us." —*Morning Register*. "We know of no publication which has more fully | ratified the promises held forth by its conductors at the first, than the Farmer's and Gardener's Magazine."—*Derry Sentinel*.

EMIGRATION.

THE EMIGRANT'S DIRECTORY AND GUIDE

To obtain Lands, and effect a Settlement in the CANADAS. By FRANCIS A. EVANS, Esq. 12mo, 2s. 6d. cloth.

"Once more we recommend this practical volume."—*Scots Times*. "The price of the book, as well as its style, are quite what they ought to be."—*Liverpool Times*. "Any one intending to emigrate, who fails to read this book, knowing of its existence, will be guilty of great folly. We hope it will have the wide circulation it deserves, as we feel assured, that if justly appreciated and wisely used, it will be the saving of tears, health, and property to many of our countrymen."—*Metropolitan Magazine*. "Every page of the book contains some interesting fact."—*Farley's Bristol Journal*. "The best code of instructions to Emigrants we have seen, is 'the Emigrant's Guide by Mr. Evans.'"—*Enniskillen Chronicle*. "We have no hesitation in warmly recommending this little work."—*Kelso Mail*. "It is particularly minute as to the roads, canals, &c."—*Greenock Advertiser*.

HINTS ON EMIGRATION TO UPPER CANADA,
BY MARTIN DOYLE,

With a beautiful Map of Canada. One Shilling sewed. 14,000 copies of this little work have been sold.

FIELD SPORTS OF CANADA.

AUTHENTIC LETTERS FROM UPPER CANADA,
With an Account of Canadian FIELD SPORTS.

By T. W. MAGRATH. The whole edited by the Rev. T. RADCLIFFE, with etchings by LOVER. 12mo, 6s. cloth.

"We do not hesitate to assert that amongst the very numerous publications respecting America and the Canadas which have of late years issued from the press, there is not one superior to this volume."—*Kilkenny Moderator*. "The volume is practical, judicious, and full of important information."—*Scots Times* "The letters are written in an amiable, confidential spirit, and leave upon the mind a most favour- | able impression of the writer."—*Atlas*. "These letters may be had for less than the Canadian postage, and yet, an emigrant of the superior, that is to say, the wealthier and educated classes, would freely give five pounds or more for the information of a practical kind they contain."—*Spectator*. "We heartily recommend this volume to the notice of our readers, | and can assure them it will afford both entertainment and information, which will abundantly repay the perusal."—*Manchester Courier*. "Every thing is here set down; not only the business of life, but the pleasure; not only the trouble of the world, but the sport. The anecdotes are well told, and the book is particularly interesting from the evident authenticity of the letters."—*Tyne Mercury*.

CLASSICAL AND MATHEMATICAL BOOKS.

PLATO'S APOLOGY OF SOCRATES, CRITO AND PHÆDO,

With the Latin Version of PICINUS, and numerous English Notes.

By the Rev. C. S. STANFORD, A. M. 8vo, 10s. 6d. cloth.

"It is fortunate that such a work has fallen into the hands of an editor, possessing the varied acquirements requisite for its illustration. Mere scholarship is the least of Mr Stanford's merits; he possesses a high sense of moral beauty, and an intimate familiarity with the mazes of metaphysical investigation. It has rarely been our fortune to meet a Classical Work so ably edited as these dialogues; they are equally valuable to the Scholar and the Philosopher, and both will derive pleasure and profit from Mr. Stanford's la. bours."—*Athenæum.*

A TRANSLATION of the above.

'By the Rev. C. S. STANFORD, A. M. 8vo. 6s. 6d. cloth.

"The translation is executed with spirit and fidelity, and we cannot but notice the manner in which the metaphysical subtleties of Plato's arguments for the immortality of the soul are unfolded, without loose paraphrase on the one hand, or imitating the scholastic mysticism of the original on the other."—*Athenæum.*

ELEMENTS OF EUCLID, the first Six Books,

With Notes by Dr. ELRINGTON. Tenth Edition, 7s. boards.

ANALYTICAL TRIGONOMETRY,

Intended as an Appendix to Simpson's Trigonometry.

By WM. HARTSHORN, A. M. 8vo. 1s. sewed.

GREEK TESTAMENT, (the Gospels and Acts, being the Historical Books,)

With copious English Notes and a Lexicon

By the Rev. E. J. GEOGHEGAN, Editor of Xenophon, &c. &c. One thick vol. 12mo, 7s. 6d. bd.

"The plan adopted in the work may be explained in a few words The text is given from Vater's correct Edition (Halle, 1834) The notes have been selected from the works of the most eminent Commentators, with reference to the necessities of the class of readers for whose use the edition is intended." "A Vocabulary of words which occur in the text has been subjoined, in order that this important auxiliary to the study of the language may be consulted with ease and convenience. It has been compiled chiefly from the Lexicons of Wahl and Parkhurst."—*Author's Preface.*

HOMER'S ILIAD, Books 1 to 8,

Carefully Printed from the Text of Heyne, with copious English Notes, and a Preliminary Dissertation on the Greek Digamma.

By D. SPILLAN, A.M. 8vo. 9s. boards.

A GREEK GRAMMAR,

On a New and Systematic Plan, according to the Analytic Method.

By the Rev. THOMAS FLYNN, A.M. *New edition, improved.* 3s. 6d. bound.

A CHART OF GREEK GRAMMAR.

By the Rev. WILLIAM BURGH, A. M. 1s. 6d. on a Sheet.

OVID'S FASTI,

With very numerous English Notes by the Rev. C. S. STANFORD, A.M. 12mo. 5s. 6d. cloth.

VIRGIL'S GEORGICS,

Translated into English Prose; with an Appendix of Critical and Explanatory Notes.

By ISAAC BUTT, LL.B. M.R.I.A. Ex-Scholar of Trinity College, Dublin.

The Notes have been so arranged as to supply information in those points of general literature with which it is necessary for the candidate for honors, under the new system, to be acquainted.

12mo. 3s. 6d. cloth.

LIVY, Books 1 to 3,

With English Notes by JAMES PRENDEVILLE, late Scholar of Trinity College, Dublin.

Third Edition, corrected. 12mo, 5s. 6d. bound.

LIVY, Books 4 and 5,

With English Notes by the same Author. 12mo, 5s. bound.

SELECT SATIRES OF JUVENAL,

With a Paraphrase and Notes in English,

By JOHN HAWKESWORTH, LL.D. Head Master of the Feinaghan School, Luxembourgh. 12mo, 4s. bound.

INITIATORY EXERCISES IN THE LATIN LANGUAGE,

Extracted from Classic Authors, and arranged progressively; together with a system of Rules, explained and illustrated, completely developing the principles of Latin Syntax.

By THOMAS PHILLIPS, A. M. 12mo, 2s. 6d. bound,

THE METRES OF TERENCE EXPLAINED.
By the Rev. RICHARD HOBART, A. M. 8vo, 1s. 6d. sewed.

A LATIN GRAMMAR.
By the Rev. THOMAS FLYNN. 12mo, 1s. 6d bound.

A CHART OF LATIN GRAMMAR.
By the Rev. WILLIAM BUROH, A. B. 1s. 6d. on a sheet.

A SPELLING BOOK,
On a new Plan, containing all the common Words in the language; to which is prefixed an Introduction, in three Parts, exhibiting—I The Sounds of the Letters—II. The Quantities of the Syllables—III. A Rythmical Classification of Words, with an Appendix, containing several useful Tables.
.By the Rev. RICHARD ROE, A. M. 12mo. 1s. 6d. bound.

A SYNOPSIS OF ROMAN ANTIQUITIES;
Or a Comprehensive Account of the City, Religion, Politics, and Customs of the Ancient Romans. With a Catechetical Appendix.
By JOHN LANKTREE. New Edition, plates, 18mo. 3s. bound.

Specimen of the Illustrations.

THE DUBLIN UNIVERSITY CALENDAR for 1836.
Containing, besides the usual lists, the Examinations for Fellowships; Bishop Law's Mathematical Premium; Divinity and Moderatorship Examinations; and all the Prize Examinations for the Year. Small 8vo, 5s. cloth.

DUBLIN UNIVERSITY EXAMINATION PAPERS for 1834.
Small 8vo, 2s 6d. sewed.

AN ADDRESS
To the Members of the COLLEGE HISTORICAL SOCIETY, delivered at the termination of the Session 1834-5.
By W. ARCHER BUTLER, Scholar of Trinity College, President of the Society. 8vo, 1s. sewed.

AN ADDRESS
To the Members of the COLLEGE HISTORICAL SOCIETY, delivered at the opening of the Session 1835-6.
By WILLIAM RIBTON, Scholar of Trinity College. 8vo, 1s. sewed.

AN EPITOME OF ASTRONOMY,
With a Treatise on the Use of the Globes: to which are added the Rules of Mathematical Chronology, and the Construction of Maps, according to the different projections of the Spheres.
By JOHN GREGORY, Author of " Philosophy and Practice of Arithmetic," &c. &c. &c. In 12mo, 2s. 6d. cloth.

THE PRINCIPLES OF PLANE GEOMETRY AND TRIGONOMETRY
and their Application to Practice. 12mo. 4s. 6d. cloth.

WORKS FOR TOURISTS IN IRELAND.

To be Published in July,

In small 8vo, with a new Map of Ireland, and numerous engravings on steel by Mr MILLER,

THE TRAVELLER'S GUIDE THROUGH IRELAND.

This work has been in preparation nearly two years, and the utmost pains have been taken to produce a book useful to the Tourist, and creditable to the country.—Above all, conciseness and correctness have been studied, and it is hoped the Tourist in Ireland will now, for the first time, possess a book upon which he can rely, while the beauty of the embellishments will render it worthy of a place on the drawing-room table

New edition.   Small 8vo, with a plan of the City and 13 Views, price 7s. 6d. cloth,

THE PICTURE OF DUBLIN; OR GUIDE TO THE IRISH

METROPOLIS, containing an account of every object and institution worthy of notice, together with a brief description of the surrounding country, and of its Geology.

"This volume is truly what it professes to be, 'A Picture of Dublin.' Every stranger coming to this Metropolis should purchase this Guide, and carry it with him in his researches, and if he do, we will be bold to say he may see more of the beauties of Dublin in one week than many of its inhabitants have seen in their lives."—Dublin Evening Mail.

"A volume which, in every sense, demands our warmest admiration."—Derry Sentinel. "We can at length announce a complete Picture of Dublin   The publishers really merit praise for the careful and truly graphic character of this new Picture of Dublin."— The Warder. "A book to be read in England or Scotland as well as Ireland: we

are bound to give our warmest praise to the work, which is alike creditable to the city and the spirit of the publishers "—Dublin Morning Register. "A geological paper on the vicinity of Dublin, by Dr. Scouler, adds much to the value of this estimable little volume."—Athenæum.

GUIDE TO WICKLOW.

Small 8vo, Map and Plates, 5s. cloth.

GUIDE TO KILLARNEY AND GLENGARIFF.

Small 8vo, Map and Plates, 5s. cloth.

GUIDE TO GIANT'S CAUSEWAY.

New Edition, corrected.   Small 8vo, Map and Plates, 5s. cloth.

"No tourist ought to set foot in Ireland without these little volumes They are worth a dozen living guides, such as the inns supply. Our personal knowledge of the routes described, enables us to speak confidently of their correctness."—Sun "The Volumes are neatly got up, are illustrated

by engravings after the designs of Petrie, and will be found very useful and convenient to tourists in Ireland."—Printing Machine. "They deserve the notice of the tourist, the geologist, and the antiquary—" Edinburgh Weekly Chronicle.

AN ACCOUNT OF THE CAVES OF BALLYBUNIAN, County of Kerry.

By WILLIAM AINSWORTH, Esq. With Engravings on Copper and Wood. 8vo, 4s. cloth.

TEN VIEWS OF PICTURESQUE IRISH SCENERY.

Engraved by W. Miller, from drawings by George Petrie, R.H.A. India Proofs, 8vo, 7s. 6d.

SKETCHES IN THE NORTH AND SOUTH OF IRELAND.

By the Rev. CÆSAR OTWAY. Post 8vo. 10s. 6d. cloth.

"An able and delightful Volume."—Quarterly Review.

A HISTORY OF THE SIEGE OF DERRY AND DEFENCE OF

ENNISKILLEN, in 1688-9.

By the Rev. JOHN GRAHAM, A.M. &c New Edition, with Map and Plates, 12mo 6s. cloth.

"We can recommend it with the greatest confidence to our readers, assuring them that it is a work of no ordinary importance, and is by far the best History

of James's expedition in Ireland which has appeared." —Edinburgh Literary Gazette.

A HISTORY OF THE RISE, PROGRESS, AND SUPPRESSION

OF THE WEXFORD REBELLION, in 1798.

By GEORGE TAYLOR. Third Edition. 12mo, 3s. 6d. cloth,

"It gives a lively picture of the scenes in that rebellious period of which it treats."—Glasgow Free Press.

A HISTORY OF IRELAND,

CHIEFLY FOR THE USE OF YOUNG PERSONS.

By JOHN JAMES M'GREGOR, Author of a "History of the French Revolution," "History of Limerick," &c. 3 vols. 18mo, 10s. 6d. half bound, or 13s. 6d. embossed, with gilt edges.

GUIDE TO THE CONTINENT.

LETTERS FROM FRANCE, SAVOY, SWITZERLAND, ITALY,

GERMANY, DENMARK, HOLLAND, and the NETHERLANDS.

By GEORGE DOWNES, A.M. 2 vols. crown 8vo, £1 1s. cloth.

These volumes contain copious and accurate details connected with the countries which the author visited, and will be found extremely useful to any one meditating a Continental Tour.

THEOLOGICAL WORKS.

BY THE REV. EDWARD HARDMAN.

I.

EXPLANATORY AND PRACTICAL COMMENTS,

Being a Series of Short Lectures on the New Testament, designed as an Assistant in Family Worship, and suited to the capacity of all ranks. 2 vols. 8vo. 21s. cloth.

II.

FAMILY PRAYERS.

Small 8vo 4s. 6d. cloth.

"These prayers were originally written to accompany the Explanatory and Practical Comments, and are now published separately in consequence of repeated requests."—*Publisher's Advertisement.*

"Simple in construction, scriptural in expression, and evangelical in sentiment."—*Christian Examiner.* "They are short, plain, simple, scriptural, with | much of that unction which is so desirable, yet so difficult to introduce into written prayers."—*Edinburgh Christian Instructor.*

BY THE REV. HUGH WHITE, A. M.
CURATE OF ST. MARY'S PARISH.

I.

TWENTY SERMONS,

Preached in St. Mary's Chapel of Ease.

Fifth Edition, 2 vols. small 8vo. 10s. 6d. cloth.

"They are pervaded by a faithfulness of sentiment, a gentleness, but earnestness of spirit, and a beauty of expression, which will be found to interest and instruct, in a very high degree."—*Presbyterian Magazine.* | "The present volume we earnestly recommend to the attention of our readers, as characterised by a fine stream of hallowed eloquence, fitted at once to rouse the thoughtless sinner, and to animate and refresh the devout believer.—*Presbyterian Review.*

II.

MEDITATIONS AND ADDRESSES,

Chiefly on the Subject of Prayer. Second Edition, small 8vo. 5s. cloth

"They are truly excellent, simple, devotional, and scriptural." — *Church of Scotland Magazine.* " In reading this volume we were at once carried back to the days of the olden theology. There is the same elevated spirituality of thought and feeling, the same searching closeness in applying the truth, and | the same continual reference to Scripture at every turn, which distinguish the puritanical theology." —*Presbyterian Review.* " Few men of the present day have succeeded so well as the author of this work in combining popularity as a preacher of a deservedly high order, with an hum- | ble, bland, and devotional spirit. His recently published Volume of Sermons afforded a fair specimen of his pulpit exhibitions; and their almost unparalleled success -but corresponded with the admiration which, when delivered, they invariably produced." — *Christian Examiner.*

III.

PRACTICAL REFLECTIONS ON THE SECOND ADVENT.

Small 8vo. 5s. 6d. cloth.

This book is written in a very beautiful spirit ; perhaps few religious publications are calculated to meet a larger number, more calculated to interest generally than that which we now so cordially recommend.—*Christian Examiner.*

IV.

AN ADDRESS

To those attending the RELIGIOUS ANNIVERSARIES. 12mo, Six-pence, sewed.

BY THE REV. WILLIAM BURGH, A. B.
CHAPLAIN TO THE DUBLIN FEMALE PENITENTIARY.

I.

LECTURES ON THE SECOND ADVENT

Of our Lord Jesus Christ, and Connected Events; with an Introduction on the Use of Unfulfilled Prophecy. In small 8vo. Second Edition, 5s. cloth.

" He advances much which is worthy of serious consideration, and throws great light on various passages of prophecy."—*Investigator.* " There is a candour, a clearness, and a meekness in | his manner of writing on these things, that we cannot but admire, and most heartily desire to see imitated by all that enter the arena of religious controversy." —*Christian Examiner.*

II.

SIX DISCOURSES ON THE NATURE AND INFLUENCE OF FAITH.

Originally Preached in the Chapel of the Dublin Female Penitentiary, and now Dedicated to the Congregation assembling there. In small 8vo. 3s. 6d. cloth.

" These discourses supply valuable food to the contemplative mind, and constitute, in our opinion, a most valuable gift to the religious world —*Dublin Record.*

III.

AN EXPOSITION OF THE BOOK OF REVELATION.

Third Edition 12mo 6s. cloth.

.BY THE REV. MORTIMER O'SULLIVAN.

GUIDE TO AN IRISH GENTLEMAN
IN HIS SEARCH FOR A RELIGION.
Being an Answer to Mr. Moore's " Travels of an Irish Gentleman in Search of a Religion."
In small 8vo. 7s. 6d. cloth.

PRIMITIVE CHRISTIANITY IN IRELAND,
In a Letter to Thomas Moore, Esq. exhibiting his Misstatements in his History, respecting the Introdu
of Christianity into Ireland, and the Religious Tenets of the early Irish Christians.
From HENRY J. MONCK MASON, LL.D. Small 8vo. 3s. cloth.

THE BOOK OF REVELATION.
With compendious Notes, according to the Exposition which has been most generally received in the Chu
By the Rev. ISAAC ASNE, A.B. Small 8vo. 5s. cloth.

"This volume, though very un-
pretending, possesses some rare
excellencies. It is free from all the
wild theories of the early and modern interpreters of prophecy. The
author has availed himself of the
labours of the most solid and enlightened writers on prophecy,
both on the continent of Europe,
and in this country, and has so condensed the result of his reading as to
present, in a very brief and convenient form, all that is worth possessing in the voluminous writings
of those who have addicted themselves to the study of the pro-
phetic Scriptures." —Evangelical
Magazine.
"We have found it to be not only
instructive, but exceedingly en
taining."—Edinburgh Christia
structor.
"We much admire the calm
and candour of the hook, the to
Christian feeling which pervad
and the plain unambitious styl
which the observations are
veyed."—Presbyterian Review

AN ANALYTICAL ARRANGEMENT OF THE APOCALYPSE,
Or REVELATION, recorded by St JOHN; according to the Principles developed
under the name of Parallelism, in the Writings of Bishop Louth,
Bishop Jebb, and the Rev. Thomas Boys.
By the Rev. RICHARD ROE. 4to. 15s. cloth.

THE IRISH PULPIT,
A Collection of Original Sermons, by Clergymen of the Established Church in Ireland.
Second Series. 8vo. 10s. 6d. cloth.
CONTRIBUTED BY
Rev. HUGH WHITE.
Dean of ARDAGH.
Rev. H. WOODWARD.
Rev. F. B. WOODWARD.
Rev. ALEXANDER ROSS.
Rev. H. HAMILTON, D D.
Rev. THOMAS WALKER.
Rev. WILLIAM HARE.
Rev. HENRY MAGRATH.
Rev. PATRICK POUNDEN.
Rev. HENRY BROUGHAM.
Rev. HANS CAULFIELD.
Rev. W. K. TATAM.
Rev. J. C. LLOYD.

" A most gratifying specimen of the pulpit eloquence of the sister Kingdom......we hope to see the
Series continued to many Volumes, and that it may
meet with the cordial support of the Establish
in this, as well as our sister Country."—Christian
membrancer.

THE MEDIATOR OF THE NEW COVENANT;
A Series of Sermons on the Sacrificial and Mediatorial Character of the Saviour, as revealed in the Epistl
Paul to the Hebrews.
By the Rev. JAMES SPENCER KNOX, A.M.
Rector of Maghera, and Vicar-General of the Diocese of Derry.
In 8vo. 9s. cloth.

" We have read this volume with great delight.—
The style is elegant, full, simple, and often tender,
never weak or vapid ; figurative without being
flowery."—Church of Scotland Magazine.
" There is no lack of high ability in them, and a rich
and pleasing strain of pious principle and devoti
feeling runs through them all. The doctrine is of
most sacred and scriptural character, and is bro
forward in the simplest and clearest manner."—E
burgh Christian Instructor.

NINE SERMONS
On the Scriptural Evidence of the Doctrine of the Trinity,
Preached in Rostrevor Church.
By the Rev. E. J. EVANS, A.M. Vicar of Kilbroney. In 8vo. 8s. cloth.

THE TRUE NATURE AND DESIGN OF CHRIST'S PERSON A
ATONEMENT stated, in reply to the unscriptural Views of the Rev. Edward
Irving, " On the Human Nature of Christ."
By WILLIAM URWICK, D. D. In 12mo. 5s. cloth.

" We know not when we read such a refreshing
Work in controversial theology. If any one can read
this volume with attention, and after all adhere to the
awfully corrupt views of Mr Irving, he must be
the reach of argument and conviction."—Evange
Magazine.

PARENTAL RESPONSIBILITY ;
Addressed to those who profess to be Followers of the Lord Jesus Christ.
Second edition, enlarged. Small 8vo. 2s. 6d. cloth.

PRACTICAL REMARKS ON THE BOOK OF GENESIS,

For Family Worship, with a Prayer and Hymn adapted to each chapter.

By M. MURRAY. New Edition, improved. 8vo. 7s. 6d. cloth.

" We wish the author all success in his pious undertaking. The Remarks are plain, practical and judicious. evidently flowing from a mind embued with the love of God, and his fellow men, and throughout, well adapted to the end in view."—*Presbyterian Review*, No. 11.

PRACTICAL REMARKS ON THE BOOK OF EXODUS,

For Family Worship, with a Prayer and Hymn adapted to each chapter.

By M. MURRAY, Author of the Remarks on Genesis 8vo. 7s. 6d. cloth.

" The design, the plan, and the execution of the work are excellent "—*Wesleyan Methodist Magazine.*

LECTURES ON THE FOUR LAST BOOKS OF THE PENTATEUCH,

Designed to show the divine origin of the Jewish Religion, chiefly from internal evidence.

By the late Dean GRAVES, Regius Professor of Divinity, Trinity College, Dublin. Fourth Edition. 8vo. 14s. cloth.

" Indispensibly necessary to the Biblical student." —*Horne's Introduction.*
" Dean Graves' Lectures may be referred to for much valuable information equally illustrative of

the wisdom and of the difficulties of the Mosaic Code. ' —*Bridges' Christian Ministry.*
" Much important information." — *Bickersteth's Christian Student.*

TOWNSON ON THE GOSPELS.

Discourses on the Four Gospels, chiefly with regard to the peculiar design of each, and the order and places in which they were written ; to which is added, a Discourse on the Evangelical History, from the Interment to the Ascension of our Lord and Saviour Jesus Christ.

By THOMAS TOWNSON, D. D. late Archdeacon of Richmond. , *Fourth edition*, edited by the Rev. Dr. ELRINGTON, 8vo. 10s. 6d,

AN ANALYSIS OF BISHOP BURNET'S EXPOSITION OF THE THIRTY-NINE ARTICLES, with Notes.

By the Rev. THOS. NEWLAND, A. M. 12mo, 9s 6d. cloth.

AN ANALYSIS OF BISHOP BUTLER'S ANALOGY OF NATURAL AND REVEALED RELIGION.

By the Rev. RICHARD HOBART, A: M. Small 8vo. 4s. cloth.

A FAMILIAR SURVEY OF THE CHRISTIAN RELIGION,

And of History, as connected with the introduction of Christianity, and its progress to the present time.

By THOMAS GISBORNE, A.M. 8vo. 8s. cloth.

AN EPITOME OF THE GENERAL COUNCILS OF THE CHURCH,

From the Council of Nice, A D. 325, to the year 1563, when the Roman Council of Trent finished its sittings, with incidental mention of other Councils, &c.

By RICHARD GRIER, D. D. In 8vo. 9s. boards.

" The Author has supplied a very important desideratum in our Ecclesiastical Literature, and produced a work which should always be read in connexion with such Histories as those of Mosheim and Milner— it is, we believe, the first Work of the kind that has appeared in our literature, and is entitled to a place

in every Theological Library,"—*Wesleyan Methodist Magazine.*
" A very useful Compendium, particularly to those who have not the opportunity of consulting the great Collections."—*Bickersteth's Christian Student.*

A COMPENDIOUS HISTORY OF THE COUNCIL OF TRENT.

By the Rev. B. W. MATHIAS, A. M Chaplain of Bethesda. In 8vo. 10s. 6d. cloth.

FAMILY PRAYERS,

With Meditations and Hymns suitable to a Christian Family.

By the Rev. AUGUSTUS M. TOPLADY, A.B. late Vicar of Broad Hembury, Devon. New and beautiful Edition, corrected and revised. 18mo. 2s. neatly bound, or 3s. silk.

THE COMMUNICANT'S SPIRITUAL COMPANION,

Or, an Evangelical Preparation for the Lord's Supper ; with Meditations and Helps for Prayer, suitable to the Subject.

By the Rev. T. HAWEIS, LL.D. New Edition, beautifully printed in 32mo. 1s. 6d. cloth, 2s. 6d. silk, 3s. 6d. morocco.

BY THE REV. J. C. LLOYD, A.B.
CHAPLAIN OF THE MOLYNEUX ASYLUM.

I.
FIFTEEN SERMONS.
8vo. 7s.

II.
SERMONS, DOCTRINAL AND PRACTICAL.
8vo. 7s.

III.
DISCOURSES ON THE LORD'S PRAYER.
8vo. 7s. 6d.

IV.
LENT LECTURES ON PETER.
12mo. 5s.

SACRED POETRY AND MUSIC.

CHRISTIAN MELODIES,
A Collection of Hymns for Public and Private,Worship, published under the sanction
of His Grace the Archbishop of Tuam.   Fifth edition, beautifully printed
in 32mo.   1s. 6d. cloth, or 2s. 6d. silk.

THE DAY OF REST, and other Poems.
By a Clergyman. 12mo. 2s. 6d. boards.

PSALMS AND HYMNS AND SPIRITUAL SONGS.
By ELIZABETH BLACKALL. 18mo. Two Shillings, cloth.

A SELECTION OF PSALMS AND HYMNS
For Public Worship, under the sanction of the Lord Bishop of Limerick. Second Edition,
32mo. 1s. 3d. cloth, 2s. 6d. silk.

THE CHRISTIAN CHOIR,
A System of Christian Psalmody, for Public and Private Worship, comprising, I. Liturgic Hymns, in a
Easy Method for Chanting, with Music of Chants and Sanctuses, partly original —II. Selections
of Psalms, Anthems, and Hymns, with Arguments and Annotations, Practical and
Devotional ; also, some account of Psalmody in Public Worship, especially in the
Established Church, since the Reformation, with evidence that the
Psalms in Metre, and *Hymns* are in the same position with
respect to the laws of the Church.
By a Clergyman of the Established Church. 18mo. 3s 6d. cloth.

THE POCKET PSALMIST,
A Selection of Seventy Psalms, the words from the Authorized Version of Tate and Brady;
adapted to the Services of the United Church of England and Ireland ; together with
the Morning, Evening, and Festival Hymns ; also several Chants, the Music
by the best Composers.   Edited by the Wife of a Clergyman.
Second Edition, 18mo, 3s. neatly bound.

THE PSALTERY,
A Collection of Psalm and Hymn Tunes, carefully selected from the works of the most
eminent Composers ; arranged for one, two, three, and four voices.   In a
neat pocket Volume, 2s. 6d. cloth.

" This beautiful little book, which is of the size suited for binding with the ordinary class of Hymn Books, is quite a curiosity in musical publication. It contains within a few of ONE HUNDRED of the most favourite hymn tunes, engraved by Kirkwood, in a style which for elegance and distinctness we h never seen equalled,* * * as a portable volume congregational singing, it could not be improved. *Christian Examiner.*

HYMNS FOR THE USE OF SUNDAY SCHOOLS,
Collected and arranged by the Committee of the Hatch-street Sunday School, with Prayers, &c.
18mo. 2s. 0d. cloth.

THE IRISH CHURCH.

FACTS AND CIRCUMSTANCES

Relating to the CONDITION of the CLERGY of the ESTABLISHED CHURCH, and to the PRESENT STATE of IRELAND

By the Rev. T. S. TOWNSEND, Rector of Timogue. 12mo. 2s. sewed.

AN APOLOGY FOR THE ESTABLISHED CHURCH IN IRELAND,

Being an attempt to prove that its Present State is more pure than in any Period since the Reformation. In a Series of Letters addressed to the Earl of Mountcashel.

By HENRY NEWLAND, D.D. Vicar of Bannow. 12mo. 5s.

"Mr Newland's book contains more valuable and authentic information upon the state of the Church in Ireland, than can any where else be met with."— *Bishop of Ferns.*

"Those who wish for information concerning the Irish Church, may consult with advantage 'Newland's Apology for the Church in Ireland.'"—*Dr. Dealtry's Charge, p. 76.*

AN EXAMINATION .

OF THE EVIDENCE AND ARGUMENTS ADDUCED BY DR. DOYLE, before the Committee on Tithes in Ireland, in Defence of the supposed Quadripartite or Tripartite Division.

By HENRY NEWLAND, D.D. Vicar of Bannow. 12mo. 3s.

CORRESPONDENCE BETWEEN THE LORD BISHOP OF FERNS

and the EARL of MOUNTCASHEL, on the Church Establishment; to which is prefixed a Report of the Proceedings of the Lay Meeting at Cork, out of which the Correspondence arose. 8vo. 3s. 6d.

CUI BONO? ·

A Letter to Lord Stanley, on Church Reform.

By HENRY COTTON, LL.D. Archdeacon of Cashel. 8vo. 2s. 6d.

FIAT JUSTITIA.

A Letter to Sir Henry Hardinge, on the Present Circumstances of the Established Church in Ireland.

By HENRY COTTON LL.D. Archdeacon of Cashel. 8vo. 2s.

ROMAN CATHOLIC CONTROVERSY.

A COMPARATIVE VIEW OF THE CHURCHES OF ENGLAND

AND ROME, from the earliest period; and a Development of the Errors of the latter, with their Dates of Introduction to the Christian Church.

By a Clergyman of the Church of England. 12mo 7s. 6d. cloth.

A SUMMARY OF POPISH ERRORS,

With a Refutation of them in Express Texts of Scripture—written originally in French, by CHARLES DRELINCOURT, Minister. New Edition, 12mo. 1s. 6d. boards.

THE WORD OF GOD WEIGHED AGAINST THE COMMANDMENTS OF MEN.

By the Rev. CÆSAR OTWAY, A. B. 8vo. 1s. 6d. sewed.

THE FRAUDS OF ROMISH MONKS AND PRIESTS,

In Seven Letters from Italy, Descriptive of the Mock Miracles, Monasteries, Confraternities, Processions, Superstitious Observances, &c. of the Church of Rome.
12mo. 3s. 6d. boards.

FIVE SERMONS ON THE ERRORS OF POPERY.

Preached in St. Peter's Church, Dublin.

By the late Rev. C. R. MATURIN. Second Edition, 12mo. 3s. boards·

AN AFFECTIONATE ADDRESS

To the Roman Catholics of Ireland. 12mo. Sixpence, sewed.

A BRIEF VIEW OF THE VERSIONS OF THE ROMAN
CATHOLIC AND PROTESTANT BIBLES.
18mo. 1s. 6d. cloth.

MOTIVES FOR LEAVING THE CHURCH OF ROME.
By James Godkin, formerly a Roman Catholic, and now Minister of the Gospel
at Armagh. 8vo. One Shilling and Sixpence, sewed.

THE GOSPEL OF LUKE AND ACTS OF THE APOSTLES,
The Protestant and Roman Catholic Versions in Parallel Columns. 24mo.

AN AUTHENTICATED REPORT OF THE DISCUSSION
at Londonderry, between Six Clergymen and Six Priests. One large Volume, 8vo. 10s. 6d. boards.

SERMONS, PAMPHLETS, &c.

THE VOLUNTARY SYSTEM;
A Sermon preached at the Visitation of the Diocese of Armagh, on Wednesday, the 23rd September, 1
By the Rev. Richard Allott, A.M. Precentor of the Cathedral of Armagh,
and Fellow of Trinity College, Cambridge. 8vo. 1s.

A SERMON
Preached at the Annual Visitation held in the Cathedral of Derry, 9th October, 1834.
By the Rev. John Hayden, Rector of Lower Cumber. 8vo. 1s. 6d.

A SERMON
Preached in the Parish Church of Killurin, on the 4th October, 1835;
Being the Third Centenary of the Publication of the first Bible in the English Language.
By the Rev. John Booker, A.M. Vicar of Killurin, Diocese of Ferns. 8vo. 1s. 6d. sewed.

THE DUTIES MORE IMMEDIATELY CONNECTED WITH T
PRESENT CRISIS;
A Sermon preached in the Cathedral Church of Londonderry, on 29th September, 1835, at the Trienni
Visitation of His Grace the Lord Primate.
By James Smith, A.M. Rector of Camus juxta Mourne. 8vo. 1s. sewed.

THE CHURCHMAN REMINDED,
Concerning some Important Doctrines and Duties of his Profession;
A Discourse preached in the Cathedral Church of Cashel, at the Visitation held there in August, 1827,
Notes and Illustrations.
By the Rev. W. A. Holmes, A.B. Rector of Moyne, &c. 8vo. 5s. cloth.

A SERMON
Preached in the Cathedral of Christ Church, at the Ordination held by His Grace the Archbishop of Du
on the 19th December, 1824.
By J. H. Singer, D.D. F.T C.D. 8vo. 1s 6d. sewed.

TWO SERMONS ON THE HUMAN NATURE OF CHRIST.
By James Thomas O'Brien, D. D. Archbishop King's Lecturer on Divinity, Trinity College, Dublin
Second edition, corrected. 8vo.

PREPARATION TO MEET GOD;
A Sermon preached in Rostrevor Church, on Sunday, 31st August, 1834, occasioned by the Death of th
Hon. Justice Jebb.
By the Rev. E. J. Evans, A.M. Vicar of Kilbroney. 8vo. 1s. 6d.

SCRIPTURE EVENTS AND CHARACTERS.
NO. I.—THE FALL OF PETER.
By the Rev. James Carlile, of the Scots Church, Capel-street.
Small 8vo. 6d. sewed.

A REPLY to a Pamphlet entitled "CHRIST OUR LIFE,
Or, the Scripture Doctrine concerning Immortality; by a Clergyman of the Church of England."
By the Rev. PATRICK POUNDEN, Rector of Ballinasloe. Small 8vo. 1s. sewed.

THE SYSTEM of the NATIONAL SCHOOLS in IRELAND considered,
In a Letter to the Rev. Dr. SADLEIR, S.F.T.C.D.
By an Irish Clergyman. 8vo 1s.

A LETTER TO HIS GRACE THE ARCHBISHOP OF DUBLIN,
On the Nature of the Christian Sabbath.
By the Rev. WILLIAM FOSTER, Vicar of Collon. 8vo. 1s.

A PRACTICAL EXPLANATION OF THE NATURE AND ORIGIN
OF THE ORDINANCE OF CONFIRMATION.
By the Rev. THOMAS NEWLAND, A.B. 12mo. 6d. sewed.

PESTILENCE ARRESTED BY PRAYER,
An Address to the Rulers and People of Great Britain at this alarming Crisis. 8vo. 1s. sewed.

SCRIPTURAL EMBLEMS AND SPIRITUAL REALITIES,
In three Sermons from the Song of Solomon. Translated from the German 8vo. 2s. 6d.

RELIGIOUS NARRATIVES.

VILLEROI;
OR, RELIGION FOUNDED ON PRINCIPLE, NOT ON EXCITEMENT.
By the Author of "The Valley of the Clusone," &c. &c. Small 8vo, 5s. cloth.

" In short, the work is a good one, and there are thousands of people who think themselves exceedingly religious who may peruse it with the greatest advantage."—*Edinburgh Christian Instructor.* " We have great pleasure in announcing this interesting work to our readers, assured that those who have read and admired the former productions of this lady's pen, will not be disappointed in this." — *Christian Examiner.* " A most interesting book; there is scarcely a page in it that does not contain something wholesome. The sentiments are strikingly Just, abounding in clear doctrinal truth, which, much to the author's credit, and the reader's advantage, never lacks a right practical application. We may add, that the characters are well drawn, and the story attractive."—*Christian Ladies' Magazine.*

TALES OF MY COUNTRY,
Containing ROSE MUIROON, EVELEEN O'CONNOR, a Tale of MONAN-A-GLENA, SIX WEEKS AT THE RECTORY.
By the Author of " A Visit to my Birth-Place," &c. Small 8vo. 5s. boards.

A VISIT TO MY BIRTH-PLACE.
By the Author of " Early Recollections," &c. with Frontispiece 18mo. Third Edition, 2s. 6d. half bound.

MY OWN STORY.
By the Author of "A Visit to My Birth-place," &c. 18mo, with Frontispiece, 2s. half bound.

THE INDIAN BROTHERS;
Facts and Authentic Sketches Illustrative of Eastern Manners and Character, as connected with the Progress of Christianity in India. 18mo. 2s. 6d. boards.

" It is exceedingly adapted to school, parish, and district Libraries; to such we commend it as calculated to promote the spirit of missionary labour."—*World.* " The whole Tale is one of the deepest interest, and could only have been penned by a spectator of similar scenes."—*Sunday School Teacher's Magazine.*

THE PASTOR'S DAUGHTER.
By the Author of " Little Mary." 18mo. 1s. 6d. boards.

THE MARTYR OF PRUSA,
A Tale of the Early Christians. 18mo. 1s. 6d. boards.

" Many ponderous quartos might be proud of the talent which is displayed in this unassuming little Volume. We cordially recommend it to the perusal of our readers."—*British Magazine.*

FATHER BUTLER AND THE LOUGH DERG PILGRIM—Irish Sketches.
By the Author of "Traits and Stories of the Irish Peasantry." 18mo. with Frontispiece, 3s. 6d. cloth.

ELLMER CASTLE,
A Roman Catholic Story of the Nineteenth Century.
Fourth Edition, with Frontispiece. 18mo. 3s. 6d. half bound.

NATURE AND GRACE EXEMPLIFIED.
By the wife of a Clergyman. Second Edition, improved. 1s. sewed.

INDEX.